LONELY
POWER

LONELY
POWER

Why Russia Has Failed to Become the West
and the West is Weary of Russia

LILIA SHEVTSOVA
TRANSLATED BY ANTONINA W. BOUIS

CARNEGIE ENDOWMENT
FOR INTERNATIONAL PEACE
WASHINGTON DC · MOSCOW · BEIJING · BEIRUT · BRUSSELS

Carnegie Endowment for International Peace
1779 Massachusetts Avenue, N.W.
Washington, D.C. 20036
202-483-7600
www.ceip.org

The Carnegie Endowment does not take institutional positions on public policy issues; the
views represented here are the author's own and do not necessarily reflect the views of the
Endowment, its staff, or its trustees.

To order, contact Carnegie's distributor:
Hopkins Fulfillment Service
PO Box 50370, Baltimore, MD 21211-4370
1-800-537-5487 or 1-410-516-6956
Fax: 1-410-516-6998

Library of Congress Cataloging-in-Publication Data

Shevtsova, Lilia Fedorovna.
 Lonely power : why Russia has failed to become the West and the West is weary of Rus-
sia / Lilia Shevtsova.
     p. cm.
 Includes bibliographical references and index.
 ISBN 978-0-87003-246-2 (pbk.) -- ISBN 978-0-87003-247-9 (cloth) 1. Russia (Federation)--
Foreign relations. 2. Russia (Federation)--Politics and government--1991- 3. Russia (Fed-
eration)--Relations--Western countries. 4. Western countries--Relations--Russia (Federa-
tion) I. Title.

 DK510.764.S545 2010
 327.47--dc22   2010022943

Cover design by Zeena Feldman
Composition by Oakland Street Publishing
Printed by United Book Press

© **Mixed Sources**
Product group from well-managed
forests, controlled sources and
recycled wood or fiber
www.fsc.org Cert no. BV-COC-070702
© 1996 Forest Stewardship Council

CONTENTS

FOREWORD

Russia has made a tradition of puzzling the world with its ups and downs, its sudden course changes, and its shifting masks, thus forcing the West to constantly ask itself: Is a new policy a change of tactics or a change of paradigm?

Tough Russian policies toward its neighbors earlier this decade, culminating in the 2008 war with Georgia, have given way to a seemingly new approach in the wake of the global financial crisis and the Obama administration's "reset." Today, the ruling tandem presents a far more cooperative face to the world. Yet the question remains: Does this new face represent a genuine change in direction?

In *Lonely Power*, Lilia Shevtsova examines the relationship between Russia and the West, the domestic roots of Russian foreign policy, and the myths that both Russia and the West maintain about each other. She provides a comprehensive assessment of the interaction between foreign policy and domestic developments in Russia and how, as she sees it, the Russian elite is using foreign policy as a tool to reproduce the traditional Russian state.

In the midst of optimistic views about Russia's modernization and its rapprochement with the West, Shevtsova invites the reader to ask some probing questions: Can Medvedev's modernization be serious and sustainable when the nature of the regime has not been altered? Can rapprochement be real when the system continues to rely upon anti-Western sentiment to consolidate itself? Are political and expert communities in the West rushing to endorse an imitation democracy?

Shevtsova makes it abundantly clear that transforming Russia is a project that belongs to Russians themselves. Like any country, Russia cannot be modernized from outside. But, she believes that Russia can't succeed with its transformation when the West chooses either to stand back as a neutral observer or to actively support the status quo. "Delaying change under the guise of modernization from above," she writes, only makes transformation harder. And it may compromise Western values in the process.

Shevtsova, long one of Russia's most prominent and insightful political observers, sees Russia today as adrift in a sea of uncertainty. Parts of Russian society demonstrate that the country is ready to live in a new world. Many Russians believe that autocracy and hostility toward the world are not Russia's destiny. Yet powerful forces of history and contemporary politics push in the opposite direction. These tensions could be resolved, Shevtsova believes, sooner than many imagine. The West, by seeking to understand Russia's dilemmas, can make the process of resolving these dilemmas less painful.

Jessica T. Mathews
President, Carnegie Endowment for International Peace

LETTER TO THE READER

What you are about to read are polemical essays prompted by a growing number of questions about Russia—questions not only about its behavior in the international arena and its relations with the West, but also about the attitudes and perceptions Russia and the West hold about one another (including, not least, stereotypes). Much ink has been spilled on these topics in Russia and the West, but usually it has been spilled by writers concerned primarily with issues of the balance of power, security, and geopolitics.

However, the logic and toolkit arising out of the study of international relations do not explain much about the issues I've mentioned. Indeed applying foreign policy categories to them can sometimes be disorienting. Foreign policy logic does not answer the question: Why does Russia so often act contrary to common sense and undermine its own positions? Consider one example of such behavior. From 2004–2008, the Russian ruling team seemed to be doing everything in its power to exacerbate the crisis in relations with the West, choosing political confrontation with the United States and deciding to snub Europe. By the end of the Putin presidency there was probably more distrust between Russia and Western nations than there had been in the final stages of the existence of the Soviet Union. What did Moscow earn by this muscle-flexing? Respect in the Western capitals? The trust of its neighbors? A solution to the ongoing problems of transformation? No, no, and no. Trying to explain Russia's behavior by studying its foreign policy will not tell us why Russia seems continually to shoot itself in the foot.

Traditional foreign policy categories are equally futile for answering other questions as well. Why did Russia provoke the "gas wars" with Ukraine, when that move only convinced Europe to get serious about seeking alternative sources of energy? What problems did the war with Georgia solve? Or Moscow's recognition of the independence of South Ossetia and Abkhazia? How can Moscow simultaneously view NATO as a threat and seek partnership with its members? Why does the majority of the Russian elite continue to regard the West with suspicion?

While the study of foreign policy often fails to provide satisfactory answers to such questions, the study of the domestic sources of foreign policy offers much greater clarity. We must examine Russia's foreign policy as a factor in the overall equation that describes the traditional Russian system's efforts to reproduce itself, and thus come to some understanding of the internal constraints on relations between Russia and the West.

When the global financial crisis hit Russia, the Russian ruling elite began to seek new ways to survive. It returned to Peter the Great's formula of re-energizing by using the West—a formula Stalin used effectively to pursue Soviet industrialization. To use the West in order to save an anti-Western system exemplifies the highest possible degree of pragmatism—and cynicism as well.

The Kremlin's change in survival tactics necessitated a change in the way it behaved toward the outside world. The Russian ruling team came to understand that smiles are better than scowls for securing help, but could their smiles be trusted if they were only skin-deep—that is, if they had not changed the nature of the traditional Russian system?

"One has to believe that positive change will happen, and if you believe, it has to happen!" one European observer said to me. But if hope is the sole basis of the new Western optimism, then we are really in trouble. If Russian "modernization" with Western help fails, one can easily guess who will be blamed for subsequent failures as well.

I argue that we cannot expect stable cooperation, much less partnership, as long as Russia remains under a system of personalized rule, which consolidates itself through anti-Western sentiment, whether that sentiment is expressed openly (as it was in the past) or secretly (as it is today). The political regime in Moscow may change in the future (and it will change in 2012), but if the nature of power remains the same, then the new regime, smiling all the while, will continue to either reject Western norms or merely imitate them. No foreign policy "reset" based on economic and security cooperation can change Russia's behavior unless Russia rewrites its genetic code: personalized power.

Will Russia be able to do this by itself? If it can't, how might the West help? At the moment, the West is actually helping the Russian elite maintain the status quo. Bogged down by its own problems, the political West has no time or inclination to think about a challenge as daunting as Russia's transformation. Its present dream is merely to find a *modus vivendi* with Russia. There are, however, people in Russia today who believe that their country needs to change its trajectory (and they are not a minority anymore), and while they know there is a limit to what the West can do, they expect at a minimum that the West should stop hindering transformation by propping up the traditional state.

Every day, the disparity between reality and the imitation scenery in Russia is growing. The rhetoric of modernization and leaders' attempts to look self-assured can't conceal the fundamental deterioration of the Russian system or the regime's increasing inability to respond to pressing challenges. The more the ruling elite loses control over the present and the future, the more it tries to recreate the past in the form of a rosy picture reminiscent of the late Brezhnev era. This decay might continue indefinitely, or it might suddenly end in collapse. Imitation stability, fake modernization, artificial consensus, and a "let's pretend" foreign policy make predicting Russia's future impossible. But whatever the future is, from our vantage point in the present, it looks grim.

"These are the same old fears and flights of fancy about Russia. The political class is pragmatic enough to keep things from unraveling," my Western reader may argue. I would answer that pragmatism can't compensate for a lack of vision or a plan for the future. I have the impression that the political West is not prepared (and it wouldn't be for the first time) for Russia's tottering on the brink of turbulence. The unpredictability of Russia's future, even its near future, is reason enough to have this conversation.

In this book, I summarize the discussion in Russia about the West, I expound on Russian expectations regarding the West, and I discuss Russian disillusionment with the West. While it has long been known that Russian nationalists, statists, and even pragmatists hold suspicions of the West, the fact that the majority of Russian liberals now holds a critical view of the West, its leaders, and its Russia experts is a rather new phenomenon. Our Western counterparts do not always pick up on this view, or perhaps they prefer not to notice, but the sense of disappointment is palpable.

I do not rule out the possibility that my Western colleagues will find my frankness—in tone, in formulation, and in exposition—too emotional, perhaps even unfair. "This is grist for the mill of Russophobes, and it undermines mutual trust," an esteemed Western expert on Russia, who has spent years trying to create partnership between Russia and the West, said bitterly. "Don't talk about what separates us," he explained. "Let's seek what unites us." But this only served to convince me more than ever that it is time to talk about the growing chasm between Russian liberals and quite a few Western experts. Before we can ever bridge that gap, we must determine how wide it is—or in other words, exactly where and how the two sides do not correspond. In the following essays, I will spell out the issues on which the two sides have different positions.

I do not pretend to represent all Russian liberals—of course not. Moreover, I admit that Russian liberals do not yet have a unified understanding of what they don't like about the West and what they would like to change. But I think that many of them will at least support the questions I ask of Western politicians and experts. And if we actually get answers to those questions, that may help us overcome our naïve hopes and come to a better understanding of the West's intentions toward Russia and its transformation. I do not rule out the possibility that our hopes for the West and our disillusionment with the Western political and expert community are the result of incurable Russian idealism, as well as our own inability to influence Russian development. But before accepting that bitter truth, I would like to see what our Western colleagues have to say about the questions that Russian liberals are raising.

I quote a lot of people in this book, both Russian and Western, experts and politicians. I do this in order to show the content and direction of the current discussion in the Russian political community about Russia and its role in the world. I would also like to demonstrate how the Western view of, and policies toward, Russia are perceived by the pro-Western Russian audience. I argue with and contradict many people in this volume, including colleagues and even friends, but I am not arguing merely for the sake of argument. I believe that cordial but honest debate will bring understanding more quickly than polite agreement and feigned unity.

These essays are in no way meant to settle the issue. On the contrary, this book is an invitation to start the discussion.

This book would have never appeared in print without the support of a wonderful group of people. I am grateful to Jessica Mathews, president of the Carnegie Endowment, for her unwavering encouragement. I appreciate the support of Executive Vice President Paul Balaran and vice presidents Thomas Carothers and Peter Reid. My special thanks go to James Collins, director of the Russia and Eurasia program, for his insights.

I thank all my friends and colleagues, whose conversations or articles and books were exceptionally important to me in the course of writing this book. I express sincere gratitude to Leon Aron, Anders Åslund, Ronald Asmus, James Goldgeier, Rose Gottemoeller, Thomas Graham, Jr., Sam Greene, Arnold Horelick, Andrei Illarionov, Donald Jensen, Igor Klyamkin, Andrei Kortunov, David Kramer, Andrew Kuchins, Robert Legvold, Edward Lucas, Roderic Lyne, Michael Mandelbaum, Michael McFaul, Mark Medish, Sarah Mendelson, Marie Mendras, Arkady Moshes, Robert Nurick, Robert Otto, Nikolai Petrov, Steven Pifer, Andrei Piontkovsky, Peter Reddaway, Blair Ruble, Eugene Rumer, Stephen Sestanovich, James Sherr, Angela Stent, Strobe Talbott, Dmitri Trenin, Andrew Wood, and Yevgeny Yasin.

I appreciate the collegiality of those colleagues with whom I have disagreements, as well as their willingness to continue our debates.

I am grateful for the support of the Carnegie Corporation of New York, the Charles Stewart Mott Foundation, the Open Society Institute, and the Starr Foundation for the Carnegie Moscow Center.

I thank Antonina W. Bouis, who also translated my *Putin's Russia,* and who has once again rendered my words into English with subtlety and understanding.

I would also like to thank the great team who prepared this manuscript for publication.

My thanks go to Ilonka Osvald, senior publications manager at Carnegie, for her unwavering support, for making this book a priority, and for shepherding it through the production process. I am also grateful to Daniel Kennelly, my editor, who gave the manuscript an expert and invaluable polishing and prepared it for an English-speaking audience. I appreciate the help of David Donadio, who helped with the editorial process. Carlotta Ribar was a great proofreader. Thanks to Zeena Feldman for the cover design, as well as for her enthusiastic promotion of the book.

And finally, my thanks to my family—mother, husband, and son—for their patience and their understanding.

1   INTRODUCTION

There have been not one, but many, "milestone" years in the history of the new Russia. The first and perhaps most familiar, 1991, marked not only the birth of post-communist Russia, but also the stillbirth of its democracy. In 1993, the Boris Yeltsin constitution created the framework for a new "personalized power." Yeltsin's victory in the controlled elections of 1996 marked an embryonic form of what would later become Russia's imitation democracy. In 2003, the destruction of YUKOS signified a turn to bureaucratic capitalism. In 2004, the "orange revolution" in Ukraine hastened Russia's return to a statist matrix. And finally, the August 2008 Russo-Georgian war heralded a period of open political confrontation between Russia and the West.*

This final milestone marked the end of an important path in Russia's development—a path that began with Mikhail Gorbachev's perestroika and was supposed to end with Russia's integration into the community of liberal democracies. But there had been too many diversions from this course over the last two decades. No diplomatic thaws, no détentes, and no "resets" between Russia and West will now be able to return it to the track of integration with the West—at least not until Russia rejects the principles on which its political system and state are being built.

All successful democratic transformations since World War II occurred because conditions *within* the respective societies had matured enough to make them possible. At the same time, none of these transformations took place without the influence of Western civilization. In some cases, the very existence of the West as a model was enough to inspire authoritarian

---

*In this book I use "the West" to refer to a civilization, that is, a community of states that organize themselves on the basis of liberal-democratic principles. The relations between Russia and the West interest me primarily from the point of view of norms and principles and how Western liberal civilization can influence the Russian transformation.

and totalitarian societies to open themselves up to the world, but even those transformations had to be consolidated by means of diplomatic and economic links to developed democracies, as occurred in Latin America, South Korea, and Taiwan. In other cases, the West put direct pressure on dictatorships like those in Portugal, Greece, the Republic of South Africa, and in a number of Asian and Latin American countries. The most successful transformations have been the ones in which the West took an active role in the internal life of states transitioning from totalitarian and authoritarian systems, as occurred in conquered Germany and Japan, in Southern Europe, and in the former communist states of Central and Southeastern Europe and the Baltic states. Admission to the North Atlantic Treaty Organization (NATO) and the European Union (EU) became the ultimate guarantee of a state's successful transformation. In these cases, the West—as a community of liberal democracies—became both an internal and an external factor of reform. It should be noted that such intimate engagement only worked when Western experts and politicians actually understood what was going on in the countries they were trying to help.

For Russia in the 1990s, the West was not just a mentor and a guide on the path of reform; it was a participant. Today, a broad spectrum of political and social forces in Russia, including human rights activists and liberals, view the West with skepticism, if not antipathy. Of course, the West itself no longer greets Russia warmly, but Western politicians and commentators are loath to acknowledge this uncomfortable truth, fearing it will only further cool relations with Moscow. But neither polite smiles nor clarion calls to "reset" the relationship can disguise it: Russia and the West are further apart today than they have been at any time since Gorbachev's perestroika.

This uncomfortable truth raises several questions: What role did the West, as a liberal civilization, play in Russia's transformation? How does Russia's internal evolution influence its relations with the West? What do Russian and Western observers think about the relationship? What is the liberal interpretation of this recent history? And finally, what can we expect from Russia in the future? Let us explore how the civilizational factor— that is, the method of organizing power and society, norms and principles—affects relations between Russia and West, and how those relations ease or hinder Russian reforms.

2 COLLAPSE OF THE USSR: THE WEST CAUGHT UNAWARES

There is an astonishing historical irony embedded in the disintegration of the Union of Soviet Socialist Republics (USSR)—so astonishing, in fact, that it raises doubts about the global elite's ability to predict and prepare for the future. For many decades, the West marshaled its finest minds to the task of devising strategies to contain and neutralize its Cold War opponent. However, it was the possibility no one had prepared for—a Soviet collapse—that preoccupied the West's key leaders at the end of the Cold War.

During the Soviet Union's dying years, George H. W. Bush, François Mitterrand, Helmut Kohl, and John Major were all feverishly searching for a way to keep it alive. All of the Western powers, and especially the Americans, feared that Mikhail Gorbachev was losing control of a nuclear superpower. Secretary of State James Baker publicly called on the United States to do whatever was needed to "strengthen the center," namely Gorbachev. President Bush shocked an audience of pro-independence Ukrainians in August 1991 by telling them that "freedom is not the same as independence," and that Americans would not support those who sought independence in order to trade tyranny for "local despotism." Brent Scowcroft later explained Washington's position during the late 1980s and early 1990s:

> We tried to act in a way that did not provoke in Eastern Europe another cycle of uprising and repression. We wanted to move liberalization forward, but at a pace that would be under the Soviets' reaction point. Of course, we did not know exactly what that pace was. But we tried to avoid causing either a crackdown by the Soviet Union or an internal disruption within the Soviet Union in which the hardliners would kick Gorbachev out because he wasn't tough enough.[1]

In Europe, the Soviet demise caused confusion, even panic. Leaders who had for many years feared Soviet imperialism now found that they couldn't decide whether they could live without it. Should they support independence for the former Soviet satellites? Or should they help Moscow rein in the chaos of its crumbling empire?

These concerns were understandable, especially when seen in the context of unguarded nuclear stockpiles. But there was another reason the thought of a Soviet disintegration made Western leaders so nervous: The West had grown accustomed to a world order that relied on the idea of *mutual containment* for its stability. For some influential corporative interests—economic, military, and ideological—the struggle against international communism and the Soviet Union gave meaning to their existence. The disappearance of that struggle meant there was no longer a civilizational alternative by which the West could set itself apart. As Robert Cooper put it, "Today's America is partly the creation of the Soviet Union.... The USSR presented a challenge that went to the core of America's Enlightenment identity." The existence of the USSR had hastened the process of European unification and given Europe's leaders a foil against which they could set their own course. The Soviet Union, which had cemented the West and forced it to perfect itself, was disappearing. After it was gone, the West was unlikely to find another such organizing principle. It wasn't clear what kind of Russia would appear in the place of the former Evil Empire. A new world was in the making, and the West wasn't ready for it.

Bewildered, Western leaders continued to bet on Mikhail Gorbachev up until the very end, reluctant to negotiate with Boris Yeltsin. Neither Yeltsin nor the new Russia he represented were trusted in Western capitals. The West found Yeltsin and his people, who were busy pushing Gorbachev out of the Kremlin, suspicious.

Nevertheless, Western leaders were not prepared to support Gorbachev when he began to lose ground. Only Germany rendered aid to the USSR in the form of payments for the evacuation of Soviet troops from the former East Germany and Moscow's acquiescence to German reunification. With that exception, the countries of the West had no intention of offering Gorbachev help. When the USSR began to come apart at the seams, they sought only to fill the niche left by the disappearance of the Soviet Union. It looked as if the West's leaders liked having a weaker, less aggressive USSR. They clearly did not lend any credence to the prospect of its transformation and did not plan to offer Gorbachev any serious help to restore the Soviet state, even in a new form.

At the same time, the West no doubt understood that the USSR could not stand on one leg with the other dangling over a cliff for very long. It just couldn't figure out what to do and preferred not to think about it. I remember those years, when the iconic Russian question—"What is to be done?"—became a Western preoccupation, too. Western elites had no answer to it. Gorbachev, meanwhile, was desperately pinging the West with requests for loans. Western leaders heard him and demanded in return, "Give us a plan. Tell us how you intend to use the money." And then they did nothing.

Grigory Yavlinsky, one of the future leaders of the Russian democratic movement and a close confidant to Gorbachev at the time, came to the United States in 1990 to propose the idea of a Grand Bargain—a plan that would invite the West to take a major role in cooperating with Soviet reforms. Yavlinsky's proposal met with polite evasions and deferrals. "Money can't compensate for the lack of strong foundations for a new system," the skeptics in the Bush administration told him. "And we're not going to help you revive what is rotting away." The skeptics were right, but the West was caught in a Catch-22: It feared a Soviet collapse, but it also couldn't bring itself to do what it took to preserve or reform the Soviet Union. Gorbachev's dream of renewing the state or creating a new kind of community of states was slipping away. Of course, no one knows what would have happened if Gorbachev had received the Western support he needed to implement radical reforms. No one knows whether Gorbachev would have embarked on these reforms if he had gotten the support he desired. But since that support was never very likely to materialize, we can only engage in idle speculation about what could have happened.

In July 1991, when the economic situation in the USSR was critical, Gorbachev attended the Group of Seven (G7) meeting in London. It was the first time a Soviet leader had been invited to the annual summit of global grandees. As his press secretary Andrei Grachev later recalled, Gorbachev's fellow elite treated him "like a supplicant, politely but indifferently." He "did not touch the hearts of the pragmatic members of the G7."[2]

When I asked Gorbachev about the Seven Plus One summit, he replied bitterly,

> I did not ask for grants. There was no talk of the Marshall Plan. We talked about loans with very specific conditions. Some of the Western leaders were ready to give us this urgent aid. Mitterrand spoke hotly and emotionally in our support. But then Bush took the floor

and announced that perestroika was not a credit-worthy undertaking and there was no need to talk on that topic further.[3]

That pronouncement effectively ended Gorbachev's mission in London. The elder Bush had hammered the last nail in the political coffin of the father of Soviet liberalization, and the other leaders of the West buried him. The club of Western democracies no longer believed in perestroika. They had decided to wait and see what would unfold.

Of course, fear of global chaos would eventually force Western leaders to loosen their countries' purse strings, albeit slowly and reluctantly. Under pressure from Germany and France, the G7 issued the Soviet Union a loan of $11 billion, but the funds didn't begin to arrive in Moscow until late 1991 and early 1992, when Yeltsin and his team, not Gorbachev, were the ones to enjoy them.

Many in the West regretted the departure of Gorbachev and the USSR, and they regarded the new faces filling Kremlin offices with distrust. Unexpectedly deprived of a foe, the West was not prepared to be a friend to the new Russia. Zbigniew Brzezinski analyzed the mood of the Western political and intellectual community during the USSR's collapse:

> When it began, there was no model, no guiding concept, with which to approach the task. Economic theory at least claimed some understanding of the allegedly inevitable transformation of capitalism into socialism. But there was no theoretical body of knowledge pertaining to transformation of the statist systems into pluralistic democracies based on the free market. In addition to being daunting intellectually, the issue was and remains taxing politically, because the West, surprised by the rapid disintegration of communism, was not prepared for participation in the complex task of transforming the former Soviet–type systems.[4]

Eliot Cohen broadly echoed this analysis: "At the end of the Cold War, the US unexpectedly found itself in a situation where it had enormous power and influence, but unlike 1947–1948, it had no idea how to use them."[5]

Only when it became obvious that the collapse of the USSR was inevitable did Western leaders suddenly awaken to the need to avert its most catastrophic potential consequence—namely, an unsecured Soviet nuclear arsenal. But beyond this task, the West simply didn't know what to do with Russia. Russians today who blame the West for the Soviet disintegration of the late 1980s and early 1990s are widely off the mark. The Western elite feared the collapse of the USSR more than the Soviets themselves did; the Soviet elite, after all, were the ones who elected to dismantle their own state. We must therefore put aside conspiracy theories and analyze Western intellectual and political attitudes toward Gorbachev's perestroika and the Soviet collapse calmly and dispassionately.

It's a much simpler matter to understand how the Russian elite failed to foresee the likely consequences of Gorbachev's reforms; independent and strategic thinking skills had languished after decades of Soviet rule. But why were Western intellectuals and politicians so unprepared for the avalanche of events preceding and following the collapse of the USSR? Why were Western experts and political leaders unable to begin a discussion either about Russia's place in a new world order or about how the West could support Russian reforms? Answering these questions calls not for a rush to judgment but for responsible consideration from Western experts themselves.

Notes

1. Zbigniew Brzezinski and Brent Scowcroft, *America and the World: Conversations on the Future of American Foreign Policy* (New York: Basic Books, 2008), p. 158.

2. Andrei Grachev, *Gorbachev* [Gorbachev] (Moscow: Vagrius, 2001), p. 360.

3. All direct quotations without corresponding footnotes are from personal conversations with the author between 2008 and 2010 or from personal diaries.

4. Nikolas Gvozdev, ed., *Russia in the National Interest* (New Brunswick and London: Transaction Publishers, 2004), p. 31.

5. Francis Fukuyama, *America at the Crossroads. Democracy, Power and the Neoconservative Legacy* (New Haven: Yale University Press, 2007), p. 162.

3 THE WEST REGARDS YELTSIN WARILY

From the first days of its existence, the new Russia expected to be embraced and helped by the West. Elite and public attitudes were marked by quite a bit of naïveté, provincialism, and feelings of inadequacy. In 1991–1992, one of the most popular topics for discussion in political and intellectual circles in Russia was the idea of a Marshall Plan.[1] Very few proponents of this plan saw the inherent contradiction between their desire for Russia to be recognized as the inheritor of the Soviet Union's great-power status and permanent Security Council seat, on the one hand, and its status as a supplicant for Western aid, on the other. Russia's leaders, desperately trying to avert the pending economic collapse, gave no thought to political nuance or the need to adjust to Russia's new international role. Indeed, they were in unanimous agreement that the West should reimburse Russia for the collapse of the Soviet Union. The entire political spectrum from left to right agreed that by giving up its empire and its antagonistic position, Russia has saved the West a lot of money. "Why, then, shouldn't the West spend some of that money on supporting Russia?" they asked.

The Marshall Plan idea did not resonate in Washington. Even if it had, there is no guarantee that such aid would have helped Russian reforms. A similar plan for Latin America passed under the Kennedy administration in 1961 (Alliance for Progress) failed to stimulate progress among America's southern neighbors. Another key factor working against the success of a Marshall Plan for Russia was motivation: In the 1940s, the United States had a vital national interest in reviving the economies of Europe and the vanquished nations of Germany and Japan. In the 1990s, no such vital national interests were engaged. Russians overlooked another important aspect, too: A state receiving massive aid on the scale of the Marshall Plan would have to accept limitations to its own sovereignty; Russia was not prepared to accept Western domination.

The West remained divided. Some politicians continued to support a balance of power strategy. They believed that a country's external behavior did not depend on the nature of its political regime. Thus there was no need to spend money to support Russian reforms. Other politicians believed the opposite: that the internal character of a regime mattered, and that it would be easier to deal with a democratic country with a market economy.

However, even those who wanted to help did not know what to do. In 1991 and early 1992, a defining moment for post-communist Russia, the West was only prepared to assist in two ways: helping Russia to maintain control of its nuclear stockpile and easing the pain of the disintegration of the USSR with humanitarian aid. The West's main task, as its leaders saw it, was to guarantee the stability of the emerging new world order. Very few people—at least, very few at leadership level—put any serious thought into how to integrate Russia into that order. Russia quickly moved to take up the Soviet Union's place on the Security Council, but no one knew what form that succession would take. Nor was anyone in Russia ready to think about these questions.

Today, as I think back to what seems not so long ago, I feel bitterness and hurt. So many opportunities were lost—primarily by Russian intellectuals and politicians. How easy it would have been for them to look to their neighbors in Poland or Hungary who had already undertaken dramatic reforms. But the new Russian elite, concerned only with itself, did not show any interest in the world around it, especially its neighbors. At a unique moment in history, when the Russian people trusted the new ruling team and hungered for change, the Kremlin's new denizens could not rally around a consensus about the principles of state-building or Russia's new role in the world. In 1991–1992, quite a few of Yeltsin's comrades sensed that moving "into Europe" was the right direction, but what that meant in practice they did not know. Meanwhile, democrats and liberals whose own intuitions carried them in the opposite direction increased in numbers, and they called for a new, Eurasian mission for Russia within the former Soviet space.

In 1992, the foreign policy quarterly *National Interest* reprinted an article by one of Yeltsin's closest allies, Sergei Stankevich, that stunned Western observers. Stankevich's essay merely said publicly what many people in the democratic camp in Russia already thought privately. Stankevich wrote that the "Atlantic jacket was too tight for Russia's broad shoulders" and that Russia needed "to seek a new balance of Western and Eastern orientations." He was merely humming an old, familiar song in a new key, but the very fact that people close to Yeltsin were dredging up old tunes was a troubling sign. Evidently, the Kremlin was contemplating forming a new Russian identity in the usual way: Neglecting Russia's domestic problems in pursuit of geopolitical exploits and a grand role on the world stage.

Indeed, Francis Fukuyama, Jim Hoagland, Leon Aron, and Bruce Porter, who commented on Stankevich's views in the same issue of the *National Interest*, interpreted them in this way as well. Aron correctly identified the idea of Russia's new "mission" as merely the latest copy of the old Slavophile doctrine of Russia's "special destiny as a bridge between East and West." Porter spared little patience for this notion in his comment:

> Russia the conciliator? Russia the connecting and combining? This is neither idealism, nor a plausible statement of a Russian national mission. It is sheer fantasy and bad history to boot.... A country steeped for nearly a millennium in self-isolation, a people with only the most limited knowledge of the outside world, a culture still struggling to rid itself of xenophobia—this is hardly a country that can play the role of world conciliator and harmonizer.

Harsh, but true.

Not everyone in the West reacted so negatively to the dream of turning Russia into a new "bridge" between East and West. Quite a few commentators issued calls for an understanding of the reasons behind Russian nostalgia, and for treating the Russian elite more gently. Meanwhile, having neglected to discover a new modus vivendi, the Russian elite fell into old habits. While nationalism pushed the former Soviet satellite states in Eastern Europe toward the West, it was once again pushing Russia in an imperial, anti-Western direction. A few years later, Russia's return to its Soviet-era role would be all too obvious. And it pains me somewhat to confess that Russian liberals and democrats not only were unable to stop it; they even willingly jumped on that bandwagon.

Western leaders, unable to keep up with events as they unfolded, had no idea what to discuss with Yeltsin. And whenever they did figure out something to say, they did not always have good suggestions. John Major, British prime minister at the time, wrote in his memoirs:

> Some of our European partners, for so long fearful of Russia, were less sensitive to her plight. When Boris Yeltsin dined with the lead-

ers of the G7 or the European Union, he sometimes found himself interrogated on his progress in implementing economic reform by heads of the government, none of whom could have carried out similar measures in their own democracies. It was, I felt, both bad policy and graceless behaviour.[2]

In order to really help Russia, the West had to come to an agreement on the fact that the transformation of Russia and the former Soviet space was its new mission. There were quite a few people in the new Russia who dreamed that the West would take on this transformational role. Instead, the West saw the decline and fall of its former opponent as a sign that it should move on to other issues—not an unreasonable interpretation.

Today, I find myself asking why the West should have spent any time and money on Russian reforms. I can understand the Western pragmatists who saw that a Russia mired in the abyss of an economic crisis could no longer challenge the West. Why should the West strengthen and revive a country that might pose a threat to its existence once again? There were no guarantees that a strong Russia would also be a friendly Russia. Indeed, the new Kremlin did not bother concealing its dreams of a return to Russian messianism.

Some politicians in the West expressed support for aid on the condition that Russia demonstrate its readiness for transformation. There is a kernel of logic to this reasoning that, at the time, we Russians did not understand. After the wave of universal love for the West, the Russian elite, including the democrats, became increasingly disillusioned with the West, which had no intention of embracing Russia. There was another sense as well: The Russian elite wanted to blame the West for what it could not do itself.

Recalling the reaction to Russia in Western political circles at the time, Yegor Gaidar admitted, "The initial attitude toward Russian economic reforms in the Western political-financial elite was very cautious and cool."[3] Anders Åslund was even more blunt: "The leading powers in the West did not give Russia the necessary financial help when Russia started economic stabilization."[4]

The West was wary of the new Russian elite and the plans of the Russian reformers. Much depended on the line the United States would take toward Russia, for it was the only country that could bring the West around to a new global mission. The elder Bush remained true to a policy of "realism"—that is, a policy focused on interests and maintaining the balance of power, a policy that ignored Russian internal processes as much as possible. Bush's attitude toward Russia was understandable: Russia as an actor on the global stage was now a manageable problem, so why open up the Pandora's Box of its domestic problems? Washington did open a few channels of aid to Russia and the newly independent states, but the aid was limited and could be seen more as a manifestation of political correctness, or as a show of magnanimity and sympathy for a former foe. In trying to explain Washington's position, Derek Chollet and James Goldgeier wrote that Bush and his advisers "understood that the United States had an interest in steering Russia's transformation the right way, but they had no big ideas on how to do it."[5] In Russia's eyes, the elder Bush would be remembered as a leader who not only did not know how to help Russia at a watershed moment but also one who couldn't even decide whether it *should* be helped. There are perhaps some American experts who can disprove this perception. There are at least a few, however, who agree with it. Charles Kupchan wrote, "The United States plodded ahead with little change of course. The foreign policy of George Bush (the elder) was aptly dubbed 'status quo plus'."[6] That foreign policy meant the United States would preserve everything as it was, minus the USSR. The transformation of Russia did not fit into that picture.

Notes

1. The Marshall Plan (officially named the European Recovery Program), a program for aiding Europe in the aftermath of World War II, was established by the United States in 1947. Seventeen European countries, including West Germany, received aid. The total aid provided by the United States was $100 billion (the equivalent of $700 billion today).

2. John Major, *John Major: The Autobiography* (London: HarperCollins, 1999), pp. 501–2.

3. Gaidar has said that two ambassadors at the time—Sir Rodric Braithwaite, the British ambassador to Russia, and Robert Strauss, the U.S. ambassador—did much to ease mistrust toward the government that succeeded Gorbachev. See Yegor Gaidar, *Dni porazhenii i pobed* [Days of defeat and victory] (Moscow: Vagrius, 1999), p. 168.

4. Anders Åslund, *Rossiya: Rozhdenie rynochnoi ekonomiki* [How Russia became a market economy] (Moscow: Izd-vo Respublika, 1996), p. 381.

5. Derek Chollet and James Goldgeier, *America Between the Wars* (New York: Public Affairs, 2008), p. 118.

6. Charles A. Kupchan, *The End of the American Era* (New York: Alfred A. Knopf, 2002), p. 22.

4 HELP OR WAIT?

In early 1992, several politicians called on the West to pay attention to Russia. The first was Helmut Kohl, perhaps out of a sense of gratitude for Russia's agreeing to the unification of Germany. Yeltsin's advisers recalled that Kohl was the first Western leader who had used the familiar form of address (*ty*) with Gorbachev to switch to the same (*ty*) with Yeltsin. He was also the first to address Yeltsin by his first name, Boris, and helped his new friend enter the elite club of world leaders.

The second politician to begin lobbying for Russia's interests in 1992 was John Major. He supported Russia's entry into the International Monetary Fund (IMF) and attempted to persuade his colleagues in the G7 to give Russia financial aid. Major later admitted that he had trouble convincing Japan to support Russia due to the Kuril Islands dispute. The Americans, too, were in no hurry to spend money on Russia.

Nevertheless, the United States also had its own surprising advocate for aid to Russia: Richard M. Nixon. The conservative Republican former president called on America to support the new Russia. Nixon warned that if the reforms in Russia failed, historians would ask the United States, "Who lost Russia?" In March 1992, Nixon sent the elder Bush a memorandum that warned: "Yeltsin is the most pro-Western leader of Russia in history ... whatever his flaws, the alternative of a new despotism would be infinitely worse."[1] This was amusing revelation; while Nixon did not believe in Yeltsin's democratic nature, he believed in his pro-Western orientation. Soon after Nixon, yet another advocate for Russia appeared: Presidential candidate Bill Clinton included the idea of helping Russia in his campaign platform. This was a dramatic reversal of the West's attitude toward Russia.

It is at this point that we must take note of a significant fact. The active assistance of a united Europe was much more important to Russia than any other kind of aid. Only the European Union could help Russian society understand and internalize new principles and standards. This was the kind of aid—not money—that a country building an entirely new political and economic system really needed. To facilitate this kind of relationship, Europe had to create a new framework for relations between the European Union and Russia that would allow Brussels to use the mechanism of conditionality to influence how Moscow adapted to its new principles. The only time this framework could have been created was late 1991, when the Russian elite was beginning the task of creating a new state. Alas, the very idea seemed like madness to Europe's elite. America could have convinced them otherwise, but Washington wasn't ready to take such a conceptual leap in the dark either. Clinton might have been able to pull it off, but by the time he came to Washington it was too late.

Candidate Clinton's efforts weren't entirely in vain, however. Running for re-election, Bush couldn't allow Clinton to portray himself as Russia's savior, so on April 1, 1992, he announced his intention to put together a $24 billion aid package.[2] This announcement came just before the populists and nationalists in the Congress of People's Deputies, the Russian parliament, in Moscow had planned to begin another series of attacks on Gaidar and his government. Unfortunately, once again, the aid came too late, as money only began to flow into Russia's coffers after Gaidar had left the government.

Anders Åslund has calculated that the United States saved $1.3 trillion in reduced military spending at the end of the Cold War. Timothy Colton noted that the collapse of the USSR allowed the United States to cut its armed forces by 30 percent. Between 1993 and 1999, however, U.S. aid to Russia was no more than $2.50 per person for the whole period. That figure amounts to just 1 percent of the U.S. defense budget for a single year, 1996, or in other terms, one fourth the price of a Nimitz class aircraft carrier.[3]

In his book *Across the Moscow River*, former British ambassador Rodric Braithwaite wrote regretfully: "Determined Western leaders could have tapped into the general sympathies for Russia and put together a genuine stabilization scheme which would have mitigated the pain of transition and relieved much of the distress which ordinary Russians were to suffer over the next few years."[4] Responding to those who thought the money would just have been pilfered by corrupt Russian officials, Braithwaite wrote, "Mechanisms of corruption were not yet in place, and Western aid at the right moment might well have helped turn the corner. It is another of the 'ifs' of history." Now, years later, quite a few representatives of the

Western world share his view when they think about why things turned out as they did in Russia. I should add that even massive aid might not have been enough, if the West had not also conditioned that aid on the Russian elite organizing the regime and the state around new principles. Without such conditions, Western aid most likely would have given rise to those "mechanisms of corruption."

The bewilderment of the Western political community and its lack of a Russia policy were a reflection of the disorientation and paralysis gripping the West at the time. Jim Goldgeier spoke mournfully of "the West's intellectual weariness after the Cold War." Traditional Sovietologists, focused on confrontation between the West and the USSR, could not bring themselves to think in new categories. They merely reclassified themselves as supporters of Realpolitik rather than experts on the transformation of the former USSR. Nor did the traditional course of "democracy promotion" work any better in relation to Russia. The transformation of an empire and a superpower required a special approach.

The West's inability to comprehend post-Soviet reality was in many ways the result of confusion in Russia. The Russian political and intellectual classes did not know which way to go. The emotions that overwhelmed them when the USSR fell quickly gave way to disorientation, even despair. James Collins, U.S. ambassador to Russia in the 1990s, recalled, "Many people from the Russian power structures came to us and asked us for advice on what to do. And what could we offer?" I should clarify one thing: The new Russian leadership had no idea how to find answers to existential or transformational questions, but they quickly found a way to monopolize the lifeboats for themselves when the Soviet *Titanic* began to sink, as would soon be revealed.

There was another factor restraining the West from helping Russia. As Thomas Carothers explained during a recent conversation, "After World War II, Germany and Japan were included in the American world without any questions. But it was not clear who needed a strong Russia and why." Thus doubts that the new Russia would be both anti-communist and Western in its outlook explains much of the West's recalcitrance at a critical period for Russia. The West was in no hurry to strengthen a potential rival, instead using the time to restructure the world order. And since the Western elites were not prepared to make bold decisions, the only choice was to avoid rocking the boat.

The West's position toward Russia in 1991–1992 was tied to the policy of the Bush administration. That policy was to focus on America's current interest—namely, security, not integrating Russia into the community of liberal democracies.

Western aid in the early 1990s was compensatory. It sought to help a weakened Russian state maintain stability and avoid a collapse that would endanger the whole world. At the same time, it sought to help guarantee statehood for the newly independent countries in order to avoid the possibility of a restoration of the Russian empire. These two goals defined the limits of policy. It was as if the West was saying, let's stop right here and see what happens next.

What did Yeltsin want in those years? At first, he wanted Russia to be part of the West, and even dreamed of a partnership between Russia and America. In February 1992, at a summit with Bush at Camp David, Yeltsin pleaded with Bush to declare that Russia and the United States were allies. Bush's refusal upset and disappointed him. But he did not back down. Indeed, at every opportunity he tried to get the West and especially the United States to be Moscow's partner.

The new administration in the Kremlin believed its first priority was gaining membership in all the Western clubs, first of all the International Monetary Fund and the Council of Europe. Andrei Kozyrev, then-minister of foreign affairs and the most pro-Western minister in Russian history, repeatedly said that Russia intended to become a "normal country" and a "responsible partner" of the West. But the Russian elite felt that Russia's efforts to break with communism had already earned it a free membership in the Western clubs, even before it considered adapting itself to the rules of those clubs. Talk to the effect that Russia needed to adapt to anyone's rules deeply irritated members of the Russian political class, even those who considered themselves democrats.

The most contentious point for the Kremlin and Yeltsin's team were the questions of Russia's "national interests" and whether they should be subordinated to Russia's westward-leading trajectory. Even democrats like Vladimir Lukin, who would become one of the founders of the democratic party Yabloko, thought that Russia must maintain a "multivectored" policy and not "subordinate" itself to the West. That meant that Russia should continue to be, in the words of one of Kipling's *Just So Stories*, "the cat that walked by himself." From the very beginning of the new Russia, the Russian elite maintained ideas that would soon create obstacles on the path to Europe.

For Yeltsin and the Russian elite, there was no doubt that the West was the only force that could avert the looming economic collapse. Yeltsin asked for help from Western leaders at every opportunity. Of course, he did not like to admit it. He would later write, "I believe that we should never put Russia in the position of a country that receives help and has others trying to solve its problems."[5] The fact nevertheless remains that he appealed to the West many times. Yet in all those supplications, he left out one request: forgiveness of Soviet debt. The debt was a crippling burden on an already feeble Russian economy. By late 1993, Russia owed the West close to $119.3 billion, 43 percent of its GDP. Most of the debt was owed to Germany (only $2.8 billion to America). Yeltsin did not ask, nor is there evidence that Western leaders gave any serious consideration to easing Russia's debt burden at that pivotal moment for the new Russia (1991–1992). On the contrary, when it became clear that the USSR was doomed, representatives of the G7 rushed to Moscow with a single goal in mind: to demand that Russia and the former Soviet republics promise to repay Soviet-era debts. In a few words: business, not philanthropy, was the order of the day.

As I mentioned, this was a pivotal moment for Russia: when the Russian elite could have chosen to turn to the West; when Western leaders could have advised Yeltsin about the principles on which he should build both state and regime. Yeltsin, who didn't know what to do with the enormous state that had been thrust suddenly into his hands, would surely have been receptive to Western advice. Indeed, he begged for it. But no one in the West was prepared to accept the responsibility of offering it. And the advice that Yeltsin did get, as Major wrote, was never very likely to help.

Notes

1. Strobe Talbott, *The Russia Hand: A Memoir of Presidential Diplomacy* (New York: Random House, 2002), p. 31.

2. The bulk of the aid had to come from Europe and Japan. The United States was prepared to appropriate $5 billion, and the World Bank, $4.5 billion. Most of the U.S. aid was in the form of tied loans, which require that the recipient purchase American exports. But the Americans also sent Russia sixty-five transport planes, increasing the value of the aid by $189 million.

3. Timothy J. Colton, *Yeltsin: A Life* (New York: Basic Books, 2008) p. 129.

4. Rodric Braithwaite, *Across the Moscow River* (New Haven, Conn.: Yale University Press, 2002), p. 315.

5. Boris Yeltsin, *Prezidentskii marafon* [Midnight Diaries] (Moscow: Izdatel'stvo AST, 2000), p. 181.

5   CLINTON TURNS THE WEST AROUND

In early 1993, there was an unexpected shift in the attitude of the "collective West" toward Russian reforms. That watershed moment was the election of Bill Clinton to the U.S. presidency. "The world cannot afford the strife of the former Yugoslavia replicated in a nation as big as Russia, spanning 11 time zones with an armed arsenal of nuclear weapons that is still very vast," the president announced in April 1993.[1] Clinton believed that he needed to prevent Russia "from blowing up in our faces" as the former foe began feeling its way forward toward an uncertain political future.[2] Clinton was the first Western leader to think about how to keep Russia from becoming the "sick man of Europe." Unlike his predecessor, George H. W. Bush, Clinton seemed to understand that safeguarding the West from an unpredictable Russia required doing more than just preserving the status quo; rather, global security depended on Russia's ability to reform itself. Clinton's leadership style was an attempt to combine two traditional American approaches to foreign policy: the need to protect America's interests with the desire to promote its values. As for America's interests, one could get an impression that he believed they would be better served by a strong Russia, not a weak one. However, his motives in refashioning Russia policy weren't really important. What did matter is that he tied international relations into domestic political processes in Russia, based on his understanding that Russia could become a responsible partner only if it reformed itself. And Clinton's rhetoric and actions proved that he was prepared to invest serious resources in his vision for Russia, making reform one of the main goals of his foreign policy.

Before his April 1993 meeting with Yeltsin in Vancouver, Clinton said, "You know and I know that, ultimately, the history of Russia will be written by Russians and the future of Russia must be charted by Russians. But I would argue that we must do what we can and we must act now. Not out of charity but because it is a wise investment...."[3] Strobe Talbott, who helped ignite Clinton's interest in Russia, defined the administration's goals in the memorandum "Strategic Alliance with Russian Reform": "Russia is on the path toward becoming a modern state, at peace with itself and the world, productively and prosperously integrated into the international economy.... It should be the US policy not just to prevent the worst but also to nurture the best that might happen in the former Soviet Union."[4] America had stopped vacillating. It was now signaling to the rest of the West that it was time to hasten to Russia's aid.

However, there was one major problem with this approach. By the time Clinton was ensconced in the Oval Office, the Gaidar reforms were done and the new head of the Russian cabinet, Viktor Chernomyrdin, did not intend to continue the reformist experiment. In 1993 Russia was entering a new stage of development, not transformation, but the creation of a system of personalized power. Yet again, the West's support for reform came a day late and a dollar short.

The main thrust of the West's aid to Russia was support for its market reforms. At Clinton's urging, the West offered Yeltsin a mechanism of aid through the IMF. Besides supporting reform, the IMF was supposed to help Russia pay foreign debt, buy food, and address social problems. The conditions were more generous than the ones the IMF usually imposed on countries with which it worked. For its part, the Russian government had to rein in inflation, create positive conditions for investment, attract foreign capital, collect taxes, and implement macroeconomic stability. Aside from the IMF, the European Union, the World Bank, the European Bank for Reconstruction and Development, and a number of nongovernmental organizations (NGOs) also provided aid.

The received wisdom in Russia's political class was that Yeltsin was spineless and the Western capitals kept his team on a short leash, to the detriment of Russia's interests. Yeltsin in fact often found himself in agreement with the West. For example, he agreed to bring Russian troops out of the Baltics, accepted the inclusion of former Soviet satellites in both NATO and the European Union, and in the end he agreed to the Western proposals for the resolution of the crisis in Yugoslavia. Of course, Yeltsin argued, threatened, and cajoled before acquiescing. But Russia simply did not have the power to resist the reduction of its sphere of influence.

As for internal transformation, the West's only opportunity to influence the direction of Russia's development came in 1991–1992, when the country was still undetermined in its path. But the West preferred not to interfere in Russian affairs during that time. When it began helping Russia in 1993, the train had already left the station. In the end, the West supported the type of transformation that the Russian political class had chosen, which prioritized economic reform. First the market, then democracy.

This raises a question: Was the market reform model imposed on Russia from outside? Quite a few Russian and Western observers maintain that the West forced Moscow to adopt the so-called Washington Consensus, which oriented the country toward macroeconomic stability as the basic precondition for forming a market (liberalization, stabilization, and privatization). During the Gaidar period, there were Western advisers working for the Russian government who favored this approach. The West, through the IMF, stressed macroeconomic criteria as a condition for its aid. So without a doubt the Western community influenced the character of Russia's economic reform. But its influence was not the determining factor. The Russian government was free to accept or reject Western advice as it pleased. Certainly Yeltsin and his team often acted as they thought fit. Gaidar insisted that Western advisers be privy only to discussions on questions of secondary importance. Most importantly, up until the middle of 1993, the West had no institutional mechanism to influence Russian reform. By the time the mechanism was created, the contours of Russian capitalism had been drawn by Russia's ruling class.

The IMF implemented support for economic reform in Russia within the framework of programs coordinated with the Kremlin. But as former minister of finance Boris Fyodorov said, of a dozen points agreed on with the IMF, Russia executed only a few and rejected the rest.[5] "We followed IMF recommendations when it suited us, because those recommendations were not always appropriate," Fyodorov later admitted. Analyzing the role of the IMF in Russian reform, Finnish scholar Pekka Sutela confirmed that most of the programs for which Moscow received money from the IMF were never completed. Nevertheless, it continued to issue loans to Russia to the point that it became the IMF's largest borrower. Thus it would be an exaggeration to say that Russia's economic model had been imposed.

One has to recognize that Western advice was not always acceptable to Russia for the simple reason that Western advisers had trouble understanding the post-communist reality—if they understood it at all. Thus Russia was often justified in ignoring their recommendations.

Notes

1. Bill Clinton's remarks to the American Society of Newspaper Editors in Annapolis, Md., April 1, 1993, http://www.presidency.ucsb.edu/ws/index.php?pid=46392.

2. Strobe Talbott, *The Russia Hand* (New York: Random House, 2001), pp. 42–43.

3. Quoted in James Goldgeier and Michael McFaul, *Power and Purpose: U.S. Policy Toward Russia After the Cold War* (Washington: Brookings Institution Press, 2003), p. 90.

4. Talbott, op. cit., p. 52.

5. As Åslund notes, Russian reformers lacked the "political muscle" to follow through on all of their commitments to the IMF. Moreover, some of the IMF's demands were inappropriate, in his view, failing to take into account the country's actual situation. See Anders Åslund, *Rossiya: Rozhdenie rynochnoi ekonomiki* [How Russia became a market economy] (Moscow: Izd-vo Respublika, 1996), p. 265.

6 HELP OUR FRIEND BORIS AT ANY COST

Western donors could grumble and groan about Russia's failure to follow their advice or fulfill its obligations, but it did not matter. Everyone understood that Washington—the focal point of influence in international financial institutions—had made a decision to support Yeltsin. Clinton would not allow Yeltsin and the reformers to be hurt. The reforms had become a priority for his presidency, and he would not accept defeat. We know, for example, that Clinton pressured international loan organizations to help Yeltsin. There was no talk of the IMF or World Bank dictating terms and conditions to the Kremlin. Any such attempt ended in Yeltsin calling up his friend Bill or, if he could not reach him, his friend Helmut, who could reach his friend Bill. And Bill would immediately call the IMF or the World Bank and tell them to knock it off. If that did not help and there were still problems with the next tranche, then Anatoly Chubais would take the next plane to Washington and scare the American gentlemen with horror stories about the communists eating up the reformers. The attitude of Western leaders to Russian reform, particularly in the United States, was always determined by political expediency. And the meaning of political expediency was defined in the Kremlin.

So rather than the West dictating to Russia, in reality it was the Yeltsin team that dictated to Western capitals, and especially Washington, by means of dire warnings about the country's instability. The West's response was to open the checkbook: Stability in Russia trumped programs and principles, and in Western eyes, the guarantor of stability was Yeltsin, feared at first, but now seen as Russia's defender against the return of communism.

Over time, even Yeltsin's newest advocates in the West began to express concern at the course of Russian reforms. Jeffery Sachs, who had helped Gaidar implement economic liberalization, called on the West to stop making loans to Russia. "In recent years," he said in the mid-1990s, "under the IMF umbrella Russia received loans from the West that merely supported a corrupt and ineffective government." In many ways, Sachs was right, but by this time, no one listened to him anymore.

No criticism, however, could stop Clinton, who kept doing everything in his power to support Yeltsin. Under pressure from the White House, the IMF decided in 1996, when the presidential election campaign began in Russia, to loan Russia $10.2 billion, a figure that was already included in the Russian budget. At Clinton's behest, and supported by Kohl, the G8 held a summit on security issues in Moscow in early 1996. The meeting, not a regularly scheduled one, was transparently a gambit to support Yeltsin's campaign. Yeltsin later recalled, "That unprecedented arrival in Moscow of the G8 leaders was an inestimable moral support for me. They made their choice much sooner than many prominent representatives of the political elite of Russia."[1] Indeed the West supported Yeltsin much more energetically in those elections than either the Russian political class or the public.

Mikhail Kasyanov, former prime minister of Russia, described in his book *Without Putin* how President Chirac and Chancellor Kohl infused Yeltsin's campaign with funds on the eve of the 1996 presidential elections, at a time when Yeltsin's ratings had dropped calamitously and he seemed to have no chance of winning. Kasyanov traveled to Paris and Berlin to negotiate these secret emergency loans for Yeltsin. The Kremlin received $3.5 billion from Berlin and $1.5 billion from Paris, support that arguably helped to secure Yeltsin's victory—and further degraded the Russian regime.[2]

I remember in the mid-1990s that politicians in Washington, Berlin, London, and Paris had little patience for criticism of Yeltsin. They refused to listen to anything unpleasant about Russia or its leader. Very few people understood Yeltsin. He confused the Western establishment with his often shocking behavior, but he was the living symbol of Russian anti-communism. As long as he was firmly in control, the character of the new regime in Russia did not worry Western leaders much, if at all. Their only concern was to stave off the resurgence of communism, which was perceived as the main anti-Western threat. I remember the indignation several Western colleagues heaped on me after reading the manuscript of my book *Yeltsin's Russia: Myths and Reality*, in which I deigned to criticize Yeltsin and his regime. "How can you let the Communists use you?" they said, barely hiding their annoyance. "Yes, Russian democracy is imperfect.

But you Russians need to be patient. Yeltsin is moving in the right direction." These reactions more or less sum up the attitudes among political and expert circles in the West at that time. A few individuals, however, did express skepticism that Russia was going "in the right direction" And I will quote some of them later. But in the meantime, I should note that, while my critics began to reconsider their positive assessments of Yeltsin's Russia in the late 1990s, none of them ever said openly, "We were wrong about Yeltsin and the Yeltsin period." It is a good thing that, in the digital age, printed matter no longer burns; these days you can always sit back, relax, and read through the archives of what people in the West thought about Russia in the 1990s. If you do, you will no doubt learn some interesting lessons about pundits' ability to understand reality.

Notes

1. Boris Yeltsin, *Prezidentskii marafon* [Midnight Diaries] (Moscow: Izdatel'stvo AST, 2000), p. 158.

2. Mikhail Kasyanov and Yevgeni Kisielov, *Bez Putina* [Without Putin] (Moscow: Novaya Gazeta, 2009), pp. 59–62.

7 EUROPE ALSO HELPS

The European Union was another channel of cooperation with Russian reforms. In 1994 it concluded a Partnership and Cooperation Agreement (PCA) with Russia. (The agreement was frozen during the Chechen War and went into force in December 1997.) Article 55 of the agreement reads, "Russia shall endeavour to ensure that its legislation will be gradually made compatible with that of the Community." Russia and Europe developed a program of technical support for Russia (TACIS) on the basis of the agreement that offered aid for market reforms and democracy promotion until 2007.

Now, I may be accused of bias, but I consider the entire experience of cooperation between the European Union and Russia embodied in that agreement as an example of how the West helped the Russian elite reinforce the traditional state, which had learned to adapt to the new rules of the game. No doubt, offended Euro bureaucrats will say that I am wrong, arguing that "There are many examples of Russia changing its behavior." To be sure, such examples exist, but they are merely proof of official Moscow's ability to imitate European principles

The elite had no intention of adapting Russian legislation and practices to EU norms, but that lack of enthusiasm for true reform had no effect on the aid Europe offered to Russia. Neither the PCA nor TACIS employed binding conditions. On the contrary, the character, forms, and recipients of the aid were defined in consultation with the Russian government. Russian bureaucrats, more experienced in manipulation, were able to persuade their EU colleagues to agree with their concept of aid. That aid was directed wherever Russian officials thought necessary. This situation satisfied both the Russian bureaucrats and their European colleagues, but it had little impact on the reform process.

For example, Brussels did not even specify how it ought to influence the development of democratic norms and principles in Russia. The PCA only referred obliquely to "the approximation of laws" and to "the integration between Russia and a wider area of cooperation in Europe." The money was disbursed to create that "approximation" and "integration." Here is what Russian human rights activists had to say about the PCA: "The text of the agreement is pompous but at the same time pathetically impotent, because it lacks specificity. There is no precise formulation of obligations or mechanisms of control."[1] In fact, there is no such formulation because Brussels could not come up with one. Europe, afraid of making a wrong move and angering Moscow, did not know what language to use. "Given time, Russia will start adapting to our rules," the Euro bureaucrats consoled themselves. How little they understood the Russian elite.

Some Western experts assumed that Brussels should have offered Russia membership in the European Union as a way of stimulating Russian reforms. The goal of bringing Russia into the Union was set by European Commission President Romano Prodi, who suggested the idea of a "common economic space." Brussels hoped that Russia would gradually adopt European principles within that space. But as Pekka Sutela said, Russia kept demanding the "impossible." It wanted to join the Western club without changing its rule-sets or sacrificing its sovereignty and traditional standards. For every compromise it made with the West, even when such a compromise tilted in Russia's favor, Moscow demanded compensation. Dealing with a former superpower is never easy, it seems.

In an analysis of the evolution of the Russian elite's views of the West, Coit Blacker recalled Alexander Dallin's famous description of Soviet foreign policy in the Brezhnev era: "It was the tension between the urge to enjoy and the urge to destroy." Blacker believed that the Yeltsin team was following the same course, trying to "integrate Russia, while preserving its independence from without and autonomy within." Blacker called it "contingent cooperation," or the strategy of "yes, but."[2] That policy of "yes, but" would be continued under Putin. But Putin, unlike Yeltsin, tended to be much more enthusiastic about pushing the "But" button.

Notes

1. Sergei Kovalev, "Oil, Gas, Political Correctness," April 28, 2008, http://www.ej.ru/ ?a=note#id=7996.

2. Coit D. Blacker, "Russia and the West," in Michael Mandelbaum, ed., *The New Russian Foreign Policy* (New York: Council on Foreign Relations Press, 1998), pp. 168–69.

8 WASHINGTON'S DICTATE OR MOSCOW'S?

From 1993 to 1994, Russia received $1.5 billion per year from the G7 countries. In 1995 (the year of parliamentary elections), Russia borrowed $10 billion from the IMF. In 1996, on the eve of the presidential elections, the Kremlin received an additional $2.4 billion from Germany and France in addition to the IMF loans; some of the money reportedly went to finance Yeltsin's campaign. By 1996, Russia had received close to $30 billion from other donors. Those were enormous sums in those days. Michel Camdessus, executive director of the IMF, liked to explain the generosity by saying, "We have a country that needs help and our moral duty is to help that country." The real question, however, was "Who got the aid? The elite or Russian society more broadly? And what was the aid for? To implement reforms or to strengthen the Russian regime?"

Western politicians and observers were not that naïve. They knew the answer to these questions. They knew that Western loans were being turned into a political bulwark for Yeltsin. The loans were given to Moscow almost completely without conditions after a single phone call from the Kremlin. Thus, in 1993, at his persistent request, the United States gave Yeltsin $500 million to conduct a referendum that reinforced his position. Western leaders supported Yeltsin despite the Chechen war and the increasing corruption of his regime. At a press conference in Moscow in April 1996, Clinton tried to persuade journalists not to criticize Yeltsin for the war in Chechnya on the basis that even Abraham Lincoln waged a war and sacrificed his own life so that "no state could leave our Union." That was too much. Clinton had shocked even his own administration by how far he was willing to go to support his Russian friend Boris.

After the elections, Yeltsin's Western colleagues once again came to his aid. The next time the West and his friend Bill helped Yeltsin was in May 1998, at the height of the financial crisis. The IMF and World Bank leaders were no longer hiding their annoyance that Russia was neither observing the conditions of its loans nor pursuing reforms. But Washington, worried that Russia would collapse, insisted on continuing the funding. In July 1998, facing pressure from Washington, the IMF, the World Bank, and Japan announced that they were giving Russia a stabilization loan of $22 billion. The loan required Moscow to prepare an anti-crisis program and at long last begin economic reforms. In the meantime, the IMF issued Russia a $4.8 billion loan to help it stay afloat. Once disbursed to Moscow, the loans vanished without a trace. (Of course, no one looked for them in Moscow.) The West's efforts did not help; the Russian economy collapsed.

What if the West had not given Yeltsin those loans? Would Yeltsin have turned to economic reforms out of desperation? It's hard to say, but perhaps that might have given the Kremlin an incentive to at least think about reform.

When the Russian economy failed, Yeltsin was forced to change the government. His new choice for prime minister, Yevgeny Primakov, sent Western officials into mourning. They hated Primakov. A left-wing government was formed and included communists, who now also had a majority in the parliament—a surprise move that obviated all Western expectations for Russia. However, the greatest surprise turned out to be the fact that Primakov's government managed the market much more responsibly than had any of the previous governments led by liberal technocrats. This was one of many Russian paradoxes.

Officials of the international credit organizations—the IMF, the World Bank, and the European Bank for Reconstruction and Development—do not have fond recollections of the partnership with Russia in the 1990s. Russia, for its part, feels no gratitude toward its Western donors. Blaming the IMF for the failures of Russian reforms is a common refrain in both Russia and the West. It is with this context in mind that I should mention one of the most energetic critics of IMF policy toward Russia. The Nobel Prize-winning economist Joseph Stiglitz, vice president of the World Bank in the 1990s, issued a string of well-founded complaints against the IMF. He never missed an opportunity to fault the IMF for opposing the devaluation of the ruble in 1998, when it was absolutely necessary. The IMF instead gave Moscow billions of dollars to support the ruble, fearing, according to Stiglitz, that any change in the exchange rate would lead to a new spiral of inflation because they assumed that Russia had no reserves. They failed to notice—or chose not to notice—that Russia had redundant production facilities that were not working because the price of the ruble was too high in 1998. The leaders of the IMF, backed by the U.S. secretary of the treasury, as Stiglitz mentioned frequently, ignored the World Bank's calculations. The World Bank team felt that new IMF loans would not lead to economic growth in Russia but would only increase the country's foreign debt. Subsequent events proved Stiglitz and his team right.

Stiglitz scathingly summed up the results of the IMF's work in Russia:

> In the years of implementing IMF programs, the market economy with high interest rates, illegal privatization, bad corporate management and liberalization of the capital market merely created convincing reasons for bringing assets abroad. Russia's economic growth came about only as a result of the changes in the economy that Russia subsequently made independently.[1]

Of course, it should be noted that without the financial help of the IMF, which made up a significant portion of the Russian budget, Russia would not have survived those difficult years. But therein lies a paradox: the same Western aid that helped Russia survive also destroyed any incentives to reforming its economy.

Stiglitz was no less harsh in his assessment of the Russian reformers. He believed that they were the ones who did not understand the need to create institutions. Furthermore, not only did they not manage to separate power and property, they effected a new merger of the two. "It's not such a big deal to implement privatization," Stiglitz said, mocking the privatizers. "You can always do it, just by giving property away to your friends. It's another thing to create a private market economy. But that requires an institutional framework, a set of reliable laws and rules." Stiglitz maintained that privatization "in an unregulated milieu" instead of "blocking political intervention in market processes created an instrument that made it possible for special interest groups and political forces to retain power." The Washington Consensus, he concluded, had helped to strengthen the new alliance of power and property.

Not only Western economists criticized the IMF's policy toward Russia; Russian liberals did too. Among them was Boris Fyodorov, a member of the Russian cabinet who spoke out against the mass influx of money into Russia. Fyodorov believed that money corrupted the state and its managers and hindered the implementation of reforms. He was right, but who could possibly refuse an avalanche of dollars, especially one that comes with no strings attached? In the 1990s the money from the IMF and other international institutions played the same role in Russia that petrodollars played in the Putin regime: It destroyed any incentives to reform the economy. Of course, the question remains: Who bears greater responsibility for the ineffectiveness of Western aid? The ones who asked for help and then frittered it away, or the ones who handed over that aid without strict conditions?

The international financial organizations, including the IMF, were unprepared for the mission the Western governments saddled them with. They could help Russia resolve technical problems of macroeconomic stabilization, and they could help it finance individual projects. But Russia needed another kind of help, one that would have incentivized the creation of new institutions. Western financial organizations were helping Russia form mechanisms that could not succeed outside of a certain institutional environment that Russia lacked. Thus, the West helped Russia introduce macroeconomic mechanisms into an alien environment that would serve only to mutate and deform them. Even before Western aid arrived, Russia had started re-creating a system of personalized power and returning to a merger of power and property. Under those conditions, the mechanisms that the international financial institutions were helping Russia to build wouldn't work like they did in Western economies. Indeed, as Stiglitz said, they would inevitably begin to advance anti-liberal goals. Thus the West and the IMF were supporting a system that perverted market principles. They were not guilty of creating that system, however. The blame for that falls squarely on the Russian elite.

Note

1. Joseph Stiglitz, Kto potierial Rossiyu [Who Lost Russia?], *Ekovest*, 2004, N1, edition 4, pp. 4–37, http://www.portalus.ru/modules/ruseconomics/rus_readme.php?subaction=showfull&id=1130407959&archive=&start_from=&ucat=12&.

9 MOMENTS OF TRUTH FOR RUSSIA

There were three moments in post-communist history when the West could have at least halted Russia's return to the past: 1991, 1993, and 1996. In each of those years, Russian leaders not only listened to the opinions flowing out of Western capitals; they actually sought out and heeded that advice. Moreover, Russia depended on Western financial aid, so the West actually had leverage over Yeltsin and his team. In 1991, it could have influenced Russia's choice of development model. The old system was falling apart and the contours of the new one had not yet been defined. The Russian elite was looking to the West as the main factor of development. In those conditions, Western leaders could have advised Yeltsin to push through a new constitution that would have liquidated the remnants of the Soviet state—namely, the Supreme Soviet and the Congress of People's Deputies, the main centers of power in Russia. A new constitution would have made it possible to avoid an exhausting battle for power between Yeltsin and the Supreme Soviet. Western leaders could have also dispelled Yeltsin's illusions about privatization. He and his team regarded privatization as a miraculous instrument that would solve Russia's market problems, summon institutions from thin air, and guarantee the primacy of law. Western leaders could have told Yeltsin otherwise, but at the time, they hadn't decided whether it was worth it to support the new Russia. Nor did they really even understand what was going on there.

Opportunities to influence Russia's trajectory diminished after 1991, but there were still several irrevocable mistakes and misapprehensions that the West could have helped Russia avoid. In 1993, Western leaders could have at least tried to prevent Yeltsin's violent confrontation with the parliament, which resulted in the emergence of a new authoritarianism in Russia. They could have advised him to solve the conflict by holding new elections for both president and parliament simultaneously. Yeltsin and his team would have easily coasted to victory, and Russia's democratic institutions would have been guaranteed. Western leaders, however, chose to support Yeltsin's attack on the Supreme Soviet and his monopolization of power. Blair Ruble's account sums up the incident well: "For many people in the West, Yeltsin saved Russia in 1993 from a return to communism. For many in Russia, it was a moment when violence set back the arrival of democracy."

The West missed yet another opportunity to shepherd Russia's transformation in 1996. The Yeltsin administration, having lost public support due to its rampant corruption, was facing a real possibility of defeat at the ballot box. The West opted to do everything in its power to back their protégés in the Kremlin at the expense of free and fair elections. Thus 1996 marked the beginning of democracy's discrediting in the eyes of Russian public opinion. "But free elections would have led to the victory of the Communists!" say the "defenders" of democracy. Most likely they would have. But here we ought to remember that Yevgeny Primakov's 1998–1999 government, which relied on a left-wing majority in parliament, not only did not bring Russia to the brink of catastrophe, it even rescued it from the crisis brought upon it by the liberal technocratic government.

What would have happened if the West had brought pressure to bear on the Kremlin to adhere to clean elections? We do not and cannot ever really know such counterfactuals. However, we do know what happened in Russia when the Kremlin rejected democratic principles. The electoral shenanigans of 1996, through which Yeltsin's corrupt team maintained its grip on power, led to the formation of a new authoritarian regime that soon locked Russia into an anti-Western path. Naturally the Russian elite, including those who considered themselves democrats and liberals, bear the most responsibility for this turn of events. But the West shares at least some of the blame for failing to understand the processes at work in Russia at the time.

The past cannot be changed or repealed. Any attempt to step backwards in time and try to imagine an alternative course of events would violate the principles of sound historical judgment. Nevertheless, understanding the illusions we labored under in the past and the mistakes we made as a result of those illusions can help us avoid similar missteps in the future. Training ourselves to see what opportunities we missed prepares us to see them, and seize them, in the future.

Looking back at the West's role in Russia's development in the 1990s, we can come to this conclusion: You can help a country transform itself, but only if you understand what's going on there in the first place. If you don't, it's better to just stand back, watch, and learn. But there is one problem with this conclusion: how to understand what you don't understand!

10 WESTERN DISILLUSIONMENT IN RUSSIA AND REPUBLICAN ATTACKS ON DEMOCRATS IN THE UNITED STATES

The year 1999 was another watershed in the relations between Russia and West. Western governments finally realized that the system that had arisen in Russia was not only undemocratic; there was also no guarantee that it would be friendly toward the West. With the reform process at a standstill, Western leaders began to question whether aid should continue to flow into Russia.

This epiphany was most difficult for the European Union, which was in the process of transmogrifying into a sluggish organization incapable of quick reactions. Brussels was disillusioned with Russia and Yeltsin, but it found that it was harder to close down a program than it was to start one, and so the partnership coasted along, fueled by nothing but inertia and the Russian bureaucracy's masterful imitation of European norms. For the Eurocrats, that ersatz activity was the price they were willing to pay to keep the relationship friendly—or at least to give it the appearance of amicability.

The IMF, too, was still working in Russia, but Washington's message to it was that the money faucet should no longer be turned on without good reason and strict conditions. Suddenly, everyone was concerned with accounting for where all the money was actually going. New winds were blowing. Clearly, the time of unconditional support for the Yeltsin regime was coming to a close. In 1999, the IMF stopped making loans to Russia. Other international institutions and American banks soon followed suit. The Export-Import Bank, which had given loans to Russian companies, stopped a promised payment of $500 million to TNK, the Russian oil company.

The West's policy re-evaluation wasn't just the result of an awakening by its leaders; elections in the United States also played a role. The Democrats in the White House were under siege by Republicans, who were asking voters, "How could Clinton have spent so much time supporting Yeltsin's reforms and have produced so little to show for it?" Republicans rallied around the banner "Who Lost Russia?" and the Democrats fell back in disarray.

A Congressional committee chaired by Republican Congressman Christopher Cox published a report ominously titled, "Russia's Road to Corruption. How the Clinton Administration Exported Government Instead of Free Enterprise and Failed the Russian People." The committee had shown incredible energy in putting together the report, meeting not only with White House staff in charge of implementing policy toward Russia but with numerous representatives on the Russian side, from Prime Minister Mikhail Kasyanov to the leaders of the main political parties. The final verdict of the report was harsh:

> The West's victory in the Cold War presented America with its greatest foreign policy opportunity since the end of World War II. Just as America's defeated enemies, Nazi Germany and Imperial Japan, had become free enterprise democracies and close U.S. allies, so too might the new Russian Federation. The U.S.–Russian relationship that President Clinton inherited could only have been dreamed of by his predecessors from Truman to Reagan.[1]

Instead of supporting Russia's transformation into a normal democracy, said the report, the United States had emphasized "strengthening Russia's government rather than deconstructing the Soviet state and building from scratch a system of free enterprise; close personal association with a few Russian officials, even after they became corrupt, instead of a consistent and principled approach to policy that transcended personalities."[2]

The Clinton administration, the report continued, had supported Russia's attempts to build democracy by undemocratic means and had proven unwilling to correct its policy even when its failure was obvious and corruption was on the rise in Russia. "Worse, by using massive lending and aid to plug the gap in the Russian central government's operating budget, the Clinton administration exposed these funds to theft and fraud." The Republican congressmen were especially incensed at the administration's attitude toward its friends in Moscow. "The Clinton administration's enormous political stake in its Russian partners gave it an overwhelming incentive to ignore and suppress evidence of wrongdoing and failure by officials ... who had come to personify the administration's Russia policy."[3]

The Cox Commission was especially scathing in its denunciation of Vice President Al Gore, who allegedly had ignored a 1995 Central Intelligence Agency (CIA) report containing a dossier on Prime Minister Chernomyrdin, his co-chairman in the Gore-Chernomyrdin Commission. The CIA report maintained that Chernomyrdin had accumulated billions of dollars dishonestly. According to the Cox Commission, when Gore was shown the CIA report, he refused to read it, writing "Bullshit" on the cover page. This story circulated widely throughout Washington at the time. The Cox Commission claimed that the Clinton administration reacted similarly to other CIA reports on Russian officials, including some well-known liberal democrats.[4]

To put it bluntly: the Cox Commission was strongly exaggerating the role of the Clinton administration in the Russian reform process. Some of its charges were fair, to be sure, but much of it should be taken with a grain of salt. When the Republicans succeeded Clinton in the White House, they kept to the same course of personal relations with the Kremlin— albeit with one difference: They cared not a whit what happened in Russia. Nor did the problem of democracy in Russia concern them, not even on the rhetorical level.

Notes

1. *Russia's Road to Corruption* (Washington: U. S. House of Representatives, 106th Congress, September 2000), p. 4.
2. Ibid., p. 6.
3. Ibid.
4. Ibid., p. 79.

11 THE DONORS COULD NOT RESIST TEMPTATION

Western law enforcement agencies quickly were becoming very interested in the goings-on in Russia. Their main concern was the fate of Western aid. In August 2000, a Swiss court began investigating Russian officials' alleged laundering of IMF loans through Swiss banks in 1998. There were also suspicions that portions of other IMF and World Bank loans from the 1990s had ended up in secret foreign bank accounts. Western political circles were finally awakening to the strangeness of the situation: Russia was asking, sometimes even begging, for financial aid at a time when more than $15 billion was flowing *out* of Russia and back into the West every year.

Evidence soon surfaced that some Western donors had been unable to resist the temptations of the official Western largesse flowing into Russia and the murky reality on the ground. The biggest scandal involved the Harvard Institute for International Development (HIID). The U.S. government had made HIID the operator for its program of aid for economic reform and privatization in Russia. HIID controlled substantial sums: $57.7 million for Russian economic reform and $20 million for legal reform. Indirectly, HIID coordinated a packet of aid from the American government totaling $300 million. This was an important channel for disbursing aid to support economic reform in Russia in the first half of the 1990s, and HIID project managers also acted as advisers to the Russian government.

In a 2000 lawsuit, a U.S. court found that economics professor and HIID adviser Andrei Schleifer and his assistant Jonathan Hay "used their position and substantial influence on Russian officials in this decisive moment in Russian history to achieve their own financial interests and the interests of their spouses." Harvard University, on whose behalf these gentlemen acted, and the managers themselves later settled the suit and agreed to compensate the U.S. government for damages, including reimbursement for false invoices that Harvard billed in the amount of $31 million.[1] "Protecting the integrity of U.S. funded international development programs is essential to their success and to ensuring our government's credibility among other nations," commented U.S. Attorney Michael Sullivan. "The defendants were entrusted with the important task of assisting in the creation of a post-communist Russian open market economy and instead took the opportunity to enrich themselves. Such conflict of interest activities only serve to undermine important development programs. As evidenced by the hard fought five-year litigation of this matter, the U.S. Attorney's Office is committed to protecting federal funding from misuse and ensuring the adherence to the requirements of government contracts."

What had Schleifer and Hay done? The U.S. government contended that they had collected inside information about the Russian government's decisions regarding privatization and other economic measures and passed that information along to their spouses, relatives, and friends, who then used the information to make lucrative investments. Essentially, they enriched themselves exactly as their Russian colleagues were doing. Rather than imparting Western norms, these advisers were adopting Russian ones. "Improper use of federal grant programs for the purpose of self-enrichment will not be tolerated," said Peter D. Keisler, Assistant Attorney General for the Civil Division, in August 2005. "Today's settlement demonstrates our commitment to fighting fraud and abuse against the United States wherever we find it."[2] I imagine Muscovites would have smirked to hear those words: In Russia, state funds existed for the purpose of personal gain.

. Russian law enforcement never cooperated with their American counterparts in this case. Nor did Russian government officials issue any statements. While Moscow wasn't especially eager to air its dirty laundry in public, by and large it couldn't care less about its image being tarnished by corruption in the privatization process.

Washington, on the other hand, was concerned about the tarnish on its image. It is a fair bet that these two Americans were not the only ones to take advantage of the "Wild East" climate of the 1990s to line their pockets, but these two offered a convenient way for the United States to polish its brand.

Many Western experts believed that the improper use of Western aid would cast deeper shadows over the rules of the game. Janine Wedel, who studied Western aid in Russia, suggested the term "transactorship" to explain the practice of exploiting American-Russian relations for personal gain. In their book *The Tragedy of Russia's Reforms: Market Bolshevism Against Democracy*, Peter Reddaway and his co-author Dmitri Glinski argued that Western aid was being used to reinforce a system that was not the least bit liberal. "Western recipes failed to stabilize the ruble, halt the steep plunge in investments; they also created a humiliating dependency on the West's aid, promoted crony capitalism, fostered corruption and capital flight," concluded Reddaway and Glinski.[3] Charles Flickner, a veteran staffer of the U.S. House Budget Committee who was involved in aid to Russia, was also critical of its results. He placed the blame for its inefficiency on the donors, rather than the bureaucracy that executed the aid. "The main local beneficiaries of American aid were the luxury hotels of Moscow billing an endless stream of visiting delegations at the rate of $300 per night," he said indignantly. Realistically, though, the main problem with Western (in this case, American) assistance to Russia was not the uses to which consultants put it; the main problem was that Western aid was premised on an erroneous model that guaranteed it would be misused. Why didn't the West put a stop to the abuses? Perhaps Russian realities were too overwhelming. Perhaps Western donors were too weak-willed to stand up to it. But whatever the reason, Western aid frequently enabled Russia to fall back into the pattern of corrupt bureaucracy and its traditional fusion of power and property. Having successfully co-opted liberalism and partnership with the West to suit their own needs, the Russian elite saw that the public had become disillusioned with both and was now falling back into old habits. As a result, the outside world's suspicions of Russia grew strong once again.

Toward the end of Yeltsin's term, both Russia and the West desperately tried to pretend that they were still partners, but maintaining that charade was becoming increasing difficult.

Notes

1. "Harvard Defendants Pay over $31 Million to Settle False Claims Act Allegations," USAID press release, August 3, 2005, http://www.usaid.gov/press/releases/2005/pr050803_1.html.

2. Ibid.

3. Peter Reddaway and Dmitri Glinski, *The Tragedy of Russia's Reforms: Market Bolshevism Against Democracy* (Washington: United States Institute of Peace, 2001), p. 310.

12 THE RESULTS OF THE 1990s: WHO IS TO BLAME?

As we have seen from the foregoing analysis, the West had missed several opportunities to act as a transformational force in Russia's development. To be sure, it had influenced Russia, first as a model for emulation, but also by means of its attitude toward Russia. That attitude, however, was not always constructive. In the 1990s, the Western community allowed the Russian elite to turn its banks and business structures into a laundromat for dirty money. Western politicians and businessmen understood what was going on. They couldn't have *not* known; it would be insulting to suggest that they were so naïve. Some businessmen took part in the corruption, a phenomenon that reached well beyond Russia's borders. The Harvard aid scandal is proof enough of how tempting the opportunities for graft were for enterprising Westerners in a wild and disordered Russia.

The worst part of this story is that the West, through its own elites, had supported a system whose foundations would soon be exposed as anti-Western. Strobe Talbott admitted,

> I think, we can only be self-critical ... [E]conomic reform could have used a lot more major up-front support from the outside world. We and other Russian reformers should have paid a lot more attention to the kind of structural side of what was necessary in economic reform and ensuring that there would be real rule of law.[1]

Zbigniew Brzezinski wrote about the West's role in Russia's evolution on several different occasions. In his book *Second Chance,* he sounded a more critical note than had anyone else up to that time:

> More deliberate U.S.–EU cooperation might have spilled into other strategic domains. The effort to draw Russia into closer relationship

41

with the Atlantic community might have been more successful if the United States and the European Union had made a joint endeavor to engage Russia.... It was never made to feel that it would be genuinely embraced in some special association with these institutions. Worse still, the Western allies never made it clear to Moscow that it risked isolation if it chose to reestablish authoritarianism.... Instead, Russia was continuously flattered as a new democracy and its leaders personally propitiated.[2]

Later, Brzezinski also said of that period, "We could have perhaps done more to create some sort of shared institutions in which the Russians would feel more a part of the major European adventure that is so important globally today."[3]

Regarding America's role in Russia, Arnold Horelick and Thomas Graham wrote:

Close identification [of the White House] with an increasingly feeble Yeltsin; strong support for radical reformers with their thinning popular support base; public insistence on reform programs most Russians believe led their country to ruin ... have caused increasingly more Russians to question the wisdom, judgment, and benevolence of the United States.[4]

As we can see, the West has not deluded itself about its own role in Russia's evolution.

In the 1990s and especially in the early part of the decade, the United States and the European Union were in an exceptionally good situation geopolitically. The challenge of international terrorism existed but was nowhere near as explosive an issue as it would become in later years. The capitalist model, too, seemed triumphant, its present troubles nowhere in evidence at the time. For America, this was a period of global preponderance, one that may never come again. Unfortunately, the West lacked the intellectual, political, and strategic potential to seize that historic opportunity and use it to bring Russia into its orbit, to find the institutional solutions that could have prevented Russia's regression.

In the second half of the 1990s, the character of the new system emerging in Russia, or at least its basic elements, was becoming clear to Western political and economic analysts. So why did they stubbornly continue to support Yeltsin and his regime? There are three reasons.

First, they supported Yeltsin because, in a sense, they feared the devil they knew more than the devil they didn't know. That is, Western leaders feared the communists' return to power more than they feared the rise of a new authoritarianism. Many Western leaders believed that only Yeltsin could keep the communists out of the Kremlin, and so they followed the lead of the Yeltsin team and the liberal technocrats close to the Kremlin, who had learned to skillfully manipulate that fear. It's Yeltsin or the communists, they said. That dilemma allowed them to successfully manage both Russia and the West's attitude toward it.

Second, the West had invested so heavily in Yeltsin that Western politicians did not want to go to the trouble of seeking out and propping up another candidate. Western observers saw no alternatives to Yeltsin. He was head of state: Whom else were they supposed to deal with?

Third, they supported Yeltsin because, despite his unpredictability, he was predictable enough. He entered into agreements with the West on foreign policy and almost always kept his word. Despite his vacillations and his longing to return to old stereotypes, his foreign policy still tended to lean toward the West. Supporting Yeltsin thus seemed like a wise investment in positive relations between Russia and the West. Western politicians were prepared to accept Russian authoritarianism as long as Russia continued to be a productive partner in international affairs. What the West had failed to foresee was that the Russian system of personalized power would sooner or later consolidate itself by means of playing up anti-Western feelings.

Western leaders often compromised their principles in dealing with Russia. Most did it with their eyes wide open, for understandable reasons of political expediency. They were betting on an individual who started to centralize power, supporting a market model that turned out to be oligarchic. There were many, however, who from the beginning clearly saw the vulnerability of the paradigm stressing the market and privatization and ignoring the independent institutions. Ralf Dahrendorf wrote in 1994, "When economic values prevail over political ones, there is a risk of loss of freedom. The new economy of capitalists is just as illiberal as the previous economy of Marxists."[5] Juan Linz and Alfred Stepan came to a similar conclusion. "In our opinion, the fact that Yeltsin decided to implement economic reform before a democratic state was formed weakened the state, undermined democracy, and in the final analysis, deformed the economy."[6] Despite having obtained unprecedented freedom of action in Russia and direct access to the Russian decision-making centers, the West had effectively put the economic cart before the democratic horse. Market reforms could not work without new institutions and an emphasis on the rule of law.

The actions taken by Western governments depended on how their analysts perceived reality in Russia. In the 1990s, the majority of these analysts were optimistic, stressing the success of its democratization and market reforms. The skepticism of analysts like Peter Reddaway or Stephen F. Cohen was the exception. To express optimism about Russian reforms was merely to affirm the world victory of liberal civilization, to celebrate a kind of "end of history" in the Fukuyama sense. No one in the West wanted to acknowledge the possibility that the Western brand of civilization would suffer a defeat in Russia. Indeed, it often seemed as though some thought they could hasten change in Russia merely by the force of their own optimism. The uglier tendencies that became apparent in Yeltsin's Russia were dismissed as mere footnotes in the Russian success story. The majority in the West believed that capitalism would lead Russia to democracy sooner or later, but even those in the minority who knew better preferred to keep quiet. They did so for a variety of reasons. Some didn't want to venture too far from the protection of the herd. Others didn't want to appear Russophobic. Perhaps others had pecuniary interests in expressing unjustified optimism. But it's not my task to bring up the question of motives.

In an assessment of the state of the American analytical community in the 1990s, Charles Kupchan wrote,

> Not only has there been little demand for Americans to think about broad questions of grand strategy, there has also been little supply. The Cold War generation continues to debate matters of geopolitics, at least in the pages of academic journals. But there is little in the way of a rising generation of strategists.[7]

This remark of course applied to Russia experts, too—in the United States and in the West as a whole.

Let's assume for a moment that the West had somehow managed to create a Marshall Plan for Russia and had sold the Kremlin on the benefits of constitutional reforms, the creation of independent institutions, the rule of law, and regular, democratic transfers of power. Would all of that have changed Russia's trajectory? It's hard to say. A Marshall Plan that excluded Russia from the Western system of international institutions would have failed. But if there had been a common strategy to include Russia in that system, then Russia would have had more opportunities for transformation and, accordingly, its return to the past less likely. Only Russia's direct integration in European institutions would have guaranteed success. However, the European Union, burdened by its absorption of East Germany and the former communist countries of Eastern Europe and the Baltics, could not have gone that far. The West could have offered Russia membership in NATO, but that ship had long since sailed.

The West offered Russia participation in a number of transnational forums in order to help it adapt to Western standards (for example, cooperation with NATO, the European Union's PCA, and membership in the Council of Europe and the G8). But these were passive instruments to bring Russia "into the West." None of them involved conditionality—that is, mechanisms tying Russia's gradual entry into the West with its mastery of successive liberal-democratic norms. The West never developed such a carrot-and-stick system.

Europe had successfully used conditionality to push former communist countries to adopt reforms in order to gain entry into the European Union. The West's failure to set conditions sent a signal to Russia that it could successfully use a policy of blackmail and imitation of the West. Would conditionality have worked with Russia the way it did with Bulgaria and Hungary? Theoretically yes, but on one condition: Russians had to relinquish the idea of their nation as a great power. The idea that the West could set conditions on the behavior of a "Great Russia" was a nonstarter. Thus the fact that Yeltsin had sought to establish Russia as the successor to the USSR on the world scene limited the West's ability to influence its development.

The West's experiences helping instill democratic institutions and market rules in other countries show that it would have been naïve to hope that the West could be a determining factor in Russia's transformation. Democratization and marketization can succeed when the society in question achieves a national consensus on the decision to move toward liberal democracy. In those cases, Western aid can accelerate and ease the transition. But without such a consensus, Western pressure and aid has rarely turned out well.[8]

So perhaps it was foolish ever to think that the West would be a key factor in Russia's transformation. However, if the West had formulated a common strategy, it might have created opportunities for change. But instead of doing this, the West decided to legitimize an oligarchic model of capitalism and a personalized system of power. Some individuals in the West were not aware that they were doing this. Others were compromising their principles to secure what they saw as a pro-Western regime. The West needed a manageable, friendly Russia in order to implement its own foreign policy agenda. As subsequent events would soon show, support for Russia's new authoritarianism would have the unintended consequence of encouraging its evolution in an anti-Western direction.

Notes

1. Strobe Talbott, interview conducted by Mary B. Warlick from the Bureau of European and Eurasian Affairs on March 22, 2009. The videotaped remarks were shown by the State Department on May 24, 2005. Transcript and video available at http://www.state.gov/ p/eur/ci/rs/200years/122762.htm.

2. Zbigniew Brzezinski, *Second Chance* (New York: Basic Books, 2008), pp. 188–89.

3. Zbigniew Brzezinski and Brent Scowcroft, *America and the World: Conversations on the Future of American Foreign Policy* (New York: Basic Books, 2008), p. 9.

4. Arnold Horelick and Thomas Graham, *U.S.-Russian Relations at the Turn of the Century* (Washington: Carnegie Endowment for International Peace, 2000), p. 19.

5. Ralf Dahrendorf, *Posle 1989. Razmyshleniia o revoliutsii v Evrope* [After 1989: Morals, Revolution, and Civil Society] (Moscow: Ad Marginem, 1998), p. 109.

6. Boris Yeltsin, *Prezidentskii marafon* [Midnight Diaries] (Moscow: Izdatel'stvo AST, 2000), p. 54.

7. Charles A. Kupchan, *The End of the American Era* (New York: Alfred A. Knopf, 2002), p. 24.

8. Assessing the net results of Western aid in the development of democracy, Thomas Carothers concludes that most efforts "have had neither a transformative nor a decisive effect." See *Confronting the Weakest Link: Aiding Political Parties in New Democracies* (Washington: Carnegie Endowment for International Peace, 2006), p. 161.

13 THE ARRIVAL OF PUTIN AND HIS WESTERN PROJECT

Putin's ascent marked the beginning of a new stage in the development of the system that Yeltsin had begun building. Putin stabilized the system by reinforcing its linchpin—personal power—and by strengthening bureaucratic control over property. At first, Putin seemed, like Yeltsin, to hope for partnership and perhaps even greater integration with the West as a means of securing Russia's modernization. The president was getting a sense of the limits of his new position. A novice in politics, Putin was open to influence, and he sought out contacts with the West.

In March 2000, while still prime minister, Putin sat for an interview with David Frost. When Frost asked him about his attitude toward joining NATO, he said, "And why not? Invite us." His response was delivered lightly enough that it could have been taken as just a joke. But the levity contained a question to the West, an attempt to get a sense of what his fellow world leaders thought about him. In effect, he was saying: "We are prepared to talk about this."

In the fall of 2000, Putin traveled to Berlin, where he gave a well received speech to the Bundestag. He called on Germany to start a new page in relations between Russia and Europe. Here was a fresh and inspiring leader who seemed ready for a rapprochement with the West. Putin called Lord Robertson, Secretary General of NATO, and, according to Robertson's colleagues, said, "Come to Moscow. We have things to discuss." He proposed reviving Russia's relations with NATO. Robertson and his advisers excitedly hurried to Moscow, convinced that a new era in international relations had come.

Putin's actions bespoke more than just a desire to put an end to the mutual alienation afflicting relations between Russia and the West toward the end of the Yeltsin era. Clearly, Putin was seriously considering closer ties with the West, but to what end? What did the Russian leader expect to achieve by demonstrating his intention to move toward the West?

Soon Putin set about developing relations with the world centers of influence. He was in a sense his own minister of foreign affairs, and the priority of his foreign policy from 2000 to 2001 was the West.

In June 2001, Putin met with George W. Bush, and they developed a personal relationship. It was during their meeting in Ljubljana that Bush uttered his famous words, "I looked the man in the eye. I found him to be very straightforward and trustworthy, and we had a good dialogue. I was able to get a sense of his soul[!]." By the way, I am convinced that Bush was not as simple-minded as his statement would otherwise suggest. I doubt that he saw, or even wanted to see, into Putin's soul. And if he did see anything, it almost certainly wasn't inspirational. Rather, Bush's statement was a reflection of Washington's desire to resolve its problems with Moscow (in particular, to get out of the Anti-Ballistic Missile Treaty) by means of a personal relationship with Putin. By and large, Bush's gambit successfully turned the U.S.–Russian relationship onto the right track. A cynical move? Sure, but that's how geopolitics works.

The September 11, 2001, al-Qaeda attack on America inaugurated a new stage in the Moscow-Washington relationship. Brushing aside his advisers' objections, Putin decided to directly cooperate with the U.S. anti-terrorist campaign. The United States and Russia were now military allies. This unexpected, albeit short-lived friendship still puzzles many observers. How did it happen? And why did it end so quickly?

The answers to those questions soon became obvious. Putin wanted to prove that his Chechen war, unpopular in the West, had also been provoked by international terrorism. Putin, after all, had been talking about the global arc of instability well before Bush's crusade against Osama bin Laden and al-Qaeda. After 9/11, Putin felt a certain satisfaction in telling the West, "I told you so." But even more than understanding for his actions in Chechnya, Putin wanted reciprocity—full-fledged partnership for Russia and the United States.

The Kremlin, however, understood partnership with America (and the West) not as an opportunity for Russia to adopt its principles but as a condition for securing the West's acquiescence to Russia's course of action. There was no civilizational dimension to Putin's formula for partnership; rather, it contained a rejection of the values of Western civilization, which he proved by his actions inside Russia, such as building his "power vertical" and purging his political opponents. While he was willing to cooperate with the United States, Putin had no intention of giving up his attacks on the independent media or his centralization of domestic power. He was certain that his new formula for partnership with the sole remaining global superpower would be built purely on geopolitics and realist principles.

Western leaders, meanwhile, were drawing their own conclusions about Putin. George W. Bush, Schroeder, Chirac, and Blair saw it this way: Since Russia's transition to liberal democracy had failed, there was no point in wasting their breath on lectures about principles. They placed the blame for the failure of reform not on their own erroneous model or the Russians' failure to execute it, but in Russia's unpreparedness for liberal democracy. "Russia can't be made to resemble the West, and we shouldn't even try," was the prevailing opinion as Putin came to power.

There were even some who maintained that Putin would succeed in reforming Russia where Yeltsin had failed, but this delusional optimism lay in tatters by the end of Putin's first term.

Western decision makers chose the path of least resistance in dealing with Putin's Russia: Bet on the new guy and avoid lecturing him about democracy. So even if there had been a way to influence the new boss of the Kremlin, no one tried it. After all, Putin's predictability and measured tone was a breath of fresh air compared to the emotional and unbalanced Yeltsin. As Andrew Wood, the British ambassador to Russia, put it, "The West, in short, bought into the foundation myth of the Putin era that the new president had brought stability and prosperity after the troubles of the Yeltsin era." Wood added, "Western business interests urged them to continue to believe in the idea that Russia would continue to develop in its own way into a responsible and economically integrated member of the international community."[1] And in fact, the Western business community was an important player in influencing relations between Putin's Russia and the West. Understandably, businessmen weren't interested in lectures on liberal democratic values and freedom; they wanted to make money. By stabilizing the situation in Russia, Putin had created much more ideal conditions for enterprise than had existed in the Yeltsin period. Putin was free to tighten the screws.

Western leaders thus compartmentalized domestic and foreign policy, interests, and values, and energetically sought common ground with Russia. Realpolitik triumphed once again, only this time without the former hostility. The most vivid example of the new approach toward Russia was in the policy of the younger Bush, who continued his father's policies.

Bush was not interested in Russia's domestic issues, and he saw no connection between the character of Russia's regime and its attitude toward
the West. The fact that America had strong ties with states like Saudi Arabia and Pakistan apparently persuaded Bush that authoritarian regimes
could be loyal allies of America. The Bush administration was counting on
good relations with Russia's new leader.

The years 2000–2002 marked the height of Putin's pro-Western orientation, which was evidenced by his active cooperation with NATO and his
partnership with Washington in the war on terror. Moscow agreed to let
the United States establish bases in Central Asia and even directly cooperated in America's military action in Afghanistan. In 2002, at the Moscow
summit, Bush and Putin signed a joint declaration on strategic stability in
which the South Caucasus and Central Asia were viewed as a sphere of
common interest for the security of Russia and the United States. This
declaration said:

> In Central Asia and the South Caucasus we recognize a common
> interest in supporting the stability, sovereignty, and territorial
> integrity of all states of this region. Russia and the U.S. reject the
> model of competition of 'superpowers,' which has shown its unsus-
> tainability and which can only intensify the potential for conflict in
> these regions.

At this stage, the Russian leader accepted the West's presence (that is,
America's presence) in traditional spheres of Russian influence. Putin
signed documents that today he would call humiliating "unilateral concessions," perhaps even a betrayal of national interests.

The Kremlin's interest in partnership with the West did not prevent its
efforts to reduce freedom inside Russia. From the outside, it might have
seemed like Russia was turning into a country ruled by a soft authoritarian regime with a pro-Western orientation. Western leaders accepted the
unspoken terms of the deal, trying not to react as the regime moved to roll
back democracy, liquidate the independent mass media, and prosecute
the second Chechen war. The arrangement suited all concerned parties.
Western politicians, who had recently criticized Clinton and Kohl for being
too friendly with Yeltsin and personalizing relations with the Kremlin,
were now doing much the same with Putin. They now believed that warm
personal relations with Putin would be enough to help them to resolve several troubling issues, primarily security issues, and create a more ideal climate for Western businesses. For his part, Putin must have thought that

he had at long last found a model for partnership with the West that was acceptable to the Kremlin.

Putin was clearly placing an emphasis on Russia's partnership with the United States. He was particularly proud of his warm relations with Washington. In November 2001 he said, "If anyone thinks that Russia could become an enemy of the United States again, he clearly does not understand what has happened in the world and what has happened in Russia."

Note

1. Andrew Wood, *Reflections on Russia and the West*, November 21, 2008, http://www.chathamhouse.org.uk/files/12710_1108russia_west.pdf.

14 HOPES THAT ONCE AGAIN DID NOT COME TO PASS

This was a time of great optimism. Russian analysts were writing about "mutual integration," supposedly meaning that the West and Russia would adapt to one another. Western analysts had no particular objection to that approach. Some had even begun to recall the Soviet liberals' old dreams of an East-West convergence. Of course, it was not clear which principles the West would borrow from the East in this arrangement. Personalized power? The merging of power and property, perhaps?

Still, there was hope aplenty for constructive partnership in those years. As Angela Stent and I wrote then: "What appears to be evolving is the new transatlantic partnership, unimaginable before the collapse of communism."[1] We were not alone in our optimism. Robert Legvold thought Russia was ready for asymmetric partnership with America, concluding, "The Russian leadership had to make a crucial strategic choice.... Putin was reconciling himself to what could only be called a junior partnership with the US."[2]

Many in the West hoped that partnership with Russia would push Russia's domestic evolution in a more democratic direction. But the opposite happened: Warm relations with the West, and with Russia's eternal foe, America, did not keep the Kremlin from tightening the screws on the few remaining opponents, or from herding the miserable remainders of the liberals into a political ghetto.

None of this dissuaded the West's leaderships from singing Putin's praises. In a joint statement at the July 2002 G8 summit in Kananaskis, Canada, they declared, "Russia has demonstrated its ability to play a weighty and significant role in solving the global problems we are facing. This role reflects the amazing economic and democratic transformation [!] that took place in Russia over recent years, primarily under the leadership of President Putin." Under pressure from Washington, they reversed their earlier decision that Russia would not be permitted to chair the G8 until it had joined the World Trade Organization and met other political and economic criteria. Perhaps they thought their courtship would woo for them a convenient partner in international affairs. None of them gave any further thought to the Kremlin's attack on mass media, its destruction of independent television, or its erection of the authoritarian "vertical." When Western leaders visited Moscow, they refused to meet with representatives of the opposition and civil society, lest anything interfere with the construction of their "horizontal" relationships with the Kremlin. The policy was to keep the Putin team happy in order to promote Western interests.

The West's advances under Yeltsin had reflected its hope that Russia would not only be a loyal foreign policy partner but also would evolve to a higher democratic plane. Under Putin, the West's advances had the sole aim of securing the Kremlin's cooperation on issues that worried Western leaders. What they did not realize, however, was that Moscow had no intention of reciprocating the West's generosity. Putin believed that Russia deserved all the respect, honors, and emoluments by right. The Kremlin was not about to make concessions that would undermine the foundations of its personalized system.

When in the fall of 2003 the Putin team moved to arrest the troublesome Mikhail Khodorkovsky and crush YUKOS, perplexed Western leaders issued cautious queries to the Kremlin. Secretary of State Colin Powell published an article in the Russian newspaper *Izvestia* on the eve of his January 2004 trip to Moscow in which he expressed Washington's concern about the course Russia was taking, but never breaking from a measured and polite tone. "Certain developments in Russian politics and foreign policy ... give us pause," he wrote.[3] Such gentle rebukes were the limit of the Western response. Constructive relations with Putin still trumped any concerns over his domestic political actions. The West would forgive Putin anything, just as it had forgiven Yeltsin. Putin forged a relationship of mutual understanding not only with Bush, but with Chirac and Schroeder as well. Indeed, he developed an especially warm and confidential friendship with the latter.

Schroeder's attitude toward Russia and its leader were a product of not only his personal preferences and political views but also of the views of Germany's social democrats. Those views might be summed up as follows: "Russia cannot be changed quickly, and progress is still slowly marching on today. All Germany needs to do is be friends with the Kremlin and everything will be fine." In his memoirs, Schroeder later characterized his friend Putin this way:

> In the period of his presidency Putin started building viable state institutions. It was Putin who created a solid base for the vital activity of citizens, enterprises, and investors.... It would be a mistake to make unrealistic demands of Russia regarding political reform and democratic development.[4]

What were these "viable institutions" Putin built in Russia? It is not clear. Apparently Schroeder's partners in the Kremlin convinced him that Russia was not mature enough to handle a more developed democracy. Schroeder took them at their word.

The love affair between Putin and the West as a whole ended quickly, but not in Berlin, Paris, or Rome. By the end of Putin's first term, the West and Russia were quarreling once again. The Kremlin was unhappy because Russia had received neither most-favored-nation trade status nor a special partnership from the West. Despite all their friendly gestures, Western leaders would not accept Putin as an equal at their gatherings. The West, for its part, was unhappy about Russia's temperamental, demanding nature. The courtship at the summit level most likely could have continued anyway, except for two factors. First, though they themselves were indifferent to Russia's democratic deficit, Western leaders were forced to take into account domestic public opinion, which was not so accepting of it. But the second, more important factor was Moscow's expansion into the post-Soviet space. That was something to which Western leaders were decidedly not indifferent.

Notes

1. Angela Stent and Lilia Shevtsova, "America, Russia, and Europe: A Realignment?" *Survival*, vol. 4, no. 4 (winter 2002–2003), p. 122.

2. Robert Legvold, "U.S.-Russian Relations Ten Months after September 11," *U.S.–Russian Relations: A New Framework*, vol. 17, no. 5 (Washington: Aspen Institute Congressional Program, 27th Conference, August 15–21, 2002), p. 12.

3. *Izvestia*, June 20, 2007, http://www.izvestia.ru/archive/26-01-04.

4. See *Nezavisimaya gazeta*, http://www.ng.ru/world/2006-10-25/9_shreder.html.

15 WITH THE WEST AND AGAINST THE WEST

Starting in 2004, Moscow began experimenting with the new strategy of using foreign policy to maintain political power. Its domestic foundation was proposed by Vladislav Surkov, Putin's deputy chief of staff, who called it "sovereign democracy." Essentially, his idea held that "Russia is a democracy. But we have the right to understand that term as we wish. No one can teach us how to live." This conceptual innovation gave the Kremlin the justification for pushing away the West and developing its own version of liberal-democratic standards. From that moment forward, those standards would give way to pronouncements about Russia's "special" path and the need to "respect Russian traditions."

The Russian elite was returning to the ideology of *derzhavnichestvo* in foreign policy. There is no good translation for this purely Russian phenomenon, which refers to the elite's desire to retain Russia's great-power status, to propagate its missionary impulses, to preserve its imperial designs, and to propound the belief that Russia's destiny is to be the "pole" of its own geopolitical galaxy. The quest for great-power status and personalized power are mutually reinforcing. Authoritarian leaders justify their grip on power by the need to preserve and defend Russia's great-power role on the world stage, and *derzhavnichestvo* legitimizes the autocracy.

Partnership with the West had not paid out the dividends the Russian elite had expected. As long as oil prices continued to rise, the elite felt confident. High oil prices gave the new energy state a sense of its weight and self-sufficiency.

But the great-power aspirations of the political class demanded more. Nuclear might and energy resources—perceived in Russia as hard-power factors—weren't enough. The elite's instinct for self-preservation required it to focus on the rest of the Russian matrix: militarism, fostering a siege mentality to consolidate society, and imperial pretensions that presume the presence of spheres of influence. This was merely another iteration of an old story in Russia, in which the elite marshaled its forces against real or imaginary enemies in order to retain centralized power. The security of the state within that matrix required the existence of defensive barriers made up of satellite states.

The Kremlin's return to the great-power formula needed ideological framing. Minister of Foreign Affairs Sergei Lavrov conceptualized Russia's foreign policy by tying it to a civilizational context. His statements illuminate the thinking of the Russian elite and the direction they chose for Russia's development. Here are the basic points of Russia's foreign policy strategy as Lavrov formulated it in 2004–2007: The old global order was obsolete. Russia proposed the creation of a new world government, a 'troika' of the main centers of power—Russia, the United States, and the European Union—that "could sail the world boat." The world must switch to "network diplomacy" and dismantle outdated alliances (primarily NATO). Finally, "Russia cannot take anyone's side in a conflict of civilizations. Russia is ready to play the role of a bridge between them." The choice of words here—"middleman," "bridge," "superpower," "network diplomacy," and "geopolitical triangle"—testify to the mood prevailing among the Russian elite. Interestingly, the authors of this doctrine sounded very much like American neoconservatives and George W. Bush during his first term. They, too, had proclaimed the twilight of outdated global institutions, as well as the beginning of a new chapter in history. The Kremlin evidently wanted to show the world that it could be just as unilateral as America.

Russia unveiled the new Putin doctrine at the February 2007 Munich Security Conference. The Russian leader announced that "the world has approached a decisive moment, when we must think seriously about the entire structure of global security." Putin was showing an almost Bushian capacity for bluntness. With jaw clenched, he threw his words in the faces of the hushed Western audience sitting before him:

> Today we are witnessing an almost uncontained hyper use of force— military force—in international relations, force that is plunging the world into an abyss of permanent conflicts.... One state and, of course, first and foremost the United States, has overstepped its national borders in every way.[1]

This was an ultimatum. The Kremlin was ready to sour relations with the entire Western world if America did not accept the Kremlin's rewriting of the post-1991 world order. Putin's rhetoric left no doubt that Russia had become what Leon Aron and Dmitri Trenin called a "revisionist state." Trenin wrote,

> Munich and [what] followed was a demand for partnership on the Kremlin's terms. In condensed form, the terms boil down to this. Take us as we are, don't interfere in our domestic issues; recognize us as your equals.... We will make concessions if you do.[2]

Putin's bluntness in Munich came as a shock to many in the West, but their surprise only shows how inattentive they had become. Indeed, they should have been surprised that Putin's challenge had not come sooner.

It would be a mistake to conclude that the Kremlin had decided to free itself to move only in a single direction—that is, to contain the West. It wanted to create a platform that would enable it to maneuver in many directions. On one hand, it wanted to position Russia outside of the West—that would allow Russia to act on its own. On the other hand, Moscow wanted to guarantee itself a place in the ruling triumvirate with the United States and the European Union. That meant reviving the post-Yalta division of the world while at the same time building Russia's partnership with the West. These were incompatible desires: One cannot have a balance of power system with mutual deterrence that also secures Russia's absolute freedom of action—and then, in addition, friendship with the West. The point of a balance of power is that the actors work to limit everyone else's freedom of action while maximizing their own.

The majority of Russian politicians and experts supported the new Russian revisionism for geopolitical reasons: Russian might was growing, the West was weakening, U.S. hegemony was waning, and Russia needed to seek redress for past humiliations as well as recover its spheres of influence. Sergei Lavrov chose the values approach. Speaking in June 2008 as the foreign minister of the new government formed by the new president, Dmitri Medvedev, he declared, "There is no doubt that with the end of the Cold War, a stage of world development has ended, the 400 to 500 years in which the European civilization was dominant." This was a bizarre reading of history: The collapse of the USSR heralded not the victory of Western civilization but its "conclusion." How had everyone gotten this so wrong?

So what should we expect now? According to Lavrov, the world faces a dilemma: either to "accept Western values and become the Big West," or "another approach, which we promote." This other approach means that "competition becomes truly global, taking on civilizational dimensions and the object of the competition become[s] values-based models of development."[3] It is unlikely that Lavrov would have improvised such a grandiose statement. As such, the official representative of the ruling administration in Russia had declared that his country planned to offer the world a new value system and a new model for development. The official thinking inside the Kremlin was that Russia could once again become a civilizational alternative to the West.

Just before Lavrov's speech, members of the Russian elite had spoken of the possibility of accepting liberal principles but implementing them in accordance with Russia's special character. Now they were saying they were prepared to offer the world an entirely new value system. It wasn't clear what that system was: the one that had collapsed in 1991?

Apparently Lavrov himself got mixed up in ideological constructions. No later than 2007, he explained the causes of the Cold War this way, "Bipolar confrontation was a conflict within a single civilization and the opposing forces were the product of tendencies, albeit different ones, of European liberal thought."[4] Therefore, the USSR and the West belonged to the same civilization, and both America and the Soviet Union were products of European liberal thought! The minister would have had a hard time proving this thesis. But open polemics with the regime had ended in Russia, so Lavrov did not have to worry about finding proof—at least for his Russian audience.

Here is another confusing thought: If the West and the USSR were part of the same European civilization, as Lavrov assured us in 2007, then why did the West and Russia start competing in the "civilizational dimension" just a year later? Lavrov demonstrated the mental flexibility of a top-class diplomat, maintaining in the very same speech (June 2008) that even though "we" are offering the world "another approach," "Russia considers itself as part of the European civilization, with common Christian roots."

These bewildering paradoxes must weigh heavily on the consciences of the speechwriters in the foreign ministry, but let's leave them aside for a moment. The important thing is that Lavrov himself was claiming that a nation's foreign and domestic policies were intimately connected. Many people in Russia had preferred to maintain the illusion that the differences between Russia and the West have nothing to do with norms and principles. But here was the Russian minister saying, "Yes, they do!" And ironically enough, on this issue, he was right.

Remember this statement. Write it down. Keep it safe in your wallet or purse. For as surely as the sun rises in the East, Lavrov will change his mind on this issue yet again. His vacillations expose the Russian elite's tortuous search for an explanation for the Russian system and for the country's behavior on the international scene. The elite desperately wants to prove that Russia does not differ at all from the West, even that the West was just like Russia. It also needs to throw a sop to the traditionalists, who say that Russia does indeed differ from the West and can even compete with it—without specifying how. One can only sympathize with anyone who has to explain Russia—to explain that stagnation is movement, that convulsions are really a conscious strategy, that the private wishes of the ruling class are national interests, and that a total lack of principles constitutes a new form of pragmatism. You must really have to work yourself into a lather to convince the world of something you yourself don't believe.

Conceptual confusion aside, the Kremlin had made clear what it expects from the West: noninterference in domestic affairs; recognition of its right to spheres of influence in the post-Soviet space; the inclusion of Russia in the collective "governance" of the world; and long-term contracts for energy delivery and beneficial conditions for Russian business in Western markets. In response, Moscow was ready to cooperate with the West on security and to respect the interests of Western businesses operating on Russian territory. If the West were not prepared to accept these proposals, Moscow would follow its own rules of the game.

This was a survival strategy, allowing the political class to enjoy the benefits of the Western world while rejecting its standards. In this model, situational pragmatism is everything; principle is nothing. As I have written elsewhere, it is "being with the West and against the West simultaneously." Without flinching, Moscow can defend the unity of Serbia, undermine the unity of Georgia, and threaten to do the same with Ukraine. Russia belongs to the NATO-Russia Council, participates in joint maneuvers with NATO, and even cooperated in peacekeeping missions in the Balkans; yet it never stops labeling NATO as its main foe. The Kremlin undermines international stability in order to preserve the domestic status quo. To be dogmatic and revisionist at the same time is the one remaining hallmark of the Putin era. Putin may one day bow out of Russian politics, but the paradigm he created will exist indefinitely unless the Russian system is radically restructured. Even then, it will take a long time to shed the habits now ingrained in the Russian political mind-set.

Western leaders have met Russia halfway yet again, accepting several elements of the Putin-Lavrov doctrine. They refrained from interfering in

Russia's internal affairs. They even tried to look away as Moscow attempted to restore control over its "near abroad." If not for ever-recalcitrant public opinion, they (or at least Europe) might have success-fully forgotten the newly independent states.

Thanks to petrodollars, Russia no longer needed Western financial aid or its troublesome requirements for reform. But the West continued send-ing it anyway—and in large amounts. U.S. aid to Russia and the newly independent states increased from 20 percent of all foreign aid in 2000 to 36 percent in 2007. Let's look at what the United States gave Russia dur-ing Putin's second term, when the Kremlin began regarding America as a foe. The United States spent about $4 billion to support Russia's eco-nomic development between 2004 and 2007; Russia got $264 million for "improving [!] state administration"; $35 million in humanitarian aid; $100 million for "investing in people" (another form of humanitarian aid); and $3.556 billion for Russian security.[5] Most of this aid went to programs approved by the Russian authorities. Democracy promotion was the least significant line in the budget of official American aid to Russia. Most of the money went to disarmament projects and programs to strengthen Russian security.

Thomas Carothers sought to dispel the idea that Bush was interested in "democracy promotion" in Russia:

> ... the notion that Bush policy represents any kind of all-out democ-racy crusade is an illusion, fueled by the exceptional and confusing case of Iraq. President Bush's prodemocratic rhetoric is grand, but his policy is semi-realist. Its main pillars—the basic framework of strategic relations with Russia and China, the war on terrorism, and the quest for good relations with foreign energy producers—are real-ist endeavors in which democracy plays at most only a minor role.[6]

However, neither the West's sensitivity to Russia's feelings nor its contin-uing aid to Russia halted the deterioration of relations. In 2008, Russia and the West found themselves in open political confrontation. Relations dur-ing the Putin era had ended worse than they had in the Yeltsin era.

Notes

1. English translation of Putin's February 10, 2007, speech available at http://www.securityconference.de/archive/konferenzen/rede.php?menu_2007=&menu_konferenzen=&sprache=en&id=179&.

2. Dmitri Trenin, "Prinuzhdenie k partnerstvu" [Russia's Coercive Diplomacy], Carnegie Moscow Center, Briefing Paper, vol. 10, no. 1, January 2008.

3. Speech on June 24, 2008, transcript available at http://:://www.mid.ru/brp_4.nsf/2fee282eb6df40e643256999005e6e8c.

4. Sergei Lavrov, "Global'noi Politikie Nuzhny Otkrytost' i Demokratiya" [Global Politics Needs Transparency and Democracy], Izvestia, April 30, 2007, http://www.izvestia.ru/politic/article3103583.

5. "U.S. Government Funds Budgeted for Assistance to Russia," http://www.usaid.gov/pubs.

6. Thomas Carothers, U.S. Democracy Promotion During and After Bush (Washington: Carnegie Endowment for International Peace, 2007), p. 11.

16 ALTRUISM AND PRAGMATISM

As long as we're talking about the aid that the West has provided and continues to provide, it's worth discussing, at least in broad outlines, what sort of aid we're talking about. Aid packages have evolved significantly since 1990. In the late 1990s, it had become clear that the old forms of aid to Russia—humanitarian aid, technical assistance, and help in developing market and democratic institutions—were no longer working. In some ways they were even proving counterproductive. When Putin came to power, it became clear that the most contentious kind of aid was that which was directed toward democracy promotion. It harmed opposition movements by making them look like a Western "fifth column" and, furthermore, it irritated the Kremlin. The things the aid was supposed to promote—competition, a genuine multiparty system, an independent judiciary, political and civil liberties, civilian control over security forces, government accountability, and limitations on government intervention in the economy—all had the effect of undermining the foundations of the current state.

Clearly, democracy promotion was threatening to undermine dialogue with the Kremlin on issues of vital national importance to the West. Additionally, the West's other means of gaining leverage over the Kremlin—namely, loans and other forms of economic assistance—were now obsolete.

Until recently, Western donors had many different reasons for providing aid to Russia. Some saw it as a way to help the West implement its strategic or economic interests, but most viewed political, economic, humanitarian, and technical assistance as a way to help Russia draw closer to Western society. But little by little, pragmatism and altruism began to converge. For example, Falk Bomsdorf, the Friedrich Naumann Foundation's representative in Russia, explains the purpose of aid thus: "It's not

out of altruism that I work in Russia, but out of enlightened self-interest."
For Bomsdorf, who has devoted 20 years of his life to Russia, "enlightened
self-interest" means that he wants to help Russia become a liberal country because that would guarantee security for Germany and the whole of
Europe:

> In Europe, we have an interest in a predictable and knowable Rus-
> sia. And that kind of Russia can come about only once the country
> is built on liberal principles. Therefore, we have to convince the Rus-
> sians that those principles are in its own interests, as much as they
> are in ours.

The basic Western programs for technical, humanitarian, and political
aid to Russia were drawn up in 1992–1993, and by the middle of the
decade they were in full swing. Aid during the previous decade had been
largely compensatory—that is, designed to compensate for inadequate
levels of state support for social services like education, culture, science,
health, and so on. The second most important area of Western aid was
assistance in market development and improving governance. "Political
aid," or democracy promotion, has never been a primary focus of aid for
Western donors in Russia. Far from it. Only about 2 percent of all Western government aid to post-communist Russia has been directed toward
democracy promotion. Western governments and Western nongovernmental donors alike have always tried to avoid giving the Kremlin grounds
for accusing them of political interference.

Initially, donors directed political aid mainly to a broad spectrum of
political parties, as well as to efforts promoting judicial and administrative
reform. At a time when Russia's new political system was just being built
and its revenues for such purposes were limited, this aid played a positive,
if not decisive, role.

Russia's nongovernmental organizations had the West's unequivocal
support—not just in financial terms, but also as a source of wisdom and
experience about building civil society. Without Western aid Russia's
human rights organizations surely would not have been able to survive.
And whereas human rights activists in the 1990s also received assistance
from Russian businesses, in recent years the chief resource keeping them
alive has been Western contributions. It's depressing to note that an
organization like Memorial, which is dedicated to preserving Russian
society's memory of its own history, survives only because of Western
donations.

All too often, Western programs in Russia have died the moment the West ceased funding them. The same goes for most of the nongovernmental organizations that owed their existence to Western financing. Conversely, the West's failure to understand Russia has also meant that Western money and efforts have been wasted on movements and organizations with no future.

The most effective programs have been those that have not been directly tied to Western governments. Unfortunately, the United States has viewed democracy promotion as a form of foreign policy to be coordinated by the State Department. This has had a negative impact on the effectiveness of U.S. government assistance to Russia. Aid from the European Union faces a different challenge. European donors themselves admit that the excessive bureaucratization of the aid process puts up major obstacles to implementation. However, Russian observers believe that aid ineffectiveness is the result of its being tied too closely to the Russian government.

Aside from these difficulties, since 2002 Moscow has demanded that the European Union no longer approach Russia as a country in need of "help"; it deserves to be dealt with in the context of a partnership, receiving not guidance from a mentor, but advice from a friend. In fact, there are economic grounds for such a turnabout. Russia has become a self-sufficient country. Its government knows what it wants, and that does not include the adoption of Western standards.

And to be blunt, few Western donors, for their part, take any pleasure in working in Russia. Donors wait for months for the government to approve a new project, only to endure constant and petty monitoring of its implementation. Many donors have observed that, even when times were hard in Russia, the government didn't know what to do with Western donors or their aid, and they didn't particularly welcome it, even when it was nonpolitical. Later on, after Russia "got up off its knees," Moscow was even less desirous of assistance from abroad.

When Putin assumed the presidency, Russia began phasing out all forms of Western assistance. This was inevitable for two reasons: The first was that the regime didn't want to put up with interference by the Western donors. The second reason was socioeconomic: indigenous sources of funding emerged within Russia. Western donors, for their part, saw the petrodollars flooding into Russia as evidence that Russia could now solve its own aid problems. But the fact was that private businesses in Russia were slow to fill the aid vacuum or confined themselves to financing government projects. While it is true that, according to some estimates, Russian businesses had given approximately $1.3 billion to philanthropic missions by 2009, they were much less likely to offer political aid without government say-so. And in 2008, after Russia fell into what has all the signs of being a protracted economic crisis, Russian business philanthropy has fallen off sharply.

Russian authorities no longer conceal their suspicion toward Western aid, even when that aid isn't connected with politics. Andrei Kortunov, who has a long history of involvement in Western aid to Russia, now admits,

> Unfortunately, in the minds of the Russian elite, even the West's social investments, i.e., the transfer of Western experience in organizing social and public life, is considered useless, at best, and subversive, at worst.... That is, 'We'll take the money from you, but we're not going to let you tell us what to do.' The indiscriminate rejection of Western experience—which, incidentally, is still being offered to us on very easy terms—does not bespeak great statecraft on the Russian elite's part.

The same Western donors who have been working with civil society have begun encountering outright hostility from Russia's official institutions. This is hardly surprising. Putin has distrusted Western donors, Russian nongovernmental organizations, and their activities for some time. Putin seems sincerely to believe that any assistance to Russia in the development of democratic mechanisms and civil society is an attempt by "foreigners in pith helmets," as he called Western representatives, to bend Russia to their will. Thus they perceive any nongovernmental organizations that receive outside aid as instruments of influence from hostile forces. Putin has openly and repeatedly fulminated against "so-called 'nongovernmental organizations,'" which he says are "formally independent but are purposefully financed from outside, which means they are beholden."

With the Russian elite behind him, Putin has been particularly harsh in his opposition to Western human rights organizations. The Russian government has labeled the activities of such organizations as "interference in internal affairs,... the imposition on another state of how it ought to live and develop."[1] As of this writing, there is no reason to conclude that this attitude has changed under the presidency of Dmitri Medvedev.

Since 2005, Russian authorities have tried to rigidly control both Western donors and Russian nongovernmental organizations receiving Western aid. In 2006, the government adopted a law that dramatically limited the activities of Western donors in support of civil society. It later eased the strictures on nongovernmental organizations in the summer of 2009, but those changes did not apply to either Western donors or NGOs that use Western funds.

There is today a belief in the Western donor community that Russian democratic reforms have failed. But the community as a whole has not yet decided whether it should continue efforts to support transformational processes in Russia, or, if it should, how it ought to carry out such efforts in the context of the new political climate.

Note

1. Vladimir Putin, speech at the Munich Security Conference, February 10, 2007, http://www.securityconference.de/archive/konferenzen/rede.php?menu_2007=&menu_konferenzen=&sprache=en&id=179&.

17 WHERE WESTERN MONEY GOES

In the years since the new Russia began to emerge in 1991, the West has given the country an impressive amount of aid. U.S. government aid to Russia between 1992 and 2007 totaled $15.95 billion. Yearly amounts ranged from $328.42 million (1992) to $1.04 billion (2007). The peak year was 1999, when the United States tried to help Russia weather the economic crisis and avert financial collapse. That year's total, delivered through a variety of channels, surpassed $2.13 billion. It bears remembering that this was the year that power in the Kremlin changed hands.[1]

But what did an average year look like? In 1997, Washington provided Russia with $542.52 million in aid for economic development, social stabilization, governance, and security. The largest portion, $456.2 million, went to security assistance. Another $38.45 million went to promoting "democracy and fair governance"; $31.65 million went to support economic development; $930,000 to humanitarian assistance; and $18.29 million to "investment" in individual citizens.

How do these numbers compare with those of 1999, the year in which power was transferred from Yeltsin to Putin? Of a total $2.13 billion given that year, $790.05 million went to security assistance; $85.64 million to promoting "democracy and fair governance"; $65.06 million to economic development; $1.17 billion to humanitarian assistance; and $24.38 million to "investments" in citizens. These totals suggest that the United States was by no means interested in rocking the boat.

How much official U.S. financial assistance went to the "democratic package"? A negligible amount, it turns out. To show this, let's see how American aid was apportioned through USAID (United States Agency for International Development). In 1997, USAID earmarked $173 million for Russia. The largest part of this, $43.35 million, went to promote private enterprise. The second-highest amount, $31.6 million, went to health and the environment. Assistance to government and local authorities implementing finance and tax reform came to $6.75 million; $5.2 million went to energy sector reform; $6.5 million to judicial reform; and $4 million to improving local governance. As we can see, the bulk of the assistance in this "package" went to the improvement of government at various levels. Only $5.4 million was allocated to "citizen participation"—that is, projects related to civil society. All of the remaining aid money went to social and technical assistance. The breakdown was more or less the same in other years. Clearly, it cannot be said that the American administration was all that interested in promoting democracy in Russia.

Even as U.S.–Russian relations have plummeted, USAID has kept up its Russia program, albeit not on the same scale. In 2006, the United States earmarked $74.5 million for Russia; in 2007, $78.3 million; in 2008, $52.2 million; and in 2009, $56.3 million. The basic components of the aid include children's health, combating AIDS and HIV infection, antiterrorism, good governance, "investing in people," economic development, and civil society.

America provides significant resources to Russia to deal with security issues. Annual funding in this category during Putin's presidency ranged from $790 million to $954 million—impressive sums when one considers that the Kremlin embarked on its anti-American campaign during this period. The main elements of this aid go toward implementing the Nunn-Lugar program, which aims to help Russia dismantle strategic weapons and their means of delivery, as well as to enhance the security and storage of nuclear materials. The program also funds the storage and disposal of radioactive waste, the dismantling of decommissioned submarines, and upgrades to Russia's arms export system. To date, the program stands as a model of effective and constructive cooperation between the two countries. And in addition to and complementing the Nunn-Lugar program, the United States has helped 8,000 Russian nuclear scientists and engineers find employment in civilian projects. For all intents and purposes, during the 1990s the United States was issuing these workers their paychecks.

As part of the Peace and Security package, the Americans are continuing to fund cooperation between Russia and NATO, as well as efforts to achieve compatibility between Russian and NATO armaments. Funds from this "basket" are also used to combat organized crime and modernize the Russian judicial system. As we can see, despite the fact that the Russian government considers America to be its chief adversary and a disagreeable entity in every respect, it doesn't turn down American aid, even in areas of vital importance to the state. Russian officials have successfully compartmentalized or ignored these facts in their calculations.

The U.S. government has allocated a less significant portion of its total aid ($40–80 million annually) to democracy promotion and effective governance, and this aid has dwindled even further in recent years. For the development of "just and democratic governance," the U.S. government gave Russia $21.87 million in 2007, $31.18 million in 2008, and $18.78 million in 2009.

America is not Russia's main benefactor, however. The European Union and individual European countries have also delivered significant aid to Russia. From 1991 to 2007, the European Union offered Russia economic and technical assistance totaling €2.7 billion. Most of these funds were delivered as a part of the TACIS program and were aimed at developing cross-border cooperation; nuclear security programs; aid for the North Caucasus; food aid (between 1998 and 2000); mitigation of the social consequences of reform; agricultural development; institutional, judicial, and administrative reform; and development of civil society and democracy. About 40 percent of TACIS funds were aimed at building a "common economic space"; about a quarter of the total went to developing a "common space for education, research, and culture"; and approximately 15 percent was directed at development in Kaliningrad Oblast. The negligible remainder went toward other areas, including civil society. As we can see, the bulk of EU assistance has been aimed at promoting social and economic transformation. Beyond that, Brussels sent €25 million annually to Kaliningrad Oblast, and €20 million to the North Caucasus. The North Caucasus number is in addition to the €172 million in humanitarian assistance that the Caucasus region as a whole has received from Brussels since the start of the second Chechen war in the fall of 1999. EU aid to Russia declined from €146 million in 2002 to €30 million in 2008. Those amounts are likely to remain at similar levels for the foreseeable future.

What specific projects does the European Union fund in Russia? All kinds, ranging from the construction of a water purification system in St. Petersburg to the allocation of credits for small business and tourism. The European Union is also focusing on converting former military cities and territories to civilian use, as well as destroying chemical weapons stockpiles. Between 2004 and 2007, about €100 million went toward the construction of nuclear waste storage facilities and improved security at Russian nuclear power plants. The European Union gives Russia about

€7 million annually to support civil society projects, including environmental initiatives—in short, not much.

Individual European governments also offer aid to Russia. Among the more successful projects has been a program launched by the Ministry of Defence of Great Britain in 1995 that helps Russian military retirees obtain a second college or technical education at five Russian institutions of higher education. Great Britain has invested more than £18.6 million in the project during its ten-plus years, benefiting about 25,000 retired Russian officers.

In 2004, the Danish government allocated 110 million kroner to initiate an economic development program in Kaliningrad and Pskov oblasts. One of the program's aims is to help de-bureaucratize local government and create a competitive business atmosphere. In addition, the Danish Refugee Council has been active for years in the North Caucasus. Danish nongovernmental organizations also give aid to the indigenous peoples of the Arctic.

The government of Finland has provided €26.6 million for collaborations, especially of a socioeconomic nature, with adjacent regions of Russia. The Finns prefer to fund small projects with quick returns—among them, humanitarian projects such as those aimed at children. These are just a few examples of how European government money is being spent in Russia.

From 1991 to 2001, the government of Japan gave Russia about $136 million for humanitarian assistance, including food, medical equipment, medicine, and technical assistance. It also created several Japanese centers in Russia that offered everything from Japanese language classes to assistance in qualifying for work or study in Japan. Since 1994, 44,000 Russians have used the centers and 3,500 have visited Japan to take professional courses. From 2004 to 2008 Japan spent about $22 million in operational costs for these centers. Aside from this spending, the Japanese Ministry of Foreign Affairs has spent about $9 million bringing Russian officials to Japan to study government there. Japan also sent aid to the disputed Kuril Islands totaling $5 million from 2004 to 2008. (This aid was discontinued in 2009 when Russia refused the funds.)

Along with international organizations and Western governments, there are a multitude of nongovernmental organizations of all shapes and sizes operating in Russia. Beginning in the early 1990s, thousands of volunteers came to Russia with a noble purpose in mind: to help Russia overcome its crisis and become a free and liberal country. It would be hard to tally the financial contribution of Western NGOs toward this goal, but the figure is surely in the billions of dollars. Even more important than money, however, has been the enthusiasm, dedication, and sincerity of these volunteers. Larry Diamond believes that nongovernmental organizations and private foundations have proved much more effective and nimbler than the large government aid agencies. These organizations include the Open Society Institute, the Mott Foundation, the MacArthur Foundation, the Carnegie Foundation, the National Endowment for Democracy, the Konrad Adenauer Foundation, the Friedrich Naumann Foundation, the Friedrich Ebert Foundation, the Eurasia Foundation, and many other large and small nongovernmental organizations, as well as private citizens.

In the 1990s, many of these organizations provided crucial assistance in building democratic institutions—notably, a multiparty system. Today, the focus is on aiding the institutions of civil society, particularly environmental groups, human rights organizations, anti-racism and xenophobia groups, independent media, educational institutions, the Academy of Sciences, and local governments and officials. Moreover, Western nongovernmental donors continue to provide social and humanitarian assistance.

One of the first donors to come to Russia was George Soros, who became a philanthropic institution in his own right. Soros explained his interest in philanthropy: "My personal wealth was around $30 million at the time, and I felt that it was more than sufficient for me and my family. I thought long and hard about what I really cared about."[2] Soros wanted to accelerate the change in transitional societies and help make it irreversible:

> I was in a unique position to accomplish this. I had political convictions, financial means, and an understanding of the importance of the moment. Many people had one or two of these attributes, but I was unique in having all three.... Other Western foundations moved so slowly that it took them years to overcome the legal obstacles; I plowed ahead without paying much attention to legal niceties.[3]

Soros also worked to preserve and reform Russian scientific institutions, spending $100 million on this goal during the 1990s. During the same period, he devoted $20 million to assisting individual Russian scientists. He then founded the Open Society Institute in Russia to strengthen the institutions of civil society. Some 1,199 Russian NGOs took part in the institute's activities. Soros financed numerous other projects as well, from judicial reform to support for libraries. Notwithstanding such unprecedented personal generosity (and indeed in some cases because of it) Soros eventually fell out of favor with the Kremlin. Today, he is afraid to visit the "open society" he labored to create in Russia.

Western nongovernmental organizations continue to operate in Russia, but not on the scale that they once did, no longer providing direct support for political movements, for example. The nongovernmental organizations that once supported political parties and the electoral process in the 1990s now work with civil society, focusing instead on fashioning a new political culture and cultivating political dialogue. "We offer you our experience. Whether you accept it or not is your business," they say. These organizations' long-standing experience in Russia has convinced many of them that the creation of a favorable social atmosphere must precede the creation of new institutions.

Europeans were the first to begin looking for indirect ways of influencing Russian life, and American donors have also begun to move in this direction. In recent years, Western NGOs that previously provided political assistance have all switched their focus to supporting Russian civil society. But owing to increasing governmental pressure on both civil society and Western donors, many have begun phasing out their activities in Russia.

Has Western aid contributed anything to Russia's development? The simple, if unsatisfying, answer is, "It depends." It has helped to sustain the important work of human rights organizations. Lyudmila Alexeyeva, the chairman of the Moscow Helsinki Group, told me, "The Western community has unquestionably been helpful in establishing Russian human rights organizations. Western aid was particularly important in the early 1990s, when Russia was just beginning to develop civil society. Arseny Roginsky, head of the NGO Memorial, echoed Alexeyeva:

> Certainly the West has been a help to our civil society. Western foundations have played a great role, especially in the early stage (the first half of the 1990s). For nascent civic groups and movements, the most important thing at the time was procuring at least some resources of their own, independent of government. Or course it's true that there weren't a lot of Western foundations supporting nongovernmental organizations....

Alexeyeva emphasizes that

> ... it wasn't so much Western funds that were important—though certainly they were necessary to laying the groundwork for our

human rights activists. What was important was the actual experience of the human rights organizations—their mission, how they were organized, how they interacted with the authorities. It would have been very hard for me to have created the Helsinki Group from scratch, had I not had American expertise, which was hugely helpful to me. Yes, we modeled the Helsinki Group on American network-type movements.

Alexeyeva and Roginsky both admit that interactions between Western donors and their partners in Russia have not been without problems. Alexeyeva is loath to overstate them, but she nevertheless had this to say:

> The West helped us on a "leftover principle"; you certainly couldn't say the aid poured in like a river. Often Western donors expended some 90 percent of their budget for Russia on their own advisers—advisers who had to have expensive hotels and tickets.... We had to make do with 10 percent. Still, it was very important for us.

Roginsky is rather more critical:

> Of course I'm itching to rip into those Western foundations—some for the superficiality of their analysis of the Russian reality, some for their red tape, some for timidity and eagerness to maintain a 'balance' to support independent organizations and be pro-Kremlin at the same time, without regard to values (some foundations dealt only with the government outright, or NGOs that were close to it, afraid of getting too chummy with the others). There's certainly no need to overstate the extent of Western support. The foundations spent far less on civil society proper than on the rest of their activities (for example, culture and education). However, one has to take into account the atmosphere in which the Western foundations were operating. After all, the Russian government managed to instill in the mind of the public the idea of 'hostile encirclement' outside the country (Georgia and Estonia, Poland, Ukraine, and other countries—and most certainly the United States), and of a 'fifth column' within. And of course this 'fifth column' (all those independent NGOs, some of the media, and certainly the opposition politicians, who were completely repressed), this 'fifth column' was operating, by the government's lights, on the funds of those same hostile powers. Obviously, foreign foundations can't feel confident and free in circumstances like that: on the contrary. But still I'm grateful to all the

foundations that have supported the structures of Russia's civil society over the past 20 years, and I believe that they've done important and necessary work.

Alexeyeva is of like mind, although she is more inclined to criticize Russians' apathy regarding civil society. "We shouldn't be criticizing the West but ourselves," she told me.

Let's take a look at ourselves and ask why our foundations and businesses aren't prepared to support human rights organizations and are indifferent to civil society. But really the answer is clear: as soon as a businessman is "incriminated" in supporting civil society, he's slapped down. So we're left to rely on Western aid.

Reflecting for a moment, she adds bitterly, "Not long ago I was at Solovki, the site of the infamous Solovetsky Island Gulag camp, and I saw Swedes and Norwegians restoring an Orthodox church. For shame! The West is even taking care of preserving our historical memory!"

My own thoughts on this subject are mixed. At first, in the 1990s, Western aid to Russia helped create a party system and a new political culture among certain political and social groups. But this wasn't enough to avert Russia's U-turn to the past. By the mid-1990s, it had become clear that the earlier forms of Western aid, both the political and developmental ones, were out of date. We needed more flexible means of supporting Russia's ever-shrinking free space. Alas, no one ever discovered these new forms of aid.

The chief obstacle to a reconceptualization of Western aid today is Russia's political elite. They perceive any kind of Western activity in Russia as a threat. Thus, in recent years, many have begun to talk about replacing the aid model (indeed, does a resurgent great power need "aid"?) with a cooperation and mutual engagement model, which presupposes a mutual exchange of experience with the West. It's an idea that has some support among Western donors, albeit possibly under duress. But this begs the question: What kind of Russian experience could be useful to Western society?

Having spoken with many Western volunteers and donors still in Russia today, I sense how disappointed they are in the course of Russia's development. Some now see all their efforts as having been for naught. Liberal-democratic principles in Russia today do indeed seem to have been completely discredited, and Russian society, morally and politically broken.

But seeds often take a long time to germinate in cracked and dusty soil. Russia is entering into a new political phase, in which the exhaustion of the old system is becoming plain. Sooner or later, the search for alternative courses will begin. Only at that point will we see what will become of the volunteers' efforts on Russia's behalf.

If this new stage of political revitalization does indeed come about, we will need a new model for cooperation between Russian society and the West. Russia won't need funding, perhaps not even the political experience of the "old democracies"; it will need to learn from the experiences of the new post-communist democracies in creating a liberal system and modernizing economic and technological life.

Notes

1. See U.S. Government Funds Budgeted for Assistance to Russia, http://www.usaid.gov/policy/budget.

2. George Soros, *The Age of Fallibility* (New York: Public Affairs, 2006), p. 53.

3. Ibid., p. 58.

18 THE MEDVEDEV-PUTIN TANDEM BEING TESTED BY FOREIGN POLICY

The Putin era introduced new elements to the way society and power are organized in Russia, as well as changing the nature of Russia's relationship with the West. The principle of imitation democracy became the basis of the political system, and a dual-track policy of partnership with the West and containment of the West formed the basis of Russian-Western relations. This model was exceptionally effective at securing the interests of the Russian elite. It preserved itself by personalizing power and mimicking the process of reform; externally, it sought to give the appearance of cooperation with the West while simultaneously reviving old imperialist claims.

Let's examine how Medvedev influenced domestic and foreign policy in Russia. Did he change the regime's survival strategy or its relations with society? Did he change Russia's foreign policy model? If so, how did they change? If nothing changed, why not?

Medvedev's arrival in the Kremlin marked the emergence of a new political regime in Russia. This new tandem of two leaders—Putin and Medvedev—was the elite's solution for the problems of continuity and legitimization. It was an unusual form of personalized rule that demonstrated the regime's adaptability. The ruling tandem became a way of keeping Putin in power, thus guaranteeing the status quo established by both Yeltsin and Putin. Medvedev's presidency shows us that the Russian elite has mastered the art of ensuring continuity by imitating change.

This is not the first time in Russia's post-communist history that a "dual regime" has held the reins of power. From 1991 to 1993, Yeltsin struggled with the Supreme Soviet, and from 1998 to 1999, the Kremlin moved to form a strong government under Prime Minister Yevgeny Primakov in an attempt to get out of the economic crisis before turning around and ousting him. These brief periods show that authoritarianism in Russia tends toward its classic form—that is, personalized rule by one leader. There is no reason to think that this most recent two-headed leadership will emerge as a stable institution.

We can see signs of this in the asymmetrical nature of the Putin-Medvedev arrangement: Putin has been controlling the basic financial, administrative, and law enforcement functions, leaving Medvedev with constitutional powers that are impressive on paper but mean little without control of resources. Of course, it's unlikely that Medvedev and Putin could have ever shared power on an equal footing. The duumvirate has reached agreements that helped it avoid overt conflict, but however amicable its internal relations may be, such an arrangement will inevitably fail within the framework of a personalized regime centered around autocracy and the fusion of power and property. Its failure does not necessarily mean open conflict, although the principle of personified rule would seem to suggest it. Instead, various political forces may back one member of the duumvirate or another in order to aggrandize themselves and diminish their enemies. Autocracy genetically does not tolerate ornamentation, conditionality, fragmentation, or violations of the "vertical" structure of power under a single leader. The real question is whether the struggle among the competing factions will lead to elite pluralism or to an even harsher rule under a single leader. This struggle can be tamed under one condition: if one of the leaders demonstrates that he is the real boss, pushing the other to a pathetic role of chair-warmer.

How did Russia react to the political innovation of the Putin-Medvedev duumvirate? In 2008, both the political class and a significant part of the public believed that keeping Putin in power in one form or another guaranteed stability. But the economic crisis that swamped Russia in the fall of 2008 changed that calculus and observers began to think that solving Russia's problems might require Putin to step down. But by late 2009, the economy began to show signs of recovery. Not only had the duumvirate survived an acute crisis, but Putin got his breath back. The Russian regime would, however, undergo profound changes. Even members of the ruling elite believed that the existing system could no longer preserve Russia's stability, much less promote economic modernization.

Crisis itself, or the regime's inability to deal with it, always leads to a search for scapegoats in Russia. In such situations, the natural choice for the scapegoat role is the previous political regime, in this case, Putin himself. By remaining the dominant partner in the tandem, Putin had prevented Medvedev from legitimizing himself as the new face of leadership in Russia. The longer the Putin past dominated, the more it smothered the political class's ability to renew itself. Yet at the same time, the Putin past was undermining the old stability as well. The bitter irony is that the opponents of personalized power were unlikely to be pleased by this state of affairs: By blocking change, Putin was increasing the threat of systemic collapse—a turn of events that no one wanted to materialize.

Most thought that, sooner or later, the Kremlin would revert to traditional autocracy (unless the system collapsed or was reorganized). Thus it mattered little who was the face of Russia's personalized power. Under normal circumstances, the new regime would have used anti-Putinism as the basis for consolidating its hold on power. This is how it works all over the world, even in democracies. The George W. Bush administration took office repudiating the Clinton legacy. Obama in turn repudiated Bush. In Europe, Sarkozy purged Chiracism, Brown pushed out Blair, and Merkel said goodbye to Schroederism. Putin himself did the same with Yeltsin.

It was hard to avoid the feeling that such a moment was coming in Russia, too. Parts of the political class had already expressed interest in turning the last page on the Putin chapter. Putin's future hinged on the depth of the economic crisis and the conclusions that Russian public and elite opinion reached about it. Putin's departure might have allowed Russia to start looking for the ways out of the current uncertainty and daunting problems. Paradoxically, Putin was not only killing any chance for renewal, his presence limited the field for maneuver for the very system he had created. There seemed to be two possibilities: Putin's efforts to cling to power could hasten the system's end, or a real transition of power to Medvedev could extend its life. For all the hopelessness of both scenarios, the second, at least, might have opened the door to new possibilities.

Did this mean that Putin would be forced to descend from his lofty throne on Mount Olympus in the near future? In the past, leaders had clung to their thrones long after their eras had ended, due to Russian society's inertia and lack of imagination. In all likelihood, Putin will remain solidly entrenched when this book goes to press. He may try to stay on through new presidential elections in 2012 for another two six-year terms, extending his reign to 2024. In fact, it became clear in early 2010 that Putin had already begun campaigning to return to the Kremlin. The fact that Putin realistically has a chance to extend his rule into yet another decade (indeed, to infinity and beyond?) is a sign of the profound demoralization and listlessness afflicting Russian society.

From Medvedev's first days in the Kremlin, a popular discussion topic was whether he could somehow beat the odds and become a full-fledged leader. Soviet history gives ample proof that a seemingly weak leader can occasionally outmaneuver his puppet masters. Putin was obviously aiming to defend against that possibility with his choice of successor, but given the inevitable trials and tribulations and economic disruptions ahead, such an outcome remains a possibility. However, how the fate of the ruling tandem is resolved is not really important. As long as the system itself is not reformed, the personalities who staff it will hardly change its trajectory.

The questions that foreign journalists so like to ask, and Russian observers like to answer, are: "Who's in charge, Putin or Medvedev? And who's going to win?" The answer really isn't all that significant. As long as the principles undergirding the present system remain in place (primarily the absence of competition), even the most liberal leader in the Kremlin will have to follow in Putin's footsteps, unless social or political turmoil forces him to take a different route.

The preservation of personalized power in Russia, even in its present "duumvirate" form, means the continuation of the old paradigm of Russian foreign policy—one of the key pillars supporting autocracy. There was never any reason to assume that the new regime would change this foreign policy paradigm, especially given that Putin remained in power. As long as the system remains focused on great-power status, power monopoly, and the fusion of power and property, the broad contours of Russian foreign policy will remain the same whatever tactical juggling the Kremlin may undertake.

The Russian political regime has remained a hybrid, and so its foreign policy was also pulled in two separate directions. But these abrupt shifts from aggression to amity with the West did not signify a change of course within the Kremlin. Rather, the Russian elite had mastered the art of mimicry.

After Medvedev came to power, the West anticipated a change in rhetoric and a greater willingness to compromise on issues that frequently caused irritation or confrontation. His seemingly gentler leadership style had raised hopes of a diplomatic thaw in the West and among liberal circles in Russia. But the events of 2008, primarily the August war with Georgia, showed that Medvedev was not only still working within an autocratic framework, he was also continuing the Putin model of diplomacy with the

West. This was only natural, as Medvedev's role in the ruling duet was to perpetuate the status quo. It remains to be seen whether Medvedev will ever be able to gather the resources necessary to venture outside the boundaries drawn around him by Putin.

19 THE WAR IN THE CAUCASUS AND WHAT IT SAYS ABOUT RUSSIA

Russia's war with Georgia in August 2008 confirmed that Medvedev continued to pursue the foreign policy doctrine developed by Putin and Lavrov.[1] Moreover, the Caucasus debacle showed Moscow's readiness to move from anti-American rhetoric to open political confrontation. The Russian elite viewed Georgia as an "American project," and thus a convenient proxy to show its defiance of the United States. This proves that Moscow still perceived the United States as the leader of a community that was existentially alien to Russia. In fact, Georgia was mainly a pretext for the Kremlin to secure a more assertive Russian role in the world, reformulate its relations with the West, and force the United States to agree to the new order, at least in the former Soviet space. Demonstrations of military might and the readiness to use it were instrumental in achieving this agenda.

The Russo-Georgian war is a story that many, both Russian and non-Russian, would rather forget. We ought to resist this temptation, for the episode revealed much about how Russia positions itself for survival, and how the West reacts. Why did the Kremlin risk political confrontation with the West at a moment when its power in society was largely secure? Few among the Russian political elite sensed the looming financial crisis, so that couldn't have been the reason. Rather, the Kremlin chose to undertake its "little adventure" in Georgia because it sensed that the conditions were ripe for securing Russia's geopolitical interests as its elite understood them. A policy of vengeance and assertiveness had served the Kremlin well since 2004, and it was enticing Moscow to expand its influence—this time in a spectacular way. Economic success and unprecedented high oil revenues were restoring Russia's sense of power just as weakening American leadership was putting a stop to NATO's plans to expand further into former Soviet domains. Aside from that, Moscow had several scores to settle with Tbilisi.

Obviously the military conflict could not have played out as it did without Georgia's open overtures to Europe and the United States, without Europe's inability to come to agreement on Georgia policy, and without America's contradictory desire to both support Saakashvili and avoid irritating Moscow. Russia was even likely to come to favorable terms with Georgia on the question of its separatist enclaves, apparently. On this very question, Medvedev said, "I met with Mr. Saakashvili and told him that we are ready to help in the restoration of territorial integrity of the state. For that, they must behave in the right way."[2] What was "behaving in the right way" in this context? Quite simply, agreeing to follow Moscow's lead. Moscow had just as little concern for the fate of the Ossetians in 2008 as it had in 2004, when terrorists had killed hundreds of schoolchildren in the North Ossetian city of Beslan. As a matter of principle, the Kremlin had never been a strong supporter of the independence of self-proclaimed republics, a fact amply demonstrated by Moscow's rejection of independence for both Chechnya and Kosovo. In essence, Georgia had become a proxy for the systematic incompatibility between Russia and the West. Preserving Russia's imperial great-power status required that Western civilization be contained, and that the other newly independent states, Ukraine most of all, be made to see the heavy price to be paid if they opted to turn to the West. Georgia had to become the whipping boy and the example for the other newly independent states.

Saakashvili's suicidal adventurism gave the Kremlin not only the ideal excuse to enact this agenda but also the opportunity to justify its actions in the court of public opinion. As former Georgian president Eduard Shevardnadze has convincingly explained, over the years the Russian elite had given Saakashvili many excuses to become an excuse himself.

Could military conflict have been avoided if Saakashvili had not acted rashly? Moscow would almost certainly have found another excuse to show the intransigent Georgians and their Western benefactors that the Kremlin could neither be ignored nor challenged. Nevertheless this does not exonerate Saakashvili for his role in the fiasco.

The Caucasus clash merely confirmed the tightness of the connection between domestic and foreign events for Russia. Independent Russian commentators explained the origins of the war in this way:

Russia wanted to teach the outside world, especially America, a lesson—let them see that you can't joke with Moscow; shape up the CIS, demonstrating that you can have the misbehaving presidents of neighboring countries removed; and no less importantly, consolidate your own citizens in a united wave of enthusiasm and also scorn for foreign enemies.[3]

The consequences of the Caucasian war will be with us for a long time. The conflict provided ample proof that the disintegration of the former Soviet empire is far from over. Russia's recognition of the independence of the two separatist Georgian enclaves, South Ossetia and Abkhazia, is clearly part of an effort to restore the old Soviet borders in a very volatile region, raising many questions about the future of the Russian Federation.

The Kremlin was greatly mistaken in at least one aspect of its calculations about the Georgia war: its expectation of support from its allies. Even Belarus and Armenia, long-standing, loyal dependents of Russia, refused to recognize the new statelets of South Ossetia and Abkhazia, despite pressure from Moscow to do so. Russia's refusal to respect the principle of territorial integrity had unnerved its neighbors, convincing them to seek support from other power centers, including the West. Additionally, Moscow failed to unseat Saakashvili and failed to create a schism in the West. Thus, despite Russia's military victory, the Georgia war had exposed even further that Russia's foreign policy was merely a return to Soviet policy clichés.

Within Russia, the war marked the revival of the old tactic of rallying the population around a common foreign enemy, thus distracting them from their real problems. A year later, in August 2009, 71 percent of Russians said that Russia "had acted correctly" toward Georgia (11 percent did not). However, they were supporting the new militarism without the former enthusiasm. Only 29 percent thought that the war "was beneficial to Russia" (in 2008, 40 percent thought so). Nevertheless, rallying the populace against an enemy was still a viable political strategy: In late 2009, 63 percent expressed disapproval of Georgia, 47 percent disliked Ukraine, and 40 percent expressed hostility toward the United States. The war had thus eclipsed any hopes for Medvedev's liberal credentials.

The Georgia clash also forced Western observers to look more closely at the evolution of Russian policy. After August 2008, the West's insouciance regarding Moscow was replaced with concern. "The brief conflict marked a major turning point in European security affairs as well as US–Russian relations," wrote Eugene Rumer and Angela Stent. "It represents the unfinished business of the collapse of the Soviet Union."[4] As Rumer and Stent saw it, the war reflected the unsolved problems of the Russian transformation and attitudes toward the former Soviet republics.

During the war itself, Russia had concerns that it might be isolated and acquire a negative image in the West, but only a year later, the Russian elite had persuaded itself that the West had swallowed it all. "For Russia, August 2008 became the time of acquiring a new face and dignity," wrote pro-Kremlin observer Vyacheslav Nikonov. "It was the Russia that does not let its friends be hurt and was ready to slap the hands of brazen criminals." Russia's representative at NATO, Dmitri Rogozin, concluded, not without satisfaction, "The isolation of Russia, of which so much had been said, did not take place. We have a few problems with the West, but they are not dramatic. The West needs us more than we need it." Other pro-Kremlin commentators took pleasure in the Georgia war as confirmation of the wisdom of Russia's course: "The West had to recognize the new geopolitical reality in the Caucasus," and "Georgia has no chance of becoming a member of NATO—most likely, neither does Ukraine."

A year after the war, Putin claimed that Europeans were actually blaming Georgia for the war but were afraid to say so because of U.S. intimidation. "In the West, we have plenty of supporters," he told Abkhaz journalists in August 2009. "They are all under a certain pressure from NATO's leading country, the United States. And to put it bluntly, many of them don't publicly state their positions, because they would diverge from the US position."[5] It's hard to judge whether Europeans were actually whispering this to Putin or if he came to the conclusion on his own. He may have heard what he wanted to hear, or other leaders might have told him what they thought he wanted to hear.

The pro-Kremlin pundits readily presented the example of Taiwan and North Cyprus, neither of which has ever received support around the world for a formal declaration of independence, in an attempt to prove that the Kremlin didn't need to worry very much about securing global recognition of South Ossetian and Abkhazian independence. Perhaps the Russian elite was consoling itself that it had not lost anything in the Caucasus clash. The Kremlin did believe that Russia had acted correctly and that the West had admitted as much. This perception speaks to the Russian elite's evolution toward incongruity and impunity. Russian liberal commentators worried that "the Kremlin will now legitimize its power by wars around the world." The West, for its part, never did find a formula for responding to the Georgia war that would have forced Russia to acknowledge that certain lines should never be crossed.

In October 2009, an EU "fact-finding mission" presented a report on the causes of the Russo-Georgian war that demonstrated Europe's impotence in the face of the problems of the post-Soviet space. The report concluded that Georgia did indeed initiate the conflict, but only after suffering years of provocations from Russia. Russia, whose major concern was to pin the blame for the conflict on Georgia, hailed the report. The commission did not evaluate the contradictory events that led up to the conflict, nor did it attempt to answer why Georgia thought it wise to pursue such a precipitous military action. It also made no efforts to assess the consequences of the effective revision of Russia's territorial borders, and proposed no mechanisms to prevent a new conflict in the region.

The Europeans, in other words, chose to follow the path of political correctness and avoided expressing any opinions that could annoy Moscow. "The only thing the commission does is to conclude that Georgia says one thing and the Russians another," wrote Russian journalists. "Thanks for the valuable information, but we all knew this without any help from the commission."[6] The report proved that there are events that cannot be evaluated from a "technical" point of view—that is, who attacked whom, and who is to blame. Events like the Russo-Georgian war raise issues of systemic and civilizational dimensions and question whether Europe is ready to respond to challenges from failed transitional societies.

"Let's just move on and start a new chapter," suggested many Western observers who believed the incident was over and should be forgotten. I would argue, on the contrary, that we have to reflect on what had happened because the consequences of this conflict go beyond the relationship between Russia and Georgia and are not limited to the fact that the conflict revised post-Soviet boundaries. In seeking to justify its operations in Georgia, Russia appealed to internationally approved norms and legal principles (the right of self-defense against an armed attack, the prevention of genocide, humanitarian intervention, the "responsibility to protect," sovereignty, and the right of secession), invoking them selectively for nakedly political purposes. This precedent could serve to undermine adherence to international norms and laws in future conflicts.

During the Russo-Georgian war, the Russian Federation Council did not authorize the use of military force outside of Russia's borders. A year later, President Medvedev proposed amendments to the federal law on defense that permit the use of the Russian military force abroad "to prevent aggression against other countries" and to protect Russian forces or citizens. Analyzing the Russian attempts to use normative claims as "a diplomatic resource" and to "modify norms on the legitimate use of military force," perhaps cast in terms "of preventive self-defense," Roy Allison has ample justification to conclude:

This would risk a destabilizing rift between Russia and other major powers on how sovereignty and international order should be upheld. Russia would risk becoming further isolated internationally, and the anxieties of its immediate neighbors about the campaign in Georgia and Russia's readiness to privilege separatism would be enhanced.[7]

This scenario should worry those who want to relegate the Russo-Georgian war to the trash heap of history.

Further events in the former Soviet region confirmed that the 2008 war was neither random nor extreme but an aftershock of the earthquake that brought down the USSR and placed Russia on its current path. One cannot exclude the possibility of subsequent "cold wars" between Russia and Ukraine over fuel or over some other issue. No one can exclude tensions and conflicts between Moscow and other newly independent states if these states express reluctance to become part of the Russian area of "mutually privileged interests."

At the moment Georgia and Ukraine are the litmus test that will show how far the Kremlin may go in its new expansionism and expression of its bruised ego and what forms it could take. True, Georgian and the Ukrainian elites cannot claim that they have been without blame for the previous conflicts, or that they could not have foreseen their particular circumstances. Both countries keep giving Moscow excuses "to worry" about the fate of the former Soviet satellites. The relations between Russia and these neighbors comprise a volatile mixture: money, "pipeline politics," corporate interests, personal ambitions, mutual distrust, and thirst for revenge. But for Russia, its conflicts with Georgia and Ukraine boiled down to the law of self-preservation for an isolated and forlorn state. During the Putin administration, the Russian state returned to its traditional survival strategy still favored by its political class: repression, fear, containment, and vengeance. The fact that the Russian elite is returning to such tactics reveals that the West, Europe in particular, failed to create mechanisms that could have prevented Russian revisionism or at least made it less aggressive.

Russia's conflicts with the neighbors took the new President Medvedev hostage, limiting and perhaps destroying his inclination to modernization. If not for the Caucasus conflict and the Ukraine natural gas dispute, Medvedev might have been able to legitimize himself as a reformist leader. The conundrum in today's Russia is that only a Westernizer can be a reformer, but no pro-Westerner can be the leader of a great power ready to smash its neighbors' windows. Medvedev was forced to pretend that Russia was still a great power, but this time the burden was his own, not one that he inherited from Putin.

The global financial meltdown of 2008 saved the Russian ruling tandem by quickly diverting attention from the Caucasus and from Russia and its damaged reputation. But the events of August 2008 will continue to haunt Russia and its leaders for a long time.

Notes

1. On the causes, nature, and implications of the military conflict between Russia and Georgia, see Garry Kasparov, "Voina Ambitsii i dieneg" [War of Ambitions and Money], www.gazeta.ru/comments/2008/08/13_a28101112.shtml; Andrei Illarionov, "The Russo-Georgian War," *Continent*, no. 140, 2009; and Ronald D. Asmus, *A Little War that Shook the World: Georgia, Russia, and the Future of the West* (New York: Palgrave Macmillan, 2010).

2. Dmitri Medvedev, remarks at a meeting with students and professors of the London School of Economic and Political Sciences, April 2, 2009, http://www.kremlin.ru/transcripts/36.

3. Andrei Kolesnikov, "Vystrel iz budushchego" [The Shot from the Future], http://www.gazeta.ru/column/kolesnikov/2815484.shtml.

4. Eugene Rumer and Angela Stent, "Repairing U.S.-Russian Relations: A Long Road Ahead" (Washington, D.C.: INSS and CERES, April 2009).

5. Ellen Berry, "Putin Promises Abkhazia Economic and Military Support," *New York Times*, August 13, 2009, http://www.nytimes.com/2009/08/13/world/europe/13russia.html.

6. Yulia Latynina, "A Murder With No Killer," *Moscow Times*, October 7, 2009.

7. Roy Allison, "The Russian Case for Military Intervention in Georgia: International Law, Norms and Political Calculations," *European Security*, vol. 18, no. 2, June 2009, pp. 192–193.

20 THE KREMLIN STARTS REBUILDING BRIDGES WITH THE WEST

The global financial tsunami that engulfed Russia came as a complete surprise. The Russian economic "miracle," supported by petrodollars and cheap Western loans, began to implode before our very eyes. The instability of the Putin petrostate was painfully obvious. As Anders Åslund wrote, "The Russian economy Titanic met its iceberg. Captain Putin could not believe his eyes." Fall of 2008 sent still more shockwaves across Russia. In September, the stock market fell by about 75 percent. By November, Russian foreign exchange reserves plunged by $36 billion, from $516 billion to $480 billion. Gazprom saw its capitalization fall two-thirds, from $320 billion to $100 billion. Western investors fled in panic, pulling about $147 billion out of the country. The disaster was relentless and brutal. In 2009 Russian GDP fell by 7.9 percent, while the drop in GDP in France was 2.2 percent, the United States saw its GDP drop by 2.4 percent, Italy by 4.7 percent, Britain by 4.8 percent, and Japan and Germany by 5 percent. China posted growth of 7.1 percent and India 4.1 percent. Inflation was 8.8 percent in Russia, 2.8 percent in Britain, 2.7 percent in the United States, 1 percent in Italy, and 0.9 percent in both Germany and France (Japan posted deflation of 1.7 percent in 2009). Russia's industrial production fell by 24 percent. According to government sources, unemployment in Russia in 2009 was roughly commensurate with that of developed economies at 8.2 percent (Japan posted 5.1 percent unemployment, Germany 7.5 percent, Britain 7.8 percent, Italy 8.5 percent, and both France and the United States 10 percent).

Panicked, the ruling tandem began blaming the West, primarily the United States, for provoking the economic collapse. To admit that there had been domestic causes as well would have been both inconvenient and unwise. Instead, Medvedev told the Russian public, "The problems are not in our economy, but on a different plane. In essence, we are paying for the irresponsible decisions that heated up another economy [the U.S. economy], creating colossal risks and leading to global consequences."[1] He would repeat that mantra several times. The new president tried to divert attention from Putin's failures even though he shared responsibility for these failures.

After laying the blame at the feet of the West generally and the United States in particular, Medvedev then switched gears and made a few conciliatory gestures during his November 2008 visit to Washington. He declared that Barack Obama's election "opens new possibilities" in relations between Russia and America, and he tried to smooth over the abrasions caused by his harsh statements in Moscow. The Kremlin tandem realized that confronting the West and especially Washington made no sense at this stage.

Confirmation of these new winds came in Medvedev's speech at the Council on Foreign Relations in Washington. The moderator was former U.S. secretary of state Madeleine Albright, a thoroughly disliked character in Moscow. Albright asked the Russian president what he had meant when he referred to Russia's sphere of "privileged interests." Evidently, Russian imperialism worried the West more than did Russian authoritarianism. Strange, but true: Not everyone in the West makes the connection between Russia's autocratic system and its need to make neo-imperialist gestures. Medvedev's reply to Albright's question was memorable:

MEDVEDEV: I mentioned Russia's privileged interest ... when I formulated the five current principles of Russia's foreign policy. One of them is the principle for developing relations with nations which traditionally have been connected with the Russian Federation. Or we can say that the Russian Federation has privileged interests there. This does not imply that this is an exclusive zone of our interests. This is not the case. But those are nations which are very important for us, with which we have lived side by side for decades or centuries, with which we are connected by the same roots. I am referring to the states that at one point were part of the Union of Soviet Socialist Republics. Before that they were part of other nations. Those are countries where Russian is spoken, where they have economic systems which are similar to ours, and where cultures are similar to ours. But those are not only nations that neighbor on the Russian Federation, there are other states that are traditional partners. This is what I imply when I speak about "privileged interests," or our "advantaged interests," with regard to those nations.

ALBRIGHT: May I follow up? What are they, when you say not just those on our borders, but partners. Who, what countries does that include?

MEDVEDEV: Well, those are nations that for decades or centuries have enjoyed ongoing contacts and exchanges with us that are important for us, both economic and political. This is a large part of European countries. And this could be the United States of America. [Laughter.][2]

Medvedev's geniality and affability at this event were no accident. Putin would have answered Albright's question in his usual attack mode. Medvedev had retreated into an ambiguous interpretation of "spheres of influence" (which, incidentally, greatly amused the audience). Many Council members found his explanation clumsy, but Medvedev simply couldn't tell his American audience the blunt truth: that Russia regards its neighbors as inferior states that must follow Russia's lead. His explanation of the principle of "privileged interests" reflected the contradictory thinking of the Russian elite: its unwillingness to give up traditional stereotypes and its desire to appear liberal to the West.

In the first half of 2009, the intensifying economic crisis was forcing the Kremlin to rebuild bridges to the West. The Russian *rentier* class—which both desires to be a part of the Western community and to make money from it by skimming profits from the sale of raw materials—realized that its ability to live simultaneously in the East and the West would be threatened if Russia's image became too tarnished. The Russian political class had wanted to frighten the West, not create a nightmare. The problem was not in the enormous debts the Russian elite owed to Western banks and corporations (the corporative debt of Russian companies, including state companies, to Western lenders was more than $500 billion at the time, and more than $110 billion was due in interest payments). Moscow could have defaulted on its debts as easily as it had in 1998. The more serious issue was that the Russian raw-materials state, built on anti-Western principles, could not survive in isolation from its consumers. The Russian *rentier* class needed to be able to sell raw materials to the West and feel secure about leaving its profits in Western banks. When the Russian political class gradually realized its dependence on the West it was forced to mute its assertiveness.

There was one more factor that influenced the behavior of the Russian elite: the Obama factor. The new U.S. administration heralded either new unpleasantness for Russia or a chance for a new, less contentious stage in U.S.–Russian relations. One of Obama's campaign slogans, "The Change We Need" ought to have made the Russian elite anxious, as the idea of changing course was inherently alien to Russia's commitment to the status quo.

The Russian elite, however, hoped that Obama would be preoccupied with the financial crisis and the Bush legacy in the Persian Gulf and Afghanistan. Obama would need Russia's cooperation to deal with these problems. Having already successfully used anti-Westernism to consolidate power domestically, the Russian elite hoped that this naïve new American leader's need for cooperation with Russia would allow it to climb still higher on the great-power ladder.

Two events in early 2009 confirmed the new trends in Russian relations with the West. The first was Putin's speech at the World Economic Forum in Davos. Putin astonished his audience with his confidence, which stood in sharp contrast with the confusion shown by other speakers. Only one other leader could compete with Putin's radiant sense of optimism: Chinese premier Wen Jiabao. Putin stunned Davos with his new "liberalism," too. This was not the unpleasant, bitter man, the defender of paternalism and imperial leanings that Davos-goers might have expected. Rather, Putin was speaking like a Western politician. He warned of the threat of excessive state expansion into the economy. He worried that provoking military and political instability, and regional and other conflicts would distract people from social and economic problems. He called on people to "seek support in the moral values that assured the progress of our civilization."[3] It was as if an alien abduction had occurred: Putin was condemning his own past actions.

Putin impressed people in the improvised question and answer period, as well. He outclassed the panelists with skillfully employed irony. He basked in the flattery of the plenary session members, which seemed to justify his own sense of superiority. He remained aloof from Western businessmen, often with a suppressed grin. A similar scene was playing out with Wen Jiabao. Indeed, why Westerners are attracted to the holders of absolute power is a question for psychologists.

Drawn to him though they were, the participants seemed to have no illusions about Putin personally. This was unexpectedly demonstrated during former U.S. president Bill Clinton's speech. Moderator and founder of the Davos forum Klaus Schwab asked Clinton, "Putin spoke before you, and he announced support for private entrepreneurship. What do think of that?" Clinton gave Schwab a knowing smile, and then turned to the overflowing audience and quipped, "Well, I can only wish him luck!" The sarcasm dripped so heavily from Clinton's voice the audience couldn't help but break up in laughter. This was the reaction to Putin in Davos: People politely and respectfully heard him out and then showed what they really thought.

Putin's appearance at Davos spoke volumes about the mood in the Russian government in January 2009. When he had ruled alone, Putin had refused to go to Davos, so his appearance was evidence that Moscow was changing its tactics. After its anti-Western muscle-flexing, team Moscow needed to backtrack.

When the G20 convened in London in April 2009 to discuss the global financial crisis, it was Medvedev who took to the stage. He continued the tone Putin set in Davos: a readiness to cooperate with the leading countries. It was here that Medvedev had his first meeting with Obama. In an article published in the *Washington Post* on the eve of their meeting, Medvedev confirmed his desire to normalize relations with America, noting, "The need to renew our cooperation is dictated by the history of our relations, which includes a number of emotional moments—the diplomatic support Russia gave the US in critical moments of American development, our joint struggle against fascism, and the era of détente."[4] Such a statement from a Russian leader would have been unimaginable just six months earlier.

Perhaps to lower expectations, the Russian president felt compelled to repeat some classic clichés. He put all the blame for worsening relations on Washington: its decision to deploy missile defense bases in Eastern Europe, its desire to bring Ukraine and Georgia into NATO, and its refusal to ratify the Conventional Forces in Europe Treaty (CFE). Those factors "undermined Russian interests," according to Medvedev.

Medvedev confirmed the Kremlin's desire to reestablish spheres of "special responsibility" for Russia and the United States in world affairs and also to make trilateral cooperation between the European Union, Russia, and the United States the "basis" of world politics, a recitation of the Putin doctrine. This rhetoric contained the seeds of new misunderstandings between Moscow and Washington. As long as the Russian ruling team refused to reassess its foreign doctrine, the underlying factors complicating the return to a cooperative relationship would remain.

Meanwhile in London, Medvedev expressed satisfaction after his first meeting with Obama, as did the American leader. Television reports showed that Medvedev not only was confident in the company of Obama and the others; he was also friendly and warm. He smiled continually for the camera, offering a more human and open image. Medvedev was clearly impressed and enjoyed being included in such elite company. There was none of Putin's sense of wariness and pugnaciousness. Medvedev's warm reception showed that Western power brokers hoped to see him not as Putin's "left hook" but as the alternative partner who could guarantee cooperation with the West. One politician commented, "We'll do everything we can to support Medvedev, and we will deal only with him." The international club hoped that its backing would raise Medvedev's influence back home. But the reality is that such Western support could backfire, complicating Medvedev's position in the Kremlin.

For the time being, the new strategy forced the Russian anti-Western camp to change its rhetoric and some of them did so with gusto. Dmitri Rogozin, appointed by Putin to represent Russia at NATO and well known for his ability, in the words of one NATO representative, "to give his Western counterparts nervous attacks," was suddenly cooing like a dove. "NATO needs us and we need NATO," Rogozin declared. "We are fully committed to cooperation with the West on common threats and challenges," he insisted in a stream of articles submitted to Western publications.[5]

Those who heard the continual two-track voice of Russian foreign policy must have also heard echoes of the previous firmness in these new, more pacific statements: "We want higher status and recognition of our rules of the game." There were nuances in such Russian demands. Some Russian politicians demanded equality with the West. Others demanded recognition of Russia's right to have special responsibility for the world. These demands were not compatible. No Russian politician could explain what the guarantees of Russian "equality" should be or what constituted "inequality." But what was meant by "special responsibility" was clear. They were the same old spheres of "privileged interests."

Of course, Russian politicians, understanding the negative reaction to that demand, came up with a new term, "mutual privileged interests." Foreign Minister Sergei Lavrov explained in an interview in the *Financial Times* that "our relations with these countries [Russia's neighbors] could be described as privileged relations. The word that frightened so many people, but which reflects only that it is a privileged partnership. We have special interests going deep into centuries in these countries, and they have the same deep interests in the Russian Federation...."[6] This may have meant that Ukraine could not join NATO or the European Union without Russia's approval. But could Ukraine demand that Moscow leave the

Shanghai Cooperation Organisation? Of course, it's not clear what would happen if the Ukrainians really did make such demands on Russia, but all of the foregoing suggests that the Russian elite was now stressing the first part of the "partner-opponent" formula without forgetting the second.

Western leaders watching the warming of relations with Russia must have felt a surge of optimism. Many believed that the extended "Putin winter" was over, that they could start thinking again of a new stage of cooperation, maybe even partnership. How little Western optimists understood the logic of Russian development!

But to be fair to them, I have to admit that the global financial crisis has changed not only the international economic environment; it has also had an impact on several myths about Russia maintained by both Westerners and Russians. This may further influence the relationship, but it is difficult to predict how. Here is what Bobo Lo thought about this question:

> The global financial crisis, for all its disruptive impact, has had three salutary consequences. The first is to take much of the heat out of tensions between Moscow and Washington. The second is to explode the myth of Russian invincibility (epitomized in the triumphalist slogan, 'Russia is back'). The third, and most important, is to emphasize the extent to which we are all interdependent. These realities allow us to hope for a more constructive relationship between Russia and the West, one based on positive-sum modernization rather than a mutually debilitating *realpolitik*.

I would add here one premise for the hopeful turn of events that Bobo Lo has been describing: It may happen only if the Russian elite stops faking modernization and does it for real, and the West decides to support it.

This brings our chronological narrative up to the present. I will now turn to the analysis of the foreign policy mechanisms created by the Russian elite to survive the present by prolonging the past. These mechanisms were started by Yeltsin, completed by Putin, and continue to be finely tuned by the Medvedev-Putin ruling tandem.

Notes

1. "Vystuplenie na zasedanii Pravitel'stva 29 dekabrya 2008 goda Moskva, Dom Pravitel'stva" [speech at a government meeting], December 29, 2008, http://euroasia.cass. cn/2006Russia/Russia/speech_President/2008/1804_type63378type82634_211155.htm.

2. A Conversation with Dmitri Medvedev, November 15, 2008, http://www.cfr.org/ publication/17790/conversation_with_dmitry_medvedev_audio.html.

3. Putin speech on February 29, 2009, transcript available at http://www.premier. gov.ru.

4. Dmitri Medvedev, "Building Russian-U.S. Bonds, *Washington Post,* March 31, 2009. .

5. Dmitri Rogozin, An End to Cold Peace, *Guardian,* March 30, 2009, http://www.guardian.co.uk/commentisfree/2009/mar/30/dmitry-rogozin-nato.

6. Transcript: "FT Interview with Sergei Lavrov," March 25, 2009, http://www.ft.com/ cms/s/0/d32b732e-1920-11de-9d34-0000779fd2ac.html.

21 HOW TO FORCE THE WEST TO WORK FOR RUSSIA

The growing problems between the Kremlin and the West didn't keep the Russian elite from creatively using the West to promote its corporative and individual interests. The Russian elite has demonstrated an extraordinary ability to survive and adapt, moving from whining about American arrogance and how Russia was "humiliated" and "ignored" to a much more effective psychological approach: namely, forcing the West to justify itself, to explain, apologize for, and remedy its own defects. They not only expanded into Western economic and political space, but also manipulated the West into supporting a system whose principles are alien to it. Such a feat requires imagination and artfulness.

The Putin regime co-opted representatives of the West into its network structures, both formal and informal; played on contradictions within Western countries; skillfully deployed threats and intimidation; and used Western double standards to justify Russian ones. The Medvedev-Putin tandem continues to use these tactics.

Co-optation usually involves bringing prominent Western politicians to work for the Russian regime or its businesses. Russia perfected this policy on former German chancellor Gerhard Schroeder, whom it made chairman of the board of directors of Nord Stream (a Gazprom subsidiary) and an "independent" director of TNK-BP as well. The Russian shareholders of TNK-BP then executed a management coup, pushing out the British, a maneuver that they would not likely have made without the support of the Kremlin, which keeps a close eye on its leading oil companies. The company needed an "independent" director like Schroeder who is always ready to follow the Kremlin line.

The former German chancellor works the trust he has been given on all fronts, including politics. He travels around the world with the message that Russia is a democratic country whose administration should not be criticized for its lack of democratic zeal. Schroeder claims that, "Russia is a European country and there are enormous opportunities for us in Russia." At difficult moments for the Kremlin, Schroeder is always ready to offer a hand to Putin. He attacked Washington for supporting NATO membership for Georgia and Ukraine. After Russia annexed Abkhazia and South Ossetia, Schroeder assured Europe, "Europe must accept Russia as any other country defending its security interests.... Russia is a responsible and stable country, so close to Europe."[1] Covering a Schroeder talk about Georgia at a Berlin gathering, a reporter for the *Sueddeutsche Zeitung* wrote, "It was as if the Russian ambassador were speaking." The Germans like to joke that "the parrot on Schroeder's shoulder speaks with a Russian accent."

Schroeder represents a great success story for the Kremlin, proving that the West's moral principles can be bought for the right price. Schroeder's appointment generated almost unanimous condemnation in Germany. A few other Western politicians, notably former prime minister of Italy Romano Prodi and former U.S. commerce secretary Donald Evans have received offers to become lobbyists for the Kremlin like Schroeder. (After some consideration, both Prodi and Evans refused.) Other Western politicians agreed to work as Russian lobbyists without publicizing the fact or including it in their resumes. These include former prime ministers and even former secretary generals of NATO. "So what," one might say. "Maybe they're introducing openness and other Western norms into Russian corporations." Perhaps so, but if they are, the results are still nowhere in evidence.

Note

1. Judy Dempsey, "Schröder Urges Europe to Warm to Moscow," *International Herald Tribune,* http://www.nytimes.com/2008/09/17/world/europe/17iht-germany.4.1624 7633.html?_r=1&scp=16&sq=Gerhard%20Schroeder%20on%20Russia&st=cse.

22 THE VALDAI CLUB, OR THE KREMLIN AND WESTERN COMMENTATORS

The Valdai Club is a format in which Western journalists and experts meet with Russian leaders to hear their explanations of Russian politics. This is yet another example of the Kremlin's policy of co-optation. My colleague at the Carnegie Moscow Center, Nikolai Petrov, once addressed a question to the participants in the Valdai Club:

> How justified from the moral point of view is it for Western analysts to participate in Valdai, a project used as blatant propaganda by the Kremlin? I'm not the only one who has this reaction to the Valdai Club. I hope that many participants in the Valdai meetings will decline the next Kremlin invitation.[1]

There was no evidence that Petrov's appeal had any effect.

Rarely has any Western participant in the Valdai Club publicly criticized the event. Some have made ironic comments, however, as Andrew Kuchins did in an interview in *Kommersant*. "My head is spinning after a week in Russia as a guest of the Valdai Club, one of the most effective Kremlin PR projects," Kuchins said. "I came away with the impression that the Kremlin boss is like the Wizard of Oz, who is revered and feared, but who actually is improvising desperately, pulling various levers in the vague hope that his efforts will be effective."[2] Such sarcasm is the exception for Valdai Club members: Go too far, and you might not be invited next year. For many Western guests, an invitation to the Kremlin and face time with Russian leaders is the event of their lives. In my experience with Valdai Club members, they grow quite upset if they don't get an invitation early and fret about their place in the inner circle.

Before 2008, you might have been able to convince yourself that the club really did provide journalists and experts with valuable information about Russia. And who wouldn't be curious to see the objects of your research in person? However, if this were really the clubgoers' motivation, one visit would be enough. I would have no issue with the Valdai Club members if they used that one opportunity to tell Russia's leaders how the outside world views them and their country's foreign policy. But judging from the transcripts, which are available to the public, the guests are too embarrassed to discuss problems that the Russian elite might find too uncomfortable to answer. Perhaps they do not wish to appear rude, but in that case I would ask what purpose these meetings serve, and who really benefits from them.

Valdai-2008, however, had a goal that even the most naïve or idealistic Western experts couldn't miss. In the fall of that year, the Russian regime desperately needed to break out of the international isolation that followed the war in the Caucasus and the Kremlin's recognition of South Ossetian and Abkhazian independence. The Kremlin needed to do more than just retouch its image. It was fishing for any signal whatsoever that the West supported Russia's aggression toward Georgia. The Valdai-2008 attendees did not disappoint. They came. They listened. They met with the leaders of the unrecognized republics and the Chechen President, Ramzan Kadyrov, a man even Russian politicians try to avoid. By listening, nodding, and openly complimenting the Russian leaders, they agreeably helped Moscow solve the problem of legitimizing the war and the annexation of Georgian territories.

For the last several years in a row, the most grateful, naïve, or, perhaps, least perceptive Western experts have willingly parroted the arguments they heard at Valdai. I have attended several talks by Valdai attendees whose voices swell with pride at their own importance and regard those of us without access to the Kremlin throne with pity. "As Putin told me recently," they say, or "Putin promised me that he would not stay in the Kremlin," or "You don't understand what Medvedev and the Kremlin really think. Let me explain," and so on. It is as if the Kremlin had implanted a one-way radio in place of their voice boxes. You have to give Russia's regime credit for creating such an effective propaganda machine—the Kremlin proved to have a keen sense of the intricacies of the human soul.

I could understand it if Western experts wanted to ask Russian leaders questions that would clarify what they can't find out through the usual analytical channels. But I don't understand how otherwise respectable people suddenly find themselves kowtowing to such a laughable degree. One could easily imagine that Putin's scorn for the West was something he developed as a result of meeting with the Valdai attendees. What other conclusion could he draw from statements like this one by Thierry de Mont-brial, director of the French Institute of International Relations, who said at his 2007 meeting with Putin:

> Mr. President! You will be the first leader in Russian history to be very powerful but who knows how to share power with others and refuses to change the constitution. Of course, this is proof that you are a democrat. [!] But whoever becomes the next president, he will have to co-exist with you to some degree, since you said that you do not want to retire.

I hope this is merely an example of French politesse and nothing more. But how humiliating for the expert community! Unfortunately, de Mont-brial is not alone is expressing such refined feelings for the Russian lead-ers. Here is German political scientist Alexander Rahr at a meeting with Medvedev in 2008:

> Thank you, Dmitri Anatolyevich. Yesterday Vladimir Putin said that the West missed an enormous opportunity in not extending a hand to such a liberal and modern politician as you. I believe that our Valdai meeting today is the start of such a dialogue. You truly are a liberal.[3]

I think that the Russian leaders are too smart to enjoy such blatant flattery.

How has the Russian regime used the Valdai club? To answer that ques-tion, I must quote the attendees' impressions in dealing with the Kremlin. Journalist Jonathan Steele of the *Guardian*, who by the way is quite sym-pathetic toward Russia, admitted that the speeches by Putin and Medvedev at the Valdai Club radically changed his attitude toward Moscow's recog-nition of Abkhazia and South Ossetia. "At first, I thought it [recognition of independence] was a mistake. But then, after hearing the arguments of your prime minister and president on the reasons for that step, I think that now I will approve those steps."[4] British expert John Laughland was even more charmed. Here's what he wrote about Vladimir Putin:

> No matter how much Putin is criticized in the West, he is still a great leader. His career is like an old spaghetti Western: a stranger comes to a small town in the Wild West, cleans out the bandits, and then having done his work, gets back on his horse and disappears into the sunset. Anyone who sees this thinks it's incredible that rela-tions between the West and Russia could deteriorate under Putin."[5]

Vladimir Putin as Clint Eastwood: Could the Kremlin propaganda writers do any better?

Let's look at a few more observations. Here is Italian journalist and member of the European Parliament Giulietto Chiesa:

> Medvedev stressed that today Russia is not the same as the one of the 1990s or even the start of the twenty-first century. The president was expressive and looked very confident. He did not fail to stress that he made all the difficult decisions during the Caucasus crisis himself.

Here is Ariel Cohen, a frequent critic of the Kremlin:

> I practically do not know of a similar situation in world practice, for heads of states and governments, people so responsible and busy, to spend so much time and explain the policy of their country in such detail. Of course, for us as experts who more or less influence the development of public opinion, this is exceptionally important.

Exceptionally important, indeed. But how much do those "who influence public opinion" really understand about why they were invited, or how much their independence was compromised? "The main benefit for Russia is that this forum adds to the transparency and openness [!] of the country," claims British expert Alena Ledeneva, thereby confirming that the Russian leaders have successfully mastered their job as image makers.[6]

I can't resist quoting *Independent* columnist Mary Dejevsky, whom I like very much personally. Here are Dejevsky's impressions after visiting Ramzan Kadyrov and Grozny in September 2008, as well as commentary from one of her British readers in response, which gives us reason to hope that you can't trick the Western public as easily as the Kremlin might hope.

Mary Dejevsky describes a visit by Kadyrov and the Valdai attendees to the Grozny zoo's lion exhibit. She then moves on from there to the Chechen president's successes. "You have to give Kadyrov (and the Russian government[,] which largely financed it) their due. Grozny ... is a phenomenal achievement, which has generated confidence, encouraged exiles to return and made Grozny a place with an increasingly acceptable quality of life." Meanwhile, Dejevsky frets that things are much worse in Baghdad. That Baghdad and its problems are even mentioned ("even Baghdad was still suffering regular power cuts") in a story about Kadyrov suggests to the reader who is the better manager, Kadyrov or the United States.

Here is the reader's response to Dejevsky:

I can't believe you are lapping up Kadyrov's PR slop. Taking an interest in lions, my foot! Being a man-eating lion himself, small wonder he's taking interest. Do you know what happens to people who displease Kadyrov? Rumours abound, yes, because no one dares to say anything openly. As for rebuilding Grozny, the United States could not have achieved a similar result in Baghdad even if [it] could stick to Kadyrov's methods, simply because the United States is foreign culturally and [its] repressions are perceived in a completely different frame.[7]

All of this is really just a warm-up for the professional flatterers. According to Alexander Rahr, most Valdai-2008 attendees shared Russia's position on Georgia. Answering a journalist's question after his meeting with Medvedev on whether Russia's position had become any clearer, Rahr said,

> It was always clear to me. I think that 80 percent of the members of the Valdai club now share it [the Kremlin's position] and understand after the emotional talks by Vladimir Putin, Dmitri Medvedev, and Sergei Lavrov.... and after our rather frank conversation with the presidents of the newly recognized [by Russia] republics of Abkhazia and South Ossetia, there are arguments enough for it.

This admission, which was not contradicted by the other participants, means that either the Russian authorities were extremely convincing or the Western experts were exceedingly receptive. Perhaps both.

Finally, let me cite a sincere, touching statement: Members of the Valdai Club, according to Richard Sakwa, are forced "to be careful." He explains why: because "some people, who do not show good will toward Russia" accuse them of participating in a propaganda campaign. "I would not stay here a minute it that were so, if this [were] brainwashing," Sakwa assured us. "We felt the evolution, the self-confidence of this country, its consolidation."[8] The British expert found the right name for the procedure he underwent. I could continue quoting other esteemed Valdai Club members, but I will stop here without embarrassing anyone else.

Recently, however, Valdai's critics (on the Russian side, the event was criticized by Boris Nemtsov, Nikolai Petrov, Yevgenia Albats, and others) have apparently managed to convince its organizers to make the event look less like propaganda. They have begun inviting independent experts and even voices from the opposition as speakers. Thus Vladimir Ryzhkov was among the participants at Valdai-2009. Regardless, the essence of the event is unchanged. Foreign guests come to the Valdai meetings to absorb the opinions of Russia's leaders and then transmit to the rest of the world.

Finally, I would like to mention one last amusing fact: Valdai-2009 showed the world that the Kremlin has figured out how to involve Western experts in their games. Thus, the Valdai attendees themselves did not hide the fact that most of the questions they posed to the Russian leaders had been cleared in advance by the organizers. Some of them even envied the position of Nikolai Zlobin, a Russian-American expert who always had the honor of asking Putin the most important question—one about his plans. The reply to this question typically became the subject of lively discussion in the Russian and foreign press, so Zlobin became the most popular attendee. This time the Russian prime minister used Zlobin's straight line to demonstrate with pleasure who was boss in Russia and who would determine the fate of the next elections. In fact, the whole lunch with Putin had been organized to convene an audience that would hang on his every word and disseminate Putin's message *urbi et orbi*. At that meeting, Putin, through his volunteer assistants, told the world that he, and he alone, not Medvedev or anyone else, would decide what would happen in Russia. Why did he choose to humiliate President Medvedev in such an extravagant way?

I hope that at least some of the Valdai attendees will heed the critics and I would be happy if my colleagues and I can help them avoid risking their reputations. Of course, the Kremlin itself has picked up on the negative publicity the Valdai meetings have generated and may change the format. So: Valdai attendees, be prepared! You soon may be invited to join a different propaganda show.

More Refined Seduction of Western Intellectuals

The Russian regime sometimes uses Western experts in much more subtle ways than what we've seen from the Valdai Club. For example, in summer 2009, the Russian Institute, founded by leading Kremlin spin doctor Gleb Pavlovsky, and the Centre for Liberal Strategies (Sofia), held a conference in Moscow in cooperation with the European Council on Foreign Relations (London) and the German Marshall Fund of the United States that appeared to be the beginning of a series of such events.[9] The majority of the Russian participants were with a few exceptions analysts close to the Kremlin. The exceptions were lost in an unfamiliar crowd. How the Western co-organizers of this event benefited from it isn't clear to me, but the Russian side certainly improved its image through meetings with the Western participants, some of whom clearly had no idea where they were. Such meetings between Western observers and pro-Kremlin experts might be useful if their Western colleagues were not afraid to argue with their hosts. But I suppose political correctness and politeness prevented them.

Here is yet another example of subtle manipulation. European analysts Ivan Krastev, Mark Leonard, and Andrew Wilson, under the aegis of the European Council on Foreign Relations, published a collection of essays by some of their pro-Kremlin interlocutors called *What Does Russia Think?* I would have merely regretted these efforts, if not for a chance meeting I had at Davos. An influential member of the Davos community showed me the brochure and asked, "Have you read it? Amazingly interesting thoughts! Does Russia really think this way?" I had to explain that there are various "Russias," and the thoughts presented in the book not only fail to fully convey the spectrum of debate within Russia; but they don't even convey the range of opinion within the Kremlin itself.

Mulling over what I should tell my readers about this subject in this book, I decided that I must honestly and openly explain how esteemed European experts are propagandizing Kremlin ideas—and not even very fresh ones at that. I've always been intrigued by what European intellectuals found attractive in Russian authoritarianism and why they flirted with it. This is a long-standing phenomenon predating the examples I've presented above. Those people had celebrated predecessors in Romain Rolland, Henri Barbusse, Lion Feuchtwanger, John Reed, and George Bernard Shaw, who expressed sympathy for the Soviet Union and had direct contact with the Soviet regime. They were drawn in by the allure of the leftist idea and the hope that it could be realized in the Soviet Union. They were victims of their own naïveté. But the European intellectuals propagandizing the ideas of the current Kremlin authoritarianism can hardly be accused of such political inexperience.

But let's return to Krastev, Leonard, and Wilson's anthology. They wrote in the introduction, "If we want to influence and deal with Russia, we need to understand it." A promising start. One needs the help of a guide to navigate Russia's seemingly inexplicable movements. In order to simplify their task, the authors proposed "an attempt to look at the internal logic of the Russian political debate." That's the right approach, but the problem was that there wasn't even a hint of a debate in the book. Except for a few articles, the book mainly explicated the position of the Kremlin camp. Wasn't the Kremlin doing enough to propagandize its views without all this help? Well, all right, perhaps there was a need in the West to expand the audience for a discussion of the Kremlin position, but then why not offer comments on it?

The editors, however, never got past the conclusions of their Kremlin colleagues: "Russia does not want to be like the EU"; "Russia's distrust of Europe is growing." Yet that is not true! The Kremlin establishment does not trust the European Union; however, more than 70 percent of Russian respondents in a survey considered Europe a desirable partner for Russia. Following their authors' lead, Krastev, Leonard, and Wilson claimed, "Whatever the regime's origins, Putin has come to embody some lasting hopes." Meanwhile in the real world, a poll of Russian public opinion found that only 19 percent thought that Putin's policies had been successful. What "lasting hopes" did they mean? The esteemed European colleagues wrote inspiring words about "sovereign democracy" as "the most powerful explanation for the enduring popularity of Putin." Meanwhile in the real world, both Putin and Medvedev had already rejected the idea of sovereign democracy as incompatible with Russian reality. As for Putin's popularity, how stable was it since it was based on the absence of alternatives?

The delight both the authors and the editors felt for the "Putin consensus" made me smirk: They had devoted so much space to it at a time when the consensus was falling apart, and even its former adherents among the authors of this book—Pavlovsky, for one—were calling Putin "deadwood."

I think the most amusing part of the book is its Afterword by Gleb Pavlovsky. He used his eloquence to prove that Russia had soft power, political strength, and global know-how—in particular when it came to working with "new nations in Eastern Europe in creating identities of their own." I don't know what "soft power" he had in mind, given that even Russia's closest allies were trying to escape Moscow's stifling embrace at the time. And the Eastern Europeans would probably have been surprised to learn that Russia had helped them form their national identities. Then again, perhaps Russia's assertiveness did speed the process. Some soft power!

"In order to solve other problems, we need to go beyond Russia," warned Pavlovsky. That meant that Moscow, with the help of Pavlovsky and his co-authors, intended to teach its neighbors how to live. What a pity that the European experts did not respond to the thoughts of their Russian colleague. Their silence can thus be construed as agreement. In that case, they should read President Medvedev's speeches, where he criticizes many of the Putin-era ideas in the collection. This means that even in the Kremlin, not everyone agrees with them. But even if the "ideas" presented in the anthology were still popular among the Russian political class at the time of this writing, couldn't the editors have at least thought through how adequate these "ideas" are and what lies behind them?

We can only guess at the motivation of esteemed experts who would repeat the views of Russian traditionalists so uncritically. One thing is clear: This sort of mechanical retransmission of official Russian propaganda is unlikely to deepen the West's understanding of Russia.

Besides *What Does Russia Think?* there are many more examples of Westerners who consciously or unconsciously (more of the latter, I hope) hum along to the Kremlin's tune. Sometimes these intellectuals and politicians share their thoughts with their Russian counterparts without thinking about the context or the consequences. For example, an influential representative of the European elite, Robert Cooper, the European Union's Director-General for External and Politico-Military Affairs, said in an interview with the aforementioned pro-Kremlin Russian Institute,

> Sometimes I think that the word 'democracy' becomes problematic. I would prefer to talk about responsible, open government that defends the rights of nations ..., but having enough legitimacy to use repressive administrative measures when there is a need for them.

Such an understanding of democracy expressed by a Western politician is exactly what the current Russian government is looking for. Cooper went on to make several more revelations in the same interview: "I personally like the Chinese government: it has done amazing things for its people. And it continues to transform the country. In the end the state will be transformed as a result of this activity."[10] I understand that Cooper said this in the context of global developments, but in the current Russian situation, the words can mean only one thing: legitimation of the Russian reality. I can't believe that Cooper wanted his comments to be interpreted this way.

The Kremlin authorities—and especially those responsible for cracking down on Russian intellectuals, primarily Westernizers—express unusually warm feelings toward Western intellectual gurus, inviting them to Moscow for a pleasant chat. Let's see what one of them, Alvin Toffler, says, "I met with Vladislav Surkov, who helped me understand that he sees the need [for Russia] to move toward becoming an information society based on knowledge. Russia needs 'to jump' into the third wave, as Japan and China have done already."[11] I wonder whether Mr. Toffler believes that Russia can really "jump into" the information age while the Kremlin is busy using militias to disperse rallies in defense of the constitution. I wonder whether he asked Mr. Surkov whether he thinks that an "information society" is feasible in a situation in which the state controls the flow of information. Indeed, I wonder whether he understood why he was invited to Moscow by the Kremlin. And if he did understand, was he comfortable taking part in the building of the Russian Potemkin Village? If he was unaware of the role he was playing, then perhaps we could send him some books on Russia to read before his next trip to Moscow.

Notes

1. Nikolai Petrov, "Valdai Voodoo," *Moscow Times*, September 16, 2008.

2. Andrew Kuchins, "Piar po-kremlevski ili niechto bol'sheje" [The Kremlin PR or Something Much Bigger?], http://www.inosmi.ru/translation/230002.html.

3. See http://www.kremlin.ru/transcripts/1383; "Bol'shinstwo chlenov kluba "Valdai" razdieliajut pozitsiju Rossii po Kavkazu" [Majority of Participants of the "Valdai" Club Share Russia's Position on the Caucasus], http://www.valday2008.rian.ru/news/20080912/52333652.html.

4. "Klub Valdai" pozvolil zarubiezhnym ekspertam luchshe poniat' politiku RF" [Club "Valdai" Has Helped the Foreign Experts to Better Understand Russia's Policies], http://www.valday2008.rian.ru/news/20080914/52333682.htm.

5. John Laughland, "Putin Has Been Vilified by the West—But He Is Still a Great Leader," *Daily Mail*, September 23, 2007, http://www.dailymail.co.uk/news/article-483321/Putin-vilified-West—great-leader.html.

6. Nadezhda Sorokina, "Politologi Valdaiskogo Kluba Rasskazali o Svojei Vstreche s Vladimirom Putinym" [Political Scientists of the Valdai Club Discussed Their Meeting With Vladimir Putin], http://www.rg.ru/2007/09/15/politologi.html; Viktor Zozulia, S Valdaya Luchshe Vidna Rossija [Russia Is Better Seen from Valdai], http://www.izvestia.ru/politic/article3117907.

7. See Mary Dojevsky, "Russia Notebook: How a Lion-Fancier Got Grozny Back on Its Feet" (article and reader comments), http://blogs.independent.co.uk/openhouse/2008/09/russia-notebo-1.html.

8. See Interfax, September 12, 2008, and RIA Novosti, September 14, 2008; "Club Valdai pozvolil zarubezhnym ekspertam luchshe ponyat' politiku Rossii" [The Club Valdai Has Allowed the Foreign Experts to Understand Better the Russian Politics], The Meeting of the Valdai Club, http://www.rian.ru/politics/20080914/151242542.html.

9. In early 2010 the German Marshall Fund hosted another event in Washington, D.C., with the participation of the Kremlin pundits.

10. "Yaroslavskaya Initsiativa. Umnaya Politika v Post-Zapadnom Mirie" [Yaroslavl Initiative. Smart Politics in the Post-Western World], Special Edition of the Russian Institute, Moscow, December 25, 2009.

11. Alvin Toffler, "The Governments Often Hinder Modernization," interview in *Itogi*, January 11, 2010, p. 21.

23 AND NOW FOR THE MAJOR VICTORIES

All the events I've just described are but minor Kremlin victories achieved at little cost. Indeed, the Kremlin has shown itself to be capable of much more. One such major victory has been the Kremlin's efforts to play the individual members of the European Union off against one another and to exploit their dependence on Russian energy. By establishing a special relationship with Berlin, Paris, and Rome, Moscow has successfully torpedoed both a unified EU energy policy and a common strategy toward Russia. It has also used other European countries (such as Hungary, Bulgaria, Greece, and Serbia) as Trojan horses for its energy policy. The Russian elite spends enormous amounts of effort and money not to unite Russia with Europe but to keep it fractious and distant. It has succeeded because the European elite is all too ready to pursue its own narrow, short-term interests in dealing with Russia.

Russia has been just as successful in its policy of issuing selective threats. To name just a few occasions when it has skillfully employed this policy: Moscow has cut off gas to both Ukraine and Belarus, stopped oil deliveries to Lithuania along the Druzhba pipeline, halted energy supplies to the Czech Republic, introduced sanctions against Moldova and Georgia, and issued ominous threats to Estonia.

Moscow was unquestionably wise to move its relations with its neighbors and energy customers onto a commercial footing. But the fact that a fair "market price" seems to track closely with a consumer's loyalty to Moscow shows that political considerations, not free-market principles, are really running the show. "But one would expect the same kind of behavior from virtually any resource-rich country," one might counter. Perhaps, but none of those other countries also have pretensions to membership in the club of liberal democracies. And so it is that the developed democracies' enabling creates an almost irresistible temptation among

Russia's leaders to use the vast energy wealth they control to achieve political goals.

As for Russia's threats (against Estonia) and sanctions (against Georgia and Moldova), these are just symptoms of a classic neo-imperial syndrome. Neo-imperialism doesn't mean that Russia has to restore direct rule over neighboring states. Why would it want that headache? Rather, it wants its neighbors to willingly limit their own sovereignty and return to Russia's sphere of influence. But why does the Kremlin want even that much? Again, because it needs not only to feed its ego but also, and most importantly, because the Russian state cannot sustain itself without satellites, even illusory ones.

The Kremlin threat-machine didn't just operate on neighbors; it even made attempts on major Western players, especially Britain. Bristling in the face of London's refusal to extradite former Chechen separatist leader Akhmed Zakayev and self-exiled oligarch and Putin supporter-turned-critic Boris Berezovsky, the Kremlin decided to retaliate. It refused to extradite a Russian citizen suspected in the poisoning of Alexander Litvinenko in London. It allowed, if not directly ordered, the thug-like, Kremlin-backed Nashi movement to harass British Ambassador Anthony Brenton. It closed the British Council offices in Russia, and it put pressure on Shell and BP. It got so bad that Sergei Lavrov, according to the British Press, used vulgar language to lecture Foreign Minister David Miliband. It's hard to imagine that Lavrov would have done this without carte blanche from the Russian leader.

All this chest-thumping was intended to sound out the depths of Western sensitivity. How far could Moscow go and still avoid reprisal? Very far, apparently. London's inability to come up with a commensurate response reinforced the Kremlin's sense of its own invincibility and Britain's relative weakness. "The weak get beaten," Vladimir Putin once said in explaining Russia's brutal behavior on the world scene, Clearly, Britain was one of the weaklings he might have had in mind. Finally, the war with Georgia, which Moscow openly called an "American project," was meant as the ultimate demonstration of Russian strength: its readiness to challenge the world's only superpower, America.

Confronted with economic hardships, the Russian leadership, beginning in 2009, has tried to soften its bullying ways and has made efforts to smooth over its differences with neighboring states and the West. Unfortunately, this kinder, gentler phase probably won't last. Once you get used to kickboxing, it's hard to go back to chess.

But beyond boasts and threats, one of Russia's greatest victories has been its ability to imitate all of the institutions that compose the foundations of democracy in the Western world, up to and including a Kremlin-fashioned "civil society" that remains loyal to the regime. These imitation institutions effectively disguise the reality of personalized power in Russia. Russian leaders actively employ liberal rhetoric and the government counts people who present themselves as liberals among its members, both of which complicate not only the development of real democracy but also liberal criticism of the Russian system. Moreover, even some Russian intellectuals tend to confuse Russia's stage-prop parliament, multiparty system, and liberal-sounding public organizations with a genuine liberal order, and so they long for the purity of authoritarianism. "Why should we support these chatterboxes!" goes the refrain. "Better to have just one person in charge."

Yet another major victory for the Kremlin has been its ability to exploit the West's "double standards" and shortcomings. "See!" the propagandists tell the people. "They have corruption, crime, and human rights violations, too." The United States has become the main target of these efforts, thanks in no small part to the Bush administration. "Why does America single out Belarus for criticism when Saudi Arabia and Pakistan are no better?" And really, are they any better? "Why Russia and not China, or Kazakhstan?" Few Westerners have a satisfactory answer to these questions, yet one does exist—at least as it pertains to China and Kazakhstan. Neither of these two countries belongs to the Council of Europe or the G8, nor did they sign documents promising to observe democratic values; Russia did.

The Kremlin's final and perhaps most important victory has been its capture of Western business, which it has successfully embroiled in a system that makes no distinction between the regime and the economy. The recipe for success in Russia is clear: You play by the Kremlin's rules, or you fail.

I should note that playing by the Kremlin's rules is a necessary but not sufficient criterion for success. Sometimes you fail even if you become a Kremlin apologist. Take the case of William Browder, president of Hermitage Capital, who became a defender of the Kremlin's methods with regard to Mikhail Khodorkovsky. I recall arguing fiercely with Browder about Khodorkovsky at the World Economic Forum in Davos in 2006. A few years later, Browder received a taste of those methods himself. His business activities had run afoul of the Kremlin. The state refused him entry into Russia, and reminiscent of the Khodorkovsky story, his company was charged with tax evasion and tax fraud and his people were harassed by Kremlin officials. Hermitage Capital lawyer Sergei Magnitsky died under tragic and suspicious circumstances in his pre-detention cell in Moscow.

Today, Browder has been reborn as a Kremlin critic. "Russian sharks are feeding on their own blood," he bitterly concludes. "Simply put, Russia is not a 'state' as we understand [it]. Government institutions have been taken over as conduits for private interests, some of them criminal. Property rights no longer exist, people who are supposed to enforce [the] law are breaking it, innocent people are victimized[,] and the courts have turned into political tools."[1]

Bill Browder has my sincere sympathy. I am sure that he has reassessed his attitude toward Khodorkovsky, whom he had berated so eloquently. He and his people had to pay a heavy price for the lesson. Browder's case shows that political loyalty and even support of the Kremlin's actions are no surefire guarantee for entrepreneurial success in Russia. However, there are no signs that Bill Browder's painful experience has served as a warning for the Western business community.

Of course it doesn't hurt, which is why many Western businessmen have become virtual lobbyists for the Russian regime in their home countries, lest deteriorating relations between Russia and the West cut into profits. Some have even joined the corrupt oligarchic-bureaucratic system by directly participating in informal deals with the authorities. Some Western companies have even adopted traditional Russian business practices: A German court recently investigated the multinational conglomerate Siemens for bribery of Russian officials. In Siemens's defense, it was merely playing by the rules of the game—rules written and enforced by the authorities to maintain their opaque, corrupt system.

All of the above victories—the threats, the sanctions, the bullying, the co-optation—represent a masterful synthesis of the traditional with the contemporary, modernism with post-modernism. Here is James Sherr's description of that synthesis:

> Today Russia is pursuing a number of classically nineteenth-century aims—great-power status, diminution of the rights of small powers and the formation of "regions of privileged interest"—and it is doing so with a mixture of classical and twenty-first-century tools—intelligence and covert penetration, commerce and joint ventures, "lobbying structures" and litigation, energy and downstream invest-

ments, and, in the former USSR, Russian diasporas and other "civilizational" forms of soft power.

This amalgam, of course, is a temporary and transitional phenomenon.
But it is hard to predict just how "temporary" it will be.

All the above "victories" have helped the elite survive and guarantee
itself a place in the West while at the same time cutting off the bulk of
Russian society from the West. But they are also serving to discredit Russia in Western eyes.

Note

1. William Browder, "Russian Sharks Are Feeding on their Own Blood," *Financial
Times*, July 6, 2009, http://www.ft.com/cms/s/0/2172e246-6a53-11de-ad04-00144feabdc0.
html?nclick_check=1.

24 HOW RUSSIA WAS HUMILIATED

How Russian experts and politicians rate relations with the West, especially the sharp cooling of relations between 2004 and 2008, tells us about more than just Russian foreign policy; it gives us a window into the minds of the political elite, its understanding of the present, and its agenda for the future. It also influences Western perceptions of Russia, often inducing Westerners to repeat Russian clichés in the belief that they either reflect the genuine feelings of the Russian public or represent an accurate picture of Russian realities. More often than not, however, they're merely a reflection of the interests, phobias, fears, and ambitions of the Russian establishment.

Once you see what I mean by "clichés," you will be able to come to your own conclusions about the originality of what passes for good commentary on Russia in the West. Don't be misled by the fact that the Russian and Western commentary often appears to be unanimous; this is merely a demonstration of how effective the Kremlin propaganda machine has been.

So what is the general thrust of Russian thinking about the West: quite simply, that all the blame for the poor state of relations, the mutual misunderstanding, and the disillusionment belongs to the West alone. What exactly were its transgressions? The standard laundry list of Russian grievances, which has been memorized and repeated by every representative of the Russian elite, is as follows:

- the West encroached on Russia's legitimate sphere of influence and took advantage of its weakness in the 1990s;

- it forced Russia to make unilateral concessions;

- it saw Russia through ideological (read: "democratic") lenses;

- it was unwilling to re-evaluate the rules and norms that developed after the fall of the USSR;

- and, of course, it refused to take responsibility for all its transgressions against Russia from the 1990s onward.

These grievances unite representatives from across the political and ideological spectrum, demonstrating that the elite in Russia has arrived at a consensus on its approach to the West. Otherwise fractious forces have joined forces under the banner that the West is at fault for the poor relations and for the fact that "things are not right" in Russia. This consensus held strong even when Moscow and the West began to look for points of agreement in early 2009. Thus there is no reason to think that this state of affairs will change anytime soon.

There are both political and psychological causes for the unanimous blame the Russian ruling caste heaps upon the West. In large part, it is the result of the caste's failure to move beyond a framework that places a high premium on loyalty to the state and the regime, and its fear of taking its own, independent position. Even regime critics hesitate to question Russian foreign policy for fear of being accused of "betraying" national interests. According to Russian public opinion, the state is the sole legitimate voice for Russia when it comes to relations with the outside world.

The absence of a new idea of national accord also plays a part. Without such an accord, politicians must rely on the tried and true strategy of rallying the people around an external threat and deflecting blame for their own inability to offer a constructive alternative for development. In any case, asserting the West's collective guilt for all Russia's woes is a convenient tool for many.

None of this is to deny that the West does bear some responsibility for this situation; indeed I pointed out some of the missteps made by Western leaders earlier in this very book. But most Russian analysts and politicians today accuse the West of an entirely different set of sins than I have. There are, to be sure, Westerners who exhibit a condescending or aggressive attitude toward Russia, wishing only to further isolate it, but these are marginal voices in the debate. The problem is not that the West interfered in Russia's affairs, dictating concessions, badgering, humiliating, and gloating over Russia's difficulties, but rather, that Western civilization has not been principled enough—either unable or unwilling to stand up to Russia's ruling class and its agenda at key points in Russia's development. In effect, the West legitimized imitation democracy in Russia and turned a blind eye to the increasing aggression of the Russian traditionalists.

The blatantly propagandist anti-Western rhetoric of the Russian traditionalists, which at times takes on a truly clinical dimension, deserves little in the way of response here. Let's listen, however, to what the moderate, balanced, or even Westernizing voices in Russia are saying.

Alexei Arbatov expressed the most widely held point of view on the basic reason behind the mutual distrust between Russia and the West: "It is Moscow's attempts to change the rules of the game in relations between Russia and the West, which formed in the 1990s, and the unwillingness of the West, primarily of the U.S., to allow Russia to do this." He is referring to Moscow's rejection of "the paradigm of relations [...] which Russia followed in the wake of the U.S., when its interests were not taken into account."[1] Sergei Karaganov characterized "the content of the new era" as "the counterattack of the old West, trying to preserve or restore lost positions and stop the re-division of the world that has begun." What prompted the West's "counterattack"? Karaganov explained, "Moscow started re-examining the rules of the game that formed in its relations with the West in the years of Russian chaos."[2]

Konstantin Kosachev, chairman of the Duma's Committee on International Affairs, insisted that continuing relations with the West along its previous track would have led to "foreign control over Russian resources" and the "de-sovereignization" of Russia.[3] The West's avarice for Russian resources has long been a concern for Prime Minister Putin, who likes to accuse the West of trying "to impose dishonest competition on us and guarantee access to our resources."

And finally, here is a list of additional irritants for Moscow: the expansion of NATO, up to and including proposed membership for Ukraine and Georgia; support for, and formal recognition of, Kosovo's independence; and the Bush administration's push to deploy an anti-ballistic missile system in Eastern Europe. More recent irritants include economic aid for Georgia; the decision to build the Nabucco pipeline; and Eastern Europe's and the Baltics' refusal to accept the Kremlin's version of recent history, particularly that of World War II. Every day, new grievances are added to the list. Sometimes it seems as though the Kremlin has a secret army of propagandists tasked with coming up with new grievances and accusations against the West and Russia's neighbors.

This army directs most of its hostility against the United States, naturally. In fact, the only reason any other Western countries take flak is because they have the occasional misfortune of standing near the United States. Former minister of foreign affairs Igor Ivanov defined the common denominator of virtually all Russia's grievances in this one quote: "America built its unipolar world. But that construction either did not take into account Russia's interests or was directed against them." The American "axis" of world order outrages the Russian political class, despite its having built its own "axis of power" inside Russia. Strangely, in calling for global democratization the Russian elite refuses to consider the democratization of its own political regime.

How sincere are the above grievances? Some are so absurd that one wonders why their purveyors don't blush at their cynicism. Others have been recited so frequently that their purveyors might even believe them by now. The problem is that after spending so many years nursing these grievances, turning away from them would feel too much like a retreat.

Notes

1. Alexei Arbatov, "Moscow and Munich: A New Framework for Russian Domestic and Foreign Policies," Carnegie Moscow Center Working Paper no. 3, 2007, p. 13.

2. Sergei Karaganov, "Novaya epokha protivostoyaniya" [A new era of confrontation], October 23, 2008, http:www.rg.ru/2007/07/06/karaganov/html.

3. Konstantin Kosachev, "Rossiya i Zapad, nashi raznoglasiya" [Russia and the West: Our Differences], Rossiya v global'noi politike, http://www.globalaffairs.ru/numbers/27/8066.html.

25 IS THERE REASON TO TAKE OFFENSE?

Russian politicians trot out all of the above grievances at almost every opportunity, even when Moscow believes that collaboration with the West is in its best interest. So it makes sense to see how justified these accusations and grievances really are—especially in light of the fact that some of my Western colleagues have seen fit to repeat them to their own audiences.

I don't wish to idealize Western elites or their attitudes toward Russia. They themselves admit that some of their leaders treated Russia arrogantly, reinforcing the country's neuroses. Any serious observer of international relations must acknowledge that, at times, the West ignored Russia's interests and set it up for humiliation.

The key question, however, is whether it did so intentionally. Roderic Lyne, British ambassador to Russia and adviser to Prime Minister John Major, answered this charge:

> Of course, the attitude of Western countries toward Moscow in the early 1990s showed a large dose of naïveté, where the desired was taken for reality. In many ways, the West was tactless and patronizing, even though it was not intentional. But we must remember that by the early 1990s, Russia had been accepted in a number of democratic "clubs," it was offered the broadest participation in all kinds of international organizations. Moscow became a member of the IMF and the Council of Europe. The Treaty on Partnership and Cooperation between the European Union and Russia declared a "strategic partnership based on common interests and values." President Boris Yeltsin was invited to summits of the G7, which turned into the G8.[1]

Are these the actions of a group who scorned Russia, or sought to weaken it? Ronald Asmus, too, is surprised by the Russian elite's constant complaining, especially about NATO expansion: "Since the first new members entered a decade ago, NATO has not conducted a single military exercise directed against Moscow."[2]

But what do independent Russian researchers have to say about all this? I'll turn to Andrei Kortunov, who shared his thoughts in a personal conversation:

> The G7 leaders did open the doors for Russia to join Western structures. This invitation was made under Yeltsin and confirmed under Putin. But the actual process of entering Western structures demanded constant and persistent efforts from Russia. We could have used the opportunities that the West offered—within the G7 and in relations with the EU and NATO, the Council of Europe, OSCE, and so on. But we did not do so. We lacked the political will, the persistence, and the continuity. We wanted to solve issues on the level of summits and general declarations—but that did not work. In practice, we did not want to do anything. So whose fault is it that Russia is all alone?

Having seen that it's no simple matter to assign blame, let's take note of a curious detail in the arguments of both Russian and Western defenders of "wounded Russia." Typically, when they bring up the concessions forced on Russia by the West's expansionism, they are referring to the Yeltsin period. All former taboos about criticizing Yeltsin have fallen away completely; indeed many of his detractors now lay into him with gusto. He is constantly criticized for "softness" in relations with America, or for shamefully retreating in the face of "provocations" from the West. Yet Putin himself was no less "soft" on Washington during his first term. On Putin's watch: NATO occupied Kosovo; the United States unilaterally abrogated the Anti-Ballistic Missile Treaty; the Americans began training and arming the Georgian army; the largest expansion to date of NATO took place, bringing former Soviet republics into the alliance; and America built military bases in Central Asia, with Putin's approval. Yet none of these actions soured the friendly relations between Putin and Bush. Far from being a critic of American expansionism, Putin encouraged it. If one were to apply the Kremlin's current criteria of softness to then-President Putin, then one would have to find him guilty of implementing a policy of concessions that ran counter to Russia's national interests.

Let's assume for a moment that my opponents are correct, and that the West tried to wrest "unilateral concessions" from Russia (and continues to do so) in order to weaken Russia and take over its spheres of influence. Of what possible use to the West would a weak, rancorous, and nuclear-armed Russia be?

I always like to ask politicians and experts of the "wounded Russia" camp, as well as their allies in the West, the following question: Is it not in Russia's interest to have stable and successful states for neighbors? If so, and if their movement into Europe allows these states to become stable and successful, then how is Russian security threatened? I haven't gotten an answer to these questions yet.

The same measures that those who nurse Russia's grievances indignantly call "unilateral concessions" were in fact a rejection of imperial longings that Russia simply could not afford to support in the 1990s. Should they have irrationally—and quite futilely—fought to preserve the Soviet Empire? And if these concessions were so unjustified, then why not hold those who acceded to them responsible—namely, the ruling administrations under Yeltsin and Putin. Most of them are still in power; why not take them to task for their actions?

For its part, the West, including the United States, was making concessions of its own to the Kremlin. Western leaders, for example, hesitated to pressure Putin about the second Chechen war and the brutality it engendered. They turned a blind eye to violations of rights and freedoms in Russia. As Stephen Sestanovich reminds us, it was the Bush administration that recognized Russia's status as a country with a market economy, supported its entry into the World Trade Organization, asked Putin to be chairman of the G8, agreed to have the G8 summit meeting in St. Petersburg, raised Russia's status in the NATO-Russia Council, and initiated a multi-billion-dollar aid packet to Russia in the form of a new version of the Nunn-Lugar program.[3] And what has America gotten in return for these concessions, save a short-lived period of cooperation during the war in Afghanistan, which Moscow regretted and began scaling back almost immediately?

Another Russian grievance holds that the West has refused to change the rules of the game established in the 1990s following the collapse of the Soviet Union. Yet some of Moscow's demands have been met (albeit grudgingly). The West moved slowly in response to Ukraine's and Georgia's requests to join NATO, hesitating to offer them even a membership action plan. European nations continue to make bilateral agreements with Russia on energy security—agreements that take into account the interests of Gazprom. The West doesn't interfere in Russia's internal affairs. It discusses with Moscow even ideas that are hardly feasible: for example, Dmitri Medvedev's initiative to create a new European security architecture.

But Moscow wants more! Does the Russian elite really believe it can have the dissolution of NATO, the cessation of democracy and election monitoring by the Organization for Security and Co-operation in Europe (OSCE), or a guarantee that Gazprom will be Europe's only energy supplier for perpetuity? Be assured, dear readers, that the Russian elite does not suffer from excessive naïveté. They know you don't get half a loaf of bread by asking for half; you ask for a full loaf. By constantly pushing the envelope of demands, the Kremlin keeps the West off balance, in the hopes of forcing it in the end to give up its own plans and compromise with the Kremlin. The Russian elite survives and thrives on uncertainty, instability, provocation, and blackmail.

There is yet another rationale for Russian "revisionism." By forcing the West to reject impossible demands, the Russian elite creates the impression that the West is the intransigent and unfriendly one. By forcing the West to play the part of Dr. "No," it creates a constant justification for hurt feelings and calls for revenge.

Given this context, how should we view President Dmitri Medvedev's demands in 2008 for the world to recognize Russia's "spheres of privileged interests"? I doubt the Kremlin strategists ever believed that even its most loyal neighbors, Armenia and Belarus, would jump at the opportunity to become Russian satellites. The Kremlin knew the complex feelings and reactions such statements would stir up in the newly independent states. No one realistically hoped that Alexander Lukashenko would don the boyar caftan of a Kremlin steward. Nor did officials in the Kremlin care about their neighbors' reactions. Rather, it was a trial balloon sent up to gauge what kind of concessions the West might possibly make. Note that this trial balloon was floated when high oil and gas prices had inflated egos in Russia, making the elite think it could bring the whole world to its knees. As the economic crisis intensified, this euphoria died down, but the grievances and demands for "deliverables" kept coming; to backtrack on those demands would have been tantamount to an admission of weakness.

As for the Russian elite's desperate craving for spheres of influence, I should point out that Russian allies feel no ties or gratitude toward their patron. Even when they are in the Russian sphere of influence and being helped by Russia, they're always shopping around for new sponsors. Take, for example, the behavior of the presidents of Belarus, Uzbekistan,

Kyrgyzstan, and even Armenia. In recent years, the Kremlin bestowed enormous sums of money on these countries, yet these so-called allies continue to demand more and more, despite having dropped any pretense of being loyal to Moscow. Thus instead of strengthening its prestige and raising the esteem of its ruling class, Russia's "spheres of influence" have resulted in humiliation for Russia's ruling tandem. Nevertheless, the geopolitical masochism continues.

Today the Russian elite, apparently understanding that the idea of "spheres of influence" appears to represent a return to the Brezhnev doctrine, has started to talk about "spheres of interests." But how one can pursue interests without attempts to influence?

"Russia was not given a chance to fight for its national interests," some Russian experts insist. But which doors did the West slam shut to stop them? And here is an even more important question: What were, and for that matter what are, Russia's national interests? To maintain influence over the Baltics? To keep Ukraine out of NATO? To drive Western influence out of Russia? If this is what the Russian elite considers the national interest, then its aim seems to be a revival of the Soviet past. Does it really believe that is possible? This is not reality-based behavior; it's the old Leninist maxim that says, "Let's jump in the water and then see what happens!"

Let's consider who benefits from the "wounded Russia" narrative. The Russian public? Hardly. "Humiliation" is useful to Russia's rulers. It detracts attention from domestic problems, from the anti-national essence of the *rentier* class, and from the fact that the country has been turned into a raw materials state. The public becomes too preoccupied with suspicion and feelings of hostility toward the outside world. No détente in relations with the West will convince the political class to give up this advantage. Doing so would require it to find another way to rule Russia, and I don't see any signs of its having had such an epiphany. Besides, the grievance racket isn't just a regime survival strategy; it's become a well-paying profession in its own right. Why would they give this up when they don't know anything better?

Notes

1. Roderic Lyne, "Ot megafona k mikrofonu" [From Megaphone to Microphone], *Rossiya v global'noi politike*, no. 6, November-December 2008, http://www.globalaffairs.ru/numbers/35/10833.html.

2. Ronald D. Asmus, "Dealing With Revisionist Russia," *Washington Post*, December 13, 2008.

3. The Nunn-Lugar Cooperative Threat Reduction Program was adopted in 1992; its purpose was to help Russia and the other former Soviet states dismantle weapons of mass destruction on their territory.

26 ON THE "CENTER OF POWER," "DE-SOVEREIGNIZATION," AND OTHER THINGS

The Kremlin thrives on reminding the West about Russia's humiliation, a song that plays too sweetly for some Western listeners. Sincere and honest Westerners who have sympathy for Russia hear that song and begin to feel guilty. Then they call on their governments to treat Russia with greater understanding, with gentleness and tolerance. In practice, these admonitions usually lead to one thing: a policy of leniency toward the Russian regime.

Russian politicians, joined in chorus by the experts, readily bring up the West's slights or threats, but they tend to fall strangely silent about the real threats facing Russia: the demographic catastrophe, social and economic inequality, nationalism, the troubled North Caucasus region, and Russia's unstable southern borders. It suits the ruling class to have Russian citizens shed tears over the lost grandeur of the state and hurl curses westward rather than to have them dwell on the regime's corruption or their own poverty.

The Kremlin experts consider it their mission to keep Russia from forgetting its grandeur and global mission. "Russia remains an independent center of power, maintaining its sovereignty in domestic and international affairs," Vyacheslav Nikonov assures us.[1] Thanks to its nuclear status and energy resources, Russia is indeed a center of power. Unfortunately, the Russian elite, enthralled by its own boasting, doesn't see that its "satellite" states rarely display a respect befitting its self-assessed status. For example, not a single Russian ally recognized Abkhazia and South Ossetia, leaving the Kremlin isolated in the aftermath of the 2009 war with Georgia.

The Russian elite prefers not to think about the fact that Russia is a mere "petrostate," a raw materials appendage of other "centers of power." During the gas wars between Russia and Ukraine in 2009, Moscow was forced to ask Europe to help it settle the conflict. Even that humiliation didn't ease Russian strategists down from the pretense that their country was "an independent center of power."

Russian revisionists encounter significant problems when they attempt to combine the "wounded Russia" thesis with their view that Russia is a major power. They don't seem to be able to decide where "humiliation" ends and grandeur begins, or how the two could coexist. Usually, they count the 1990s as the era of humiliation and the Putin period as the era of Russia's return to great power status. But if this is true, then why did the sad songs about past humiliations begin in the present, supposedly brighter era. Why open old wounds? And if independence for Kosovo, the abrogation of the Anti-Ballistic Missile Treaty, and Western support of Ukraine and Georgia were humiliations, then how can we say that present-day Russia is a Great Power Restored? This historical doublethink gives the Russian elite a split-personality (as well as a splitting headache, one would think). Pity the poor Westerner, beset one moment with Russian whining and the next with Russian saber-rattling.

Russian politicians and experts care little for how their assertions of Russia's great-power status jibe with its grievous injuries from the global financial crisis. The very people who had assured us that Russia was virtually the only sovereign state in the world shifted seamlessly to declaring that the roots of Russia's economic upheaval could be found in America. If its economic recovery hinges solely on America's actions, then how sovereign can Russia really be? On the flip side, if Russia's rescue depends on China's economic strategy, then what does that say about its sovereignty? These would seem to be insoluble contradictions.

The Russian elite maintains another treasured thesis: the threat of the "de-sovereignization" of Russia—that is, the danger of "foreign control" of Russian resources. In reality the opposite is happening. Private investors, both foreign and domestic, are being squeezed out of the natural resources industry by the Russian state. Yet the state's expansion of its economic role didn't keep Russia from becoming little more than a raw materials appendage of developed states. For some strange reason, these same Russian experts and politicians prefer to overlook this particular example of de-sovereignization. The more Russia morphs into a petrostate whose stability depends on the export of energy resources, the louder these defenders will clamor about attempts to steal Russia's sovereignty. It's a vicious, self-perpetuating cycle.

The Russian elite has shown little interest in a different process of "de-sovereignization"—namely, the ruling bureaucracy's increasing imposition of limits on the people's sovereignty. Yet if the people were not being stripped of their sovereignty, would the Kremlin have any need to stoke fears of de-sovereignization by the West?

In June 2008, Medvedev signed a document outlining Russia's foreign policy doctrine. It declares:

> The reaction to the prospect of losing the West's historical monopoly on globalization processes is expressed, in particular, in the inertia of the political and psychological principle of "containing" Russia, including attempts to use a selective approach to history, first of all to the history of the Second World War and the postwar period.

I don't recall what Western experts had to say about this theory, but I found it notable as evidence of a return to the rhetoric of the Soviet era, when state ideology was built on faith in the inevitable failure of capitalism and the decline of the Western world. I don't need to remind you how that story ended the first time around.

So: the revamped official foreign policy doctrine under Russia's new president once again orients the country around the premise that Western civilization is in decline. What does this mean in practical terms? Rivalry? Indeed why cooperate with the West when it is supposed to be headed for history's dustbin? What will replace Western power? What can replace it? Surely not Russia, a country that, when caught unawares by the economic crisis, found it necessary to implore Western creditors to ease its debt-repayment schedule and extend more credit.

To one who takes Russian rhetoric at face value, the idea that Russia could be "captured" by an interpretation of history might seem quite odd. In his novel *1984*, George Orwell explained the process by which one might control the present and future by controlling the past. Thus if we wish to understand the mechanisms of Russian power in operation today, we should pay special attention to the regime's efforts to return to the past and to shape how that past is interpreted. Putin was the first leader to look to the past to legitimize his rule. Medvedev has continued along these lines, creating a state commission under the control of the head of the presidential administration to combat the "perversion" of Russian history. Needless to say, the majority of the commission's members endorse the regime's view of Russia's great-power status and the dangers of "pervasive Western influence."

This backward-looking mentality, this desire to protect the Soviet perspective on the Second World War and its aftermath, tells us something about the Russian elite's evolution. It tells us that Russia isn't ready to give up its imperial niche, or to turn the page on its totalitarian past. Nor is it ready to allow other states to do so.

The Russian political class has clashed fiercely with those newly independent nations that, tired of waiting for Moscow to give up the Stalinist ghost, have begun their own examinations of Soviet history. "You don't have the right to do that!" yell Muscovites to the impertinent Balts, Ukrainians, and Georgians. "It's *our* common past. You can't touch it without our permission. We suffered, too, after all. We had more famines than you did!" The neighboring capitals respond: "Well, then let's tell our peoples the truth together." But Moscow stands firm: "No. First, we need to create a commission." Creating such commissions on the past, as the Soviet experience has shown, is a surefire way to keep it buried. Taking such a hard line against historical truth and reconciliation could all but kill the potential for normal relations between Russia and the states it victimized in the past.

What a lost opportunity! Everyone had expected a liberal thaw once Medvedev assumed the presidency. The shattering of these expectations has shown that Soviet geopolitics has survived; indeed, Russia's separation from the West has grown.

Medvedev could have spoken differently. In fact, on one occasion, he even said, "Our choice is no different from the choice of other European countries. We have the same vector of development. That is why we would like to count on an equal and confidential partnership on all questions."[2] If he truly believed these words, then it would have meant one of two things: Either Medvedev had just backpedaled and contradicted all his previous statements, or he was merely employing imitation rhetoric—saying what his Western audience wanted to hear. Such doublethink exposes not only the peculiar psychology of those at the top, but also their complete ignorance as to the direction Russia is actually heading.

In that context, consider the following anecdote—just one example of the fact that some leading Russian internationalists are beginning to feel uncomfortable with their own positions. In 2009 during a meeting of the Council on Foreign and Defense Policy (SVOP), one politician (whom I have already quoted) surprised everyone, perhaps himself as well, with a devastating critique of Kremlin policy and his own past arguments. The rules of SVOP do not allow the speakers to be quoted without their permission, so I can only offer you an outline of our brave fellow's thoughts (which have already been published in the press, incidentally). The reason for Russian anti-Americanism, this politician held, lies solely in the "hurt" caused by the widening gap between Russian and American economic development. Russian foreign policy had not implemented a single item on its agenda—no global or regional leadership role, no national modernization. Instead, its agenda was built "on the denial of the agenda" of its partners. In the Caucasus, Russia merely reacted to events, the result being the August 2008 war, when it was left with no choice but to fight. Moscow understood what its partners wanted from Russia, but those partners did not understand what Russia wanted from them. He concluded his remarks by noting that it was high time to start thinking creatively, for Russia's present foreign policy program is impotent.[3]

How could a politician who had spent so much of his career justifying the actions of the Kremlin make such an outburst? Perhaps he was tired of being a propagandist. Nevertheless, after this brief but unexpected moment of frankness, our "dissident" returned to his former role as a "defender" of Russia against the West. Soon after issuing his clarion call, during parliamentary hearings on how to improve Russia's image abroad, the same politician suggested "destroying the reputation of Western opponents." In public, it seems, Russian politicians have the courage to say things that would make them blush in private. For one of the architects of Russian policy to confess that it was "impotent" proves that they knew what they were doing and understood what would happen as a result.

Notes

1. Vyacheslav Nikonov, "Doktrina Medvedeva" [Medvedev's Doctrine], *Izvestia*, February 6, 2008.

2. Dmitri Medvedev, presentation at the London School of Economics, http://www.vesti.ru/doc.html?id=27085.

3. Arkadii Dubnov, "Ot impotentsii k konvergentsii" [From Impotence to Convergence], *Vremia Novostei*, April 15, 2009.

27 AMERICA THE MODEL, AND AMERICA THE EXCUSE

The entire world has "issues" with Americans, and one's particular issues with America tend to be the most popular topics for discussion of foreign policy. In many of these discussions, America becomes either a model for other countries or an excuse for their failure to solve their own problems. America's hegemonic impulse is the persistent object of criticism for all of its allies, even the closest ones. More enlightened and influential Americans partake in such criticism, too. The late Samuel Huntington long ago spoke disparagingly of America as the "world sheriff." He also spoke of America's increasing isolation as it attempted to carry out this role.

It seems finally as if the "world sheriff" model is riding off into the sunset. With the election of Barack Obama to the presidency, global attitudes toward America are changing. Now the concern flows in the other direction, that America will be too focused on its own problems and will isolate itself. So while much of the world is hoping for America to discover a new missionary spirit, the Russian elite, stuck in the past, still accuses America of dictating to the world. This is not the first time that Moscow has played laggard.

This whining isn't just tardy; it has become persistent and habitual as well. What is it that the Russian elite so dislikes about America's behavior? Former Russian minister of foreign affairs Igor Ivanov explained: "Even during the years of ideological war and confrontation between blocs, there were elements of partnership in the relations of our countries. There were unwritten but very definite rules of the game which strictly delineated the borders of the permissible and set up 'redlines.'" But now those borders are gone, and Ivanov blames America for it. Sergei Lavrov spoke along the same lines, albeit in harsher tones. Both ministers were right in their description of the changes: There was an impression that there were no more "redlines" defining the borders of the permissible. But who erased the lines? America?

During the Cold War, Russia and America were opponents that had developed a very successful system of mutual containment. It succeeded because a step beyond the "redline" meant war between nuclear powers. It was a pact between two hostile civilizations that had compelling reasons to avoid a direct conflict. After the collapse of the USSR, a similar "redline" arrangement became impractical; Russia wanted to be accepted, and has been accepted, into Western clubs. But the new partnership isn't working, either, not because of the power differential between the two countries, but because Russia's values are still alien to America. This leaves the situation more volatile than it was during the Cold War because the Russian state struggles over its contradictory roles as both partner and opponent of the West.

Ironically, the squall of Russian accusations against the United States began when George W. Bush traded in his first-term stomping about the world stage for his second-term tiptoeing, mindful of the effect his earlier unilateralism would have on his legacy. When Bush was hurling cobblestones, Moscow took no offense. When he calmed down and Secretary of State Condoleezza Rice began her shuttle diplomacy to renew and repair U.S. relationships, Moscow suddenly felt endangered by the "unipolar world."

As to Russian denunciations of the evils and dangers of a unipolar world, journalist Yulia Latynina wrote,

> Then why do our fighters against a unipolar world, who do not wish to be on the West's leash, send their children to study in the unipolar world, buy villas in the unipolar world, drive in cars, wear suits, and use telephones manufactured in the unipolar world. They even keep their money, not in Zimbabwe or Venezuela, but in that unipolar world.

If by unipolar world, one means a structure resembling the Eiffel Tower, with a vertical arrangement of subordinate "floors," and America at the very top, then one is in the grip of a delusional fantasy. That delusion persists in the imaginations of politicians and analysts only because they have no vision to replace it. The contemporary world order is an asymmetrical structure, with elements of it, but not the whole, dominated by the United States. Those spheres of dominance remain on the political and military level, and it is clear why: The United States is still the world's most powerful nation. Its GDP is more than $13 trillion, accounting for 25 percent of global GDP.

However, influence is being redistributed to other global players in financial, social, and cultural arenas. The world is moving toward a flatter, more multipolar structure. The global financial crisis has only hastened the process of the redistribution of power and influence. Richard Haass has concluded that the world is approaching the stage of "nonpolarity."[1]

I think it's still too soon to tell. America's dominance remains, even if Americans themselves, chastened after the Iraq war and the Bush administration, no longer seem to desire it. However, this dominance has nothing in common with the "vertical" power paradigm in the Russian sense, if only because America could not erect such a structure even if it wanted to. What kind of unipolar world is it if tiny Greece has the nerve to hinder NATO membership for Macedonia against the express wishes of the United States? How we can we discuss U.S. hegemony if Paris and Berlin can just say no to the U.S. push to bring Ukraine and Georgia into NATO? Nevertheless, a U.S. global preponderance remains, because many countries, including some in Europe, rely on continuing U.S. protection.

For now, no single country seems prepared to bear this responsibility. Chinese officials repeat at world forums that "China does not want to be a pole; it is too much of a burden."[2] Most states, even those critical of the United States, prefer American hegemony, albeit in a milder form.

Russia is not prepared for life in a fully multipolar world, either. Such a model assumes the creation of one's own "galaxy" by force, or lacking that, by compromises and presenting an attractive model for a different way of life. The Russian elite does not have the ability or resources for the first; nor is it prepared for the second. Thanks to its elite, Russia is certainly not a gravitational center for its clients, cultural or otherwise; they would betray it at any moment if it were in their interests. And without American hegemony, what external power could the Russian elite use as both "threat" and model for imitation to consolidate its own society?

Nevertheless, the Kremlin continues to demand a multipolar world. Russian politicians even pretend that they are living in one. Of course, Russian demands for multipolarity are yet another manifestation of cunning. How do they jibe with the Kremlin's proposals to form a "troika" and run the world with the United States and the European Union? Sergei Lavrov never tires of saying, "We are actively collaborating in the formation of mechanisms for a collective leadership by the leading states, intended to promote the restoration of manageability of world development."[3] "Collective leadership," envisioned as a "collective vertical," actually bears little resemblance to the true multipolarity the Kremlin is demanding. It still is not clear who would elect this "collective leadership" and whether the rest of world would accept it. How would it be any more efficient than the previous one?

I'm constantly amused by the way Russian politicians and experts regard the United States. They're trying to prove that the United States is in crisis with its role in world politics withering, while at the same time condemning it for its aggression and hegemony. How can crisis and hegemony co-exist so effortlessly? Moscow hasn't bothered itself too much to come up with an answer to that question.

My intention in all the foregoing is not to defend America's actions in the international arena. I simply differ with the majority of Russian observers in one important respect: They believe that there is too much U.S. meddling in the world; I think that America, on the contrary, has lost its civilizational mission and has replaced it instead with geopolitics. There is no question that America remains very influential in the world. But what kind of influence does it now exert? I would argue that America's current international role has become a factor that sustains the traditional system in Russia.

Finally, one strong desire unites the Russian elite with regard to international relations: the desire to shift the differences between Russia and the West from the civilizational plane to the geopolitical plane. The elite claims that problems between Russia and the West arise because their foreign policy interests do not coincide and because the West is trying to interfere in Russia's affairs (which is a specific instance of interests not coinciding). Most of the problems arise for a different reason, however: Russia and the West create internal order in different ways, and thus they project themselves on the outside world in different ways.

This does not mean that purely foreign policy-based disagreements between Russia and the West are impossible. International relations have their own specific features, needs, and tools of implementation. But in the final analysis, a state's external actions have profound domestic policy roots and are determined by how the society and the regime organize themselves.

Notes

1. Richard Haass, "The Age of Nonpolarity," *Foreign Affairs*, May–June, 2008, vol. 87, no. 3, p. 51.

2. Recent Chinese attempts to increase the country's geopolitical leverage have not thus far turned China into a new "pole" of international influence.

3. "O prioritetakh vneshney politiki rosiy na covremennom etappe" [Current Priorities in Russian Foreign Policy], January 28, 2009, transcript available at http://www.mid.ru.

28 WHO DERAILED MODERNIZATION?

The question "Who is to blame?" is perhaps the most important for Russian political culture. Answering it tends to consume so much time and energy in every venue that there's nothing left over for answering the more important follow-up question, "What is to be done?" Putting the accent on blame is a national sport that perhaps explains Russia's place on the civilizational plane.

As soon as the global financial crisis demonstrated that the Russian economic miracle was yet another myth, Russian experts started looking for someone to blame for derailing modernization. In accordance with the rules of the national sport, they looked to the West. Liberals, even true liberals, bought into the idea of the West's guilt.

Since thoughtful and decent people support this conclusion, I owe it to them to very carefully examine the arguments on both sides.

Alexander Auzan, a man of well-known liberal views, maintains that the West "blurred the rules of the game" on the world stage, thereby obviating the possibility of Russian modernization, despite the fact that all the preconditions of modernization were in place when Medvedev was elected. Auzan wrote, "The political construction that arose in April-May 2008 evinced the authorities' recognition of the need for new rules. While the Putin regime was completing the redistribution of property, the Medvedev administration was preparing to secure the existing property rights. But everything broke off." Why? Auzan answers his question: "Because not only the economic but the political institutions of the post-Yalta system were being washed away. It was done by the West. Belgrade, Iraq, Kosovo—these were terrible precedents." Then, in his view, "An extremely powerful patriotic consolidation took place.... The dominant groups rejected the legal rules of the game."[1] In other words, at the start of the Medvedev term, the Kremlin was ready to secure property rights and thereby transform Russia. But the West, by undermining the rules of the game, elicited an explosion of Russian patriotism with a nationalistic flavor and ruined the plans. These views continue to carry weight, even in democratic circles.

There is no arguing with him on several points. The West, and the United States first of all, undermined some of the principles on which world order is based. The Iraq war remains an event the United States bears full responsibility for. It weakened the legitimacy of America's global role and discredited Western civilization's claims to good intentions. But the Balkan crisis, the bombing of Belgrade, and the American invasion of Iraq happened several years ago. How could these events, occurring in 1999 and 2003, respectively, affect the preconditions for Russian modernization so much later, in the spring of 2008? Why hadn't America's attack on Iraq fanned the flames of anti-modernism in Russia earlier?

Even assuming that the West's recognition of Kosovo's independence was the impetus for the "patriotic consolidation" that destroyed Russia's chances for modernization, why didn't it also stop the reforms in Bulgaria, Romania, or Serbia, the last of which has now set itself on a course to join the European Union? Were the Russians more Serbian than the Serbs? And there was no "powerful wave of patriotic consolidation" in Russia in the spring of 2008, but had there been, what would it say about Russia if events in such a small and distant enclave force such a sharp U-turn?

If the West could have derailed reform in Russia so easily, it would further prove that Putin had failed utterly to make Russia a sovereign state and a fully independent actor in international relations. It also proves that Putin and Medvedev couldn't offer the elite and Russian society a modernization agenda that could realistically become the foundation for a constructive consolidation. If the Kremlin's plans were any more sensitive to external events, they would risk being derailed by the death of Fidel Castro, or a revolution in Venezuela.

If the West did not exist as a scapegoat, the regime would have to invent it. But Western political circles should wonder carefully about why even Russian liberals are suspicious and are willing to blame them for Russia's failures.

In fact, Russia's internal processes, and especially the steps taken by its leaders, have much more impact on Russia's modernization failures than Kosovo, Iraq, and other Western actions. Russian economist Evsey Gurvich explained the internal sources of the economic crisis in Russia this way,

> events in Georgia and the Mechel affair [Putin's criticism of the company's director led to a collapse of its shares] showed that we are not

ready to observe a single set of rules. On the contrary, we are ready to reject any rules the instant they can somehow constrain our behavior. But investors cannot work in conditions when any agreement can be thrown in the garbage to suit political expediency.[2]

How can we hope for modernization if investors are too afraid to invest in a country where the prime minister can crash the market with just a few words spoken in public? How can there be modernization if there are no rules?

There are a few optimists on the question of modernization of Russia, especially among the Kremlin's defenders. They believe that modernization is not only possible but inevitable. They believe that liberal-democratic principles are not needed for modernization. Thus, Alexei Chesnakov, close to the Kremlin, tried to show in a debate with me that just because there was no example of anti-Western post-industrial modernization, it did not mean that "it cannot be because it has not yet been."[3] My response in the pages of *Vedomosti*:

> In that case, why hasn't Russia moved onto the path of modernization in recent years, when the authorities moved onto the path of anti-Western consolidation? Where is the actual program of this modernization? Where is Putin's plan, which was in the [United Russia] party's election platform? And generally, how can you modernize a country and defeat corruption while rejecting political competition, rule of law, and independent institutions? If there is a recipe for this innovation, it would be good to show it at last.[4]

The proponents of anti-Western modernization have yet to offer their plan. I guess they're still thinking.

Notes

1. Alexander Auzan, "Natsional'nyje tsennosti i rossijskaya modernizatsiya: pereshchet marshruta" [National Values and Russian Modernization: Course Correction], Polit.ru, October 29, 2008, http://www.polit.ru/lectures/2008/10/22auzan_print.html.

2. Evsey Gurvich, "Igra bez pravil" [The Game Without Rules], *New Times*, December 22, 2008, p. 42.

3. Alexei Chesnakov, "Nachalo epochi: bez starych antitez" [The Beginning of an Epoch: Without Old Antithesis], *Vedomosti*, October 8, 2008.

4. Lilia Shevtsova, "Nachalo epochi: vpered v proshloye?" [The Beginning of an Era: Back to the Past?], *Vedomosti*, October 23, 2008.

29 HOW TO COMBINE THE INCOMPATIBLE, AND WHO ARE "WE"?

Life is hard for a Russian expert, hard for all of them: the ones who stubbornly criticize the authorities and the ones who must genuflect to official propaganda while trying to retain a semblance of professionalism and dignity. The persistent ones were marginalized long ago, and the latter are forced to do battle against logic. Thus, victory is not always on their side.

One of the smartest Russian experts, Fyodor Lukyanov, has called on Russia to "increase strength" (apparently, militarily) and at the same time worry about how to avoid "unnecessary confrontation" with the United States.[1] Many Russian observers think in the same key. But "increasing strength," especially when no one is threatening Russia, is a path to confrontation. If confrontation is to be avoided, then why, you may ask, should strength be increased? This contradictory political thinking exposes the inner conflict between professionalism and loyalty to official dogma. The ultimate victim of that contradiction is clear.

Other Russian experts are also kept busy trying to reconcile the irreconcilable. Sergei Karaganov seeks to remain within the framework of the official Kremlin line while warning against hewing to that line too closely. "We must show what the economic and human price is for Ukraine joining NATO," Karaganov said. "We must use oblique methods to show Europeans and Americans the price they may have to pay for implementing blatantly hostile policies toward Russia." Such a price, Karaganov warned, "may seem unacceptable to them."[2]

So the guessing begins: How should the price be levied, in economic or military dimensions? How high should the price be? Moscow has already cut off gas to Ukraine more than once, and the results were not encouraging, especially for Russia. What about military options? Russia could try to bring in the Black Sea fleet. While it hasn't experimented with that option, it would probably make for a more daunting price.

But Karaganov has no intention of taking things that far: "The most important thing is not to be hooked by the systemic military-political confrontation, in which we will always be in a more losing position than the Soviet Union [was]." But how can you establish in advance which price the West would find "unacceptable" without the serious risk of falling into the same pattern of confrontation?

The dire impact of Ukraine's and Georgia's membership in NATO is a favorite topic for Vyacheslav Nikonov: "Events are happening and may happen that will lower the nuclear threshold to a dangerous level: they bring closer the limit beyond which a global war using weapons of mass destruction seems thinkable."[3] Well, here we are: Ukraine's accession to NATO would threaten to provoke a nuclear confrontation between Russia and the West. If NATO truly poses such a dangerous threat to Russia, what is Russia doing in the NATO-Russia Council? And what is the nationalist Dmitri Rogozin doing there as Russia's representative to NATO? Is he preparing for a nuclear war as a spy in a hostile camp?

The same experts tried to scare the West during the first and second rounds of NATO expansion, but nothing came of their efforts. We can console ourselves that this time they are just trying to spook the Americans and Europeans from even considering letting the NATO umbrella extend any farther over the borders of the former Soviet Union. What if the West doesn't understand it's all just talk? No one can guarantee that Western leaders will be able to stand firm in a game of Russian roulette forced on them by the Kremlin. There are no assurances that the Russian elite itself would not accidentally cross the line. What if someone in the Kremlin decides to use the "nuclear card" in the event that he begins to lose his hold on power?

Medvedev articulated yet another popular piece of anti-NATO rhetoric in April 2009:

> We do not always understand why there is a rush to accept countries into NATO that are completely unprepared for it, making the situation tense with other states.... It seems to me that NATO should be thinking more about how to preserve its internal unity and solidarity without creating problems for itself.[4]

These conclusions are bewildering. If you still consider NATO a threat to Russia, then why worry about the alliance's "internal unity"? If taking in new members will lead to its dysfunction, wouldn't it be smarter to support their entry as a poison pill? Perhaps the best way to neutralize NATO would be for Russia to join. That move would surely be the end of NATO's existence.

We must review these Russian arguments because my Western colleagues frequently take them on faith. Almost every Russian expert— liberal or not—who tries to explain Russia and its relations with the West speaks in the voice of the nation: "Russia will not permit" or "Russia demands" or "We do not like," and so on. Encapsulated in the use of both collective identity words, "Russia" and "we," there is an unwillingness or inability to separate personal assessment from the state position—that is, to take on an independent role in assessing the situation. Even more importantly, neither of those collective identities exists any longer. Russian society was fragmented long ago and now manifests various interests and desires. The external consensus on international issues in Russia is superficial and very unstable. It seems as if the majority buys whatever the Kremlin pronounces, but if you dig deeper, you find that the consensus can fall apart at any moment, as soon as the public gets accurate information about the price Russia pays for its foreign policy.

Whenever a Russian politician or expert uses either "Russia" or "we," ask him or her, "Which Russia and which forces are you talking about? Whom do you represent? Who are you?" Finally, "And what do you, Mr. Ivanov, think about this yourself?"

Western experts often use "Russia" in an analogous way to the Russian experts' "we." I hear the refrains so often: "The Russians are offering," "the Russians are advancing again," or "Russia does not guarantee." Who is involved? The political leadership, the elite, the general population? Western colleagues must be able to discern a more complex range of opinion within a non-monolithic Russia. They must distinguish the political regime from the society and from the various segments of the elite. On the international stage, the West must recognize that it is dealing with the Russian state and government. They are the West's partners, not "Russia" or "the Russians," who might hold very different views than those of the Kremlin.

Notes

1. Fyodor Lukyanov, "Chitaja mir, pereosnashchaja instituty" [Reading the World, Reforming the Institutions], http://www.polit.ru/institutes/2008/10/16/struct_print.html.

2. Sergei Karaganov, Borshch s pampushkami [Borscht With Fritters], *Rossiyskaya gazeta*, February 8, 2008.

3. Vyacheslav Nikonov, "Voina na Kavkazie: chego nie chochet poniat' Zapad" [The War in the Caucasus: What the West Does Not Want to Understand?], *Izvestia*, March 16, 2008, http://www.izvestia.ru/comment/article3120121.

4. Dmitri Medvedev, "Po itogam sammita Rossiya-EC" [On the Outcomes of the EU-Russia Summit], http://www.kreml.org/other/185068372.

30 THE TRIAL OF NATO AND KOSOVO

The story of how NATO expansion and the Kosovo crisis affected relations between Russia and the West is the most popular international tale told in Russia. The story itself has become so grubby from overuse that it should have been run through the wash, or perhaps dumped in the recycling bin, long ago. But, the Russian elite continues to repeat its familiar cadences because the fight against NATO is the most effective way of supporting the militaristic syndrome in Russian society, not to mention the best way to heap guilt on the Western political class. Kosovo, too, turned out to be just as successful a way of establishing Moscow's right to define its "spheres of influence" and accusing the West of double standards.

Even most liberal observers in Russia believe that these two events were a blow to Russia's democratic orientation and its relations with the West, especially the United States.

For the sake of objectivity, I would like to remind the reader that the decision to expand NATO eastward, the expansion itself, and the intensification of the Kosovo crisis all happened after the foundation for the new system of personalized power was laid in Russia, beginning with the Yeltsin constitution in 1993. These events took place after the firing on the Supreme Soviet, after the start of the first Chechen war, and after the establishment of Yeltsin's absolute rule. Thus they could not have undermined democratic reforms in Russia. However, they did provide an important argument for the Kremlin in justifying its turn toward authoritarianism.

Did these events affect the resurgence of distrust between Russia and the West? I agree with James Sherr, one of the first to notice that "the Western policy in the CIS [Commonwealth of Independent States], the Balkans, and the expansion of NATO did not play a substantive role in the formation of Russia's neo-imperial course.... That course was started earlier, and it increased when Russia First was the watchword of Western policy."[1] Sherr reminds us that back in 1993, Minister of Foreign Affairs Andrei Kozyrev began speaking of Russia's "special interests" in the "near abroad." It was then that Yeltsin demanded that the UN give Russia special powers to guarantee peace and stability in the former Soviet space. So even under a democratic regime, Russia began its return to the Soviet *derzhavnichestvo*. In April 1994, Yeltsin accused the West of struggling with Moscow "over spheres of influence," and in October 1994 he talked of the threat of a new Cold War. Moscow's return to imperial rhetoric and worsening relations started well before the events that the Russian elite and some Western commentators consider the watershed.

There is one more argument we must consider. According to data from the Levada Center, more than 40 percent of Russians who responded to surveys in the 1990s did not consider NATO a hostile institution and had a positive attitude toward it. In fact, 25 percent thought Russia should join NATO. In those years the Russian public did not consider NATO a threat. It was unlikely that the alliance itself or its expansion could have a substantive effect on the failure of democracy in Russia or worsening relations. The strained relations were the result of the failure of liberal reforms, not the expansion of the alliance.

Let's give our opponents a few free shots. Let's assume they're correct that NATO expansion and Kosovo were responsible for souring relations between Russia and the West. Relations are built and maintained by the elites, and the Russian elite had to have been displeased by those events, if only because it could not exert its influence over them. Then why did Yeltsin, on his visit to Warsaw in the summer of 1993, tell Lech Walesa that Poland's entry into NATO was and ought to be Poland's decision, not Russia's? If we assume that Yeltsin didn't really understand security issues and underestimated the threat of the alliance, then why did the entire Russian elite, along with President Putin, also maintain such warm relations in 2000–2003? Why had the Kremlin stopped worrying about "hostile" NATO after the latter's supposedly provocative expansion? And having dropped its complaints, why did it suddenly raise them again? There is only one possible explanation: NATO expansion and Kosovo are merely a diplomatic and political currency to be spent or pocketed by Russia's ruling elite as they see fit.

In any case, the Baltic states' and Poland's fears about the revival of Russian imperialism were justified. Many of my fellow Russian liberals had underestimated the possibility of that threat.

The West in the 1990s faced a dilemma: Either acknowledge Eastern Europe's fears, which seemed excessive at the time, or acknowledge Moscow's demand that NATO's eastward enlargement be halted. The West tried to satisfy both sides, but with varying degrees of success. Rejecting NATO enlargement would mean returning to something like the World War II era Yalta order, which the West could not accept. How could they tell Eastern Europe and the Baltic states that Russia would continue to have veto power over their future? How could they sell such a capitulation to Western public opinion? It was also obvious that Western leaders displayed no imagination or strategic vision for developing a new Euro-Atlantic security structure, nor for finding effective ways to include Russia, such as inviting Russia into NATO. "It would not have worked anyway: Russia was not ready to obey NATO's rules," the skeptics will say. Probably not, but if such an attempt had been made, then the Russian elite, not the West, would have had to own up to that failure. The bottom line today is that, even if it was just a hypothetical, Western leaders were at fault in missing an opportunity to link Russia with the West.

The idea of bringing Russia into NATO had been promoted in the West long ago, certainly. French President Francois Mitterrand was among those who thought it a good idea. Some Western experts supported it, too. Australian writer Coral Bell made the suggestion to bring the Soviet Union into NATO back in 1990: "It could be done by one simple though radical step: the offer of membership to Russia and other major members of the now-defunct Warsaw Pact."[2] Bell thought the scenario would help the Soviet Union in its transition to democracy.

Zbigniew Brzezinski, a target of many accusations in Russia, said in the 1990s that including Russia in the expanding transatlantic community should be a component of a long-term U.S. strategy to ensure "stability on the Eurasian mega-continent."[3] He maintained that "if Russia wants to be part of the West, it should have a variant of close association with the EU and NATO that would be acceptable for both sides." He stressed, "A formal statement to that effect [the possibility of Russia's eventual participation in NATO and the European Union] should be made, perhaps jointly by both organizations."

Subsequently, other Western experts proposed the idea, including Michael Mandelbaum and Charles Kupchan.[4] Unfortunately, their voices were not heard either. NATO and the European Union are open institutions. Russia has always had the chance to seek to join them. An open invitation to Russia could be the most effective way to combat Russian politicians' theories about the "hostile" expansion of the West.[5] "Unrealistic!" every Russian politician would say. Yet as Medvedev himself, when asked about the possibility, stated, "Never say never!" (Although he never clarified under what conditions he saw it happening.)

Notes

1. James Sherr, *Russia and the West: A Reassessment*, Shrivenham Papers no. 6, Defence Academy of the United Kingdom, January 14, 2008.

2. Nikolas Gvozdev, ed., *Russia in the National Interest* (New Brunswick and London, 2004), p. 39.

3. Zbigniew Brzezinski, "Living With Russia," *National Interest*, no. 61, Fall 2000.

4. Michael Mandelbaum, "NATO Expansion, A Decade On," *American Interest*, May/June, 2008; Charles Kupchan, *The End of the American Era* (New York: Alfred A. Knopf, 2002).

5. Four respected senior German defense experts (Volker Rühe, Klaus Naumann, Frank Elbe, and Ulrich Weisser) have stirred debate in March 2010 by arguing that it is time to invite Russia to join NATO. The authors, however, were right to stress that NATO was "an alliance of values" and Russia "must be prepared to accept the rights and obligations of a NATO member, of an equal among equals." Volker Rühe, Klaus Naumann, Frank Elbe, and Ulrich Weisser, "It's Time to Invite Russia to Join NATO," Spiegel online, http://www.spiegel.de/international/world/0,1518,druck-682287,00.html.

31 DOES NATO THREATEN RUSSIA?

For the time being, the Russian elite continues to characterize NATO as its main foe. It does so despite the fact that even the Russian military has openly admitted that the alliance presents no real threat to Russia. As retired Major General Vladimir Dvorkin wrote,

> Russia in any case—with parity or not in the potential of nuclear restraint with the United States, with any architecture of American ABM and NATO and all potential of conventional high-accuracy weapons—will retain a potential of response that will keep every madman from considering not only a military confrontation with us but even threatening Russia with an attack.[1]

General Dvorkin's opinion is confirmed by the conclusion of retired General Pavel Zolotarev, who said, "The actions of Western countries [including NATO expansion] cannot pose any real threat."[2] Russian military officers are known to speak frankly only after they retire.

The Russian experts considered to be close to the Kremlin are forced to admit that NATO is not a threat to Russia. Karaganov put it this way, "I don't think that the possible NATO expansion will lead to a qualitative increase in the military threat to Russia. From the West, it is microscopic."[3] Yevgeny Primakov, the guru of Russian traditionalists, also had to admit, "As for the prospects of cooperation with NATO, we have stable relations with that organization, within which is the NATO-Russia Council."[4] So if Russia and NATO have "stable relations," the issues that underlie these relations cannot be antagonistic.

What do independent Russian experts think? "Talk of increasing NATO's military power near Russian borders has no basis in fact. NATO expansion has not led to an increase of its military power, but on the contrary, was accompanied by a reduction of joint military potential of its members in the alliance's zone of activity," says Andrei Zagorsky.[5]

Experts such as Zagorsky could bolster their position by pointing to several examples of successful cooperation between Russia and NATO. Russian units participated in NATO peacekeeping operations in Kosovo and Bosnia and Herzegovina; in the joint military training of officers from Afghanistan and Central Asia for anti-narcotics trafficking operations; and in joint training with NATO in Wyoming on operating in post-nuclear detonation environments (these exercises have taken place three times now). Russian ships also helped patrol the Mediterranean alongside NATO ships. Official Moscow doesn't like to remind the Russian public about these things.

What does the Russian anti-NATO faction fear? General Dvorkin had a straight answer: "The process of joining NATO is a process of democratization that will lead to a civilizational schism between Russia and its neighbors, if they join the Atlantic bloc."[6] German expert Karl Kaiser confirmed this thinking, stressing the alliance's role in securing stability in Europe and in easing the transformation of new member states. Kaiser said, "It is under the NATO umbrella that the Euro-Atlantic region became a peace zone. The alliance was an effective structure for guaranteeing development and democratization of new member states."[7]

NATO membership presupposes that the new members make serious efforts to base their societies on democratic principles. NATO membership was the first step to joining Europe for most former communist countries. It was within NATO that they began the democratic reforms that proved to be much more important than solving security issues. For example, Ukraine's cooperation with NATO is more about solving political problems, namely establishing civilian control over the army, than it is about enhancing combat capabilities. According to Dvorkin, this might be just what the Russian elite fears: "the prospect of ending up in civilizational isolation" when its neighboring states join NATO.

Thus NATO enlargement is a threat not to Russia but to the Russian regime and the elite, who want to create a *cordon sanitaire* of failed or weak states around themselves. For the elite, which organizes its power around the search for enemies, NATO is the optimal foe. Therefore, those who reinforce the myth that NATO is a threat are helping the political class implement its survival strategy. "But even Russian democrats are fighting against NATO," the bewildered Western observer may say. True, many representatives of Russian democratic associations also regard the alliance as an enemy of Russia and speak out against its expansion. But I believe this only demonstrates the degree of disorientation in the Russian democratic milieu on foreign policy issues, if not the democrats' unwillingness to take a position that might be viewed by the authorities as unpatriotic.

Obviously, the Russian elite and even the Russian opposition have trouble accepting that former Soviet satellites are now independent states that have the right to pursue their own interests, including the right to manage their own security. The Russian elite today cannot or does not want to understand that the post-communist states seek to join NATO because it offers them the fastest route to Western civilization. As Primakov admitted in speaking about the USSR's former vassals, "They want to be identified as part of the West and not of the East."

My Western colleagues say not to worry. "Great Britain and France had the same difficulty giving up their imperial past. Imperial nostalgia passes with time." But neither Great Britain nor France had to change their political system in order to shake the imperialist syndrome. In Russia it is one of the building blocks of the system. Russia would have to undergo a much trickier surgical procedure to free itself from the syndrome.

Despite its being in the grip of the imperialist syndrome, Moscow doesn't wish to break off relations with NATO and so continues to cooperate with the alliance. Medvedev said, "We want normal relations with the North Atlantic alliance. We are prepared to develop partner relations with the alliance."[8] Developing a partnership with your enemy would have to be the most striking innovation in the history of world politics. Naturally, the Russian regime has the patent on it.

Notes

1. Vladimir Dvorkin, "Pochemu raschirenije NATO dolzhno trevozhit' voennych professionalov" [Why NATO Enlargement Should Worry the Military Experts], April 11, 2008, http://www.ej.ru/?a=note&id=7969.

2. Pavel Zolotarev, "Protivoraketnaya oborona: istoriya i perspektivy" [Antimissile Defense: History and Perspectives], *Rossiya v global'noi politike*, no. 4, May–June 2008, http://www.globalaffairs.ru/numbers/32/9776.html.

3. Sergei Karaganov, "Borshch s pampushkami" [Borscht With Fritters], *Rossiyskaya gazeta*, February 8, 2008.

4. Quoted in *Kommersant*, April 4, 2008.

5. Igor Klyamkin, ed., *Rossiya i Zapad. Vnieshnyaya politika glazami liberalov* [Russia and the West. Foreign Policy in Liberals' Eyes] (Moscow: Liberal Mission, 2009), pp. 16–17.

6. Vladimir Dvorkin, "Pochemu raschirenije NATO dolzhno trevozhit' voennych professionalov" [Why NATO Enlargement Should Worry the Military Experts], April 11, 2008, http://www.ej.ru/?a=note&id=7969.

7. Karl Kaiser, "For Better or Worse—Is NATO Still Relevant?" *Internationale Politik*, Summer 2008, p. 10.

8. RIA Novosti, November 16, 2008; www.rg.ru/2009/12/17/nato.html.

32 WHAT OTHER NASTINESS DOES THE WEST HAVE IN STORE FOR RUSSIA?

Now let's talk about the other Western "threats" cited by the Kremlin and elite groups close to it. They were most irritated by the George W. Bush administration's efforts to deploy an anti-ballistic missile (ABM) system. What do independent Russian experts have to say about the reality of the anti-ballistic missile threat? I will turn once more to General Vladimir Dvorkin, who explained, "The people who write or speak about the threat of the ABM for Russia's nuclear forces have no idea about this program. Otherwise they would know about the extremely high effectiveness of Russian systems for overcoming all echelons of the ABM."[1]

Serious civilian experts seem to concur with Dvorkin: "As for the ABM, it is silly to say than 10 antiballistic missiles capable of intercepting just one [!] enemy warhead could be a threat to our nuclear arsenal, which now consists of close to 3,000 warheads and by 2012 will be 1,700–2,200 warheads,"[2] says Alexander Golts. "The danger and threat coming from the future American system of antimissile defense in Europe is greatly exaggerated,"[3] confirms Andrei Zagorsky.

The Americans reminded Russia that they informed Moscow a long time ago, at least as early as 2002, when the United States withdrew from the ABM Treaty, that they were planning to create an organic defense system in Eastern Europe.[4] I remember Deputy Secretary of State Nicholas Burns mentioning this. Moscow listened to the information very calmly and then proceeded to forget about it, only to suddenly remember it at a more politically opportune time. The Russian authorities became agitated about anti-ballistic missile systems in 2007. Why, asked Leon Aron, did Moscow accept U.S. withdrawal from the Anti-Ballistic Missile Treaty in 2002 so calmly, and then get so upset about the mere possibility of placing a few components of system in 2007?[5]

I need to explain a little bit about the circumstances prevailing in Russia in 2007. It was a year in which parliamentary elections would be followed by presidential elections. The Russian authorities needed to increase the public's fortress mentality, and so the Kremlin embarked on an unprecedented campaign to whip up anti-American hysteria. The campaign demonstrated exactly how self-confident Putin and the Kremlin were at that time, but that is a separate topic. Let me just note that Putin was trying to overcome his feelings of insecurity through a search for an "enemy," in this particular case by railing against U.S. plans for an Anti-Ballistic Missile system.

It should also be noted, however, that according to independent experts, in the event of "mass expansion of U.S. missile defense based on land, sea, and space," that system might have been able to affect "the potential of Russian nuclear containment." In their opinion, the solution to the problem could have been a treaty establishing a joint development program for a global anti-ballistic missile system.[6]

This situation is surely absurd, but it is not the only one. America and Russia still function as strategic enemies within a regime of mutually assured destruction. That is why they need to sign a new Strategic Arms Reduction Treaty (START): to guarantee a predictable continuation of that regime. How, then, can mutual nuclear deterrence be combined with a joint Russian-American anti-ballistic missile system? This is just the most striking example of the kind of peculiarities that arise between states that are both partners and foes.

The Kremlin understood that the components of the American anti-ballistic missile system in Eastern Europe posed no threat to Russia.[7] In October 2008 in Evian, Dmitri Medvedev laid out his thinking regarding the system to be deployed in the Czech Republic and Poland, "It is clear that on its own, neither country is any threat to Russia." What, then, was the problem? Clearly there was no real threat, except for the threat that the Russian authorities might run out of virtual threats. Without them, Russians might believe that they live in an open and friendly world. The Kremlin cannot allow that.

In 2009, President Obama rejected the Bush anti-ballistic missile proposal and decided to reconfigure the European missile defense system. Now it would not exclude the possibility of Russia's taking part in it. Thus it seemed that the most painful irritant in relations between Moscow and Washington had been eliminated. But since that irritant was only intended to be a virtual threat to excite a domestic Russian audience, the Kremlin didn't seem too happy. Sooner or later, the elite will find another excuse, another virtual threat.

Moreover, the Obama version of missile defense, which was to have been deployed earlier than the Bush plan, above all the SM-3 interceptors that would have been placed in the territorial waters of Romania and possibly Bulgaria in 2015, became a new Kremlin headache. It seems that the Russian leaders have persuaded themselves that this plan is "even worse." The Kremlin's new concerns again appear bizarre because the American interceptors in the Black Sea region don't pose any danger to Russia's security. It would have taken thousands of interceptors to undermine the Russian nuclear missile capabilities. Do the Russian military and the Russian leaders know this? Of course they do. Then why the new fuss? For one reason: the Russian leaders need to have a pretext for their constant grumbling and dealing. A call for the construction of a joint missile defense system could be a way out of this dead end. But Russia would have to re-examine its security strategy and start rethinking its civilizational pardigm. The Russian ruling team is clearly not ready for that.

Another factor in the tension between Russia and the West is the Conventional Forces Treaty in Europe (CFE), a very important stone in the foundation of European security. Moscow continues to vigorously insist that the treaty harms Russia's security. In fact, just the opposite is true. Zagorsky says,

> A diligent execution of CFE by all participants would allow all of them not only to reduce the number of their armed forces and weapons in Europe but to go further in their reductions than the Treaty requires. The treaty guarantees the maximum degree of transparency in the situation in Europe through an annual exchange of data that were checked during inspections on site. When you see that everything is fine and in order with your neighbors, that they are complying with everything, you can calmly go on, in accordance with your budget limitations, without looking back at potential danger in the region.

Things could have continued smoothly if Moscow had not used an obviously fabricated excuse to introduce a moratorium on complying with CFE in December 2007. What were the real reasons for that step? As defense analyst Pavel Felgengauer says,

> If Russia had not withdrawn from CFE, the success of its invasion into Georgia in 2008 would have been questionable. We must

assume that the future operation against Georgia was being developed in 2007 and perhaps that was the main reason for Moscow's inexplicable withdrawal from CFE."[8]

After the moratorium, Russia stopped participating in the annual exchange of data, did not allow military inspections, and did not consider itself bound by the quantitative limits set by the treaty, especially in its southern flank. Naturally, the other CFE signatories began expressing concerns about their own security in light of the Kremlin's militant gestures, with the European countries bordering Russia being most worried. I doubt we can expect further arms reductions in Europe now. Have the Russian leadership's actions heightened security in the region? Have they heightened security in Russia? These are of course purely rhetorical questions.

Russia's "defenders" against the threat from the West like to carp on several other topics as well. They never fail, for example, to mention how menacing NATO bases in Romania and Bulgaria are. I doubt the Russian public knows that Americans are actually shuttering many of their bases in Europe. Nor is it likely they are aware that the bases America plans to build in southern Europe fit CFE in terms of size and are intended to support the American military presence in the Near and Middle East, not the European theater. These bases, which will house no more than 2,500 soldiers all told, are unlikely to be a danger to Russia. If Russian "threat specialists" are so concerned by such a paltry number of American soldiers, then how can they still believe in Russia's grandeur or its potential as a "center of power"?

Russian experts not connected to the Kremlin assure us that there is no threat to Russia from NATO expansion, CFE, anti-ballistic missile systems, or American bases in southern Europe. These threats are myths manufactured for domestic consumption, but they are not harmless myths because of that fact. If enough people begin to believe the myths, then they must be countered. Russian leaders would then be forced to react to the phony threats they themselves made up. Their reactions always take the same form: threats of a "symmetric response." For example, the Kremlin has frequently threatened to aim missiles at neighboring countries. President Medvedev himself has often found it necessary to make such threats, maintaining an even grimmer look of determination on his face with each new pronouncement. Independent experts have warned that, if Russia starts deploying new missiles or even just threatens to target Poland, the Czech Republic, or Ukraine, then it might not just provoke an arms race; it might deepen the gap between Russia and the rest of Europe as well. But who has time for "independent experts" in Moscow? The Russian elite lives one day at a time, with little concern for tomorrow. And even more troubling, there are influential groups within the elite whose guiding principle is "the worse, the better."

There are a few more explanations for Russia's menacing growls on the world stage. The architects of Russian foreign policy are apparently betting on two things.

First, they hope they will be able to intimidate the West into giving up perceived incursions into Russia's spheres of influence. They even succeed sometimes, and if you succeed once, you're all the more likely to try again.

Second, they hope that even if the West doesn't buy Russia's threats, it will still support the Kremlin's game in order to preserve good relations. As for what Western leaders think about their Russian partners and their abilities, no one in the Kremlin really cares.

The Russian campaign to intimidate the West, backed up with "light artillery" on television, has yet another goal: to lay the groundwork for a monumental distraction if the domestic situation in Russia begins to deteriorate rapidly. The militaristic rhetoric, symbolism, and pageantry (for example, the Russian navy's port call in Venezuela in 2008, or the flybys over American warships by Russian fighter jets) are clearly intended to create an enemy that Russia will bravely confront when the Kremlin finds itself unable to pull the country out of a future crisis.

Interestingly, officials in the Russian Defense Ministry and government don't buy their own rhetoric about the threat from the West, according to independent experts. Why else, they say, would Russia reduce its armed forces and consider giving up (at an unspecified future date) universal conscription and moving the military to an all-volunteer footing?

Notes

1. Vladimir Dvorkin, "Glavnoye-politicheskaya volya" [The Most Important Is Political Will], March 13, 2009, http://www.ej.ru/?a=note&id=8891.

2. Igor Klyamkin, ed., *Rossiya i Zapad. Vnieshnyaya politika glazami liberalov* [Russia and the West. Foreign Policy in Liberals' Eyes] (Moscow: Liberal Mission, 2009), p. 46.

3. Ibid., p. 15.

4. John Bolton, "Three Steps to Stop Putin ... Before It's Too Late," American Enterprise Institute, October 28, 2008, http://www.aei.org/article/28847.

5. Leon Aron, "Russia's Woes Spell Trouble for the US," *Wall Street Journal*, December 31, 2008.

6. Dvorkin, "Glavnoye-politicheskaya volya" [The Most Important Is Political Will].

7. Ibid.

8. Pavel Felgengauer, "Pervaya chast' voiny s Gruzijej" [First Part of the War With Georgia], *Kontinent*, no. 138, 2008, p. 146.

33 WHY MOSCOW NEEDED THE BALKANS

The West couldn't prevent the Kosovo crisis, and it also failed to offer a less painful ending for it. It is an undeniable fact that the NATO bombing of Belgrade in 1999 inflicted a great deal of collateral damage on pro-Western feelings in Russian society. However, the Russian elite cannot pretend that its position on that issue was unimpeachable. Russia would rather forget that Moscow's support of Slobodan Milosevic's regime intensified the Kosovo drama, thus weighing them down with some of the responsibility for both the crisis and the mode of its resolution. Of course, very few people in Russia would admit this. The official version of the events as told to the public is very different.

Today, even Russian liberals rebuke the West for its illegal actions in Kosovo. Yet Russia blocked all resolutions in the Security Council that might have checked Milosevic and made him stop his barbaric ethnic cleansing in Kosovo. The West had no choice but to do an end run around the Security Council, thus undermining it. I personally believe, even today, that the West could have avoided bombing Serbia and found a different pressure point to use on either Milosevic or Moscow, whose support he relied on.

The Russian regime continued to support Milosevic even when it became clear that he was cynically using Russia as a cover. Yevgeny Primakov admitted that Milosevic had stopped paying attention to Moscow and openly ignored the Kremlin:

President Milosevic did not keep his promises made to President Yeltsin. President Milosevic, besides that, had promised the EU that there would be no extraordinary Serbian attack. The next day, the attack began.... The [Albanian armed forces] are switching to partisan tactics. Naturally, this is the consequence of the attack by Serbian security forces.[1]

In that case, why did Moscow defend the Milosevic regime at the cost of worsening relations with the West? No need to look for complex answers here. Moscow was saving Milosevic in order to preserve the illusion of its influence in the Balkans. I doubt the Kremlin worried about the poor Serbs any more than it did about the poor Chechens.

Moscow wanted to reassert its position in Kosovo before NATO troops entered, almost triggering a confrontation with the Western alliance in doing so. In June 1999, the Kremlin (it's not clear precisely who) decided to drop Russian paratroopers in Kosovo in order to preserve the Russian sector once NATO entered the region. The paratroopers were supposed to take the Pristina airport, where additional Russian troops were to be transported. But Hungary, Bulgaria, and Romania, which had decided to join NATO and the European Union, refused to allow the Russian transport planes to traverse their airspace. Upon receiving information about the paratroopers, U.S. General Wesley Clark, commander of the NATO forces in Europe, was evidently ready to use force against them. Only the common sense of British General Michael Jackson, commander of NATO ground forces, prevented a situation that could have turned into armed conflict between Russia and NATO. Jackson informed the infuriated Clark, "Sir, I'm not starting World War III for you." When the two hundred Russian paratroopers reached Pristina, they were forced to ask for water and food from the British, who had surrounded them (to protect them from the Kosovars). The British obliged.

Strobe Talbott, who rushed to Moscow to mediate the conflict, reported that at the moment that the Russian paratroopers began their Pristina mission, neither Minister of Defense Igor Sergeyev nor Minister of Foreign Affairs Igor Ivanov had any idea what was going on. There were doubts that Yeltsin had control of the situation or of the "hawks" in the military.[2] Thankfully, there was no major incident that time, but it could have ended very differently.

Former deputy minister of foreign affairs Georgy Kunadze lamented Russia's actions regarding Kosovo. "Russia is engaged in rearguard battles in Kosovo. No one knows what goals it is pursuing. It's not clear what is more important for Russia—principles or interests."[3]

Today, however, in the wake of Moscow's recognition of the independence of Abkhazia and South Ossetia, there is no doubt that interests are more important for Moscow. There can be no talk of principles, if only because they change so quickly. It's abundantly clear, on the other hand, whose interests are important: the elite's hunger to assert itself. And if it can't influence something, the simplest and most direct method of self-assertion is to hinder it. In the most recent case, Georgia became the object of the Russian elite's tender mercies for daring to seek shelter under NATO's wing. As for the consequences of such tantrums, who's going to remember how pathetically the Pristina story ended for Russia?

The trial by war in Bosnia for Russia and the West in the 1990s fortunately ended in cooperation, although the road leading up to that point was a rocky one. The Kosovo incident in 2007–2008 was harder on relations between Russia and the West, but not because of disagreement over the principle of Serbia's territorial integrity. Indeed Moscow hasn't been consistent in its defense of the principle, supporting the separatists in Trans-Dniester and openly expressing doubts about whether Crimea is a part of Ukraine. The crowning incident in its inconsistency was Moscow's August 2008 recognition of independence for South Ossetia and Abkhazia at the expense of Georgia's territorial integrity. Clearly, territorial integrity isn't a sacrosanct commandment in the Kremlin.

Moscow's behavior during the crisis in the Caucasus allows us to conclude that its behavior in the Balkans, especially over Kosovo, had been dictated by considerations that had nothing to do with international legal principles. In fact, Russian politicians confirm this deduction. In a burst of frankness a famous Russian politician revealed, "They [the West] had the Ahtisaari plan for Kosovo. We had nothing.... Our plan was not to let them [the West] put through their plans."

In the final analysis, Moscow's policy during the Kosovo incident was a sign of the direction Russia's evolution was taking. It became clear that the Russian elite wanted to recreate its imperial nationhood by supporting Serbia. The Kosovo crisis simplified the consolidation of Russian traditionalists and facilitated the revival of old myths in the public consciousness. The Balkans were both the means and the excuse for Russian traditionalists to return to the Soviet political niche. It was the moment when Russia announced to the world that it was turning away from the West.

In turn, the Western community's actions during the Balkan crises demonstrated that its political class couldn't foresee potential trouble spots, nor could it find timely solutions that did the least damage possible to European security and the principles of international order. In other words, the West was far from without sin in its actions. However, it cannot be blamed for not doing everything in its power to keep from pushing Russia away or letting it withdraw into itself. At that moment in time, and amid many competing views about what should be done, the sober prescriptions for action prevailed; cooperation with Russia was necessary. For the first time since World War II, due to the West's initiative, the Russian military successfully cooperated with NATO troops in the Balkans as part of a joint peacekeeping operation.

After the desperate attempts to help Milosevic, the Kremlin finally had to take the West's side in the dispute in 1999. This decision was reflected in Viktor Chernomyrdin's intermediary role in negotiations with Milosevic in the final stages of the conflict. It was Chernomyrdin who convinced the Serbian leader to accept the West's ultimatum to end military action in Kosovo.

This history of cooperation between Russia and West, however, was conveniently forgotten. And it is clear why: The new Russian regime needed people to believe that you just can't trust the West.

Notes

1. Yevgeny Primakov, "Gody v bol'shoi politikie" [Years in Big Politics] (Moscow: Sovershenno sekretno, 1999), p. 303.

2. James Goldgeier and Michael McFaul, *Power and Purpose. U.S. Policy Toward Russia After the Cold War* (Washington: Brookings Institution Press, 2003), p. 261.

3. Quoted in *Kommersant*, March 13, 2008.

34 UKRAINE AS A MILESTONE

The watershed year in the deterioration of relations with Russia, and the year that revealed to all the true reasons for that deterioration, was 2004, the year of the Orange Revolution in Ukraine. The mass demonstrations on the Maidan in Kiev shocked the Russian elite into realizing that the same thing could happen to them, especially since they had always thought of Ukraine as a Russian province. Ukraine was therefore the first falling domino that began to set off other long-dormant sources of tension between Russia and the West. The Kremlin's displeasure with the West during the Orange Revolution seemed to be based on geopolitical considerations. Putin's Kremlin concluded that the West was using Ukraine to push ever further toward Russia's borders. It is hard to judge how sincere was the Kremlin's belief that the West had manufactured the demonstrations in Kiev. If they did in fact believe this, it would just be further evidence of their confusion about what really happened in Ukraine.

The level of Western aid to Ukraine immediately preceding the Orange Revolution was lower than it had been in previous years. In 1998, the United States gave Ukraine $360.24 million, $178.16 million in 2003, and even less—$144.82 million—in 2004. Most of the money was intended to support economic development, humanitarian aid, and Ukrainian security cooperation efforts. An insignificant part, less than a third of the total aid, was for "democratic administration." These figures belie the myth that America was making mass investments in the Ukrainian opposition on the eve of the elections. Russia spent vastly more money to support the pro-Kremlin forces in Ukraine and fund the expensive campaign specialists who worked for those candidates. But no amount of money could have accomplished in Kiev what the Kremlin had learned how to do in Moscow: guarantee the election of the right person. Therefore, internal causes set the Orange Revolution in motion in Ukraine. A foreign policy factor that might have acted like a detonator was the direct interference in Ukrainian presidential elections by Moscow and President Putin personally.

The Russian political class and its leaders suffered a defeat in Ukraine. They lost their most important sphere of influence—a sphere that was crucial to the preservation of the traditional Russian state. This was an intolerable turn of events for the Kremlin. More than loss of territory, it led them to lose confidence in themselves and their future. It was also a personal defeat for Putin, one he has not forgotten, as demonstrated by his direct participation in the continual "gas wars" with Ukraine, as well as the Kremlin's nervous reaction to anything that happens there.

The Russian ruling team perceived Ukraine's turn to the West under Viktor Yushchenko as a ticking time bomb under the supporting pillars of the Russian state. Ever since then, the Russian elite has repeatedly warned both Ukraine and the West, "Ukraine is the last straw. Ukraine in NATO means war!" What worries the Kremlin and the Russian elite about NATO membership for Ukraine is that it means not only the expansion of the West's security space (which doesn't worry the Kremlin much) but also the expansion of the zone of liberal civilization with which Russia cannot compete. If a pluralistic Ukraine marked by the rule of law survives, it will pose an insurmountable challenge to a Russian system that is stuck in the past.

Until now, the Russian elite has shouted itself hoarse in attempting to convince the West that it will not give up its veto over Ukraine's development path. Missteps and petty squabbling among the Ukrainian elite elicit undisguised gloating by the Russian elite. "You can't manage without us! You'll die without us!" they say. In turn, official Moscow does everything it can to make Ukraine face a sharp choice between Russia and the West. The choice has divided Ukrainian society, which to this day is made up of many former Soviet citizens who haven't adjusted well to life apart from Russia.

Moscow shut off the gas to Ukraine twice (in 2006 and 2009) in order to show that it was not to be fooled with. To the outside world, the gas conflicts between Moscow and Kiev looked like a business dispute in which Russia was right to insist that gas be paid for and loans repaid. I have to admit that, during the "gas wars," Kiev didn't always behave logically, often managing only to provoke Moscow. But in its desire to exacerbate the situation regardless of the consequences, Moscow overplayed its hand and gave proof that it was not pursuing economic aims but political ones. To put it more precisely, economics became politics for Moscow. The essence of this politics was not difficult to understand: Russia tried too hard to use Ukraine's economic problems to paint it into a corner, forcing it to admit to Europe and the world that it couldn't manage things on its own. And the more Ukraine is discredited, the Russian elite hopes, the less likely the West would be to insist on bringing this unbalanced and factionalized country into its institutional structures, especially NATO.

"Russian actions in the period of the crisis of 2009, including the unexpected shutoff of gas [at] a moment when it seemed an agreement with Ukraine was so close, shows that the motivation of these actions was not purely commercial," said Anders Åslund. "It must be sought in the political sphere and the Kremlin's desire to destabilize Ukraine, to show how bad democracy is for Eastern Slavs, while also supporting the patriotic slogan, 'The Ukrainians must pay us!'"[1] Vladimir Milov expressed a similar opinion:

> Why did Moscow need to act so harshly, threatening the reliability of Russian gas transit to Europe, the vulnerability of which was obvious as early as January 2006? Russia put everything on one card, disregarding the financial consequences (stopping European transit costs Gazprom up to $150 million a day) and Europe's possible reaction. This harshness is reminiscent of the behavior of the Russian authorities during the August conflict with Georgia. Perhaps we are dealing with a policy of a new type toward post-Soviet countries that have embraced a pro-Western course—the policy of crude pressure.[2]

Milov is right. Russian policy in the "cold wars" over gas pursued the same goals that it pursued in Georgia during the "hot war": preventing these countries from escaping to the West and punishing them for the attempt. Leonid Kuchma, the former president of Ukraine, didn't mince words in his description of the Kremlin strategy. "I am more than certain that Russia wants to punish Ukraine for its behavior, obstinate from the Russian point of view, during the Georgian conflict" (when Ukraine took Georgia's side).[3]

Even Russian leaders were forced to admit the political context of the conflict. They gave it a unique spin, though, blaming the gas war exclusively on the Ukrainian elite and a certain superpower—America, of course, which it accused of orchestrating Ukraine's actions. Alexander Medvedev, a representative of Gazprom, declared that he "did not rule out the possibility" that another country could be "controlling Kiev's action." The other country, obviously, was America. As a general rule, when the

Russian elite wants to defend its interests, it turns to America's insidious role to justify its actions.

In an interview on the German television network ARD, Putin attempted to justify Russia's actions:

> Today many people in Ukraine are disillusioned. The former leaders of the Orange Revolution have betrayed the people's expectations and the people's trust. The political struggle has turned into squabbling among clans. These clans do not want to build democracy and a market but realize their personal ambitions and get access to financial flows, one of which is trading in Russian gas, both inside and outside the country.[4]

Even if that analysis of Ukrainian reality has some basis in fact, it is strange to hear such accusations from a man who spent so much effort fighting both the Orange Revolution and democracy in Russia. Besides which, the mind reels in trying to see how cutting off gas supplies to Ukraine (and Europe) helps the Ukrainian people, whose welfare Putin professes such concern for.

Let me note in passing that it is becoming a habit for the Russian regime to spend masses of energy and resources to end up proving (yet again!) Chernomyrdin's axiom, "We wanted to do the best we could, but it turned out as usual." Alexander Ryazanov, former deputy chairman of the board of Gazprom, admitted that Gazprom lost the 2009 gas war at a stunning cost: gas production fell by 14 percent; the company lost $1.8 billion.[5] According to independent economists, the two gas wars led to a reduction of gas consumption in Europe by 5 percent overall in the first quarter of 2009. Consumption of Russian gas supplies fell by 40 percent, and Gazprom's Norwegian competitor, Statoil, increased its sale of gas in Europe in the same period. Sales of liquefied natural gas from Algeria and Libya also rose in Europe. In other words, Europe started doing everything in its power to reduce its economic dependency on the emotional state of the Russian leadership. And this represents only a fraction of the price Russia had to pay for its Ukraine strategy. Damages to Russia's image and to its future energy sales are still being tallied.

Chernomyrdin's axiom was confirmed yet again in March 2009, when the European Union and Ukraine signed a joint declaration on modernizing the Ukrainian gas transport system, an agreement that included an EU loan worth $2.57 billion for that purpose. In connection with the agreement, European consumers will have the right to buy gas at the border between Ukraine and Russia (today they are restricted to buying it at the border between Ukraine and the European Union). This step was meant as a means to incorporate Ukraine into Europe's energy and economic space, as well as a response to the Kremlin's actions.

You would think that this agreement would have pleased the Kremlin and Gazprom. After all, Europe was guaranteeing unhindered delivery and the modernization of Ukraine's gas transport system. Kiev, a chronic irritant for Moscow, was being taken out of the gas equation between Europe and Russia. But instead of sighing in relief, Moscow was infuriated. Why? Because Gazprom thereby would lose the Ukrainian pipeline as a pressure point to use against Ukraine and Europe when either of them got out of line. And even more than that, steps to normalize energy relations with Ukraine could deprive the Russian elite of one of its most important tools for pressure on Kiev. Russia's umbrage at the agreement leaves us no room for doubt concerning the real reasons for the gas wars between Russia and Ukraine.

These were not the only consequences of the gas wars. The European Union began work on finding an alternative to Russia as a leading provider of energy, allocating about €4 billion for projects to reduce dependence on Russian gas. The largest will be the Nabucco pipeline, which will transport oil from Central Asia to Europe, bypassing Russia. Despite the worldwide financial crisis and its own budgetary limitations, the European Union is pouring itself into this project wholeheartedly. In July 2009, Turkey and four European states (Bulgaria, Romania, Hungary, and Austria) signed an agreement in Ankara to build a new pipeline across their territories. Moscow should be proud: It takes a lot to get sluggish Brussels to move so quickly.

The Ukrainian elite, mired in power struggles and unable to fulfill its obligations, gave Moscow many excuses for the conflict, of course. But however clumsy and crude Kiev's actions may have seemed, the gas wars demonstrated that in the larger view the issue is a clash of vectors: Ukraine chose the Western vector, and Russia chose the opposite vector. Ukrainians had cause to declare, "We are fighting for our independence and sovereignty." Kiev tried to defend its sovereign right to choose its own model of development. If Moscow had accepted that decision, their disagreements over the gas issue would never have turned into a confrontation that left Europe out in the cold.

In other words, the gas wars were evidence of an underlying civilizational clash beneath the surface clashes over interests. The clash was prolonged by Europe's hesitation and desire to resolve the conflict without upsetting the Kremlin.

The Russian elite has no interest in the establishment of a strong and full-fledged Ukrainian state and so has become a destabilizing factor. For the elite, Ukraine is an excuse and instrument for legitimizing the militaristic and superpower paradigm within which it seeks to envelop Russia. A sad coda to this story is that Russian liberals have turned into imperialists. It is astonishing how strong superpower atavism is in people who otherwise support the idea of freedom for Russia. Would they deny the same freedom to Ukrainians?

How is it that liberals readily flock to the imperial banner when it comes to Ukraine? Perhaps they believe that Russia can only survive as an empire that needs Slavic "appendices." If so, they're forgetting that an empire cannot be a democracy and that empires are not eternal.

In an interview on the Russian radio station Ekho Moskvy, Viktor Yushchenko explained the causes of the painful relationship between Russia and Ukraine:

> I think that the problems are not in us at all. We have to forget crying for the past. We have to feel that today Ukraine and Russia are two independent peoples, free peoples, who have independent states, equal, sovereign states. Ukraine moved toward its sovereignty for hundreds of years. It is so important to have a friend here, who can offer you a hand and say, "We are not simply your neighbors, we are the first country that is interested in your sovereignty, in your development and democratization."

Alas, the Russian elite is not ready to offer Ukraine a hand.

Confirmation of the explosive relations between Russia and Ukraine, if any were needed, came in August 2009. August is always an anxious month in Russia. Unpleasant events and the consequences of fierce battles tend to surface in that month. The year 2009 was no exception. For no apparent reason, on August 11, President Dmitri Medvedev posted an appeal to Viktor Yushchenko on his videoblog. In content, the appeal resembled a declaration of war to the president of Ukraine. Standing in front of Russian warships in the Crimea, dressed in black (the color worn by Russian leaders when they want to look macho), and trying to act like

Putin, Medvedev accused Yushchenko in harsh terms of a myriad of sins: supporting Saakashvili, seeking to join NATO, breaking economic ties with Russia, interfering in the affairs of the Orthodox Church, and "playing on nationalistic complexes."

Announcing that he was postponing the arrival of the new Russian ambassador to Ukraine, Medvedev looked straight into the camera and said, "In Russia, we hope that Ukraine's new political leadership will be ready to build relations that will respond to the dreams of our peoples." Medvedev's appeal could mean only one thing: the Kremlin had no intention of dealing with Kiev until a new president had been elected (Ukraine's presidential elections were set for January 2010). This was the August bomb. There was a lot of speculation as to why Moscow set it off at precisely that time and why it needed to worsen relations with Kiev. Whatever the answers to those questions are, it was clear that Moscow was planning to continue its meddling in Ukraine. Amazingly, the Russian ruling team had not learned from its previous meddling, which inadvertently helped Yushchenko and the anti-Russian forces in Ukraine consolidate their power. Medvedev was following the line established by Putin, who allegedly told Bush in Bucharest, "You see, George, Ukraine isn't even a state!" Apparently, his heir in the Kremlin had the same view.

What will this view mean in practice? It means that new conflicts are possible over gas, the Black Sea fleet, territorial pretensions, the Ukrainian elite's desire to join NATO, or any other pretext, even seemingly insignificant ones. Since the Ukrainian elite is not going to solve its internal issues any time soon, Moscow will find fertile soil for sowing additional seeds of discord in Ukraine's domestic affairs.

The election of Viktor Yanukovych as president of Ukraine in February 2010 created in Moscow new hopes that the new leader in Kiev would be more willing to compromise with the Kremlin.[6] What naïveté! Or rather, what a stunning failure to think in novel terms! Any Ukrainian leader would be forced to pursue an independent policy in order to survive and keep the country together. The Kremlin's cold embrace would be a precursor of political death. Hence, the reasons for Moscow's frustration with Kiev remain.

What is most upsetting is the fact that the Russian elite continues to use Ukraine as just another tool to preserve Russia's traditional identity. In practical terms, this means not recognizing Ukraine as a genuine independent state. When Putin tried to persuade George W. Bush that Ukraine "is not a state," he betrayed the political immaturity of the Russian elite and decision makers in Moscow. Ukraine exposes the geopolitical schizophrenia of the Russia ruling class, making it a challenge for Europe and the West. The stability of the entire region depends on how they respond to the challenge.

However, I would agree with Mark Medish that despite the problems that Ukraine faces today, "Ukraine has a bright future.... The end of the Orange era will not be the end of Ukraine's independence nor of its Euro-Atlantic identity."[7] And Ukraine has a chance to prove to Russia that there are other, better ways it might chart its path into the future.

Notes

1. Anders Åslund, "The Gas Conflict Between Russia and Ukraine," *Handelsblatt*, January 8, 2009.

2. Vladimir Milov, "Slishkom bol'shaya tsena" [Too High a Price], January 12, 2009, http://www.gazeta.ru/comments/2257512.shtml.

3. Ukrainian TV Chanel Plus One, January 15, 2009.

4. Video of the interview is available at www.rian.ru/politics/20080830/150810743.html and www.u-tube.ru/pages/video/27976.

5. Alexander Ryazanov, "Poslieslovije k vojnie" [Afterword to the War], http://www.smoney.ru/article.shtml?2009/02/8908.

6. Moscow did not waste time in outlining what it expected from the new Ukrainian leadership. According to the Russian media, already on February 13, 2010, the head of the Kremlin administration, Sergei Naryshkin, met with Yanukovych for six hours. Moscow allegedly offered Yanukovych its requirements for better relations. Among them was the demand to discontinue relations with the U.S. CIA, renew the work of the Russian FSB office on the Black Sea Fleet, and end the military cooperation with Georgia. These were "gestures of goodwill by the new authorities that [put] Ukraine on the path to the full restoration of relations" between Kiev and Moscow. See Vladimir Solovyov, "Kotlieta po-kiyevski" [The Kyiv Cutlet], http://www.kommersant.ru/doc.aspx?fromsearch=7c510689-600e-4f21-ab66-c351d12fd500&docsid=1323691. These requirements would hardly help Yanukovych in his attempt to become an independent leader.

7. Mark Medish, "The Difficulty of Being Ukraine," *New York Times*, December 23, 2009.

35 WHERE IS THE WAY OUT?

What does the Russian elite believe it would need to do to create stable relations between Russia and the West? The Russian elite, as Dmitri Trenin has pointed out, expects the West to agree to deal "with Russia on Russia's terms, reaching for an acceptable balance of reciprocity, and not on the basis of normative principles such as democratic reform." The Russian elite and its experts assume that "[i]deology is not a good guide in a valueless yet vibrant Russian environment." In other words, the Russian elite expects the West to build its policy toward Russia on the basis of interests, not values. If that "agreement is not reached, the inertia of power diplomacy and growing anti-Western rhetoric will push Russia toward confrontation with the West."[1]

My answers to the arguments presented by Russian "realists" are given in the earlier chapters: Western Realpolitik didn't prevent confrontation between Russia and the West. Neither Clinton nor Bush tried to teach Russia about democracy, or even values or principles more broadly. This "restraint," however, didn't increase mutual understanding between the United States and Russia.

Moreover, the Kremlin and Western capitals have diametrically opposing ideas of what constitute "common interests." They see the war on international terrorism differently, and even have different definitions of whom to call an international terrorist. The United States and Europe regard Hamas as a terrorist organization. The Kremlin sees it as a potential partner and invites its leaders to Moscow. The West fears Iran and sees President Mahmoud Ahmadinejad as a threat. Russia, meanwhile, is helping Iran with its nuclear program. The two sides have different views on issues of European security and the activity of international institutions. They have different opinions on the roots of the global financial crisis. That Russia and the West have different views on a number of "common interests" merely confirms the fact that interests grow out of values. If the West were to follow the advice of the "realists" and ignore its values in dealing with Russia, the abyss between Russia and the West would only widen and consequently the threat of confrontation would grow.

In the opinion of Russian expert Fyodor Lukyanov, whom one could hardly count as a traditionalist, "the only true line of behavior for Russia is the build-up of its own strength" in order to resist "the hostile environment." That must mean that Western civilization is a hostile environment for Russia. Many Russian experts certainly think so. But they cannot explain why Russia belongs to Western institutions like the G8. Why does the Russian elite accept aid from a hostile environment? And why do their families live in supposedly hostile countries, or deposit their savings in banks on hostile soil?

Alexei Arbatov explained why Russia needs power and its concomitant "eye for an eye" policy with respect to the United States.

> What is allowed for them (the United States and its allies) will be allowed for Russia. If the U.S. Navy has the right to stay in the Black Sea, the Russian Navy will have the right to be in the Caribbean. If the United States recruits allies and builds military bases near Russia, Russia will have the right to do the same in Europe, Asia, and Latin America.[2]

And why not? Why shouldn't Russia do what the Americans are doing?

The problem is that proponents of this approach never stop to think whether Russia is ready to match America move for move. Russia, with a GDP of $1.3 trillion, has to compete with the United States, with a GDP of $13 trillion and a military budget of $600 billion (the Russian military budget is 4 percent of that).

This is how the Russian military observer Alexander Golts described the state of military resources in Russia:

> So far, there are only six of the Iskander missiles that President Dmitri Medvedev promised to place in Kaliningrad Oblast. Even more interesting is what innovative technology Russian industry is planning to manufacture, while straining every muscle. The Topol-M was developed in the late 1980s, so by 2015 the technology used in it will be 30 years old. The Iskander was developed in the early 1990s. The same can be said about the ABM complex S-400. Called the newest fighter, the Su-35 made its first flight in 1988. The fighter-bomber Su-34 is just as new. Of course, mass production of this

morally obsolete military technology hasn't even begun. At best, delivery to the army won't start for another three or four years. Thus, Putin's "innovation army" in 2020 will be equipped with military technology based on last century's technologies.

That is the "might" that Russian experts want to send to the Caribbean.

Even China's military prospects are more optimistic, largely because it spearheaded an information technology revolution throughout its military. Of military innovation in Russia, Golts says:

> Practically nothing is being done in Russia in this direction. First Vice-Premier Sergei Ivanov admitted the complete collapse of the GLONASS program, whose creators have been promising for the last year to provide military and civilian consumers with location orientation. It turns out that Russian industry cannot get production of the receivers going for lack of components.

Given this situation, what do Russian proponents of a "symmetrical" response think will happen? How do they plan to finance a build-up in the face of Russia's troubles, crawling up from the depths of the 2008 financial crisis? Perhaps, they're just trying to scare the West again out of habit. If so they're giving their Western colleagues a good opportunity to exercise their sarcasm, something many of them are already doing.

Besides lack of money, there is another problem with this response. The "eye for an eye" approach means that Russia cannot pretend to be a country that respects international law. The call for a military build-up is in fact a call to return to the law of the jungle. While public opinion acts as a check on untrammeled executive power in the United States, in Russia no such checks exist to keep "symmetrical" demonstrations of power from getting out of hand.

The "eye for an eye" policy is being disputed even among experts loyal to the Kremlin. Nadezhda Arbatova says that this is the point of view of Russian "imperialist idealists" and the "most conservative part of the 'hydrocarbons nomenklatura'" She says that they "criticize U.S. unilateral actions in international affairs, but at the same time call for following its example and seize everything Russia can take, following the Kosovo precedent." She also says—and I agree with her completely—that "Russia must defend its national interests within the framework of international law."[3]

Another Russian expert, Vladimir Baranovsky, was also concerned that the elite could take its militancy too far: "Russia must be taken into account.

But trust in Russia has diminished and the attitude toward it has worsened." In the meantime, he warned, "the key task is to keep from being pushed out of the Euro-Atlantic space." But Russia is pushing itself out of that space, not America or Europe. Its Western partners, on the contrary, are trying to keep it in, pretending that they don't take Russia's flare ups seriously, hoping that they are symptoms of a "difficult age." But Russia has been in this adolescent stage too long because of the elite's neuroses.

Interestingly, even some of the experts working for the Kremlin have started to express concerns about the course Moscow has taken. Vladimir Frolov, with some irony and humor, defined his views in the form of a joke telegram allegedly sent by Obama to Medvedev.

> Dear Dima,... I don't understand what you get out of friendship with people like Chavez and Castro. Maybe Chavez will buy some Russian weapons and pay in bolivars (I wonder what banks convert them to rubles?). And Castro can give you another radar base. But how will that help Russia modernize? And how can you trust them if they won't even recognize Abkhazia and South Ossetia? ... And what's going on with the Russian fleet in the Caribbean? Since when have we developed doubts about the balance of military power in that region? I'm happy that you guys have a chance to get a suntan. But next time you send your navy to warm seas, send them to my home state of Hawaii. I'll join them on my vacation and teach your guys how to surf.[4]

This shows that even the official expert community sees the dead-end nature of Russian foreign policy.

The more pragmatic experts have begun a cautious search for new approaches to relations between Russia and the West. The thinking of Igor Yurgens and Sergei Karaganov is a good example. They propose the idea of a "strategic union" between Russia and Europe that would be built gradually, starting with an energy union and ending with the creation of a single Russia-EU market. Their idea seems fruitful at first glance. Both have also criticized the negotiations between the European Union and Russia on a new agreement that, in my opinion, will be nothing more than a fig leaf, entirely devoid of content. Yurgens and Karaganov believe that Brussels and Moscow need to postpone their process of forging new relations in order to better understand where they stand and where they might go. It is hard not to agree with that. I also like their idea on democratizing the dialogue between the European Union and Russia. The relations between Russia and Europe must not be held hostage by two of the world's most immovable bureaucracies.[5]

Nevertheless, I question the feasibility of a "strategic union" between Russia and Europe. After all, before we create that union, we must explain why the "strategic partnership" of Russia and the European Union did not work. It failed because Russia did not want to accept European standards, and the European Union was not prepared to insist on them. If both sides don't accept the same values, then they are unlikely to agree on what constitutes common interests. Consequently, the "strategic union" will end up just like the "strategic partnership." Why should the European Union enter into a "strategic union" with Russia, if Russia continues to espouse completely different norms? How will Moscow ever be able to convince Europe to agree to an energy union after the gas wars between Russia and Ukraine? So, I agree with my colleagues: There is a real danger that we will "get stuck in the past." We need breakthroughs.

One such breakthrough could be an understanding that Russia, given its present system, is unlikely to participate in a union with the West. If it wants to get closer to the West, it will have to take the path of "subordinated" liberal-democratic development followed by the countries of Central and Eastern Europe. And if the Russian elite is not prepared to give up its "gas sovereignty," then it will just have to forget about breakthroughs and stay where it is.

To every cloud, there is a silver lining. The global financial crisis has forced the Russian political community to temper its rage. Russian experts who were until very recently rattling sabers now have toned down their attacks on the West, in light of their own country's formidable economic problems. As Vyacheslav Nikonov unexpectedly told an audience, "We truly are in the same boat [with the West]."[6] Western experts have felt their sense of optimism rekindled by the hope that the crisis will restore the Russian elite's common sense and inaugurate a new phase of cooperation. I believe, however, that their optimism is premature. Anti-Western impulses remain an integral component of the system by which the ruling stratum controls Russia.

It is true that the Russian elite can change its rhetoric and cooperate with Western countries when cooperation serves its goal of sustaining the traditional state. Occasionally, while seeking new avenues to preserve that state, the elite will entertain some discussion about reforming the world order. Russian politicians love that topic. Conversation about refashioning the universe allows them both to avoid answering concrete questions and to preserve the status quo in Russia. Thus, Russian politicians and experts have passionately taken up the cause of persuading the world that new rules of the game and new institutions to manage international relations are needed. The United Nations needs to be reformed, they say. So do the European security system and the global financial institutions. Everything must go! Time is of the essence!

When Western colleagues actually set about deciphering the Russian initiatives, it becomes clear that even their creators are unable to explain what they're for. Or it becomes clear that what they want is a return to the rules of the game as they existed before the collapse of the Soviet Union in 1991. Russian efforts to remake international relations often mask a desire to create an international order that will facilitate the survival of the personalized power and "gas" economy of present-day Russia.

We are dealing here with various attempts to formulate a *protectionist doctrine* to defend Russia's anti-liberal and anti-Western system. Foreign policy is one of the basic tools for protecting and preserving that system. While the domestic policy mechanisms in Russia are increasingly disappointing, even for the pragmatists, the elite is still largely in agreement regarding international relations. This means that the "protectors" in international relations have a lot of room for maneuver and have taken on the role of vanguard of the traditionalist state.

Do the arguments cited by the Russian "protectors," whose ranks include quite a few seemingly liberal-minded people, help us understand Russia's movement and its relations with the West? That is unlikely, since they take into account the interests of the ruling elite and not of Russian society. If they are accepted, will these arguments help build more stable relations between Russia and the West? That, too, is unlikely, because the preservation of the system requires rejection of the West as an alien civilization. Will the protectionist doctrine help Russia's modernization? Once again, no, for its goal is the defense of the traditional state, which rejects reform.

Notes

1. Dmitri Trenin, "Russia Redefines Itself and Its Relations With the West," *Washington Quarterly*, March 1, 2007.

2. Alexei Arbatov, "Double Standards in Foreign Policy," *Washington Post* (Supplements), September 24, 2008.

3. Nadia Alexandrova-Arbatova, "Russia After the Presidential Elections: Foreign Policy Orientations," in *Russian Foreign Policy, The EU–Russia Center Review*, 2007, pp. 15–16.

4. Vladimir Frolov, "Dear Dima," Russia Profile.org, December 9, 2008, http://www.russiaprofile.org/page.php?pageid=International&articleid=a1228831192.

5. Igor Yurgens and Sergei Karaganov, "K coyuzu Jevropy" [Toward Europe], *Rossiyskaya Gazeta*, November 6, 2008.

6. Vyacheslav Nikonov, "Global'nyi Krizis: riski vzaimozavisimosti," *Izvestia*, October 1, 2008.

36 LET'S MAKE A DEAL!

The art of the deal is another national game that the Russian elite enjoys playing. Often, process is more important than results. As it heaps blame on the West for cooling relations, the Russian elite loves to ask, "Where are the deliverables?" Moscow expects a reciprocal gesture from the West for every step it considers a concession or a retreat, even if that step is good for Russia itself. The West, and America most of all, must pay Moscow to shut its bases in Cuba and Vietnam, to allow American bases in Central Asia, to engage in dialogue with NATO, to allow American military cargo to pass through Russian airspace en route to Afghanistan, and to do almost anything that Moscow could arguably call a concession.

And if the West refuses to pay the piper, then the resulting soured relations are its own fault, say the Kremlin propagandists. And the Russian ruling elite expects to be paid in advance.

Putin was one of the prime architects of Russia's wheeling and dealing philosophy. "We closed our bases in Cuba and Vietnam. What did we get for it?" he demanded with sincere indignation.[1] The art of the deal suffuses the attitudes of Russian politicians and experts toward the West. Russian expert Alexander Lukin expressed the thoughts of many in Moscow when he said:

> Cooperation with the West should rest on agreements based on systems of mutual concessions. For instance, Russia can [toughen] its position on Iran, activate joint efforts on Afghanistan, not supply certain forms of weapons to certain countries, but we need an answer to the question of what it gets in return. If the West does not want to come to terms with Moscow, it is necessary to take harsh measures in response.[2]

I would like to ask those who maintain such beliefs why they think the West should pay Russia to do what it already needs to do on its own? It is

Russia that should be interested in security on its southern borders. It is in Russia's interests to have a non-nuclear Iran, a peaceful Afghanistan, and an end to military conflicts in the Middle East. Why should the West pay Russia to cooperate with it in Afghanistan, where American troops are even now defending Russia from the threat of the Taliban? Why should Moscow demand compensation from the West for ceasing all aid to Iran's nuclear program? A nuclear Iran, especially one led by its current irrational president, is a prime threat to Russian security.

It would be pointless to ask them these questions, however. Those who sincerely believe that the West perpetually owes Russia something are in the majority now. Most cynically believe that one should as a general rule always demand something from the West, and America in particular. "They will either try to deliver it, or they will feel more in our debt," thinks the Russian elite. Their entire lives are nothing but endless dealing. Not that they'll hold up their end of the bargain, of course. They're much too comfortable residing in a gray zone of uncertainty that rejects the possibility of firm agreements.

I doubt that billing the West for cooperation fits into the formula for true partnership. In fact, if Russia and the West can interact only on the basis of deal making, of tit for tat, then how exactly does one justify Russian membership in the Council of Europe and the G8, organizations meant to unite states that share common principles? Democracies do not bill one another for cooperation. The Russian elite hasn't given this simple truth any consideration.

I find most amusing the fact that ultimately the policy of deal making between the West and Russia may prove impossible. Why? Because executing a deal means solving a problem. Why negotiate and conclude deals otherwise? Yet often it is the existence of a problem and the need for deal that bolster the Russian elite's standing in the world. Why make agreements with the West on Iran, Afghanistan, and other issues if those agreements will obviate the West's need for Russia? The Russian elite has shown itself to believe that "process is everything; the goal is nothing." Those in the West who have not yet figured this out soon will.

"You are not an objective observer," someone might respond. "Many people in the West, particularly Western realists, see relations with Russia as a series of quid pro quo arrangements." That is true. Thanks for the reminder. Of course, Western politicians don't demand payment from Russia for their readiness to compromise, but that does not change things. Western realists are always hoping for deals with Moscow on Iran, anti-ballistic missiles, Afghanistan, gas, and pipelines. Sometimes these deals are possible. But most often, they are not. Responding to the realists' "let's make a deal" approach, Stephen Sestanovich wrote, "It has a tempting simplicity to it." But in his opinion, not a single deal between the United States and Russia has succeeded. Deals between Europe and Russia—for instance, on gas—are working for now, and Russia is meeting its obligations. But this is a case in which the interests of the Russian ruling clans and of Western partners coincide—for the moment. On the whole, Western partners' readiness to deal reinforces the Russian side's certainty that world politics is just a matter of deal making.

In that regard, allow me to make one more observation: The people who want relations between Russia and the West to be organized as an "exchange" are undermining the very concept of "common interests." If there are common interests between two sides, then there is no need for deals and exchanges. And on the flip side, if both sides constantly need to make deals, then there is room to doubt the existence of any common interests.

The ugly side of a deal-making approach to foreign policy is the tactic of revenge: "You did this to us, so we'll do that to you!" The West decided to hold military exercises in Georgia in 2009 involving close to a thousand soldiers, a very modest undertaking. In response, Moscow held its military maneuvers in July 2009 near the Georgian border, involving 8,000 soldiers, military aircraft, and tanks. Tit for tat. The Russian leaders were forced to respond to a stunned and bemused West because the logic of revenge dictates that the failure to respond would be a manifestation of retreat. Thus every Western act that could be interpreted by Moscow as hostile will get a response. Even if Western leaders try not to tease or irritate Moscow and do nothing at all that seems provocative, Putin and Medvedev will be forced to respond in kind. Otherwise, the elite and their entourage will no longer see them as alpha males. This is the trap they've gotten themselves into. They will have a hard time pulling themselves out of it. Indeed, it may be impossible.

Notes

1. Vladimir Putin, "O strategii razvitiya Rossii do 2020 goda" [On Russia's Strategy Through 2020], http://tours.kremlin.ru/appears/2008/02/08/1542_type63374type63378 type82634_159528.shtml.

2. Alexander Lukin, "Vneshniaya politika: ot postsovetskoj k rossiiskoj. Uroki konflikta s Gruziej" [Foreign Policy, From Post-Soviet to Russian: Lessons of the Georgian Conflict], *Rossiya v global'noi politike*, no. 6, December 2006.

37 LET'S COUNT WARHEADS

The majority of Russian experts view the normalization of relations with America as the basis for constructive relations with the West. This America-centrism reflects the superpower ambitions of the Russian elite, which continues to see the world through the prism of its own relations with America. I must admit that there is a certain logic to this view, for in recent years relations with the United States have suffered most, and America also remains the leader of the Western world.

How did the Russian elite bring relations with America out of crisis mode? By returning to the Russian-American dialogue on strategic offensive weapons. This idea became the leitmotif of Russian-American dialogue in 2009 for good reason. The START Treaty was set to expire in December 2009 (signed in 1991, it came into force in 1994). Its expiration would create a legal vacuum that could lead to an increase in mutual suspicion regarding intentions. Both sides needed to sit down at the negotiating table and decide what to do about START.

A sad and worrying situation developed, however. Washington hoped that the START negotiations would create the basis for mutual trust that could be used to resolve other roadblocks to constructive cooperation. In Moscow the mood was more skeptical from the very beginning. I recall a conversation with a well-known American expert who truly believed that the new arms pact with Russia would be the start of a new partnership. Apparently, he thought I was being too cynical when I expressed my doubts with respect to this possibility.

The irony is that in order to put an end to the aftereffects of the Cold War on U.S.-Russian relations, both sides decided to turn to the old Cold War mechanism that created the regime of mutually assured destruction. Thus Washington and Moscow found a way out by returning to U.S.-USSR negotiations, but this time without the USSR.

Did both sides really think there was a modern-day threat of a nuclear "exchange"? I doubt even the most avid hawks thought so. Therefore, these were negotiations about threats in the absence of the threats. Discouraging, as well as worrying, was the fact that no other issue in the portfolio of U.S.–Russian relations could have served as the basis for mutual trust through negotiations.

That the "nuclear dialogue" is back as the main course on the menu demonstrates that both sides missed an opportunity to change their relationship into one of real partnership, something that would be about much more than counting warheads. Both the United States and Moscow are to blame for the failures of the past 20 years. However, the main responsibility for the failure is Russia's, because it backslid into the Soviet past. It was the failure of Russian reforms that forced Moscow and Washington to return to arguments about warheads, ballistic missiles, and the means of counting and verifying stockpiles of both. If the Russian transformation had succeeded, Moscow and Washington would have moved on to much more important issues.

In the eyes of the Russian elite, the military-political dialogue with the United States was a means of raising Russia's global role and restoring a special relationship between Russia and the United States. That "specialness," or rather the hope of being special, continued to be a pillar of the Russian state.

"It's time to rid ourselves of psychological dependence on the United States," Russian observers suggested. But no! Moscow wanted to count warheads. Moscow couldn't feel secure if there weren't something to count.

What were the negotiations for Washington, then? Surely the Americans must have understood the motivations of the Russian side. If they did, then their agreement to these negotiations meant they were preparing to participate in psychotherapy sessions to cure the Russian elite of its complexes. Such was the drama of the situation: two member states of the G8 had to build up their relationship by dredging up the past. It was also ironic that quite a few people in America sincerely believed that the "nuclear dialogue" could create the basis for a more constructive relationship.

Let me quote Andrei Piontkovsky:

> The system of agreements on offensive and defensive strategic weapons was extremely important for the Soviet leaders. It legally set their status as leaders of a superpower, equal (or at least in the important military-strategic sphere) to the United States. For Russian lead-

ers, for whom the possibility of mutual suicide with the United States is perhaps the only attribute of their superpowerhood, the dilution not of that possibility but of the system of treaties that officially declares it is psychologically painful.[1]

But since the two nuclear powers continued to aim their strategic forces at each other, Piontkovsky felt their relations should be channeled into a civilized form by a new agreement that would simplify mutual control over nuclear forces and rule out any surprises.

Was there in fact any reason to hope that these negotiations would bring mutual trust? Probably not, but a different turn of events was possible. As Sergei Karaganov said:

> A return to military-political topics in the center of the dialogue between Russia and the United States brings a danger that the sides will start looking at each other as potential enemies. They will start counting up meaningless military balances and finding imbalances whose significance will be exaggerated. Constraints and reductions of weapons are not only instruments for regulating weapons races and reducing tension but, as the Cold War has shown, are successfully used to inflate tension and increase distrust. Even worse, the resumption of dialogue on security will return the old Cold War warriors with their habitual thinking. They will relish counting warheads and inventing nonexistent threats.[2]

As the range of problems associated with disarmament was identified, it became obvious that even in this sphere, where it seemed there was the best chance of finding "commonality" of Russian and American interests, there were signs of contradictions relating to fundamentally different approaches to the problem. During his first major international tour in April 2009, President Obama proposed in Prague the idea of moving toward nuclear disarmament. "We must start the process of nuclear disarmament, even if its completion will not happen, perhaps, in my lifetime," Obama announced.[3] If the American leader had only known what agitation his words would cause in Moscow! The agitation was understandable: For the Russian elite, nuclear weapons are the most important guarantee of its weight in world politics.[4] If Obama's vision were realized, Russia would turn into a normal state without global pretensions. But the key plank of the Russian platform is the maintenance of global pretensions. Dmitri Medvedev himself explained the role of the nuclear deterrent for Russia in March 2010. "… Possession of nuclear weapons is a key condition for Russia to pursue its independent policies, for safeguarding its sovereignty, for peace efforts and for preventing any military conflict and also setting post-conflict situations."[5] Clearly, the Russian elite could not support Obama's goal.

Reflecting the mood of the Russian political class, the authors of a report of the Russian Institute of National Strategy wrote:

> Today, strategic nuclear forces are the only factor for Russia that makes it an influential state and not a gigantic half-empty territory with a huge amount of natural resources. The situation is different in the US…. A reduction of strategic nuclear forces is beneficial for the US from practically every point of view. Especially since in the process of reducing them, they can increase their supremacy in conventional high-precision weapons.[6]

Thus, the Russian elite openly admits that Russia and the United States today have a different understanding of security.

Notes

1. Andrei Piontkovsky, "Funktsija strategicheskoj bezopasnosti" [Function of Strategic Security], http://www.grani.ru/Politics/m.126529.html.

2. Sergei Karaganov, "Rossiya i Zapad vo vremia krizisa" [Russia and the West in a Time of Crisis], *Rossiyskaya gazeta,* February 11, 2009.

3. "Obama Calls for Reduction in Nuclear Weapons," April 5, 2009, http://www.cnn.com/2009/WORLD/europe/04/05/czech.republic.obama/index.html.

4. Dmitri Trenin wrote, "Nearly a quarter-century later, the Russian leadership has returned to reliance upon the doctrine of nuclear deterrence…. There are at least two reasons for this. First, Russia is a relatively weak conventional military power…. Second, Russia insists on retaining the strategic independence that characterizes a great power." Dmitri Trenin, "U.S.-Russia Balancing Act," EJournal USA, February 22, 2010.

5. "Rasshiryennoje zasjedanije kolljegii Ministjerstva oborony" [High-Level Meeting of Ministry of Defense Colleagues], http://www.kremlin.ru/news/7039.

6. "Opasnost' jadernogo razoruzhenija. Perspektivy sozdanij–novykh rossijskikh jadernykh sil" [The Danger of Nuclear Disarmament: Prospects for the Development of a New Russian Nuclear Force], National Strategy Institute, Moscow, APN, March 31, 2009.

38 WHAT SEPARATES RUSSIA AND THE WEST?

Does this mean, then, that the contradictions between Russia and the West are exclusively normative in character and foreign policy issues are no longer significant? Of course not. There may be many foreign policy differences between Russia and the West that are not directly tied to standards and values—the differences one might expect to find, for example, between a supplier and a consumer of raw materials. Russia and individual Western states can have varying views on security questions in the world, Europe, and Eurasia, and different approaches to regional conflicts. Even a liberal Russia, should it develop, will be envious of former satellites and suspicious of leading Western democracies. Democracies compete with one another after all, especially economically. But must such differences take on hostile overtones? Why haven't the disagreements between, say, France and the United States, disagreements that have occasionally been very sharp, ever led to a hostile confrontation? Why didn't European anti-Americanism, especially during the Bush administration, become a flashpoint in relations between Europe and the United States? I fear I must repeat myself: Apparently, the reason lies in the identical values that form the foundation of the West and that hinder excessive differences in the foreign policy interests of individual Western countries. The converse of that truth is that the different methods of organizing Russia and the democracies of the West force them to view the world and their roles in it in different ways. This merely heightens the foreign policy contradictions and transforms those contradictions into mutual suspicions, and sometimes even hostility.

Now let's think: Why did a crisis arise in the final years of the Putin administration? After all, Russia had been moving back toward personalized power and its imperial foundations for a long time. Had Russia in the first term of Putin's presidency, when it had warm relations with the West, been a democracy? The problem was in the logic of development of *derzhavnichestvo* as a special form of existence of Russian authoritarianism (although not only there). This great-power imperialism is premised on the need to drive back the West as a civilizational force. Of course, this need doesn't always provoke open conflict. Both sides managed to avoid conflicts and even engaged in successful dialogue during the Soviet period.

There were several circumstances that led Russian *derzhavnichestvo* to turn militant under Putin and in the first year of Medvedev's term: high oil prices restored the Russian elite's self-confidence; Russian society rallied around the regime; American hegemony diminished; Europe grew more disoriented, as did the West more broadly; the West lacked a unified strategy toward Russia; and finally, the Russian leader and his comrades in arms had emotions and mind-sets influenced by their suspicion of the outside world. All these circumstances led the Russian administration to calculate that the time had come to upend the chessboard and, as the Kremlin experts themselves put it, restore things to the status quo ante 1991.

Why did the Kremlin resort to an aggressive posture? Because its system, resting on the foundation of a superpower dream, tends toward militant methods of self-affirmation. And quite aside from that reason, the people who have come to power in Russia prefer those methods of communication. They are aggressive not only because they have to obey the logic of personalized power, but also because it is a natural expression of their particular neuroses. In other words, they're tetchy and blustery because this is their way of solving their complexes.

By way of comparison, this survival strategy and these personality traits aren't shared by the Chinese ruling class. The Russian elite stresses force, spheres of influence, and the need to restrain the West. And it isn't afraid to use confrontation to secure these priorities. China, on the other hand, tries to strengthen itself and its role in the world mostly through cooperation with the West and integration into its economic and political institutions. The fact that it has become recognized by the West as a leading global player is proof enough that the Chinese have the more successful strategy.

There are several other circumstances that prompted the move toward anti-Western revisionism. A very important one is the absence of ideas that would unify the public. During the Soviet period, the consolidating mechanism was the ideology of communism. Afterward, the Russian ruling class filled the ideological vacuum with an ideology of anti-Westernism. It had nothing else to offer.

The fact that the Russian leaders flexed their muscles and tried imitation reality also played a part. The Kremlin must have come to the conclusion that Russia was strong enough to return to the international niche previously occupied by the USSR and decided to persuade or force the slow-witted West to "shove off." But the Russian ruling elite didn't realize that returning to a Soviet-era geopolitical role would inexorably lead to the West's refusal to cooperate with Russia in a broad swath of activities. The amorphous and uncertain format of relations with Russia suited Western leaders. They had learned to play imitation games with Russia, pretending that they considered Russia not only a partner but a democracy as well. Moscow's attempts to force the West to support its return to a position of global eminence necessarily undermined relations. Of course, Western capitals now have no idea how to fashion policy on Russia in a "partner-adversary" framework.

Moscow was aiming to inherit only the positive part of the Soviet legacy; it wasn't prepared to accept its negative aspect: real confrontation with the West. It is not yet clear whether the Russian ruling team fully realizes that its demands to change the global rules of the game may force Western leaders to drop their present leniency. For the time being, the West apparently prefers to smooth the rough edges in its relationship with Russia and keep up the rhetoric about partnership. So long as it continues to do so, the Russian ruling class will believe (or hope) that it has chosen the right course.

In any case, the incongruence between the reality and illusion in Russian-Western relations—that is, between the illusory "selective partnership" model and the real situation of mutual constraint—will continue to irritate Russia, even the liberal part of the establishment. Under Yeltsin, the West sought to hasten Russia's movement toward the West, and so it treated Russia as a partner and a democracy (it was neither). Western leaders expected this trust to stimulate the elite to lean westward and grow in a democratic direction. Nearly the opposite has happened, as we shall see. Let's consider, for example, the Partnership and Cooperation Agreement (PCA) between Russia and the EU, which stated that a partnership already existed between the two sides: "A Partnership is hereby established between the Community and its Member States, of the one part, and Russia, of the other part." Naturally, Moscow assumed it was just like any other country in the West, demanding full equality in its institutions and a veto on any decisions made by the West. When it didn't get this, it accused the West of disrespect. When Western politicians attempted to set aside the partnership rhetoric and put relations on a more realistic footing, Russia accused the West of hostility. Such is the price of maintaining a fiction.

This doesn't mean that the West's hopeful gestures were a mistake. I only wish to show that the Russian elite failed to respond to them in a way that benefited the public. The West can be blamed, but only for not pushing the Russian elite hard enough.

Is there any hope that Russia and the West will be able to free themselves from mutual distrust? I doubt it. Not as long as the Russian political class seeks its survival in authoritarianism and a posture of hostility to the West. As long as the root cause of suspicion between Russia and the West remains, it will invariably be reflected in international relations. Both the Russian elite and the West will always perceive their civilizations' incompatibility as a threat. The Bulgarian analyst Ivan Krastev wrote: "Just as the EU with its stress on human rights and openness threatens the Kremlin project of 'sovereign democracy,' the Russian desire to achieve a balance of power threatens the existence of the EU."[1] Not everyone in Brussels feels that way yet, but Moscow's actions, especially those of European representatives such as Dmitri Rogozin, permanent Russian representative to NATO, may convince even the most Russophilic Europeans to start treating Russia like an adversary.

What does the civilizational gap between Russia and the West mean? It means that if there were no irritants like NATO, missile defense, or Kosovo, the Russian elite would find other excuses for turning the West into the enemy it needs to shift the focus away from domestic issues.

I don't mean to idealize the West. Kosovo and Iraq raised doubts not only about its political position but also about its adherence to values and principles. Its actions damaged the international legal space and caused people to lose faith in the democratic mission.

But now the West is trying to find ways to restore international law and reinforce its civilizational dimensions in regard to both Kosovo and Iraq. The Russian political expert Igor Klyamkin, contrasting the actions of the West and Russia on these issues, said:

> The illegal policy of the West in Kosovo and the illegal policy of Russia in the Caucasus have different strategic dimensions. The conflict between the Serbs and the Kosovars can be regulated by the efforts of NATO and the European Union. And if Serbia and Kosovo are

accepted in just one of these organizations, the situation will return to the legal filed. But this can not happen in South Ossetia and Abkhazia. There cannot be legal regulation nor, moreover, any movement toward modern democracy. Under the patronage of Moscow's authoritarianism, such movement is impossible to imagine.[2]

There is no doubt that the American military campaign in Iraq was a tactical and strategic error. America now stands in agreement with the rest of the West on that issue. Nevertheless, Moscow keeps bringing up the Iraq precedent to justify its foreign policy course. And it is clear why: It allows it to dance on American bones, to deflect attention from its two Chechen wars, to justify the annexation of South Ossetia and Abkhazia and the war with Georgia, and to legitimize any future foolishness.

Let's not forget that the American war in Iraq and the Russian war with Georgia in August 2008 had different civilizational vectors. The invasion of Iraq was an (unsuccessful, to date) attempt to disseminate liberal civilizational principles. But what principles will Russia bring to South Ossetia and Abkhazia? And in the name of what standards does it object to NATO membership for Ukraine and Georgia?

Notes

1. Krastev also writes about the "polar nature" of the Russian and Western elites. "The European elites, having built a career on the art of compromise and the avoidance of conflict, deal with elites that are proud of not taking hostages." See "Rossiya kak 'drugaja Evropa'" [Russia as the "Other Europe"], *Rossiya v global'noi politike*, no. 4 July–August 2007.

2. Igor Klyamkin, ed., *Rossiya i Zapad. Vnieshnyaya politika glazami liberalov* [Russia and the West. Foreign Policy in Liberals' Eyes] (Moscow: Liberal Mission, 2009), p. 65.

39 WHAT IT WOULD BE BETTER NOT TO DO

I have argued thus far that the Russian political class has finely tuned its antennae to detect even an unintended Western slight or simply a clumsy move. So is the West justified in refusing to take this hypersensitivity into account when it acts? I have mixed feelings about this question.

On the one hand, Western leaders seem to bend over backwards not to annoy the Kremlin, and especially Putin, whom they quite correctly view as the real Russian leader and whose recklessness they clearly fear. This tendency pertains primarily to European leaders, whose obsequiousness Moscow interprets as weakness and an open invitation to be more aggressive.

On the other hand, I can think of several cases in which the West, primarily the United States, has unintentionally provoked Russian traditionalists. I found provocative Washington's decision to put anti-ballistic missile bases in Poland and the Czech Republic—a move that came during the 2007 election campaign in Russia, no less, when the Kremlin team was looking for ways to retain power. Didn't the Americans understand how that move would affect relations with Russia and Russia's domestic dynamics? If they didn't, then we're dealing with mere incompetence by the Bush administration. But if they did, then they're guilty of ignoring Russia as a potential challenge.

As a challenge to the United States, Russia falls somewhere well below Afghanistan and Iraq. But to misunderstand the character of the Russian elite, its ambitions and its aspirations, is to restrict—needlessly—America's diplomatic room for maneuver on other issues. The mind boggles to explain why the Bush administration didn't try, for instance, to create a joint anti-ballistic missile system with Russia. It's not as if the issue were a critical one for the United States. Many Americans mustered little more than indifferent shrugs in talking about the Bush administration's anti-missile plan. "I am puzzled by the project.... I am confused about the purpose of the deployment," said Brent Scowcroft. Zbigniew Brzezinski added, "... The system we want to deploy is nonexistent, and the threat against which it is to be deployed is also nonexistent."[1]

True, Russian elites, living as they do in the "hostile environment" paradigm, will seek to use virtually any U.S. action to confirm their phobias. But shouldn't Washington at least make them work for it?

The Western governments have given at least two more timely gifts to the Russian traditionalists. First, their recognition of Kosovo's independence very conveniently gave Moscow diplomatic cover to execute its experiment in the Caucasus: namely, recognizing Abkhazia's and South Ossetia's independence. Second, at the April 2008 NATO summit in Bucharest, the West gave Ukraine and Georgia a vague promise of NATO membership on an unspecified timeline.

The issue isn't whether or not Ukraine and Georgia should be accepted into NATO—a question on which I believe the West is suffering from a failure of imagination. Western leaders need to think harder about how to integrate these countries into Europe and provide them with security without provoking conflict with Moscow, and NATO is not the only way to do this.

The vagueness of the West's promises to Georgia and Ukraine, and now its vacillation, have given Russian traditionalists all the excuses they needed to use Ukraine and Georgia as part of their strategy of "containment of the West." The experts (and incidentally, Georgian politicians), believe that the West's indecisiveness and vacillation hastened the Caucasian war in August 2008 and perhaps even made it inevitable. They're probably right. Putin's team respects only overt displays of power and thus saw NATO's disunity on the issue as weakness. They didn't hesitate to take advantage of that weakness.

According to the Russian elite's operating logic, the anti-ballistic missile issue and the Kosovo incidents were net positives. They had all the arguments they needed to prove that the West had "humiliated" and "disrespected" Russia. If the West had intended from the very start to strengthen the personalized system of power in Russia, it couldn't have done any better.

"Are you saying the West has to check with the Kremlin before making any decisions?" my Western colleagues might ask. I would respond that if the West wants to avoid provoking acts of revenge by the Kremlin, it must consider reformatting its policy toward Russia. Now, I'm not saying Western leaders need to do more to appease Russia; rather, they must avoid giving Russian traditionalists any more opportunities to take advantage of their own clumsiness and myopia. If they don't, not only does the West stand to lose a great deal, Russian liberals—those who wish to lead Russia into the future as a liberal democratic partner to the West—will find themselves in an even more vulnerable position than they do now. Indeed, not even Russian pragmatists will be safe if the traditionalists continue their headlong path down into the abyss.

How might the West have handled these issues differently? They might have waited a bit before recognizing Kosovo's independence. They might have looked for a more flexible path to statehood. They might also have looked for avenues of cooperation with Serbia, seeking to integrate it into the European Union in tandem with Kosovo. Such policies might have minimized the salience of Kosovo's independence for all concerned parties, perhaps even for the Kosovars themselves.

As for Ukraine and Georgia, Western leaders might have played down official NATO membership, and focused instead on full-bore cooperation with those countries in a different format for providing security and entrée into the European community. They might have accelerated Ukraine's and Georgia's accession to the EU by turning them into associate members. However, not having chosen this course, they should have held together in solidarity, stuck to their guns, and offered a Membership Action Plan for Ukraine and Georgia. Instead, at the April 2008 NATO summit in Bucharest, the West essentially recognized Moscow's right to veto its policies in the former Soviet space. Given that precedent, defying Moscow's will on Ukraine and Georgia will evoke a much stronger emotional response in the future. In other words, not only did the West fail to appease the Russian traditionalists, it convinced them that they have free rein to further blackmail NATO.

No less important is the fact that both sides in Bucharest implied that NATO's orientation toward Russia was hostile. In that context, the Kafkaesque nature of Russia-Western relations clearly manifests itself in the activities of the NATO-Russia Council. Perhaps the West should double-down on the absurdity. Maybe it should propose accelerating Russia's accession to NATO even as it offers Membership Action Plans to Ukraine and Georgia. I can't imagine how Putin and Medvedev would react to that. At the least, they would find it a difficult thread to weave into the fabric of their preferred narrative of NATO's hostility to Russia.

Instead, Western leaders continue to supply the Russian traditionalists with ample reasons for militant demonstrations, only later to beg and cajole the traditionalists to forget those reasons. In the 1990s, the West unwittingly (and sometimes wittingly) became one of the legitimizing factors for the Yeltsin regime because it didn't believe a more liberal system was possible in Russia. Today, the West simply does not know how to react to Russia, and when it does react, it merely gives the Russian state more excuses to reinforce its anti-Western direction. This remains true despite occasional appearances that Moscow has chosen to cooperate with the West. Of course, Moscow can take any Western move and turn it into an excuse for feeling annoyed and insulted. Virtually anything and everything about the West is reason enough for the Russian elite to feel humiliated and threatened (everything, that is, except its comfortable lifestyle and conspicuous consumption).

Does Russia's persistent reliance on *derzhavnichestvo* mean that every effort to build partnership between Russia and the West will be fragile and fleeting? Unfortunately, yes. But the absence of systemic common bonds doesn't mean that Russia and the West cannot cooperate in those spheres where their interests partially or temporarily overlap. The two sides cooperated successfully not only during the Yeltsin regime but also during Putin's first term. Cooperation between contemporary Russia and the West will never extend beyond the pragmatic and situational, however, and tensions will always be prone to flare up, often seemingly without cause or motive. A stable, cooperative relationship with Russia will only be possible if the Russian system is transformed. Otherwise, the circumstances of Russia's domestic development will tend to force the elites to perceive their "common" interests with the West in their own way.

Can cooperation between Russia and the West in foreign policy stimulate domestic reforms in Russia? For now, it's hard to say. Under Gorbachev, the Soviet Union's rejection of confrontation with the West helped liberalize Soviet society. We cannot rule out the possibility that cooperation would have the same effect today. However, this would be possible only under two conditions. First, the West would have to intentionally use a policy of Western-Russian cooperation to influence the elite and Russian society. Thus far, the opposite has occurred; the Russian elite has used the West to reinforce the anti-Western system. Second, Russians themselves would have to seek a way to escape the system of personalized power. As we can see, Russia's cooperation with the West and its transformation are locked into a kind of "chicken/egg" paradox: Neither one is possible without the other.

Note

1. Zbigniew Brzezinski and Brent Scowcroft, *America and the World, Conversations on the Future of American Foreign Policy* (New York: Basic Books, 2008), pp. 192–193.

40 WESTERN "PROTECTORS"

Perceptions of Russia and its development path, in both Russia and the West, are complicated by our desire to simplify. Inevitably, we craft stereotypes to get a firm grip on the problem, only to find that those stereotypes have locked us into a warped view of reality. Some of the most popular stereotypes about Russia in Western circles come from short-term thinking, but most have been influenced by Russian political thought. The following four stereotypical lines of thought have strongly influenced Western analysts.

1) "Russia is not ready for democracy." To be sure, Russia's political consciousness is still divided on this fundamental question, and Russians still maintain mutually exclusive values regarding it. But significant numbers of Russians are capable of moving toward a freer and more competitive society. A poll by the Levada Center found that more than 60 percent of Russians are ready to live by liberal principles. Only about 25 to 30 percent of the population forms the traditionalists' political base. Even among the elite, which is the most conservative element in Russian society, there are quite a few proponents of liberal democracy. Polls of second-tier elites (for example, heads of government departments, regional leaders, medium-sized business managers) show that 45.5 percent of them support ideals like freedom and political competition. The real question isn't whether democracy is possible in Russia, but who or what will coalesce these democratically attuned Russians into a coherent political force. The claim that Russians aren't ready for democracy is a stereotype that serves only to legitimize authoritarianism.

2) "Democracy will come to Russia after capitalism, which is the determining factor." In fact, Russia provides the world's best evidence that this stereotype is wrong. In Russia, economic growth and capitalist development have gone hand-in-hand with an anti-democratic drift. And what

kind of capitalism is it when the economy is so closely tied to the regime? Recent Russian history shows that the "determining factor" in its development isn't capitalism or the economy, but politics. Radical reforms of the state and the political system are the only real prerequisites of democracy in Russia.

3) "Russia is a unique country." This is a truism; the real question is how is that "uniqueness" manifested? In the inevitability of authoritarian thought? Then why have the Ukrainians, who are genetically and culturally close to the Russians, behaved so differently? Russia's only claim to uniqueness is the way its elite has managed to hold on to power: by re-animating superpower ideology and the remnants of militarism and imperialism.

4) "Relations with Russia should be built on interests, not ideals." This thesis is as popular in the West as it is in Russia. (See, they share at least *one* thing in common!) In recent years, the West has shelved values and maintained a Realpolitik approach to its discourse with Moscow. Western political circles have elected to stand back, see how Russia handles itself domestically and internationally, and restrict itself to areas where both sides' interests coincide. Here is how one such "realist," Robert Blackwill, formulated the credo of the United States with respect to Russia: "The United States has problems, primarily with Iran. That is why we need good relations with Russia. Any criticism of Moscow and our concern over their democracy will affect our cooperation on Iran."[1]

For all its realism and reluctance to engage in values-based criticism, the West has yet to make a deal with Moscow on Iran or any substantive issue.[2] The "old" European states' course of compromise hasn't helped to avoid deep freezes in relations with Moscow, nor has it convinced the Russian elite to modify its attitude of disdain for Europe. Recall that it was during the realists' triumph in Western political circles that the worst crisis in Western-Russian (and especially U.S.–Russian) relations occurred.

Several other clichés have gained currency in the West. Among the most popular are:

- "Russia made great progress under Putin, especially compared to Yeltsin's chaos."

- "You can't rush reform; the West took centuries to build liberal democracy."

- "Russia remains one of the most attractive emerging markets."

- "Russia can be modernized only through reform from above."

- "Medvedev's presidency will create the foundation for liberal democracy."

- "The current Russian regime is as good as it gets."

- "The liberalization of Russia will lead to anarchy or dictatorship."

- "Russians have exchanged freedom for prosperity."

And so on. All these assertions come from articles and speeches by respected Western politicians and experts. I will spare their reputations and allow them to remain anonymous.

All these clichés share a common origin in the inability to believe that Russian society can function in a system of liberal democracy. One would think the elites would be humiliated by such a degrading view of the Russian people, but they encourage myths about Russian infantilism, perhaps because they're blissfully unaware about what such views say about themselves.

Let's return to Western politicians and commentators. Perhaps they're oblivious to the fact that they are parroting clichés straight from the Kremlin's propaganda handbook. Or perhaps they know exactly what they're doing but assume that the Russian regime can be trusted and that it understands its own people. Perhaps naïveté pushes Western politicians and experts into the ranks of Russia's "protectors." Or maybe it's pragmatism, or fear of seeming Russophobic, or ignorance of Russian society. The truth is that it doesn't really matter what the cause of it is. My goal isn't to dig into motives; it's to show these "protectors" what role they're playing in the hopes that they will refocus their energies. I hope my Western colleagues will recognize their own views in these stereotypes, and think carefully about whose water they carry when they make their cases before Western audiences.

Notes

1. Robert Blackwill, "The Three Rs: Rivalry, Russia, 'ran," *National Interest*, January–February 2008, p. 72.

2. Stephen Sestanovich has written about it as follows: "This 'let's make a deal' approach to diplomacy has a tempting simplicity to it." In practice, he says, "the grand bargains" favored by amateur diplomats are almost never consummated." See Stephen Sestanovich, "What Has Moscow Done? Rebuilding U.S.-Russian Relations," *Foreign Affairs*, vol. 87, no. 6, November–December 2008, pp. 14–15.

41 HOW SERIOUS WESTERNERS PERCEIVE RUSSIA

Not all Western analysis of Russia is so rife with clichés and stereotypes. Many experts try to think critically about Russia's trajectory. I will mention just a few by name here. At the outset of Putin's second term, Alex Pravda saw that the Kremlin's focus on centralization and Russia's alienation in the world were interrelated: "The more insulated and inward-looking Russia becomes, the more likely is it to continue to develop in an authoritarian direction."[1] Richard Pipes summed up his views on Russia as follows:

> Contemporary Russia, the Russia of Putin and Medvedev[,] is a country of amazing contradictions. Its leaders declare that Russia is part of European culture. But at the same time they warn the West not to teach them how to administer it because Russia has unique national traditions. They insist that Russia is a global power and at the same time they must admit that economically Russia lags behind its opponents.... They declare that Russia is a democracy and yet do everything possible to destroy democratic procedures and institutions. If you listen to what they say, a question arises: are their statements a manifestation of sincere confusion or sincere cynicism? Both are possible: cynicism masking confusion.[2]

Peter Reddaway, one of the few Western scholars who did not allow himself to be bamboozled in the heady days of the Yeltsin era, thinks along the same lines. Examining the "key pathology" of the Putin system, he said,

> Today the source of personal success in Russia is the presence of three things: enormous financial means; powerful administrative or political resources; and personal ties with individuals who are

prepared to use the "administrative resource." ... Politics in Russia is a game dominated by spin doctors, so sophisticated that they overtook their Western colleagues long ago.... Politics is a game in which what is on the surface has nothing to do with what lies below.[3]

Timothy Colton and Michael McFaul were critical with respect to the Russian political regime, saying, "Putin has diverted the country further from democratic development.... Russia's nascent democracy is on a negative trajectory...."[4] McFaul, currently President Obama's "Russia hand," has also said the following of the Putin regime:

Putin systematically weakened or destroyed every check on his power, while at the same time strengthening the state's ability to violate the constitutional rights of citizens.... Not unlike his Soviet predecessors, Putin understands the world primarily in zero-sum terms, especially dealing with the United States. Because Putin and his entourage do not embrace democratic values, they cannot be counted on to act internationally according to norms that help to coordinate the behavior of Western democracies.[5]

This is characteristic of Putin's regime. But nothing substantially changed under the Putin-Medvedev tandem.

Stephen F. Cohen has been a consistent critic of the system created by Yeltsin and perfected by Putin. Here is how he characterizes the outcome of Russia's evolution:

The most important product of the managed political system intended to exclude real alternatives is the "Putin phenomenon." It crowned the Yeltsin plan to hand over the presidency to a specially selected and little-known successor, which allowed Yeltsin to avoid criminal prosecution. Even if the administration truly was not involved in the building bombings in 1999 and other events that led to the renewal of the war in Chechnya, the cynical use of the military campaign as an election strategy is not an indicator of democracy and stability.[6]

Robert Legvold was equally disinclined to hold back his concerns about Russia's trajectory:

Russia's traumas, caused by the country's historic transformation, the gap between the status Russia would like to have in the world and the one it does have—all this does not give its leaders the opportunity to make a strategic choice and formulate a clearer vision of Russia's role and its place on the world arena.... Russia's orientation is inconsistent and devoid of a goal.[7]

Falk Bomsdorf doubted the West and Russia could reach a mutual understanding, even in spite of the recent warming of relations:

> The main danger to these relations is in the incompatibility of the political systems of Russia and the West. Europeans are trying to find answers to the challenges of the twenty-first century, albeit not always successfully, albeit with difficulty. But they are still building society on principles that have proven their effectiveness— transparency, competition, and rule of law. Russia, or rather the Kremlin, on the contrary is seeking hegemony and is building a system based on nationalism, characteristic of the nineteenth century. The Kremlin is making the old Russian mistake of striving for ostentatious might and majesty instead of thinking about how to create a flourishing society. I fear that these contradictory aims leave no possibility of true cooperation between Russian and the West.

Thérèse Delpech, a former commissioner with the United Nations Monitoring, Verification, and Inspection Commission, said,

> In the West, Moscow is perceived as a clever manipulator of internal processes, as a concentration of a "corporative state," as the center of power of a revived Soviet repressive apparatus which creates a profound and ineradicable suspicion. As far as I understand, the West analogously elicits suspicion in Moscow, which increasingly views the West as an enemy, as it declines into nationalism and xenophobia.

If Moscow judges the mood in France by the statements of French members of the Kremlin Valdai club or the geniality of the French president, it is making a mistake. It should be listening to people like Delpech.

Likewise, Moscow would do well to consider American experts like Strobe Talbott, who writes that:

> Today's Russia can be an example of the unsuccessful attempt to embody Thomas Hobbes' conviction that "war against everyone" is the national human method of existence; that a state's security requires an authoritarian ruler; that only those states that adopt the gladiator position, unsheathing their swords and standing in a militant pose, will be successful.[8]

That is how Russia looks to sincere observers. How do such observers explain the cooling of relations between Russia and the West in 2004–2008? Many lay the blame at America's doorstep. Stephen Cohen faults the West for treating Russia like a "defeated enemy." Thus Putin's foreign policy "was in many ways a reaction to the approach of Washington toward Moscow: 'Winner takes all.'" Cohen, moreover, is certain that "American actions ... promoted the renaissance of aggressive Russian nationalism."[9] Quite a few Western experts are coming to agree with Cohen that the West, especially Washington, deserves blame for ignoring and humiliating Russia.[10]

I can only thank my Western colleagues for their sincere concern, but I find it hard to agree that the United States determined Russia's trajectory. Let's assume for a moment that Washington had made no stupid mistakes in its relations with Russia and that American representatives like, say, Bush team member John Bolton and the columnist Charles Krauthammer had not behaved condescendingly toward Moscow. Would that have prevented nationalism from rearing its ugly head, the return of authoritarianism, or the general souring of U.S.–Russian relations? I wholeheartedly agree that the short-sightedness of the American political class, especially during the Bush administration, gave Russian elites ample cause to behave like sulking teenagers, but getting at the truth requires distinguishing between excuses and causes.

The causes of Russia's behavior should be sought in its domestic political development. This does not mean that the American bull in the china shop wouldn't encourage the Kremlin's aggressive tendencies or foster feelings of humiliation and suspicion among the Russian public. But for any of that to happen, Russian society already had to lack the systemic checks and balances that would have prevented those feelings from coming to the foreground. In other words, we've returned to the question of which principles form the basis for a society and its relations with government authorities. If we admit that Russian foreign policy and its failures are the consequences of American stupidity, then we absolve the Russian elite of any responsibility. And that is exactly what the Kremlin wants us to do.

Leon Aron put it rightly when he said,

> The Kremlin's foreign policy is determined by the evolution of its ideology and internal development to a greater degree than by any action of the United States.... If the advance of reactionary thought

continues inside Russia, the Kremlin will continue its aggressive foreign policy, aimed at changing the rules of the game, in particular to distract from and justify the repressive measures inside the country.[11]

Mary Mendras is of the same opinion: "Russian foreign policy is the product of the domestic political development and the domestic agenda." Andrew Wood maintains that "Western policy regarding Russia was more a complementary factor and it could not have been the determining one in the formation of Russian development."[12]

I discussed the theme of Russia's "humiliation" in an earlier chapter, where I recounted the views of Russian experts. In this context, the fact that official Russian figureheads never tire of talking about Russia's humiliation by America is an especially interesting happenstance. I wonder if those of my Western colleagues who are so keen to redress Russia's humiliations have ever asked themselves why the Russian elite pushes the "humiliation line" so hard. For my part, I can assure my Western colleagues that there are many Russians who feel humiliated—not by U.S. or Western policy, but by the actions of those who call themselves authorities in Russia.

Some Western experts, primarily European, try to shield Russia from excessive criticism, lest they or their countries be seen as Russophobic. This tendency evinces an inability to distinguish the Russian public from its elite. In rejecting a critical view of Russian reality, and especially in supporting the Kremlin's line, such Western well-wishers become the volunteer helpers of an elite that is profoundly indifferent to its people. And they're essentially serving the same ends as those who call for Russia's isolation: helping Russia's authoritarian regime solve its self-preservation problem.

If Russia's Western friends are so concerned about the health of the Russian nation, why don't they advise its elites to use a more effective means of overcoming humiliation: namely, to put aside saber-rattling, tough talk of restoring spheres of influence, and whining about humiliations, and get to the difficult work of building a flourishing society.

The crisis in relations between Russia and the United States, which reached its lows between 2006 and 2008, is an entirely separate subject. Thomas Graham considers one of the main causes of this crisis to be "a dialectic of strength and weakness." The asymmetry of power between the two states is "hardly a recipe for constructive long-term relations."[13]

Indeed, one can easily see how such an asymmetry would be considered painful by the weaker side. But one must then ask oneself why such power asymmetries don't lead to the same consequences between other countries. Why didn't America's military, political, and economic dominance get in the way of friendly relations between Moscow and Washington from 2000 to 2003?

Graham, however, also concluded that "the question of values brought a lot of irritation into the relations." I not only agree with that assessment, I would give it even more emphasis, for it is the question of values that makes the power asymmetry between the United States and Russia so painful for the Russian elite. It's not that America highlights such differences in diplomatic contexts; on the contrary, under Bush, the United States seemed to want to avoid any mention of values in its dialogue with Moscow. It is instead the very fact of America's existence as a civilization hostile to the Russian elite that creates the greatest source of its anti-Western impulses.

Graham seems subsequently to have stopped highlighting differing values as an irritant in Russian-American relations, proposing instead a curious understanding of Russian freedoms and why Russian society has become so apathetic. "There is freedom in Russia. At least, there are some personal freedoms and freedom of speech," he said in an interview in the pro-Kremlin publication *Russkiy Zhurnal*. "People take less interest in politics precisely because their standard of living is significantly higher. Probably, the public has realized that there are much more interesting things than politics."

I'm not sure how he came to these conclusions. Perhaps he was merely playing nice for his Russian hosts. Otherwise, I'm at a loss to explain how he could claim that freedom of speech exists in Russia, when even official Kremlin propagandists wouldn't go so far. As for political apathy being the result of better standards of living, one might find this to be true if he examined only a few narrow strata of Russian society. But doesn't one of the best commentators on Russian affairs understand that most Russians eschew participation in political life because politics in Russia has been liquidated? And why would he think that personal freedom without political freedom would be "enough" for us Russians, when neither he nor his countrymen would accept such a state of affairs?

David Kramer offers a more convincing portrait of the differences between Russia and America. "There is no doubt that the widening gap in values led to the differences between the United States and Russia," he wrote.

The arrest of Mikhail Khodorkovsky in 2003 affected how the American administration and the American expert community looked at Putin's Russia. But even before that, the second Chechen war and the increasing Kremlin control over mass media became a cause for concern in those circles.... Moreover, the situation in Russia was growing worse and journalists and critics of the regime were being killed more frequently.

Quite a few European experts point to the values gap as one of the main reasons, if not *the* main reason, for the cooling relations between Russia and the West. Experts like Sir Roderic Lyne understand the goal of the Kremlin's anti-Western rhetoric:

> Exaggerating the foreign threat is an old political trick.... Frequent repetition that the West is trying to overthrow and weaken Russia is used for specific goals, to justify the stronger control over society, limitations of civil and political rights, and revival of the power of security agencies.[14]

Western politicians and observers often have a hard time reining in their sarcasm when they talk about Russia. Here's how Defense Secretary Robert Gates explained Russia's increased aggressiveness:

> And the problem is now that they have regained their strength, now that they have a strong government again, now that they have stronger finances, it's almost as though they don't know how to play a broadly constructive role as a way of illustrating that they are a great power that is back. It's sometimes like they feel like they have to put a stick in the wheel to make people pay attention to them and to take them seriously.[15]

I doubt Russia would consider this attitude flattering. But give the man credit: At least he doesn't hide what's on his mind.

As a long-time observer of Russian elites, I often wonder whether they understand the impression they create when they try to force the West to respect them by means that invite mockery. Some do not, which speaks poorly of their intelligence. Others do, however; they simply hope that the West will swallow what it's fed, and more often than not, their hopes prove justified.

Andrew Wood notes that the problem lies not only with Russia, but with the West, and with the policy it chose during the Putin presidency.

[Putin] quickly took the measure of his Western colleagues and his confidence in his ability to manage them has grown over time. Had they been less accommodating at the start, perhaps he would have been less ready now to see their reactions to Russia's most recent adventure in the Caucasus as the ineffectual bleatings of Washington-led hostile sheep.[16]

Wood hits it right on the mark. Western leaders stimulated, to some degree, Putin's self-confidence and contempt. How did that happen? What spurred on Putin's ironic cockiness, even condescension, toward his Western colleagues in the G8? Were Blair, Chirac, Schröder, and Bush too easy on him, too polite, too willing to please? Did their failure to call Putin out on his pronouncements convince him of their spinelessness? Did Putin realize they had no common policy—if any policy at all—on Russia? In any case, Wood describes exactly what happened: Putin became contemptuous of his Western colleagues, sometimes mocking them openly or otherwise discomfiting them in press conferences. And he interpreted Western leaders' behavior as a license to kill.

The West, at least, has been up front about its leaders' failures in this regard. The question "Who's to blame?" is gaining more currency every day, and many are coming to reject the notion that "humiliating" Russia, ignoring it, or assuaging the Russian elite's neuroses had anything to do with it. These new voices, rather, fault the West for failing to live up to its own norms in dealing with Russia. When I asked Uffe Elleman-Jensen, former foreign minister of Denmark, about the West and Russia, he said,

> I do not support the popular thesis that the West did not help Russia in the 1990s. Let me remind you that the West gave Russia enormous help. But Russia did not have the conditions for a new Marshall Plan. I also do not accept the humiliation theory of Russia by the West, because the expansion of the EU and NATO was part of the *raison d'être* of those organizations and that expansion did not pose any threat to Russia. I am certain that the West lost when its political leaders stopped being honest in their relations with Russia. They were silent when Russia turned off the democratic path. They calmly watched Russia's serious violations of principles confirmed by the OSCE and other international institutions. I am not saying that Western leaders should have isolated Russia. Quite the contrary, they should have raised their voices when Russian leaders rejected

the responsibilities they had taken on in the sphere of freedom and human rights and in relations with independent states. The West was like the three monkeys: "see no evil, hear no evil, say no evil." I don't think that this Western position makes leaders who have a taste for authoritarianism respect Western values.

I believe that many more Western public figures would endorse Elleman-Jensen's statement today.

Notes

1. Alex Pravda, "Introduction: Putin in Perspective" in Alex Pravda, ed., *Leading Russia—Putin in Perspective: Essays in Honour of Archie Brown* (Oxford: Oxford University Press, 2005) p. 36.

2. Richard Pipes, "Putin & Co.: What Is to Be Done?" *Commentary*, May 2008, p. 30.

3. Peter Reddaway, "The Unstable Politics of Russian Diarchy: Some Preliminary Thoughts," 2008–2009 Alexander Dallin Lecture, Stanford, California, October 15, 2008, http://creees.stanford.edu/events/DallinLectures.html.

4. Timothy Colton and Michael McFaul, "Putin and Democratization," in Dale R. Herspring, ed., *Putin's Russia: Past Imperfect, Future Uncertain* (Lanham, Md.: Rowman and Littlefield, 2005).

5. Michael McFaul, "Liberal Is as Liberal Does," *American Interest*, vol. II, no. 4, March/April 2007, pp. 86–89.

6. Stephen Cohen, *Proval krestovogo pokhoda i tragediya postkommunisticheskoi Rossiy* [Failed Crusade: America and the Tragedy of Post-Communist Russia] (Moscow: AIRO-XX, 2001), p. 199.

7. Robert Legvold, Testimony Before the U.S. House of Representatives Committee on Foreign Affairs, February 25, 2009.

8. Strobe Talbott, "The Next Phase of Russia's Relations With the West," Lecture at the American Academy in Berlin, February 9, 2009.

9. Stephen Cohen, "The Missing Debate," *Nation,* May 19, 2008.

10. "For Moscow, it was payback time, payback for the national humiliation of the 1990s and what it saw as Washington's lack of respect and consideration for Russian interests," Graham wrote in the fall of 2008. See Thomas Graham, "Vzgliad poverkh geopoliticheskikh batal`iy" [The View Atop the Geopolitical Battles?], *Rossiya v global'noi politike*, no. 5, September–October. 2008.

11. Leon Aron, "Russia's Woes Spell Trouble for the U.S.," *Wall Street Journal,* December 31, 2008.

12. Andrew Wood, *Reflections on Russia and the West,* http://www. chathamhouse. org.uk/files/12710_1108russia_west.pdf.

13. Thomas Graham, *U.S.-Russia Relations: Facing Reality Pragmatically* (Washington, D.C.: CSIS/IFRI, July 2008).

14. Roderic Lyne, "Rossiya i Zapad: Konfrontatsija Nieizbiezhna?" [Russia and the West: Confrontation Inescapable?], http://www.polit.ru/institutes/2008/09/29/west_print.html.

15. Conversation with U.S. Secretary of Defense Robert Gates, "The Charlie Rose Show," PBS, December 17, 2008.

16. Wood, *Reflections on Russia and the West*.

42 ON INTERESTS AND VALUES, AND THE EXTENT TO WHICH THE "REALISTS" MAKE A CONVINCING CASE

The Western-Russian relationship will ultimately be determined by a debate taking place inside the West—the debate about how and to what degree values and interests should influence foreign policy. This debate is of long standing and encompasses a broad spectrum of opinion. Western society's native inclination toward moderation and deliberation has marginalized more extreme views along this spectrum—those of the neoconservatives and the radical liberal interventionists, who recommend either the imposition of democracy on undemocratic societies or call for the isolation and strict containment of authoritarian regimes. With these extremes having largely been extirpated from responsible debate, the discussion gets more nuanced. It's hard, however, to escape the conclusion that the subject of values in foreign policy today seems to many Western interlocutors to be of little practical relevance.

It's understandable that the values debate has fallen by the wayside. By now, the world's latest wave of democratization has rolled back out to sea, and it appears as though it will stay at low tide for some time to come. The Bush administration's simplistic understanding of democracy promotion, American aggression in Iraq, and the neocons' hubristic efforts to remake the world in their image have all played a part. Many hesitate to raise the topic of values for fear of being accused of having neocon sympathies. In many transitional and authoritarian societies, democracy promotion comes across as a tool of American interests.[1] They see its classic elements, namely, support for building a system of competing political parties and electoral mechanisms, as outsider meddling. Facing this rebuff, as well as confronting the internal crises generated by the global financial crisis, the West has been tempted to turn inward, toward an interests-based policy of realism.

If realists are merely the dominant faction in the West, then in Russia itself, they have essentially monopolized the field of debate, crowding out all other voices. This is in keeping with the nature of the Russian system. Indeed, the elites and part of the population take any talk of values as an anti-patriotic infringement of Russia's sovereignty, especially when it comes to foreign policy. Western and Russian "realists" alike are united in the conviction that foreign policy cannot be based on such principles, which manifest either a dangerous idealism or a pitiable naïveté. The heyday of the "moralists" and ideologues is gone, they claim. The driving force in twenty-first century international politics must be pragmatism alone, based on balances of power and grounded in interests. (The fact that experts and politicians who live in societies constructed on different sets of principles can be so alike in their views of foreign policy is a subject deserving of separate discussion.)

What do the "realists" argue about Russia? In 2006–2007, the *American Interest* published a series of articles on Russia that set forth the main theses of both the "realists" and their opponents. These theses remain relevant today because neither group has come up with radically new arguments.

The "realist" argument, as interpreted by Allen Lynch, came down to the following: Western civilization was shaped by a coupling of liberalism and democracy, liberalism (and the establishment of liberal institutions) having preceded modern democracy. Modern Russia's development took a different path. In Russia, democracy does not align with liberalism, says Lynch: "... the attempt to advance liberal principles has coincided with both mass political enfranchisement and mass socioeconomic disenfranchisement." As a result, "the attempt to transfer liberal values without examining their institutional and social concomitants has ended up discrediting liberalism in Russia." Russia's anti-liberal reaction "is focused on the United States," because of the perception in Russian society that its troubles during the 1990s were due largely to American efforts "to reconfigure Russian politics and society." These events have created a "hopeless" situation for the development of a liberal democracy in Russia, says Lynch. The neopatrimonial regime that emerged is quite sustainable, and it is "still the best government [that] Russians have had in a long time." Given this situation, the author says, talking with the Russians about values is nonproductive. And the more America supports the Russian liberals, the more it "angers ordinary Russians and risks driving them further toward chauvinistic nationalism."[2]

Lynch argues for a Realpolitik-based Russia policy on the basis that "a focus on the interaction of each country's specific interstate interests and a suppression of ideologically-based aspirations correspond to periods of reasonably good Russian-American relations." Finally, on the basis of these considerations, he asks, "Is a strong Russia, even authoritarian at home and operating on principles of power politics abroad, incompatible with the transaction of American interests with that country?" In answering this question he turns to George Kennan, who in 1951 defined three conditions for a normal Russian-American relationship: "Russia must renounce its messianic ideology, dismantle the totalitarian edifice of power, and renounce imperialism in the form of direct rule by those people desirous and able to govern themselves." In Lynch's view, "Putin's Russia meets those criteria." So if the United States tries to admonish Russians about values, "it would be a policy at odds with historic precedent and America's own national interests."[3]

Lynch's system of argument merits an ordered response. It's true that liberal shibboleths in Russia during the 1990s were used to legitimize an anti-liberal and anti-democratic system, in the process discrediting the ideology of liberalism and complicating the coupling of liberalism and democracy. It's true that some Russians blame the West, and foremost the United States, for their problems during the 1990s, but they have done so largely at the instigation of Russian elites. And while it's also true that Western attempts to support liberals and liberalism in Russia have aroused suspicion in at least certain elements of Russian society, I must take issue with the conclusions that the "realists" have drawn from this and other facts.

First, Russia's neopatrimonial system, which actively fosters hostility toward America and suspicion toward the West in general, would make stable and normal relations impossible, even if the West were to excise its values from its foreign policy altogether. The final years of the Bush presidency, which culminated in an adversarial relationship between Russia and America, demonstrate this. Thomas Carothers argues that Bush never ventured beyond the bounds of realism in his dealings with Russia:

> The administration ... followed a firmly realist line toward Russia and China.... It ... emphasized cooperation with both countries on the many major economic and security areas while generally downplaying democracy concerns, despite the fact that both those countries have been in a phase of political de-liberalization.[4]

So if Bush held his tongue with regard to talk of values, why did relations between America and Russia end so dismally during his term? In any case, the crisis in relations between Russia and the United States during Bush's final years belies Lynch's conclusion that "a focus on the interaction of each country's specific interstate interests and a suppression of ideologically based aspirations correspond to periods of reasonably good Russian-American relations."

Second, to what extent is liberal democracy in Russia "hopeless"? I've already introduced survey data attesting to the fact that Russian society is more prepared than we might have expected for a new way of life. Additional polling by the Levada Center in 2010 confirms that between 57 percent and 62 percent of Russians believe Russia needs democracy, and fewer than 26 percent disagree. Russians also support democratic values: 67 percent of those between the ages of 25 and 40; 75 percent of the intelligentsia; 81 percent of business executives; and 68 percent of residents of large cities. I recognize that Russians seem reluctant to organize and fight for the values that they passively support. The fact remains that Russians still dread protests and the disastrous repercussions they might bring. They also fear that the state might collapse, and they don't see any forces that could plausibly step in with an alternative arrangement. Thus this part of the population waits patiently for incentives from on high. It's important, however, to note that there are no insurmountable obstacles to Russia's adopting new rules of the game, if such rules could guarantee a non-corrupt state and the protection of human and civil rights.

The main problem lies not with Russian society, but with its elites, or rather with its ruling clique, whose existence is tied to the preservation of personalized power. Thus when Russian or Western commentators harp on the hopelessness of liberal democracy, they are effectively immunizing the elite from any challenges to its power.

Liberal democracy is far from a hopeless cause in Russia. Indeed, the mood has begun to change, even among the elite. Its second-tier representatives are coming to regard the principles of competitiveness and checks and balances as essential elements of a well-organized society.

Third, while the current regime may very possibly be "the best" in Russian history (and that depends entirely on what we mean by "best"), it is also guilty of leading Russia into a blind alley. How sustainable can the regime be if its leaders have no idea how to extract their country from the economic crisis it entered in 2008, or how to rebuild in its aftermath?

Fourth, with regard to Kennan's "three conditions" for normal U.S.–Russian relations, Russia still hasn't met them. Russia hasn't, in fact, abandoned its old ways; it has merely adapted them to new conditions. In place of the earlier, messianic ideology, the ruling group has substituted pragmatic arguments in favor of turning Russia into a "center of power." In place of totalitarianism, it has substituted authoritarianism. And in place of naked imperialism, Moscow has substituted neoimperialist attempts to guarantee areas of "privileged interests." How do these substitutions accord with American interests? That's a question for American authors to answer. For my part, I can only answer that these substitutions don't square with Russia's national interests.

Now, having addressed as best I could my objections to Allen Lynch's "realist" arguments, I would like to veer off on a brief sidetrack to note something I've observed about Realpolitik writers: They love to quote George Kennan, and all "realists," whether Russian, Western, or otherwise, inevitably know this quote by heart: "The ways by which people advance toward dignity and enlightenment in government are things that constitute the deepest and most intimate processes of national life. There is nothing less understandable to foreigners, nothing in which foreign interference can do less good." The meaning of this incantation is clear: *Leave Russia alone! She'll sort things out on her own.*

Quite right, you might think. Indeed there have been many examples in recent history when the West has tried to force-feed bliss to a country without understanding what was really going on there. (And America is a repeat offender in this category.) Kennan's admonitions with respect to Russia remain relevant today, but the naïveté and ignorance of some democratic missionaries don't mean that the West should renounce altogether its efforts to spread liberal democracy. Indeed I doubt Kennan himself would agree; nor would he approve, I think, of his admonitions being ritualistically invoked to make allowances for an anti-liberal and anti-democratic system. In short, I'm not sure the "realists" understand the godfather of realism. Kennan saw Soviet policy through a lens of communism and ideology, not simply power politics and pragmatism. It was this perspective that allowed him to recognize Soviet foreign policy phenomena much more clearly than his contemporaries.

Western and Russian realists share a commitment to pragmatism, the essence of which is to accept a starting point of Russia as it is today, not Russia as it could become in the future. "The West should build on what is possible." "One mustn't hurry the course of events. All in good time."

"Let the Russians sort out Russia." And so forth. When I hear such formulations, I like to remind their speakers that it would be shortsighted to proceed from a static picture of the world. What exists today may change tomorrow. For that reason, policy should always encompass the long term, lest one be perpetually saddled with yesterday's baggage. Moreover, by refusing to build policy on the basis of principles, hewing only to the needs of the moment, one will never discover that magical formula that can help Russia grow into a civilized European country and rejuvenate Western democracies today. Without reference to principles, development and progress are impossible.

There are supporters of both hard- and soft-line approaches among both Western and Russian "realists." The hard-line realists urge that relations between Russia and the West be oriented solely toward the balance of power; values would only muddy the waters of cooperation in the name of "common goals." Soft realists understand the importance of values but don't know how to promote them without injecting ideology into foreign policy and thus increasing tensions and meriting charges of "meddling." Thus, in practice, they too are oriented toward interests.

In recent years, the decline of the neocons has given realists in Russia and the West a second wind. The realists seem destined to succeed merely by being the clearest alternative to the foreign policy of the Bush era. In their rallying cry to the world, they argue that the current stage of global development spells an end to the twentieth-century era of ideology and its associated wars and conflicts.

Superficially, these arguments appear convincing. Who isn't tired of revolutions and turmoil, after all? Ours is an age of withdrawal into private life and local problems, and this feeling has inevitably affected the nature of contemporary politics. We hunger for the status quo.

The global financial crisis has reminded us, however, that the status quo can't last forever, and that it does not contain within itself the seeds of a renewed civilization. The downturn has awakened the world's elites and compelled them to think about new ways of organizing society, but that is impossible without cultivating new ideas and philosophies—in short, without returning to questions about society's first principles. Civilizations wither and decay when they turn their backs on ideas. This is exactly what has afflicted Russia over the past decade.

How exactly has realism helped to justify the Russian system and to hold Russia back over the past decade? Very simply, it has cooled the ardor of Western political forces that might otherwise have tried to create incentives for liberal-oriented reforms in Russia, and boosted the authoritarian regime's confidence in itself. The longer the regime's system of personal-ized rule is preserved, the more the system will consolidate itself—through hostility to the West, not openness to it. To see this for yourself, you need only look at the evolution of the Russian system under Yeltsin and Putin. It simply cannot help but maintain its suspicion of the West. This is neither the result of chance occurrences nor the product of the peculiar psychology of the Russian leadership; it is a logical extension of Russia's one-man regime. Even when the Russian government decides out of tactical considerations to reset its relations and rein in its aggressive impulses, the system's logic eventually reasserts itself.

I've taken part in numerous meetings and conferences at which the par-ticipants discussed Western-Russian security cooperation, never once acknowledging that there are internal political processes, in both Russia and the West, that determine the course of foreign policy. I will repeat here what I say at all such gatherings: A policy of realism toward Russia lacks a strategic dimension. It can only achieve transient, perhaps even imagi-nary, successes. Indeed, these successes will not only fail to ease tensions between Russia and the West; they may exacerbate them.

There is a sad irony in the fact that Realpolitik is a decidedly unreal-istic policy for Russia (and not only for Russia), and a further irony in the fact that "realists" who propose a situational course of action based on current interests are the truest (and perhaps sometimes the sincerest) idealists! Robert Kagan, who says that realism "does not fit reality," writes:

> The nature of a country's regime does matter: not only as a moral issue, but also as a strategic one. That's because ideology is often decisive in shaping the foreign policies of other nations. Ideology determines their ambitions. It is through an ideological lens that countries determine who their friends are. Even a government's per-ception of its interests is shaped by the nature of the regime.[5]

How can one purport to understand a state without first understanding its roots and its domestic agenda?

I nevertheless applaud the realists' continuing efforts to argue their position. Their acumen helps us adherents of democratic transformation to sharpen our views. Take, for example, an argument offered by Dimitri Simes and Paul Saunders in late 2009.[6] I'm reluctant to say that they don't understand the arguments of their opponents, but I'm also reluctant to accuse them of the alternative: that they've merely set up and knocked down a straw man. I'll present their arguments and let you, the reader, be the judge.

First, Simes and Saunders warn democracy supporters against "taking sides in Russia's internal debates," reminding them that Washington's open support for Yeltsin led to the discrediting of Western liberalism. Of course, I agree with them that the West should not have taken sides in the Russian political struggle, but then again I don't know anyone, at least in Russia, who called on the West to interfere directly in Russian politics. Russian liberals have always argued for something quite different: They want the West to stick to its principles rather than supporting whichever politician they happen to like at the moment. If the West, and particularly the United States, had supported liberal principles instead of Yeltsin personally, Russia's development might have taken a different turn. Even today, Russian liberals aren't calling on the West to support Nemtsov, Kasyanov, Yavlinsky, Kasparov, or anyone else; doing so would mean political death for the opposition. Rather, they merely wish the West would treat the Kremlin according to its own liberal principles and norms.

Their second argument is more curious. Simes and Saunders remind us that Alexander II's reforms didn't keep him from waging war in the Caucasus and Balkans, and that Khrushchev's "thaw" didn't stop him from attempting to stare down America during the Cuban Missile Crisis. Therefore we should not tie international relations to domestic processes in Russia.

In fact, history is much more complicated than Simes and Saunders let on. There are just as many examples to show the reverse of their argument. For example, political liberalization under Gorbachev accompanied, first, warmer relations between the USSR and the West and, later, the end of the Cold War itself. Even the historical examples they cite, when examined more closely, prove that foreign and domestic policy are intimately connected. In both historical examples (Alexander II and Khrushchev), the decompression in internal life was an alien phenomenon quickly rejected by the Russian system. Neither Alexander's Russia nor Khrushchev's Soviet Union became truly European countries after their brief dalliance with openness. Moreover, in both cases the regime was forced to relieve the resulting systemic pressures and instability using the traditional methods: expansionism and a search for a villain. The basis for a stable dialogue between Russia and the West is systemic liberalization, not a brief thaw in relations.

Here's yet another argument from the realists: "Russia doesn't have a problem with democratic governments as such. After all, its leaders seem to have gotten along better with Angela Merkel than they have with Belarus's strongman Lukashenko." This may be true, but does it mean that, all else being equal, the Kremlin prefers to deal with democracies? It's not that simple. Moscow has positive relations with Western governments only when those governments keep in mind the corporate interests of the Russian elite and of the Russian leaders personally. In broad terms, this is the policy "Old Europe"—particularly Germany—has maintained, hence the warmer relations. Nonetheless, the Kremlin hasn't given up its anti-Western propaganda.

Why does Moscow have complicated relations with Minsk? This can be explained by the fact that similar authoritarian regimes often have tenser relations than they do with regimes of an entirely different character. In this case, Moscow tries to act like a "big brother," a patronizing arrangement an authoritarian like Lukashenko can't stand. The USSR had problems with the dictatorships in Yugoslavia, Albania, and Romania for similar reasons. So in this case, the connection is even more evident between the imperial, great-power substance of the Russian system and its behavior toward its neighbors.

The final realist argument I wish to address here is the one that the West can cooperate with Russia in arms control and nonproliferation "when it views such efforts as promoting its interests." I agree: Russia can cooperate with the United States on these issues, just as the USSR did. But let me stress that Moscow does not cooperate because of the pleasure it derives from discussing arms control and nonproliferation; it cooperates because such discussions allow it to keep Russia's status at a level high enough to support the Russian system. Once again, we see the tie between foreign and domestic policy.

Readers can decide for themselves which arguments are more convincing. And as always, I will be happy to sharpen my wits against any new arguments arising from the realist camp as well.

In the meantime, let's turn to Bobo Lo, who has offered one of the clearest diagnoses of contemporary Realpolitik and its consequences. Here is what Lo wrote to me when I asked for his comment on this subject:

Just as Russia is misguided in pursuing a *realpolitik* foreign policy, so Western analysts are wrong in advocating engagement with Moscow on such a basis. Recognizing a Russian "privileged" sphere of interests in the former Soviet space, for instance, will scarcely help in developing a new quality of relationship. In the first place, it encourages anachronistic—and delusionary—strategic thinking within the Russian elite, further complicating cooperation on major security and economic priorities. Second, a *realpolitik* approach is morally dubious, in effect regarding large parts of the Eurasian continent as mere bargaining chips in some grand geopolitical game. Third, it ignores the self-evident reality that the international system can no longer be managed through a Concert of great powers or "multipolar world order." An increasingly complex and interdependent world has evolved well beyond that point.

I couldn't have said it any better.

Notes

1. Thomas Carothers, analyzing the status of U.S. aid for democracy promotion during the administration of George W. Bush, writes that "major elements of the Bush approach to the war on terror and to foreign policy in general have significantly damaged the cause not only of democracy but also of democracy promotion." Carothers, *U.S. Democracy Promotion During and After Bush* (Washington, D.C.: Carnegie Endowment for International Peace, 2007), p. 14.

2. Allen Lynch, "What Russia Can Be: Paradoxes of Liberalism and Democracy," *American Interest*, vol. 11, no. 2, November-December 2006, pp. 60–66.

3. Ibid., p. 66.

4. Thomas Carothers, *U.S. Democracy Promotion During and After Bush*, p. 14.

5. Robert Kagan, "Idealism Isn't Dead," *Newsweek*, December 30, 2009.

6. Dimitri Simes and Paul Saunders, "The Kremlin Begs to Differ," National Interest Online, October 28, 2009, http://www.nationalinterest.org/Article.aspx?id=22344.

43 HOW "OLD" EUROPE ABANDONED ITS MISSION

Let's turn now to Europe, and two questions in particular. First, how did united Europe, in spite of its intentions, become collectively "realist" in its relations with Russia? Second, does this realism facilitate Europe's interests?

United Europe provides a crystal-clear example of what a values-based approach to policy can accomplish. Its postmodern project was built on foundations that rejected the usual policy instruments and traditional understandings of power. It also has the added spur of being geographically closer to Russia than the world's other great liberal democracies. Furthermore, influencing democratic transformations comes more naturally to Europe than it does to America. The United States has often used its mission of democratization to promote its own geopolitical interests, thus undermining its democratic impulses with hegemonic habits. Russian society, moreover, is much more mistrustful of the United States. In short, the European Union thus has a better chance than any other global entity to effect the dream of Karl Popper of making freedom a guarantee of security, i.e., linking its own security to Russia's transformation.

More's the pity, then, that EU policy has facilitated attempts by the Russian elite to counterfeit democracy and liberalism. European leaders' behavior attests to the fact that they don't know how to respond to either the Russian government's authoritarianism or its great-power designs; they'd rather just plant their heads in the sand and hope the problems go away. Thus Brussels is unwittingly contributing to the Russian people's skepticism toward both European standards and Europe's willingness to defend them. Russia's ruling team, meanwhile, finds in Europe's behavior confirmation of the fact that not only can it do what it wants; it can get Europe to do what it wants, too.

Reflecting on the problem of relations between Europe and Russia, Finnish observer Hiski Haukkala writes:

> Relations between the EU and Russia after the end of the "Cold War" have been based on false assumptions. Russia was not about to transition to the liberal and democratic values that it promised to. The EU, in turn, has proved incapable of formulating a policy that would spur Russia's movement in this direction.[1]

Brussels has fallen into a trap. Lacking a coherent strategy toward Russia, it has found that Moscow's appetite for European groveling knows no bounds. "Europe today is worthy of its Barroso (the president of the European Commission)," quipped one European expert about the European Union's policy toward Russia, hinting at the weakness of the European leadership. Moscow, in turn, continues to plumb the depths of Brussels's impotence, with no obvious bottom in sight.

United Europe has never had much luck combining interests and values in its Russia policy. Its latest efforts have found it attempting to emphasize concrete measures relating to interests while restricting itself to mere rhetoric relating to values. This strategy has served neither concern particularly well. Built on technocratic principles and lacking any imagination, EU policy toward Russia has become a thin veil of wordy declarations masking an utter void. The "Road Maps for Four Common Spaces," Brussels' strategy toward Russia, not only sounds like a monstrosity of bureaucratic boredom, it is one, too. One cannot help but admire the Eurocrats' perfect achievement in creating the appearance of partnership with Russia. Only the Kremlin could rival them in spinning pretense and fantasy.

After a painstaking analysis of nearly 400 programmatic provisions of "Road Maps for Four Common Spaces," Michael Emerson, a former European Commission representative in Moscow, concluded that these "spaces" (programs of cooperation with Russia) contain nothing but empty pronouncements. None of the programs has ever been implemented. In the opinions of other impartial experts, the Common Space of Freedom, Security, and Justice largely ignores the imperative of democratic development in Russia. Katinka Barysch, deputy director of the Centre for European Reform, admitted, "Of the many technical committees established by the old PCA, only one (on customs) has met in the last five years. In its human rights dialogue with Russia, the EU has encountered "zero openness," in the words of one of the officials involved. The project to integrate the EU and Russia across four 'common spaces' ... has produced little more than anodyne reports."[2] It would not be an exaggeration to say that the European Union's master program for promoting democratization in Russia has proven ideal for abetting the Russian regime's ruling strategy. How else can one characterize these efforts, given their utter fecklessness at influencing Russia's democratic development?

The Brussels bureaucracy seems to have simply given up trying to influence the course of events inside Russia, choosing instead just to make believe that everything is perfect—that Russia is adapting to EU principles at the very moment it is moving in the opposite direction. Having witnessed Brussels's willingness to play a game of "Let's pretend," Moscow has stopped taking European institutions seriously.

Another example of the European Union's helplessness was its conduct during and after the 2008 war between Russia and Georgia. The Europeans knew perfectly well that the war was a challenge to the West and an attempt by Moscow to assert its right to return to its spheres of influence. But Brussels didn't know how to respond. Flustered and emphatically indignant, the European Union's leadership, under French presidency at the time, merely restored its old relationship with Russia, as if nothing had happened. In the Medvedev-Sarkozy plan, the EU set out its demands for a peaceful conclusion to the war in the Caucasus, including a demand that Moscow respect Georgia's territorial integrity and withdraw its troops from the territories they had occupied. These demands were never met, so Europe decided to pretend as if they had been.

I recall at the time talking to a French journalist who admitted that his president was defending an agreement that he and everyone else knew Moscow wouldn't abide by. Paul Quinn-Judge, a well-known Russia observer, then commented, "France after the war with Georgia saw an opportunity for *gloire*. Sarkozy was in too much of a hurry to get an agreement on Georgia to read the fine print." The sentiment in Brussels in August and September 2008 seems to have been, "We forgive Russia. We aren't going to rock the boat."

The European Union's conduct during the war in the Caucasus showed that its bureaucracy can't tolerate discomfort for very long. Nor can it be expected to strain itself too hard thinking about how to influence Russia. Georgia, and indeed all the problems of the Caucasus, are simply too distant from the jaded, self-satisfied life of a Brussels bureaucrat. For a time, the EU suspended negotiations over a new Agreement on Cooperation with Russia in protest of the war in the Caucasus, but before long, the EU gladly returned to the process. It was all just a big misunderstanding.

The negotiations over the new agreement afforded Brussels a small opportunity to compel Russian elites to commit to expanding the liberal-democratic field. It is important for both Europe and Russian society that the new agreement contain incentives for Moscow to adopt legal standards.

Moscow has made it clear, however, that it is not about to burden itself with such trifles. Once again, it would force a bitter pill down Brussels's throat. One can't escape the impression that the Eurocrats have again agreed not to annoy Moscow in negotiating a new deal, and simply accepted Russia's terms. This meant that the European Union, which claims in its declarations to be guided by certain values and principles, preferred in Russia's case to agree to the mere outward appearance of those values and principles.

The European Union, writes the Lithuanian Rokas Grajauskas, "returned to a business-as-usual policy in relation to Russia."[3] For Brussels that means giving priority to formalities and empty rhetorical pronouncements that would paper over the gap into which relations between Russia and Europe have fallen over the past few years. My interlocutors in Brussels have patiently, sometimes petulantly justified their actions by saying, "Our focus is on the future. The example of a united Europe should by itself persuade Russia to move in our direction." As we've seen, however, in practical terms this means willing collusion with the Russian elite in its efforts to feign European principles.

Another example of Europe's desire not to irritate the Kremlin was NATO's decision, caving to pressure from "Old Europe," to delay indefinitely the consideration of Membership Action Plans for Ukraine and Georgia. The Kremlin understood this decision as yet more evidence that the West will back down in the face of pressure. Moscow, therefore, needed only to keep the pressure turned up.

The most active proponents of the "Don't anger the Kremlin" policy are Berlin, Paris, and Rome. Even Chancellor Angela Merkel, the only "Old Europe" leader who understands and appreciates the importance of values, has been forced by political necessity to tone down her criticism of official Moscow. To be sure, from time to time she manages to say what she thinks. Merkel has been the only political leader to speak frankly with Putin about rights and freedoms. She had to walk a political tightrope to do so, jeopardizing her former coalition with the German Social Democrats. Their representative in the government, Frank-Walter Steinmeier, who was foreign minister and vice chancellor in the previous government, has constantly accused Merkel of cynically seeking to grab headlines by defending human rights. Former chancellor Gerhard Schroeder has also accused Merkel of being too emotional, saying that her past as a former subject under communist East Germany has unduly influenced her foreign policy.

Lately, however, Chancellor Merkel's attempts to forge a "strategic partnership" with Russia have left her opponents in the realist camp few pretexts for criticism. During a debate in Berlin at the beginning of 2010, a German official reacted to my criticism of the Social Democrats' stance on Russia by saying, "What is the difference between 'Schroederization' of German policy toward Russia and its 'Merkelization' today when Germany has its new coalition government?" He was referring to the fact that, under Merkel, Berlin has continued to take a soft line in its relationship with Moscow. As his question shows, the German foreign policy establishment understands the nature of its attitude toward Russia.

One of Putin's closest friends in Europe is Italian Prime Minister Silvio Berlusconi. Berlusconi is unique among Kremlin cronies in that it seems as though he stopped caring about his reputation long ago. Not to be outdone by Italy, French President Jacques Chirac refused to allow "little" European countries to criticize Putin at the EU-Russia summits. Chirac even awarded Vladimir Putin France's highest civilian decoration: the insignia of the Grand Croix of the Legion d'Honneur. (He did it in secret, so as not to infuriate the French public.) Chirac's successor, Nicolas Sarkozy, not only thinks it proper to congratulate the Kremlin after its manipulated elections; he allows the Kremlin to manipulate him, as we saw in the Russian-Georgian conflict.

Director of the Centre for European Reform Charles Grant very trenchantly observes that "Russia presents a test case for the EU's ambition to run a coherent and effective foreign policy, and it is a test that the EU is currently failing." Grant cites history and geography to explain why the European Union has such a difficult time working out a common approach to Russia. Countries that were in the Soviet Union's sphere of influence or played host to Moscow's puppet regimes are much more critical of Russia than, say, Portugal or Italy. Economic interests, and especially dependence on Russian energy, also explain why such states prefer to be guided solely by situational pragmatism in their relations with Moscow.

Grant mentions one more factor: Germany, he says, has long been "an integrationist country, and displayed real altruism, but now Germans have started to see their own interests as being different to those of Europe as a whole."[4] Indeed, the key to European policy toward Russia lies with Germany. The German political elite knows full well what is happening in Russia, but it obviously fears that any criticism of Russia's leaders (aside from occasional episodes) will get in the way of doing business with them. This is a marked departure from the recent past: When previous generations of German leaders did business with the Soviet Union, they worked to bring about change there, or at the very least, they dreamed about it. One gets the impression that the current German elite prefers the status quo.

It is possible that Germany's retreat into its own problems is one of the reasons why the European Union has no strategy with respect to Russia. German historian Wolfgang Eichwede says, "There are influential forces in Germany who believe that Russia is not yet ready for true democracy. These forces were represented by Egon Bahr when he said that Russia 'has a different culture of power.'" Eichwede has yet another explanation for Germany's efforts to exclude values from its discussions with Moscow: "It is the responsibility Germany feels for the last war and the suffering it caused Russia.... The past does not allow German politicians to criticize Russia."

One can understand that Chancellor Merkel has reason to tread lightly. Explaining Merkel's Russia policy, Constanze Stelzenmüller of the German Marshall Fund deliberated: "There has been much speculation about the chancellor's caution: Is Merkel afraid of offending Russia ... or the energy companies? Quite possible. But there is another reason for her caution that is much closer to home: pro-Russian sentiment, aloofness toward Eastern Europe, and a sense of alienation from the United States are all common in her own party."[5] That, apparently, compels the Chancellor to maintain a trust-based dialogue with the Kremlin. Anyway, Merkel alone cannot make up for the lack of a comprehensive, pan-European policy toward Russia. It remains to be seen whether Germany could craft such a policy on the basis of its special relationship with Russia, and assume the leadership of United Europe.

Returning to the theme of Europe and Russia, Eichwede confessed, "European states are trying to influence Russia through soft power. But that approach does not work. It is most likely that a certain pressure must be used in dealing with Russia." I doubt that Europe is ready for that.

As several Western observers have pointed out, the Western establishment's abandonment of its own principles has had a boomerang effect on its own interests. Edward Lucas, author of *The New Cold War: Putin's Russia and the Threat to the West*, put it this way:

> By pursuing a policy based on self-interest rather than values, the West, and particularly the EU, has undermined its allies in Russia and elsewhere; it has given encouragement to corrupt and authoritarian political forces; and it has reduced its own institutional ability to defend itself. In short, once we think that only money matters, we are defenseless when people attack us using money.

I agree with Lucas. The West, and especially the European community, often evinces a kind of helplessness when dealing with the Russian elite's high-handed bluffs. The elite skillfully makes the most of the weaknesses of the West and its representatives; money is their weapon of choice.

It's hard to avoid the feeling that underlying this policy of connivance by Western leaders toward the Kremlin are a lack of confidence in Russia's ability to reform itself and weariness over its inability to determine its own destiny. "Russia is too big," the Old Europeans tell us, the Russians, and themselves. "Russia will always be hostage to its past. It just can't be helped." Such words are music to the Kremlin's ears.

"Hold on," you might say. "What about the Treaty of Lisbon and other EU reforms? Aren't they supposed to bring about a more coordinated European foreign policy?" Yes, the Treaty of Lisbon and a more stable EU leadership—including the establishment of the post of European minister of foreign affairs—creates at least a hope for a more thoughtful foreign policy. But the way the Eurocrats filled two key EU jobs—the new president and the new "high representative" of European foreign policy—proves that Europe doesn't want any new missions, changes, or breakthroughs. So I doubt Europe will be ready anytime soon to coordinate a policy that would create incentives for Russian transformation. In any case, the future will show if I am wrong—and believe me, I hope I am.

French political scientist Dominique Moïsi only reconfirmed my doubts by concluding, "What is clear is that any ambition to define a common European energy and security policy toward Russia is slowly disappearing. From Berlin to Paris, and from Paris to Rome, European leaders may ultimately be doing the same thing, but they are doing it separately, as competitors vying for Russian favor rather than as partners within a supposedly tightknit EU."[6] Analyzing the prospects of a post-Lisbon EU foreign policy, Sally McNamara was skeptical as well: "The exercise of foreign policy by Europe is likely to remain a tug-of-war, with members pursuing their vital national interests where possible ... Europe's strategic competitors, such as Russia, will continue to encourage the aggrandizement of EU power at NATO's expense, knowing that they have nothing to fear from benign and weak leaders appointed by Brussels. The construction of EU defense and security arrangements in the absence of genuine credibility and military capacity is a recipe for disaster and an invitation to provocation."[7]

"What about the 'Partnership for Modernization' with Russia that the European Union offered Moscow? Doesn't it confirm that Europe is more ready for the transformational approach than one might have thought otherwise?" At first glance, indeed it does confirm that. In December 2009, Commission President José Manuel Barroso launched an initiative to revive the stagnating relationship that was endorsed at the EU-Russia summit in May 2010. At first glance, this initiative looks promising—launching joint, innovative projects in science and industry to restore mutual confidence, with the idea that such day-to-day cooperation would gradually promote European standards and values.

But at second glance, this is not a fresh idea. Germany's former foreign minister Frank-Walter Steinmeier had made similar attempts in 2007 and 2008, offering German help for Russian administrative, education, and health care reforms. And Sarkozy offered his own model of a partnership for modernization in 2009. None of these attempts accomplished anything.

They were bound to fail. The Kremlin sees modernization as a tool to strengthen the status quo, so it expects the West to infuse Russia with money and technology without any conditions or talk of values. But how could one expect any high-tech modernization program to succeed if the Russian leadership is not ready to allow competition or to guarantee property rights, or if it intends the state to keep a tight grip on "innovations"? If the European Union is ready to help Russia with its normative transformation, it needs to pursue a different pattern of relations, one that includes a readiness to influence the behavior of the Russian elite. It must condition its partnership on Moscow's readiness to change the rules of the game, or at a minimum, it must try to persuade the Russian leadership that their concept of modernization is a non-starter. The European Union today, however, isn't ready to irritate Moscow. Thus the "Partnership for Modernization" will amount to nothing more than partnership in a charade.

Notes

1. Hiski Haukkala, "False Premises, Sound Principles: The Way Forward in EU-Russia Relations," presentation at "Unity in Diversity? The EU vis-à-vis Russia," Brussels, April 16, 2008; published as Briefing Paper no. 20, Finnish Institute of International Affairs, Helsinki, 2008.

2. Katinka Barysch, "Can and Should the EU and Russia Reset Their Relationship?" Centre for European Reform, Policy Brief, February 2010.

3. Rokas Grajauskas and Laurynas Kasciunas, "Modern versus Postmodern Actor of International Relations : Explaining EU-Russia Negotiations on the New Partnership Agreement," *Lithuanian Foreign Policy Review*, http://www.lfpr.lt/uploads/File/2009-22/Rokas%20Grajauskas,%20Laurynas%20Kas%C4%8Di%C5%ABnas.pdf.

4. Charles Grant, "Is the EU Doomed to Fail as a Power," Centre for European Reform, July 2009, http://www.cer.org.uk/pdf/essay_905.pdf.

5. Constanze Stelzenmüller, "Germany's Russia's Question. A New Ostpolitik for Europe," *Foreign Affairs*, vol. 88, no. 2, 2009, p. 96.

6. Dominique Moïsi, "Wishful Thinking Fuels Kremlin's Temptation," *Japan Times*, March 18, 2010, http://search.japantimes.co.jp/cgi-bin/eo20100318a2.html.

7. Sally McNamara, "EU Foreign Policymaking Post-Lisbon: Confused and Contrived," Heritage Foundation Backgrounder, March 16, 2010, http://www.heritage.org/Research/Reports/2010/03/EU-Foreign-Policymaking-Post-Lisbon-Confused-and-Contrived.

44 WHY RUSSIAN HUMAN RIGHTS ADVOCATES ARE DISSATISFIED

Brussels's conduct has long disappointed Russians working for demo-cratic reform, and the Eurocrats responsible for implementing Europe's foreign policy have disappointed them most of all. Russian human rights activists openly criticize "Old Europe" and its institutions for, as they put it, their "equivocal" stance on Russia. They frequently note that Russia, too, is a member of the Council of Europe, a body whose principles include "protecting human rights, strengthening parliamen-tary democracy, and fostering the rule of law." Russia agreed to these prin-ciples when it became a member of the Council of Europe. When one of its member countries fails to live up to its agreements, the Council is sup-posed to intervene. Old Europe, it seems, would rather talk to the Krem-lin about more pleasant matters.

One of Russia's most consistent human rights advocates, Sergei Kovalev, discomfits the Eurocrats perhaps more than anyone else, accusing them of "hypocrisy, fraught with dangerous consequences." Kovalev's logic is sim-ple: The European Community affirms the idea that individual rights and freedoms are necessary not just for keeping its own house in order but also for ensuring international security and an equitable global peace. Members of the European Union claim that "human rights are not exclusively an internal affair of states." Yet when it comes to Russia, Kovalev says, Europe manifests an exceptionally "politically correct level of caution," thus nurtur-ing the invidious tendencies of the Moscow government.[1]

Can we characterize Kovalev as a maximalist? Perhaps so, but any fair-minded observer would have a hard time avoiding the conclusion that the staffers of European institutions value good relations with the Kremlin above all else, including good relations with Russia's human rights community.

I'll back up this observation with just one of many possible examples. The Council of Europe's Regional Congress of Nongovernmental Organizations took place in Penza in early December 2008, in honor of the sixtieth anniversary of the Universal Declaration of Human Rights. In organizing the Congress, the Council of Europe chose to deal with the Federation Council, rather than Russian human rights organizations. Thus Russian authorities supplied the list of participants, the agenda, and even censored the speakers' papers. Annelise Oeschger, the head of the Council of Europe's Conference of INGOs, said she saw nothing wrong with this, nor any problems with excluding representatives of most of Russia's leading human rights organizations from a congress devoted to human rights. This slap in the face led to open conflict between the Russian human rights community and the Council of Europe. Lev Ponomarev, one of the leading representatives of Russia's human rights movement, said, "This is the first time that the Council of Europe has so overtly demonstrated that the Russian powers-that-be are closer to it than are the advocates of human rights."[2] In the end, Russia's human rights organizations—in particular, the Moscow Helsinki Group, the For Human Rights movement, the Memorial Human Rights Center, the Civic Assistance Committee, and the Fund for the Defense of Prisoners' Rights—held their own conference in honor of the Declaration's sixtieth anniversary.

This incident was far being from an isolated case. Russian human rights activists increasingly complain that European institutions are bypassing Russia's civil society to work directly with the Russian authorities.

"So what?" the Old Europeans might say. "Europe can't influence Russia in the same way it influenced, or continues to influence, the 'New Europe' states seeking to join the European Union." This is certainly true, and to be expected: Russia is not about to relinquish any sovereignty in order to join the EU. Brussels thus cannot exercise direct leverage over Moscow. "We understand that," the Russian human rights activists say. "But this doesn't mean Europe has to win the Kremlin's favor at any cost."

I hasten to point out that the Russian human rights community's frustration with Europe doesn't prevent it from giving credit where credit is due. But this credit accrues primarily to European civil society and parliamentary institutions. Arseny Roginsky, head of the Russian human rights organization Memorial, says,

It's necessary to recognize that European society has an interest in Russia and an eagerness to help along our civil society. In fact, that interest is much greater than in the United States. European NGOs have a better knowledge and understanding of Russia. Europe has always been more responsive to developments in Russia. In Europe there are more institutions with which the structures of Russian civil society are in regular contact. And the Strasbourg Court of Human Rights, to which Russian citizens can have legal recourse, is also European. During the Bush-Putin era, a widespread perception arose in Russian society that America is another planet—either indifferent to us or downright hostile. Our civil society did not sense any particular support from America during that time.

There is another problem when it comes to Europe's (and indeed the West's) leverage on Russia, and this problem was on display during the 2008 war in the Caucasus. In an effort to force the Kremlin to halt its military operations, the European Union froze talks on a new Partnership and Cooperation Agreement and NATO suspended the work of the NATO-Russia Council. This punishment, however, came across as being directed at Russia as a whole rather than at its ruling elite, which didn't feel the pinch. The West needs to find pressure points that target the Russian elites specifically, forcing them to acknowledge a connection between their conduct, on the one hand, and their personal or corporate interests, on the other. To punish Russian society for the behavior of its elites is worse than useless.

Notes

1. Sergei Kovalev, "Neft', Gaz, Politkorektnost'" [Oil, Gas, Political Correctness], *Yejednevniy Zhurnal*, April 18, 2008, http://www.ej.ru/?a=note&id=7996.

2. Lev Ponomarev, "Goriachaya Liniya: Prava Chelovieka Obkornali k Ich Yubileyu" [Human Rights Have Been Limited on the Eve of the Anniversary], *Yejednevniy Zhurnal*, December 22, 2008, http://www.ej.ru/?a=note&id=8687.

45 A RECONSIDERATION HAS BEGUN

U p to this point I have largely expressed my doubts and concerns about Western policy toward Russia, but giving a full and honest account demands that I not dwell on these things without also mentioning several hopeful developments. Although "realists" in the West continue to overwhelm the debate with their numbers and influence, they haven't cleansed the Western intellectual and political scene of their opponents in quite the way that Russia's "realists" have. There still exist experts who understand the connection between foreign policy and social and political organizations—commonly referred to as "liberal internationalists," "democracy advocates," or sometimes even "idealists." They are searching for a way to combine an interests-based foreign policy with one that supports the transformation of transitional or authoritarian societies. An attempt to prove the significance of domestic developments for foreign relations has been offered by Francis Fukuyama.

Fukuyama's stance on Western foreign policy toward undemocratic countries rejects both simplistic realism and primitive interventionism. He has criticized "ambitious attempts at social engineering" and urged that the problem be approached "with care and humility," but he has also written, "What is needed is not a return to a narrow realism but rather a realistic Wilsonianism that recognizes the importance to world order of what goes on inside states and that better matches the available tools to the achievement of democratic ends."[1]

Fukuyama has called for the United States "to find a balance between what we want and what we really can achieve." At the same time, he has stressed that

> [t]his does not mean giving up on the idealistic goals of spreading democracy. But [it will be necessary] to "detoxify" the very concept of

"democracy promotion." We will have to think of ways of supporting Georgia and Ukraine other than by new alliance commitments. And we need to plan in concrete terms how to defend existing NATO members—particularly Poland and the Baltic states—from an angry and resurgent Russia.[2]

The question is: how can the West support Ukraine and Georgia without taking on additional "alliance commitments"? How can one commit to a solution without accepting the price of it in terms of both resources and responsibilities? This is an issue for further debate.

Another Western expert who appreciates the proper roles of interests and values in foreign policy is Leon Aron:

> The origin of "interests" is not an especially daunting mystery: they are a function of how those in charge of countries think their nations should live, what they [ought] to be afraid of, and what to strive for. In short, interests are defined by values, or, when ordered and prioritized, ideologies. Russia's (and the Soviet Union's, before that) behavior has furnished proofs galore. The "geostrategic" reality was no different for the Soviet Union under Andropov in 1982 than for Gorbachev in 1985, yet how differently the national interests were defined, and how stunningly different became the policies! Ditto for Russia in 2001–2002 and 2007—yet again, the ideological evolution in the Kremlin produced increasingly different, almost opposite, definitions of the country's interests, and, as a result, startlingly distinct foreign policies.

The "realists" would have a hard time explaining why the Kremlin sought partnership with the United States and the West in 2002, tried to contain them in 2007, and finally returned to seeking partnership again in 2009. The realists would be puzzled, but as Aron points out, it's no great mystery: Russia's ruling team was trying to secure its hold on power.

Recognizing the importance of values, however, brings us only so far in fashioning constructive policies toward undemocratic societies on the basis of "realistic Wilsonianism." There is as yet no convincing road map leading to a solution to this problem, but there are a few signposts. Obviously, succeeding at this task depends on the West, and above all America, abandoning the values-based approach to achieve tactical goals. As Fareed Zakaria has asked, "Does [America] want to push its own particular interests abroad, or does it want to create a structure of rules, practices, and values by which the world will be bound?" In his view, the United States' "overriding goal should be the latter." However, he says,

> For such a system to work, we would have to adhere to these rules as well. If the United States freelances when it suits its purposes, why would China not do the same with regard to Taiwan? If Washington has its own exceptions, so do other countries.[3]

This last argument is frequently employed by the Russian elite: "If all's fair for America, why shouldn't it be that way for us?"

The Europeans might take issue with Zakaria's idea that America ought to be the one proposing new rules for the world. Indeed, it would seem that Europe, which was the first collective polity to implement new political standards, is best suited to initiate new global rules of the game, Unfortunately, the Europeans have not shown missionary zeal or willingness to take on this role.

But before we get embroiled in the Europe vs. America debate, it's important that we take note of a more fundamental truth: the need for all Western actors to follow internationally recognized rules. The fact that liberal democracies themselves violate these rules remains a stumbling block to the transformation of transitional societies.

The Council on Foreign Relations in Washington has made one of the more noteworthy attempts to find a new balance between interests and values without tripping on that stumbling block. It formed a task force chaired by John Edwards and Jack Kemp, with Stephen Sestanovich as project director, that issued a 2006 report titled *Russia's Wrong Direction: What the United States Can and Should Do.*[4] The report, it almost goes without saying, displeased Moscow. Freed of the constraints of undue political correctness, the authors stated quite directly that Russia was "headed in the wrong direction" with its turn toward authoritarianism. For the first time during Putin's rule, an influential and mainstream American organization had uttered the words the U.S. administration had not dared. The report was also clear and unequivocal about the proper sources for U.S. Russia policy: "In America's relations with Russia, the choice between interests and values is a false one. It misreads the connection between internal developments in Russia and the broader foreign policy interests of the United States." Washington, said the authors, must place greater emphasis on values in its relations with Russia.

Here are a few of the principles of the new policy outlined in the report:

- increase support for democratic processes in Russia while avoiding direct interference ("Russia's course will not—and must not—be set by foreigners");

- revive the Group of Seven, without Russia;

- avoid belittling Russia "by subjecting it to double standards";

- drop the focus on partnership with Russia (partnership being "the right long-term goal, but not a realistic prospect over the next several years");

- recognize the mistakes of the 1990s; and

- form a "transatlantic consensus" between the United States and its allies with respect to Russia.

The Russian elite, of course, found these proposals objectionable, but it found yet another of the report's principles to be even more dangerous—namely, its call for the West to spell out the criteria for assessing the legitimacy of elections in Russia:

> It will be hard to treat leaders who emerge from this process as fully legitimate ... if ... opposition candidates are kept off the ballot, ... technicalities are used to deny registration to opposition political parties, ... parties are blocked from forming electoral coalitions against the "party of power," ... broadcast news coverage and advertising access are severely circumscribed, [and] monitoring organizations are kept from verifying electoral results.

The 2007–2008 elections in Russia did not meet these criteria. If one were to use the logic of the principle above, the winners of those elections (including President Medvedev) could not be considered legitimate. From a liberal point of view, the report offered constructive recommendations for influencing the behavior of the Russian elite—that is, if the West were willing to coordinate its response and act collectively. Alas, that was never very likely to be.

Let's look at another example of a Western organization seeking a new formula for relations with Russia. Around the same time as the Council on Foreign Relations report was released, the Tripartite Commission issued a report by Strobe Talbott, Roderic Lyne, and Koji Watanabe. Their report enunciated the same ideal as the Council's had, albeit in milder terms, saying that interests grow out of values. "Europe must not abandon values" in its relations with Russia, the report said. "It must abandon the pretense about values."[5] This, too, was good advice, and it was also ignored in Western capitals.

Western experts have continued casting about for a course for Russia policy that lies somewhere between partnership, which has not panned out, and containment, which the West would rather avoid. Responding to the Kremlin's formula of simultaneously "being with the West and against the West," Western observers have begun to experiment with another formula: "not overstating the kinship, but not being too confrontational either."

Will treating Russia more like, say, Kazakhstan—that is, treating it as a non-democracy ready for practical cooperation—actually improve U.S.–Russian relations?" Sestanovich asked and attempted to answer this question.[6] He proposed "determining the right balance between cooperating and pushing back—between selective engagement and selective containment." This model, I'll admit, might be productive, from the Western point of view. But speaking as a Russian liberal, I don't think it's very likely that one can sustain a course of "selective engagement." The reason why is that it provides no guidance for how the West can help foster Russia's transformation. And absent such a transformation, the West will find that its Russia policy will contain less and less "engagement" and more and more "containment." Russia's transformation certainly won't come about if the West continues to stand on the shore and take bets on whether Russia will sink or swim, and in what direction it will swim.

Eugene Rumer and Angela Stent have proposed their own model for relations between the West and Russia. Recognizing that the relationship can no longer be characterized as a partnership, they propose that the West maintain "transactional relations" with Russia. The gist of their model is to find limited areas of compromise between the two sides—a policy of small steps free of any illusions about "common interests."[7] While I welcome the appeal to discard illusions about partnership, I doubt that a tactic of limited compromise between the West and Russia can eliminate conflicts between them. After all, this tactic didn't prevent relations from cooling toward the end of Putin's term as president. Besides, Russian liberals will point to the lack of a civilizational component to this model, and to the lack of incentives for Russia to modernize. An unreformed Russia will always cast doubts on the prospects of any "transactions" with the West.

"Genuine partnership and joint membership in the democratic 'clubs' requires shared values," says Roderic Lyne. He has suggested replacing "chimeras of partnership" with the logic of "selective cooperation," which should include an element of conditionality. And what does he mean by "conditionality"? "Keeping incentives and partnership opportunities at the ready in the event that in the future Russia moves in the direction of modernization," he says.[8] This model provides for Western support of Russia's transformation, but, of course, the devil is in the details. Everything depends on exactly how the West defines "conditionality" and what incentives it proposes for Russia to begin undertaking reforms. It's not clear whether this model could work without "restraining" the aggressive tendencies on the part of the Russian elite.

James Sherr also suggests that the basic principles of Western policy toward Russia after the fall of the USSR ("engagement and partnership," he calls them) "have lost their utility." Cold War principles—containment, in particular—don't work either. Today the West should, in Sherr's opinion, build relations with Russia on the following platform: "in place of engagement, influence; in place of containment, restraint."[9] Frankly, it's not clear to me how "influence" is any more meaningful than "engagement," and in what way "restraint" differs from "containment."

As should be plain by now, I have my doubts about whether the new formula for the West's response to Russia ("not partnership and not containment, but something in between") can succeed. First, the formula is merely a reaction to Russian conduct and thus lacks strategic vision. Second, I am aware of no way it can be made to support the transformation of Russia. That said, it's essential that my Western counterparts begin seeking a new formula for dealing with Russia.

It is also important that Western observers look for a way to guarantee broad "engagement" with Russia—namely, engagement with every level of Russian society. As Andrew Wood says, "The countries of the West will and should continue to try to engage with as broad a range of Russian actors as they can. Russia is not limited to the current political elite.... The narrow and suspicious world of the political elite is not the sole reality."[10]

Ronald Asmus has reasoned along similar lines. He is confident that "NATO and the EU must articulate a need to expand the democratic West and define a new approach to Russia."[11] At the same time, he emphasizes that such an approach should by no means be about isolating Russia. "The best way to deal with revisionist Russia is to engage it," he says. "But we need to be clear on what we seek and what we want to avoid; otherwise, we will find ourselves mired in a marathon negotiation, simply playing defense as Moscow seeks to water down past commitments it now finds inconvenient."[12]

What should the West, in fact, seek for Russia, and what should the West avoid? Russian-Finnish expert Arkady Moshes answers this question and puts it in its proper context:

> Europe's top priority is the need to recognize that Russia is more than just its energy supplier. Russia is a major strategic problem for Europe, and a challenge that can only be compared to the challenge posed by the Islamic world. And the Russian challenge needs to be treated accordingly. The task facing European leaders is not to prepare papers for the next summit with Russia but to develop, for Russia, a normative vision of transformation. Democracy in Russia is more important for Europe than Europeans sometimes think. If democratization in Russia fails, Europe will find itself suddenly living alongside a "Siberian Nigeria," a country that is rich in mineral resources but is riven by social ills and poses huge security risks to its neighbors.[13]

What these statements show is that the search for a new content for Western policy toward Russia is moving toward a rejection of traditional realism. I can't exclude that failure of Realpolitik in other regions could force Western experts and politicians to rethink their "realist" approach to Russia. "I am a card-carrying realist,…" wrote Richard Haass, while deliberating on the American approach to Iran. "I've changed my mind," he admitted. Now Haass believes that "the United States, European governments, and others should shift their Iran policy toward increasing the prospects for political change."[14] At some point Western realists may come to the same conclusion regarding Russia.

No less a figure than the former German minister of foreign affairs, Joschka Fischer, has joined his voice to the chorus of those in search of a new Russia policy: "Due to its geopolitical position and its potential … Russia will remain a permanent strategic factor in Europe and Asia that cannot be ignored." Russia must be integrated within the framework of "strategic partnership" with the West, he says, suggesting that the West use Medvedev's initiative to create a new system of European security:

> [W]hy not think about transforming NATO into a real European security system, including Russia? The rules of the game would be changed and a whole variety of strategic goals could be achieved—

European security, neighborhood conflicts, energy security, arms reduction, anti-proliferation, etc. Yes, such a bold step would transform NATO. But it would transform Russia even more.[15]

It's a pity Fischer never proposed this while he was foreign minister, a time when Germany and Russia, under Schroeder and Putin, respectively, enjoyed such warm relations. But better late than never, I suppose.

On the other hand, one must admit that, without coordinated Western efforts to help Russia reform itself, such a step could easily bring about the unraveling of NATO. Some Western experts hold the opinion that the West needs to engage in dialogue with Russia on this issue, despite the risk to the Atlantic alliance. "We understand why the Kremlin needs this initiative," they say, "but still it ought to be discussed, even if it is clear in advance that Western governments are not about to implement it."[16]

If it's not serious about the proposal, I've asked such experts, what's in it for the West? Their response is typically that, even if it wouldn't bring what Moscow wants, a dialogue of that kind would at least help Russia's rulers see the contrast between their ambitions and reality. They're absolutely correct, of course, that the Russian elite needs help in seeing things plain.

In both Russia and the West, one often finds experts applying a technocratic approach to the problem of the two sides' mutual relations. Proponents of this approach argue that it is sufficient to draw up an agenda for mutual cooperation, establish a mechanism for dialogue on the pattern of the "Gore-Chernomyrdin" Commission, and then designate persons who have access to the "higher-ups" to be in charge of the collaboration. Do all this and, like magic, the process of mutual understanding will begin to grow. Or so goes the theory. In practice, as we've seen from previous cooperation agendas and government commissions, one rarely arrives at the desired result.

I wouldn't rule out the possibility that a change of leaders or administrations, coupled with the right joint initiatives, could temporarily warm relations between Russia and the West. But I assure you, my optimistic colleagues, that these measures won't dissipate the mutual misunderstanding and suspicion that have grown up over the past two decades. Those problems have systemic roots, and history has shown that attempts by Western leaders to bury, rather than acknowledge, those roots have only served to nourish Russian whims.

Everything hinges on what goals the West sets for a new phase of dialogue with Russia. If it bets on maintaining the status quo as it has tried to do all this time, then dialogue will only help Russia's authorities keep the country in a state of civilizational uncertainty. In such a state, Russia will never be a true partner for the Western community, a partner prepared to abide by its commitments. The question is whether the West can use dialogue to introduce values to the equation, thus linking the interests of the Russian elite with how that elite manages standards inside Russia. But this task requires a generation of Western leaders who think in strategic terms and act in concert with one another. For the time being, this generation is hiding, but perhaps they are only waiting for the right moment to step forward.

Notes

1. Fukuyama argues that the West should focus its policy of democratization on issues of good governance, political accountability, and democratic institutions. The main tool should be "our ability to set an example, to train and educate, [and] to support with advice and often money." However, actual reform in transitional societies must be made by the societies themselves. See Francis Fukuyama, *America at the Crossroads. Democracy, Power and the Neoconservative Legacy* (New Haven: Yale University Press, 2007), pp. 9, 183–184.

2. Francis Fukuyama, "Russia and a New Democratic Realism," *Financial Times*, September 2, 2008 http://search.ft.com/search?queryText=article+by+Francis+Fukuyama+in+2008&ftsearchType=type_news.

3. Fareed Zakaria, *The Post-American World* (New York: W. W. Norton & Co., 2008), p. 238.

4. *Russia's Wrong Direction: What the United States Can and Should Do*, Independent Task Force Report no. 57, Council on Foreign Relations, March 2006, http://www.cfr.org/publication/9997/russias_wrong_direction.html?breadcrumb=%2Fpublication%2Fpublication_list%3Ftype%3Dtask_force_report.

5. Roderic Lyne, Strobe Talbott, and Koji Watanabe, *Engaging with Russia: The Next Phase* (Washington, Paris, and Tokyo: The Trilateral Commission, 2006).

6. Stephen Sestanovich, "What Has Moscow Done? Rebuilding U.S.-Russian Relations," *Foreign Affairs*, vol. 87, no. 6, November–December 2008, p. 13.

7. Eugene Rumer and Angela Stent, "Russia and the West," *Survival*, vol. 51, no. 2, April-May 2009, pp. 91–101.

8. Roderic Lyne, "Rossiya i zapad: konfrontatsiya neizbezhna?" [Russia and the West: Is Confrontation Inevitable?], http://www.polit.ru/institutes/2008/09/29/west_print.html.

9. James Sherr, *Russia and the West: A Reassessment*, Shrivenham Papers no. 6, Defence Academy of the United Kingdom, January 14, 2008.

10. Andrew Wood, *Reflections on Russia and the West*, November 21, 2008, http://www.chathamhouse.org.uk/files/12710_1108russia_west.pdf.

11. Ronald D. Asmus, "Europe's Easter Promise," *Foreign Affairs*, vol. 86, no. 1, January-February 2008, p. 17.

12. Ronald D. Asmus, "Dealing With Revisionist Russia," *Washington Post*, December 13, 2008.

13. Arkady Moshes, "Russian-European Relations: Dualism Forever?" in K. Winther, ed., *Rusland før og nu* [Russia Before and Now. Essays in Honour of General Karsten J. Moller] (Copenhagen: Forsvarsakademiet, 2007), pp. 117–129.

14. Richard N. Haass, "Enough Is Enough. Why We Can No Longer Remain on the Sidelines in the Struggle for Regime Change in Iran," *Newsweek*, February 1, 2010, p. 33.

15. Joschka Fischer, "Finding Russia's Place in Europe," *Guardian*, January 11, 2009.

16. "The [Russians] seem to believe that a European security conference, even a European security treaty, would strengthen Russia's sphere of influence," Sestanovich wrote. "They want to show that when they speak, they get a hearing. Such aims and expectations may produce only stalemate. Yet the process would not be a waste of time if it did nothing more than demonstrate that Russia's ideas and conduct are at odds with the opinions of all other participants." See Sestanovich, "What Has Moscow Done,"pp. 27–28.

46 HOW "NEW" EUROPE IS TRYING TO REVIVE THE EUROPEAN MISSION

Perhaps they are coming forward already. Several European states are actively trying to find a new balance regarding Russia. The countries of Scandinavia, particularly Sweden, and countries of "new Europe" like Poland, Lithuania, and Estonia are showing that they understand that only the transformation of Russia can guarantee a predictable and constructive partnership between Europe and Russia. Unlike the "old Europeans," they openly criticize Russian authoritarianism and its bullying of its neighbors. They believe that Russia is not lost for liberal democracy. "If we could transform ourselves," they say, "then why can't Russia?" They admit that Russia carries an extremely heavy burden in the form of its past, that Russian society has many problems. "But we had difficulties, too, and we overcame them." Russia, too, has certain advantages, such as a relatively well-educated population, the desire for prosperity, and abundant energy resources, all of which could ease the path of reform if deployed intelligently. "[T]he East Europeans consider Russia to be as fit as they are" says Estonian expert Kadri Liik. "If there is anyone out there who considers Russia to be somehow sub-standard ... it is the Western Europeans with their endless patience, rather than the Easterners with their criticism."[1]

Commenting on the Russian dilemma dividing Europe, Polish philosopher Alexander Smolar said,

> The EU is split in its attitude toward Russia. Germany, France, Italy, and Spain want to keep partnership with Moscow, primarily using their special relations with Russia in energy policy. These countries have a rather cynical view of Russia's domestic political development. At the same time, some new members of the EU frankly speak out about violations of civil and democratic rights in Russia and those foreign policy consequences, especially for Russia's neighbors.

Smolar believes that Russia's evolution and its behavior on the international scene, in particular the Russian war in the Caucasus, "can bring closer the positions of European states regarding Russia." It remains to be seen where the two shall meet on the policy spectrum—at a point closer to acquiescence to the Kremlin's whims, or at one that approaches a concerted effort to influence the Russian elite's behavior.

At present, "old Europe" doesn't want to listen to its newer cousins, who are as irritated by it as much as official Moscow is. "New" Europe's hectoring about rights and freedoms in Russia is interfering with the mutual satisfaction of the Russian elite's and old Europe's desires.

Nevertheless, the "new Europeans" keep pushing their line. Bronislav Geremek, a leader of the Solidarity movement and later foreign minister of Poland and deputy of the European Parliament, told me in one of our long conversations not long before his tragic death in 2008,

> Poles and Swedes are doing everything they can to persuade Brussels to respond to the Russian challenge. Our reply will be bringing Ukraine and other newly independent states into the European orbit. Russia's democratic neighbors must become a role model and help Russian society understand that they must look to the future, not hang on to the past.

How tragic that this voice is now silent—the voice that embodied the moral and principled approach to politics in European circles and was readily listened to by European public opinion.

We are fortunate that there are others who have taken up Geremek's message of bringing Russian society into European civilization. They include Sweden's Minister of Foreign Affairs Karl Bildt. Thanks to the tireless efforts of Bildt and Poland's Minister of Foreign Affairs Radoslaw Sikorski, the European Union approved the Eastern Partnership program in 2009. The goal of this new program is to help Ukraine, Moldova, Georgia, Armenia, and Azerbaijan adapt to EU standards. At the March 2009 EU summit, Belarus joined the Eastern Partnership.

The starting level of financing for this program in 2009 was €450 million and by 2013, the EU plans to expend €785 million. What a united Europe failed to do for Russia, it is trying to do for the newly independent states. The "new Europeans" have criticized Brussels for its miserliness, as the budget of the new initiative is not yet sufficient for bold integrating steps. But the important point is that slumbering Brussels has stirred a bit and agreed to a new project. "We started the process and we won't stop," Bildt says.

Russia and its Western "protectors" are already sounding alarms that the new *Ostpolitik* of the Scandinavians and "new Europeans" undermines the "Russo-centric" policies of France and Germany. They are right to sound the alarm. The new policy really does threaten their cozy arrangement. Sooner or later, "old Europe" will have to come up with a policy that accounts for Russia's true national interests, rather than the corporate interests of the thin stratum of the ruling elite in Moscow.

Note

1. Kadri Liik, "Former Allies or Former Prisoners? Russia and Its Post-Soviet, Pro-Western Neighbours," November 13, 2008, http://www.icds.ee/fileadmin/failid/Kadri%20Liik%20-%20Former%20allies%20or%20former%20prisoners.pdf.

47 EUROPEAN SOCIETY IS STARTING TO SAY WHAT IT THINKS

There's much more to "Europe," of course, than "old European" politicians ensconced in their capitals. European civil society and nongovernmental organizations are increasingly a force to be reckoned with. It is thanks to pressure from this quarter that Russia was forced to relax the draconian version of its law on nongovernmental organizations.

Ordinary citizens, too, have expressed great concern to their own representatives about both Russia's internal developments and its foreign policy. Polls taken in 2008 by the German Marshall Center and the Compagnia di San Paolo Foundation in Turin showed that 84 percent of surveyed Americans and 72 percent of Europeans were worried that Russia was selling arms in the Middle East. More than 60 percent of Americans and 64 percent of Europeans were concerned that Russia wields such power being the main provider of natural gas to many European countries. Russia's policies toward its neighbor states were criticized by 69 percent of people polled in Great Britain, 68 percent in Germany, and 72 percent in Poland. Tellingly, 67 percent of polled Europeans and 58 percent of Americans demanded that the West guarantee security for Georgia and Ukraine. According to the 2009 Transatlantic Trends survey, about 67 percent of respondents in Western Europe and 52 percent in Central and Eastern Europe were troubled by the weakening of the Russian democracy. Nearly 66 percent of Central and Eastern Europeans and 70 percent of Western Europeans supported EU security assistance to countries such as Ukraine and Georgia.[1] So it turns out that the populations of Europe and America support getting involved in Eurasia.

Western populations also care about democracy in Russia. Sixty-four percent of Germans, 62 percent of Britons, and 60 percent of Americans believe that the West must not be indifferent to internal political developments in Russia. They are notably more critical of Russia's internal developments than their political leaders have been. (One hopes that their dismay is with the Kremlin regime rather than with the Russian people.) A 2009 BBC World Service/University of Maryland survey of 1,300 respondents in 21 countries found that respondents in Western societies were most critical of Russia, while the Chinese were the most positive (74 percent of those polled in China said they had positive feelings for Russia). Americans who had a negative attitude toward Russia grew from 36 percent in 2008 to 64 percent in 2009. In Great Britain, only 25 percent had positive feelings for Russia, down 20 points from the previous year. Germans expressed the least positive attitudes toward Russia, with 74 percent expressing negative attitudes. This last number is somewhat surprising, given Berlin's efforts to maintain warm relations with Moscow. Surely, the German leadership has begun to sense these shifting popular winds.

Western politicians would be prudent to register these shifts in public opinion. Consider the case of George Osborne and Lord Peter Mandelson. In 2008, the British press exploded with a story about a private meeting on a billionaire's yacht off the Greek island of Corfu. The billionaire was the Russian oligarch Oleg Deripaska, a man whose U.S. travel visa was revoked in 2006, allegedly for his possible ties to organized crime. Among Deripaska's guests on the yacht were George Osborne, the Conservative Party spokesman for economic affairs, and Peter Mandelson, the British business secretary. It was later revealed that Osborne was soliciting a donation from Deripaska, and some press accounts noted that tariffs on aluminum were reduced during Lord Mandelson's tenure as the EU commissioner in Brussels, to the benefit of Deripaska's aluminum business.[2] Proof of Mandelson's dealings with Deripaska was never unearthed, but the meeting itself was enough to invoke a firestorm in the British press and damage the political fortunes of both of Mr. Deripaska's guests. This story is more than just proof of the hypocrisy of some Western politicians; it also illustrates the effectiveness of the Western press at bringing to light this kind of corruption. These days, British politicians tend to be much more careful about which Russian oligarchs they dine with.

The year 2009 truly seems to have heralded a new dawn in European attitudes toward Russia. European parliamentarians are beginning to sense that the time has come to say what they think about the Russian regime and its policies. The Parliamentary Assembly of the Council of Europe has prepared a report on the judicial systems of various countries, focusing mainly on the problem of rule of law in Russia and the Russian courts' dependence on the executive branch. The European Court has accepted several appeals by jailed tycoon Mikhail Khodorkovsky with regard to allegedly unfair rulings by Russian courts. It also accepted a multibillion-dollar lawsuit brought by the former management of his company, Yukos, which was essentially seized by the government after his conviction.

The Parliamentary Assembly of the OSCE passed a resolution in July 2009 equating Nazism and Stalinism as totalitarian regimes. And the OSCE proclaimed August 23, the anniversary of the signing of the Molotov-Ribbentrop Pact, as an international day of remembrance for the victims of Stalinism and Nazism. The Russian authorities reacted swiftly to the measures, accusing the Europeans of trying "to ruin the dialogue between Russia and the West." Medvedev angrily declared, "The Parliamentary Assembly of Europe has placed Fascist Germany and the Soviet Union on the same slate and made them responsible for World War II. But that is, excuse me, a cynical lie." Alas, Medvedev misunderstood the declaration: It was two totalitarian regimes that were placed on the same slate, not two countries. Thus we were left with the strange spectacle of a Russian leader who had previously tried to appear liberal and modern being unwilling to publicly condemn Stalinism. We ought to have predicted his angry reaction; as long as the elite continues to use the legitimization of the Soviet past as part of its strategy to sustain the authoritarian present, we should expect more such confirmations of the incompatibility of the orientation of Europe and of the Russian elite.

The OSCE's proclamation was followed later that year by the German parliament's near-unanimous passage of a resolution in support of Khodorkovsky. For me, this news came as a pleasant surprise, as the German elite has always sought to avoid conflict with Moscow. The Bundestag's unexpected resolution would have been impossible without the energetic efforts of people like Ruprecht Polenz, chairman of the Bundestag committee on foreign affairs, Marieluise Beck, a Bundestag deputy and member of the committee on foreign affairs, and Andreas Schockenhoff, at the time a Bundestag deputy, who convinced their fellow parliamentarians that they should be concerned by the regression of human rights in Russia. The Bundestag's resolution may presage even larger changes afoot in Germany's political mood.

Liberals in Moscow appreciated the fact that Ruprecht Polenz came to Moscow to observe the Khodorkovsky trial and to try to convey to the Russian ruling elite that the German parliament was increasingly inclined to take note of this unending farce. In the sweltering European summer of

2009, Polenz and I dined with a few Russian politicians and experts in Moscow. The conversation was traditional: the Germans talked about being worried by what was going on in Russia, and the Russians talked about the grandeur of their country, managing to simply ignore their emotional Western dining companions. It was an uncomfortable meal. I tried to show the Germans that there were other, different voices in Russia still, but my voice seemed to me like a thin reed in the Russian traditionalists' gale-force winds, exerting little to no influence on Russia's authorities or its society.

During the conversation, Polenz abruptly recalled that he had sat at the very same table with journalist Anna Politkovskaya in 2006. After dinner, they had agreed to meet again in a few days for a cup of coffee. It was not to be, as Anna was murdered shortly after. As Polenz recounted his story, his eyes filled with tears; the Russians were visibly annoyed yet also completely silent. They were afraid to express human feelings about Politkovskaya's killing. What if such feelings were interpreted as disloyalty to the regime? After a few seconds of stony silence, they found a way to change the subject to Barack Obama. That meeting convinced me that we Russians have forgotten how to feel. It's as if each day those of us who work in politics in Russia lose more and more of our normal human instincts.

At around the same time I first began to arrive at these depressing thoughts, a number of analysts monitoring Europe came to a more hopeful conclusion: that sluggish Brussels was finally looking for a new approach to Russia. Heinrich Vogel, for instance, was certain that Europe was looking for a way to lessen its energy dependence on Russia, a pressure point that had been driving policy toward Moscow for a long time. A new energy policy de facto meant a new look at Russia. Said Vogel:

> Until the present moment, the EU could not formulate a consolidated energy strategy, not only because of the positions of countries like Germany and Italy, but because of the resistance of their energy companies, which had long-standing bilateral agreements with Gazprom. But now the situation has changed, and the EU has started work on alternatives to this unacceptable situation.[3]

The Europeans, however, were in no hurry to complete the processes they themselves had started.

Nevertheless, others noted the new mood inside the European Union as well, although some ascribed it to a slightly different set of causes.

Arkady Moshes believed that the global financial crisis was forcing a change in the calculus of relations between Europe and Russia. This calculus had arisen from the Europeans' belief that their relations with Russia could be based on "the priority of interests regarding values" and access to lucrative Russian markets for European business. But one day all this changed, said Moshes:

> With the crisis, the word "energy" is no longer magical. As demand declined [in Europe], the panic over Europe's dependence on Russian supply began to vanish, to be replaced by an understanding of the mutual dependence of Russia and Europe.... Russia's potential return to the international loan market or even a simple listing of Russian corporate debts reminds the West that it has instruments of influence on Russia.[4]

Indeed there are signs today that some European political circles have come to the conclusion that Russia needs the European Union more than the EU needs Russia.

In early 2010 one could see signs that the political community in some European countries had decided to use the thaw in relations with Russia to restart dialogue with Russian civil society. In this vein, Andreas Schockenhoff, coordinator of German-Russian inter-societal cooperation, has initiated discussions with the European Union and German, Russian, and Polish NGOs on how to revive cooperation with Russian civil society, and how to make this cooperation part of an EU-Russia partnership for modernization. Among the ideas generated by the discussion was a recommendation to establish a joint EU-Russian Civil Society Forum that would become a platform for cooperation by non-state actors. Any attempts to revive the European dialogue with real as opposed to Kremlin-appointed civil society representatives should be welcomed. However, the organizers of the new initiative should prepare themselves for frustration; Medvedev's notion of modernization categorically excludes an independent role for civil society. It remains to be seen which side's vision will prevail, and whether the new attempts to revive the dialogue with Russian society will genuinely help the Russian NGOs or simply degenerate into the usual game of make-believe.

There was still no reason, however, to assume that these shifts in mood and feelings would give birth to a new Russia policy. The Obama administration's "reset button" concept, borrowed by the new secretary-general of NATO, Anders Fogh Rasmussen, and the leadership of "old Europe" was creating a new desire to search for "points in common" with Moscow. Such a search, obviously, precluded any actions that could create friction with the Russian regime.

Notes

1. Transatlantic Trends 2009, a project of the German Marshall Fund of the United States and the Compagnia di San Paolo, www.transatlantictrends.org.

2. Sarah Lyall, "Loose lips Lead to Trouble for British Tories," *New York Times,* October 23, 2008.

3. Heinrich Vogel, "Russia-EU: A Dangerous Relationship?" Jean Monnet/Robert Schuman Paper Series, vol. 9, no. 4, March 2009, http://www6.miami.edu/EUCenter/publications/VogelRussiaEUlong2009edi%5B1%5D.pdf.

4. Arkady Moshes, "Diversifikatsiya Rossii" [Diversification of Russia], http://www.gazeta.ru/comments/2008/11/11_x_2879867.shtml.

48 KISSINGER VS. BRZEZINSKI

In searching for new approaches to Russia, the West has been presented with paradigms advanced by Henry Kissinger and Zbigniew Brzezinski, who have come to be seen as antagonists, at least in terms of their counsel on Russia policy. Kissinger has been warmly embraced by Moscow and has partnered with the Russian powers-that-be in discussing relations with the United States. He has become for the official political community both an icon to be venerated and an authority to be obeyed. Brzezinski, on the other hand, the Kremlin can't abide. They consider him almost an archenemy, a man whose every utterance masks an attempt to ferret out a "false bottom" that would work against Russia. Knowledgeable Russians know him as a politician who, by virtue of his Polish background, probably understands Russia better than most of his Western counterparts, but they also suspect him as someone who, by virtue of that same background, almost certainly cherishes no kind feelings toward Russia.

Kissinger continues to see, or claims that he continues to see, a positive evolution at work in Russia. After Medvedev's election to the presidency, he said:

> Whatever the ultimate outcome, the last Russian election marks a transition from a phase of consolidation to a period of modernization.... The government's operation—at least initially—with two centers of power [Dmitri Medvedev and Vladimir Putin] may, in retrospect, appear to be the beginning of an evolution toward a form of checks and balances.[1]

Of course, one does not require or expect the most famous and influential "realist" in the world, the Western statesman most respected in Russian political circles, to know all the nuances of the exercise of power in Russia. Still, someone ought to enlighten Kissinger regarding the fact that Russia's system of government doesn't even remotely resemble a system of checks and balances. Indeed it is moving in the opposite direction. As for its supposed process of modernization, Russia's leaders themselves, both Medvedev and Putin, have been forced to admit that nothing whatsoever has come of the country's reforms. But then again, one ought not to underestimate Kissinger's acumen. It's hard to avoid the impression that his attempt to accentuate the positive in Russia may be due to practical considerations, to the desire to provide a reason for the new U.S. administration to maintain a policy of Realpolitik in relation to Russia. On the other hand, maybe he sincerely believes what he has said.

Of Brzezinski, by contrast, we can be sure he is not the kind of statesman deceived by appearances. He would certainly never write that the Kremlin is gradually introducing "checks and balances." He categorically rejects the realists' contention that it is possible to come to an understanding with Russia by telling the denizens of the Kremlin what they want to hear. Brzezinski has long maintained that building sound relations with Russia is predicated on nurturing the conditions for its transformation and convincing the Russian elite that "democracy is in its interests." In a Spring 2008 essay in the *Washington Quarterly*, Brzezinski said,

> A basic lesson stands out from the West's disappointing experience with Putin: competitive courtship of the Kremlin leader's ego is not as productive as a coordinated shaping of the compelling geopolitical context for Russia.... External conditions need to be deliberately shaped so that future Kremlin leaders conclude that democracy and becoming part of the West are in Russia's interest, as well as their own.[2]

Thus Brzezinski isn't encouraging the West to interfere in Russia's internal affairs, something his opponents, especially in Russia, accuse him of doing. Rather, he is proposing a different model for Western policy: the creation of a favorable environment for Russia's transformation and of incentives that would prompt the Russian elite to begin thinking about their country, not themselves. "His plan lacks specifics," complain those who talk about "common interests" and security. Yes, but if we never change course, we will never arrive at the specifics!

Kissinger's model, on the other hand, looks to classic Realpolitik for guidance. He is forever exhorting the West "not to overdo it with attempts to influence Russia's political evolution." Naturally, the Kremlin welcomes this kind of thinking and scorns Brzezinski's. For the time being, the official West also prefers to listen to Kissinger's advice, despite its having led to an impasse in relations with Russia. Sooner or later, however, the West will have to face facts.

In the interests of giving a fair and balanced account, I should mention that Brzezinski has modified his position somewhat recently. For example, in a recent *Foreign Affairs* essay appraising Obama's foreign policy ("From Hope to Audacity," January/February 2010), Brzezinski didn't explicitly mention the need to influence Russia's internal developments. He advised the Obama administration to pursue "a dual-track policy: it has to cooperate with Russia whenever doing so is mutually beneficial, but in a way that is also responsive to historical reality." The latter meant that Washington had to persuade Russia that "the age of closed empires is over, and Russia, for the sake of its own future, will eventually have to accept this."[3] Clearly advocating a more cautious approach, Brzezinski now appears to hope that Russia's rejection of its revisionist ambitions will bring about internal political change. (Or if I'm wrong, perhaps Dr. Brzezinski will correct me?) Life constantly throws us surprises; and old paradigms sometimes do change. However, I believe Brzezinski has the causality exactly backwards. Only domestic transformation can bring the Russian elite to understand that "the age of closed empires is over."

I am encouraged in this conviction by the fact that some prominent "realists" have found themselves compelled to take a step in that direction. Condoleezza Rice held fast to a "realist" take throughout most of her tenure as secretary of state. However, toward the end of her time in office, she began to change course. In September 2008, she said

> Russia's actions ... fit into a worsening pattern of behavior over several years now. I'm referring, among other things, to Russia's intimidation of its sovereign neighbors, its use of oil and gas as a political weapon, its unilateral suspension of the CFE Treaty, its threat to target peaceful nations with nuclear weapons, its arms sales to states and groups that threaten international security, and its persecution—and worse—of Russian journalists and dissidents. The picture emerging from this pattern of behavior is that of a Russia increasingly authoritarian at home and aggressive abroad.[4]

Quite right. But one wonders whether Rice, whom I respect, understood much earlier that this was the direction in which Russia was moving, or whether she truly arrived at this epiphany toward the end of her tenure. If she did recognize the truth earlier, then why didn't she advise

President Bush to suggest to his friend Putin that he behave a bit more decently? However you answer these questions, her turnabout is all of a piece with the actions of other Western political leaders. They all tend to begin looking critically at Russia only when they're leaving their jobs and preparing to pass off the world's problems to the next comer.

Another example of this phenomenon is the evolution of the views on Russia of Gernot Erler, formerly German minister of state in the Christian Democratic/Social Democratic coalition and currently deputy head of the Social Democratic bloc in the Bundestag. Erler had for years pursued a policy of accommodation toward Russia, but became openly critical after moving into opposition. Together with Erler, I took part in debates on Russia in Berlin in late 2009. His analysis of Russian political life was devastating. "The differences between Putin and Medvedev do not influence governance"; "Where are the signs of modernization the Kremlin is talking about? Russia has failed to use opportunities to reform herself"— this was Erler's verdict on Russia. I had nothing to argue with. Gernot Erler was right. But if the German Social Democrats understood the nature of the Russian political regime, they had to know that their policy of putting up with the Kremlin "no matter what" hardly supported reform in Russia. Now that they are in opposition, will they try to form a more adequate policy on Russia?

Advocates of a values-based approach to Russia have had their own troubles justifying their point of view, much less formulating a new course of action. "Democracy advocates" universally recognize the need for a unified Western approach to Russia. But such an approach has proven elusive because many countries in the Western community have premised their relations with Russia on pragmatism, often contrary to their own strategic interests. Thus the various countries' energy interests, desires to maintain warm relations, and hunger for private Russian investment drive their policies in lieu of more unifying long-term interests.

Few Western commentators today are subscribing to the idea that Western policy needs to address Russia's liberal transformation. Leon Aron's remarks are representative of this view:

> There is a strong correlation between what we call "liberal" values that shape domestic political and economic behavior and the country's foreign policy. The West's VERY REAL "interest," then, is in a democratic and liberal Russia. The West may not always be able to promote this "interest" effectively, but realizing its immense impor-

tance and using every opportunity to act on it is something the West should keep in mind constantly and, when an opportunity arises, be ready to sacrifice to it other, less important, "interests."

Hopefully, this stance will gain more supporters.

Notes

1. Henry Kissinger, Finding Common Ground With Russia, *Washington Post*, July 8, 2008, http://www.washingtonpost.com/wp-dyn/content/article/2008/07/07/AR2008 070702218.html.

2. Zbigniew Brzezinski, "Putin and Beyond," *Washington Quarterly*, Spring 2008, p. 115.

3. Zbigniew Brzezinski, "From Hope to Audacity. Appraising Obama's Foreign Policy," *Foreign Affairs*, January-February 2010, p. 26.

4. Transcript of Condoleeza Rice's remarks at German Marshall Fund of the United States, September 18, 2008, http://www.gmfus.org/doc/2008-09-18%20Rice%20Russia %20Transcript.doc.

49 HOW USEFUL IS THE LEAGUE OF DEMOCRACIES AND HOW PROBABLE IS A GLOBAL AUTHORITARIAN REVANCHE?

In the past few years, several American experts simultaneously proposed the creation of an institutional platform for uniting the world's liberal democracies. Robert Kagan called his version the League of Democratic Countries.[1] Ivo Daalder and James Lindsay's League of Democracies was a slightly simpler name for what essentially amounts to a similar idea. These suggestions were quickly adopted by Republican politicians in the United States, particularly John McCain. Although enthusiasm for the concept has diminished somewhat today, further setbacks in Russian or Chinese relations might once again bring it back into favor.

While I appreciate the impulse behind creating a platform for cooperation among liberal democracies and am even willing to concede that a League of Democracies might help form a common Western strategy on transitional societies, I also see a serious problem with the idea. A League of Democracies would effectively relegate non-democratic states, first and foremost Russia and China, to a separate, parallel realm of international relations. I don't understand how the league would be able to neutralize the negative consequences of that division, or exert influence on that parallel system. I fear that such alienation would only increase the authoritarian vector in Russia. Of course no one knows for sure how a League of Democracies would play out if it were to come into being, but in my estimation the potential drawbacks of the idea outweigh the prospective benefits.

If not a League of Democracies, then, what about its opposite, in a manner of speaking: a global authoritarian revanche? The very idea is music to Russian ears, promising to revitalize their moribund school of authoritarianism. In his August 2007 *Foreign Affairs* article, "The Return of Authoritarian Great Powers," Israeli historian Azar Gat wrote that "China and Russia represent a return of economically successful authoritarian capitalist powers." He continued, "They may have enough weight to create a new non-democratic but economically advanced Second World.... A successful non-democratic Second World could be regarded by many as an attractive alternative to liberal democracy."[2]

I believe there is a simple explanation for the appearance of this idea in the West at that particular time. The year 2007 marked the peak of the economic renaissance in Russia, when high energy prices and a favorable economic outlook made it very much look the part of an influential global actor with revisionist ambitions. Recall that it was in February 2007, at the Munich Security Conference, that Putin stunned the Western community by laying a bill of particulars at America's feet and declaring Russia's new ambitions. There were no overt signs back then of the financial catastrophe that would soon turn moods dour in the world's capitals, including Moscow. It was also the time when China began to emerge as one of the world's leading powers.

With regard to China, if not Russia, the events of the past couple of years have also lent credence to Gat's idea. China's success in dealing with the global financial crisis has revived his thesis about the attractiveness of the authoritarian model. The idea that China can become a new power pole in the international system was expressed by quite a few participants of the World Economic Forum in Davos in 2010.

Gat's thesis had undone a seemingly long-settled issue. Until recently, it had been an axiom in political thought that, while industrial modernization was possible under authoritarianism, post-industrial modernization required a free and competitive society. China's experience seemed to suggest otherwise. Certain voices in Russia and the West maintained that it was time to give up liberal determinism and admit that the combination of authoritarianism and capitalism in China and Russia had created an alternative civilizational vector to the Western one. The proponents of this "authoritarian renaissance" began telling the world that this alternative course necessitated a return to the international paradigm of the last century. That paradigm meant a struggle between powers and an ideological division between Western democracies on one side and new authoritarian states on the other.

The current ruling group in Moscow had tried many times to convince the world that it was offering a new model of development. It counted on observers to understand Russia's economic success during the Putin period (2000–2008) as confirmation that capitalism and authoritarianism were compatible. In foreign policy, the Kremlin returned to geopolitical revanche. Just because of that, the old view of relations between Russia and the West, the "partnership" paradigm, was now obsolete. China's unprecedented economic growth only confirmed this view.

Robert Kagan, a thinker with a knack for stirring debate in the foreign policy community, formed a theory to describe the new division of the world. In his book *The Return of History and the End of Dreams*, he writes, "It is a mistake to believe that autocracy has no international appeal." Both China and Russia could become models for emulation by other states, he argues. "Today, the reemergence of the great autocratic powers, along with the reactionary forces of Islamic radicalism, has weakened the [liberal international] order and threatens to weaken it further in the years and decades to come."[3] Consequently, the Western world, headed by the United States, should begin to consolidate its power in order to respond to this new challenge.

There are Western experts who have objected to the idea of an authoritarian renaissance, and I find their arguments compelling. Their main objection is that, for now, neither China nor Russia has shown any proof that its authoritarian system can create a sustainable post-industrial capitalism. Economic growth in those countries has given no guarantees for stable economic development or a transition to a high-tech phase. Daniel Deudney and G. John Ikenberry argue that the Chinese and Russian experience not only does not disprove the link between liberalism and post-industrial capitalism; on the contrary, it confirms that post-industrial capitalism is impossible without addressing these issues: guaranteeing individual rights; fostering true competition; creating a middle class that is active in politics; establishing the rule of law; and protecting private property rights.[4] Deudney and Ikenberry maintain that authoritarianism is incapable of solving these issues. Allow me to add one additional authoritarian weakness to their list: The global financial crisis, which revealed certain weaknesses in the current incarnations of liberal capitalism, also revealed that authoritarian systems are even less well equipped to deal with such events. The supposed Chinese exception to this rule has yet to prove its sustainability. In addition, the Chinese case is dealing with an entirely different set of circumstances—an industrial economy, rather than a post-industrial one.

The idea of an authoritarian renaissance naturally led some experts to jump to the conclusion that we were about to see the rebirth of geopolitical and ideological struggle on a global scale. However, neither China nor Russia, the designated leaders of the "authoritarian internationale," is prepared to confront the West on such a grand scale.

China, for its part, has no intention of doing so; its goal is to become a more influential player within the existing global capitalist system. Perhaps one day China could become a center of a new geopolitical system, but that is hardly likely anytime soon.

Even the Russian elite, which decided on political confrontation with America in August 2008, isn't ready for full-bore confrontation with the West. Russia will not erect a new pole of authoritarian power on the territory of the former Soviet Union in the foreseeable future. We see signs, in fact, that Russia's allies are seeking support from other leading world players in order to protect themselves against Moscow's suffocating embrace.

The idea of an authoritarian renaissance was a failed attempt to explain the nature of the non-democratic systems of China and Russia in light of their economic successes of the past few years. The economic crisis, which hit Russia especially heavily, will, I hope, correct the excessive optimism regarding both its future and the idea of authoritarian renaissance more broadly.

Nevertheless, the discussion that resulted from the "authoritarian revanche" concept was a useful one, for it focused the West's attention on certain problems it had neglected for too long. It has also forced us to continue to explore new ways that the West can react effectively to authoritarian states with global ambitions—exactly what Russia is today. The West cannot return to the past model of confrontation with the "Evil Empire." Such old thinking could push the Russian ruling class toward militant dictatorship. However, the Realpolitik of recent years is also incapable of easing Russia's move toward the West, or of guaranteeing Russia's cooperation in areas of common concern.

Notes

1. Robert Kagan, "The World Divides ... and Democracy Is at Bay," *Times*, September 2, 2007, http://www.timesonline.co.uk/tol/comment/columnists/guest_contributors/article2367065.ece.

2. Azar Gat, "The Return of Authoritarian Great Powers," *Foreign Affairs*, July-August 2007.

3. Robert Kagan, *The Return of History and the End of Dreams* (New York: Alfred A. Knopf, 2008), pp. 69, 105.

4. Daniel Deudney and G. John Ikenberry, "The Myth of the Autocratic Revival: Why Liberal Democracy Will Prevail," *Foreign Affairs*, September-October 2008.

50 THE OBAMA FACTOR AND THE IDEA OF THE "RESET BUTTON"

If we're to explore new ways for the West to deal with Russia, we need to consider the "Obama factor," whatever it is and however it has moved the discussion. In the ongoing debate between "realists" and transformationalists, both sides have held out hope that Obama would adopt their case. The "realists" in America and elsewhere expected Obama to cast off all illusions and commit the United States to a pragmatic course toward Russia, unsullied by hectoring about "values." Their opponents hoped, conversely, that a president elected on the promise of change would take up the Clinton administration's unrealized dreams for Russia, reformatting them to new realities.

The Russians, meanwhile, waited for America, the bellwether of the West, to decide on its new course. Obama's victory had made it possible for the Russian elite to step back from its confrontational stance without losing face by making Bush out to be the main culprit of the crisis in Russian-American relations. This narrative suited the new Obama administration, too. But although Washington and Moscow were pleased with the state of affairs, it sowed the seeds of mutual frustration. Moscow supported Obama's idea primarily because it bought it time to solve its own problems, not to help Obama solve his. It quickly became clear that each side had its own understanding of what a "reset" entailed.

For Washington, Russia was still just another tool for addressing its geopolitical challenges, first of all Iran and Afghanistan. As Thomas Graham has been patiently explaining to a Russian audience, Moscow should have no illusions about the place that Russia holds on the agenda of the new American administration. "For the administration, rebuilding relations with Russia is not an end in and of itself; it is a means to making progress on the United States' priority interests, notably and most immediately on Afghanistan/Pakistan, Iran, and the Middle East peace process," he said.[1] Evidently, the Americans had hoped that giving up perpetual irritants like Bush's plan for missile defense in Poland and the Czech Republic and renewing the security dialogue would at least neutralize the Kremlin's recent assertiveness, if not make it a partner.

For Russian elites, on the contrary, America was their priority, the shaper of their worldview and the chief danger to their efforts to carve out a dominant place for Russia in the world. The "reset policy" was an opportunity to wind down political confrontations and give Washington a chance to legitimize the Putin-Medvedev assertive foreign policy formula. Moscow saw the very idea of "reset" as both an indulgence for Obama and a license for Russia to continue its macho policies. Did Washington realize that?

Nevertheless, three asymmetries remained that would lay the foundations for Washington and Moscow's mutual disillusionment: an asymmetry of resources, an asymmetry of perception, and an asymmetry of values. The coming meltdown was only a matter of degree and timing.

Russian liberals thus held no special hopes for the "reset." They didn't believe the Obama administration would speak to the Kremlin in the language of values. Such talk would have brought to a quick end any hopes of cooperation on security issues, a priority for Obama.

Andrei Illarionov, a former Putin advisor, was the first to give voice to the doubts that Russia's liberals had about the "reset":

> The start of the Obama presidency resembles to an amazing degree the start of the previous two administrations [Clinton and Bush]. We can see the analogous desire to improve bilateral relations, the same positive statements, the same promising gestures and visits. But since the political regimes in the two countries have not changed, we can assume that the entire cycle of their relations will be repeated: first large expectations, then deep disillusionment, and then, serious failure.

Illarionov was right. The problem in the relationship between Russia and the United States was not about foreign policy. It was about the systemic roots of the two countries' foreign policies—that is, the way in which America and Russia organized themselves. If Obama planned to offer to cooperate only on areas of "common interest," leaving aside values, he should have been prepared to find, as Bush eventually had, that Moscow had a different understanding of what their "common interests" really were. If, however, Obama had begun his entreaties to Moscow on the basis of values, then his efforts at dialogue with Russia would have been even less successful, at least in the near term. It wasn't clear how Obama could escape this trap.

Pragmatic Russian experts close to the Kremlin unanimously warned the Obama administration that it must make concessions or the "reset" wouldn't happen. Fyodor Lukyanov wrote, "Moscow does not feel that it needs to make any drastic changes to its position." Vyacheslav Nikonov was more direct: "The Russian elites ... expect concessions from America."[2]

As for Washington, the White House had never explained exactly what it would "reset" its relations to. Since the realists dominated discussion in the West in the spring of 2009, Moscow simply assumed that they had convinced the Obama administration of their views. "The Americans have understood their mistakes and are changing!" Kremlin-associated commentators proclaimed gleefully.

But the realists' rhetorical dominance was beginning to induce a response from America's liberal flank. Strobe Talbott called on the new administration to look for ways to integrate Russia into Western institutions, which would then be used to influence domestic processes in Russia. Western leaders "should focus on engaging Russia in multilateral agreements and structures that involve norms to which it must adapt if it is to be a leading player in a consensual, rule-based international order," Talbott wrote.[3] Up until that point, the West, having neither the strength nor the will to re-educate the Russian elite, had been integrating Russia into its organizations and institutions without demanding that it abide by their principles. Talbott proposed to correct this.

Other representatives of the American expert community, worried by the administration's silence on values, began to speak out as well. Thomas Carothers noted that Hillary Clinton had left out the word "democracy" from her list of America's priorities in her first speeches as Secretary of State. "President Obama and his team in the State Department should not follow the course of Realpolitk," he warned. "Despite the problems of recent years, the United States must remain a force that supports the development of democracy."[4] David Kramer wrote, "When he travels to Moscow next month, Obama should send a strong signal of support for Russia's democratic development by spending time with civil society activists and human rights defenders."[5]

In June 2009, on the eve of Obama's visit to Moscow, several conservative Republican senators sent the president a letter calling on him not to forget values. "As you attempt to set a new tone with the Russians, we believe there are issues of common interest, but we also believe it is crucial that you vigorously defend the values that have been the cornerstone of free markets and free societies," wrote Jim DeMint of South Carolina, Roger Wicker of Mississippi, and Jon Kyl of Arizona. "As you know, the interests of the Russian people and the Russian elites are not always the same."

However, many observers in Europe were convinced that such entreaties would fall on deaf ears, and that the new administration already adopted a Realpolitik approach. Andrew Wood cautioned: "Value-free Realpolitik is an illusion.... There is a limit to what can be achieved, and a limit to what Moscow can offer by way of effective help in dealing with extra-European problems." The Lithuanian minister of foreign affairs, Vygaudas Usackas, told an American audience in March 2009 of the concerns shared by many in Eastern Europe. "Dialogue [with Russia] must be a tool of strategy and not a substitute for it. We ... should engage with Russia where we can, while understanding that such engagement must be carefully graduated and met by a matching engagement by Moscow."[6] Usackas called on the United States to form "a common policy of engagement and influence" that would simultaneously draw new independent states, primarily Ukraine, Moldova, Belarus, and Georgia, into the Western orbit.

In the end these voices did not prevail. The chief proposals coming from America's "Russia hands" were clearly Realpolitik in spirit. It was an understandable choice: They realized that upending the whole apple cart to create an entirely new paradigm for relations with Russia would have required all of President Obama's attention. But the president needed to concentrate on halting the economic catastrophe. A prudent limit on America's global obligations was the obvious option. And besides this, for a new president who had little hands-on experience with foreign policy, Realpolitik was the least complicated tool in America's foreign policy shed. Right before the July 2009 U.S.–Russia summit in Moscow, I wrote: "Obama might try to pull off something that no other US president has succeeded in doing: reaching an agreement with the Kremlin on issues of common interest and at the same time offering a different world view to Russian society."[7] I have to admit that I doubted that Obama would attempt the latter. A new conceptual approach to Russia would have required great exertions in the service of uncertain prospects in the far-off future, perhaps even beyond Obama's time in office. It is a rare public official who takes short-term risks for payoffs that will only come after the next election.

Just before Obama's visit, Brzezinski published an article urging that Obama

... should have three central goals in mind when he meets Medvedev and Putin this week: first, to advance US-Russian co-operation in areas where our interests coincide; second, to emphasise the mutual benefits in handling disagreements between the two countries within internationally respected "rules of the game"; and the third, to help shape a geopolitical context in which Russia becomes increasingly conscious of its own interest in eventually becoming a genuinely post-imperial partner of the Euro-Atlantic Alliance community.[8]

It is unclear whether Obama would take up Brzezinski's call for a new paradigm for relations with Russia, much less whether he could succeed if he did so.

Notes

1. Thomas Graham, "U.S.-Russian Relations: The Challenge of Starting Over," March 11, 2009 http://www.america-russia.net/eng/security/207264932?user_session=5c49a5e3d36546dc8c; Russian version available at http://www.expert.ru/printissues/expert/2009/09/vozmozhnost_nachat_snachala.

2. Vyacheslav Nikonov, "Partial Reset," *Izvestia*, May 19, 2009.

3. Strobe Talbott, "A Russian 'Reset Button' Based on Inclusion," *Financial Times*, February 23, 2009.

4. Thomas Carothers, "Democracy Promotion under Obama: Finding a Way Forward," Carnegie Endowment Policy Brief no. 77, February 2009, http://www.carnegieendowment.org/files/democracy_promotion_obama.pdf.

5. David J. Kramer, "The Russia Challenge: Prospects for U.S.-Russian Relations," German Marshall Fund of the United States Policy Brief, June 9, 2009, http://www.gmfus.org/template/download.cfm?document=/doc/Kramer_Russia_Final2.pdf, pp. 3–4.

6. Vygaudas Usackas, "The West, Russia, and Eastern Europe: New Challenges, New Opportunities," speech at the Johns Hopkins University, March 10, 2009, www.sais-jhu.edu/news-and-events/pdf/vygaudasusackas031009.pdf.

7. Lilia Shevtsova, "A Possible Trap Awaits Obama in Moscow," *Moscow Times*, June 22, 2009.

8. Zbigniew Brzezinski, "Russia Must Re-Focus With Post-Imperial Eyes," *Financial Times*, July 1, 2009.

51 WHAT DO WE MEAN BY THE "RIGHT DIRECTION" FOR U.S. POLICY TOWARD RUSSIA?

I have to give the American "realists" their due. They not only managed to formulate their ideas and organize professional discussions, they set to work winning political support for their ideas in both Washington and Moscow. (The "values" camp certainly can't boast of having taken similar initiative.) Brigades of politicians and experts with proposals to improve relations descended on Moscow for the summit in the spring of 2009. Former senators Gary Hart and Chuck Hagel parachuted in with their own entourage, followed by yet another group of heavyweights, including former secretaries of state Henry Kissinger and George Shultz, former secretary of defense William Perry, former secretary of the treasury Richard Rubin, and former senator Sam Nunn. Former secretary of state James Baker crashed the party as well.

These American "realists" offered the new Obama administration a number of reports that had many constructive suggestions—at least, they would be constructive if the United States and Russia could ever resolve the fundamental incompatibility of their political systems. Barring such a resolution, the "realists'" proposals could have serious and detrimental unforeseen consequences.

Russian liberals were concerned by most of what they saw in the "realists'" proposals. After going over the most popular reports, Lev Gudkov from the Levada Center, Igor Klyamkin from the Liberal Mission Foundation, Georgy Satarov of the Indem Foundation, and I decided to write a response to them. We presented our thoughts in an article, "False Choices for Russia," that was published in the *Washington Post* on June 9, 2009. I believe that the "realists'" arguments, as well as our responses to them, are still relevant today. (Indeed, I believe they will be relevant for a long time to come, since neither side has come up with new ones.) Our debate also remains interesting because it culminated in a scandal.

My co-authors and I decided to react to the reports largely because we noticed that they all had one factor in common: They maintained that the worsening of Russian-American relations was caused mainly by Washington's insistence under Bush on "tying policies to values," while ignoring and humiliating Russia through unilateralist actions. As a result, the authors argued, America needed to reject the values-based approach to Russia and build a new relationship based on "common interests and common threats."[1]

This approach worried us. In our opinion, the authors had sorely misread recent history. The Bush administration had in reality ignored the problems of democracy and civil society in Russia. There was no evidence at all that Bush had ever expressed his concern to Putin that Russia was headed down an authoritarian path. The "realist" authors were thus advocating for a policy that had already exhausted itself.

The authors emphasized that "[w]e must significantly improve our understanding of Russian interests as Russians themselves define them." We couldn't disagree with that statement in the abstract, but it depends on how one understands "Russian interests." One of the authors said that Russian interests were being "a great power," "maintaining itself as the dominant influence in the former-Soviet space" and "constraining the United States." He then went on to argue that "[n]othing in Russia's understanding of its interests precludes close cooperation with the United States on a wide range of issues critical to American security and prosperity."[2] This begs the question: How can we build a Russian-American relationship based on "common interests" if Russia's leaders see fighting NATO expansion and American influence in the former Soviet space as two of their primary interests? How can you cooperate with a country that sees "constraining the United States" as one of its chief foreign policy goals? We doubt that Washington is amenable to building a relationship on these bases. Thus the attempt to apply Realpolitik to Russian-American relations falls into a paradox bordering on meaninglessness. It was inevitable that the "realists'" recommendations would do so, because they accepted the Kremlin interpretation of Russia's national interests.

My co-authors and I, on the other hand, maintained that Russian society sees its national interests in somewhat different terms. We tried to persuade our American audience that Russians are interested in making their country more open to the outside world and creating the conditions for a more effective economy. They want to limit governmental abuse and corruption and create an independent judiciary. Russians are not interested in confrontation with the West. Nor are the business and cultural elites in Russia; they understand that the Kremlin's authoritarian path leads to a dead end. So the Russian public and America really do share common interests, but building relations based on those common interests depends on finding ways of influencing the Russian elite to stop making America out to be Russia's enemy. That in turn requires America and the West as a whole to take a values-based approach to Russia. My co-authors and I suggested, therefore, that we must tie foreign policy to Russia's domestic development, not untie it.

In response, the American authors might have admitted that they were in fact basing their arguments on the Kremlin's interests because, realistically, America should interact with the Russian regime, not the Russian society. But since they insisted that they were basing their argument on Russia's interests, we were obliged to explain that they were mistaken.

The American "realists" further recommended that Obama respect "Russian sovereignty, history and traditions and [recognize] that Russian society will evolve at its own pace." Respecting Russia's "traditions" means only one thing in practice: the perpetuation of personalized power. We were also obliged to explain this fact to our opponents, because they seemed unaware that this was a typical Kremlin talking point.

The American experts also wrote that America should "establish a government-to-government dialogue on Russia's neighborhood, with a view to developing confidence-building measures." To clarify, this quote refers to a bilateral Russian-American dialogue on the fate of Russia's neighbors and, evidently, on the ways in which America and Russia might be allowed to influence this region. We suggested that this smacked of an attempt to return to the days of Yalta, a proposal that could hardly be expected to engender warm feelings among the newly independent states. This kind of retrograde, backroom deal-making, furthermore, would only reinforce the imperialist tendencies within the Russian elite.

We couldn't accept the Americans' next argument, either: "Ukraine occupies a special place in Russian thought: it is the cradle of Russian civilization and an essential element of Russia's own national identity." Similarly questionable was their proposal to "Finlandize" Ukraine. What a strange idea. The concept of "Finlandization" (imposed international neutrality) arose in the midst of a standoff between two inimical military blocs, NATO and the Warsaw Pact. But if we were to return to the past, and NATO were once again to face off against the Organization for Collective Security or the Shanghai Cooperation Organisation, then how could we talk about cooperation between America and Russia? The "Finlandization" of Ukraine would mean indefinitely condemning the country to its current status quo: bereft of stable institutions and torn apart by political conflict.

In stressing the importance of a values-based approach, we were emphatically not calling for a return to the policy of "democracy promotion," a policy that we felt had been harmful in its previous form. But we did call on our American colleagues to consider Russian domestic policy when thinking about foreign policy. We didn't try to persuade them that the West must help Russia in its reforms; we did call on them not to create obstacles to reform by aiding and abetting the Russian traditionalists. Here is what we wrote:

> If the Obama administration follows the suggestions of "realists," rather than improving relations with Moscow its efforts will lead to more mutual disappointment at best.... We believe Russia dearly needs to expand all sorts of ties with the U.S. and the West, but such cooperation must not come at the price of US refusal to understand what is happening in Russia, or allowing Washington to ignore the fundamental nature of the Russian political system and to "repackage" old concepts of tactical maneuvering as a new foreign policy strategy.

I have a few additional comments to add to this joint declaration. I understand Americans' desire to find "common interests" and bypass the realities dividing Russia and America. Senator John Kerry expressed this desire, saying that "our attempts at more constructive relations [with Russia] will fail if we condition them on resolving our differences first." But Senator Kerry and others who deeply desire a breakthrough in U.S.–Russian relations must be aware of the fact that relations based on "common interests" between the two countries have never been forged in the past. One therefore has to discover the previously unknown preconditions for that breakthrough, a dubious prospect at best.

A neutral observer might have noticed by now that American proposals for a Russian breakthrough all seem to be based on a belief in the power of personal relationships. "The new leaders just have to take that first step, and the rest will follow," they say. Why is it that a people brought up in an institutional milieu always begin with the personal when thinking about relations with Russia? One might be expected to get "personal" in Russia, where politics are built on an autocratic plane. But there's certainly no need for the United States to do so.

Regardless, such a strategy will never achieve the much-sought-after breakthrough. The regime in Moscow can accept playing at parity, defining spheres of influence, and trading concessions. And it can go for dialogue and compromise, but the compromises arrived at will inevitably be temporary and ambiguous, because Russian personalized power simply isn't interested in making life easier for American presidents. Indeed it has an interest in creating new difficulties in order to then swoop in and help to overcome them. Thus, the American authors' delicately crafted efforts to achieve a foreign policy breakthrough would crumble at their first contact with reality.

Nevertheless, the American "realists" appeared to understand exactly what kind of political regime they were dealing with. One of the authors of the report who received the widest hearing, Nixon Center Director Dimitri Simes, described the situation in Russia thus:

> We can't say anything positive about what is happening in Russia. And all because many of the things we saw in Russia [...] how to put it, at least smelled bad to me.... It's perfectly clear that today's Russia is not a democracy in our understanding.[3]

If that's so, then how did our American colleagues hope to manage successful cooperation with such a partner?

I think the most amusing proposal came from an esteemed Russia expert in Washington, who said that "we might have something to learn from the Russian experience, something that would encourage more active Russian participation." Such has always been the dream of Russian politicians, for Americans to borrow from the Russian experience. "I'd love for our American colleague to tell us what useful element he's found in Russian political practice," I thought to myself back then.

I'm not being sarcastic. As I am critical of Russian political thought and practice, including the dreams of Russian liberals, I believe that the American authors would feel insulted if they were held to a lower standard than the Russians. That is why we had to ask them uncomfortable questions. And the more we studied the arguments of the "realists," the more questions arose.

I have one parting comment on the East-West exchange inspired by the Hart-Hagel Commission's report. Russian pro-Kremlin experts actively supported the ideas of the American "realists." Andranik Migranyan, a leading pro-Kremlin commentator, wrote, "The United States will really have to change its foreign policy paradigm, which will require new approaches in the carrying out of foreign policy. In this respect, the ideas expressed in a report drafted by the Nixon Center seem fruitful."[4] Such an endorsement can mean only one thing: Their efforts suited the interests of the Russian regime. How else to explain their warm reception by the Russian leadership?

Notes

1. "The Right Direction for U.S. Policy Toward Russia," Commission on U.S. Policy Toward Russia (Chuck Hagel and Gary Hart, co-chairs; Dimitri Simes, director).

2. Thomas Graham, "Resurgent Russia and U.S. Purposes," Century Foundation Report, http://www.tcf.org/list.asp?type=PB&pubid=699.

3. Transcript: "U.S. Policy Toward Russia," Council on Foreign Relations, April 8, 2009, http://www.cfr.org/publication/19078/us_policy_toward_russia.html.

4. Andranik Migranyan, "Amerika ishchet novych soyuznikov" [America Is in Search of New Allies], *Izvestia*, May 12, 2009.

52 HOW WE WERE TAUGHT A LESSON

But what about the "scandal" I hinted at earlier? I'm glad you asked. This chapter would not exist if my liberal colleagues and I had not written that July 2009 *Washington Post* piece in the interest of starting a discussion. Unfortunately, rather than a discussion, we got a sucker punch. Let me give you a few examples of the responses our piece provoked. From Anatol Lieven, senior editor at the *National Interest* (a journal published by the Nixon Center):

- "Their criticism serves as a mouthpiece for the agendas of the most bitterly anti-Russian and geopolitically aggressive liberal interventionists and neocons who help maintain tensions between Russia and the West—and actually between the United States and the rest of the world";

- "By this approach, foreign liberal informants [*sic*] like the Russians who authored these editorials have contributed to a deep flaw in Western journalism, reflecting in turn a tragic flaw in humanity itself: namely an extreme difficulty in empathizing with those whose background, culture, experience and interests differ from your own";

- "Shevtsova and her colleagues should take a close look at this repulsive but insightful strategy and ask themselves whether they really understand the country, and the world, that they are living in."

What makes the outrage expressed in the above quotes so odd is that Lieven has had equally harsh words for the "realists":

This view of the world both tends to direct attention away from the study of societies and can act as a cover for extreme nationalism.... It is rather a comfortable doctrine for the security elite and its intellectual employees and allies, suggesting that great cultural and linguistic knowledge is not really necessary.... This belief helps demolish any capacity to put the behavior of one's own country in a wider moral perspective and encourage some of those same solipsistic weaknesses in contemporary American study of the outside world...."[1]

Too bad my colleagues and I didn't use this quote to bolster our article's case against the "realists." Then again, I find it hard to explain why Lieven was in such a hurry to defend those he had until very recently found so repugnant. In light of his confusion, perhaps it's best that we don't use his quote after all.

Dimitri Simes, coordinator of the report we criticized most severely, structured his responses to our argument more carefully, but his argument was of the same character:

- "Someone is coordinating this campaign";

- "We know that such campaigns in the past involved people tied to Mr. Berezovsky and the Yukos lobbyists, who have become very active";

- "This resembles an attempt to interfere with the Obama administration taking truly new steps in relations with Russia";

- "True liberals should not sound like petty demons from the Russian underground.... Only clean methods should be used."[2]

These statements were made in an interview Simes gave to the Russian press. Simes, who knows Russia well, had to know that connecting someone to "Mr. Berezovsky and the Yukos lobbyists," official enemies of the Russian security services, was tantamount to a political denunciation in Russia, an invitation for the Russian regime to "look into the matter." Wasn't he aware of how the regime treats people it doesn't like? This is hardly a noble method in academic discourse.

Of course, my co-authors and I are grateful to Mr. Simes for openly expressing the "realists'" favorite talking point: that "serious people" in America "are proposing building relations with Russia on a pragmatic basis like the relations between the US and Saudi Arabia and North Korea and those with Pakistan for many years." This argument once more demonstrates the lack of logic in "realist" policy toward Russia. If Russia is a country like China, Saudi Arabia, and Pakistan, then on what basis is it also a member of the G8 and the Council of Europe, clubs supposedly limited to countries that adhere to democratic principles? If we follow Simes's logic, then Russia ought to be expelled from all such democratic clubs. And in that case, the policy of "realism" toward Russia would be understandable. But if Russia wishes to retain its membership card, then it has to subject itself willingly to values-based criteria, and the logic of "realism" does not apply.

Finally, Alexei Pushkov entered the fray. Pushkov is closely aligned with the Nixon Center, an anchor of a Russian television program, and a professional anti-American. Let's look at a selection of his arguments:

- "Coordinated publications in the Western media by this group of people smack of a well-orchestrated theatre production";

- "An active group of opponents of the 'resetting' of relations who hold Russian passports have declared war on people in the USA who support the idea of 'resetting'... The fact that someone is standing behind them is obvious.... The efforts are being coordinated and directed probably from the same center."

This campaign was taken up by other Kremlin propagandists along the lines of this sample statement:

Behind the black PR spread in advance of the meeting between Medvedev and Obama are influential neoconservatives, unhappy with the turn coming in relations between the US and Russia. One of the proponents of the "old course" capable of orchestrating events most frequently mentioned is Dick Cheney.

I'll stop the quotations here rather than weary my readers with further examples of such Soviet-style propaganda.

I think our American opponents made a tactical error by bringing in such blatant Russian anti-Westerners and anti-Americans to carry water for their point of view. For example, isn't it strange to see Pushkov, whose duties include weekly televised attacks on America as Russia's main enemy, suddenly worrying about improving relations? It's as if the entire Russian media started attacking us in response to a single wave from some unseen conductor's baton. Without direct orders from the Kremlin, these things do not happen in Russia. Isn't it strange that the Russian propaganda corps, usually very busy with anti-American attacks, would suddenly and unanimously come down on us for daring to criticize (and very mildly at that) the reports of American authors?[3]

We were actually even more shocked by another happenstance. Everyone is familiar with the crude nature of Soviet-style of polemics, wherein one employs personal attacks and accusations of selling out in lieu of genuine arguments. But we had never seen Western opponents resorting to such Soviet methods before. Their basic argument boiled down to "They're on the take!" How were we supposed to prove that neither Cheney, nor Berezovsky, nor anyone else had hired us to undermine Russian-American relations? And if we were such "petty demons," then why waste so much energy and emotion on us? I imagine that the authors of the reports we criticized must have felt at least some discomfort to be defended in this manner.

The Russian philosopher Grigory Pomeranz used to say, "The style of the polemic is more important that its subject." In our case, the style of our opponents' polemic told us a great deal. It said that the Soviet style of denouncing one's enemies is alive and well—and not only in Russia.

I've drawn your attention to this episode because I think it shows two things. First, the reports' authors unfortunately could not come up with convincing answers to our questions, answers that might have allowed us to revise and reconsider the faults in our own arguments. Second, our op-ed received thousands of responses, which in itself shows that we touched on a problem that merits serious discussion.

One might ask if there weren't any serious questions at all in the objections of our opponents. There were indeed two that merit a response. The first, to paraphrase, asked how we could accuse such respected authors, including U.S. ambassadors to Russia, former congressmen and senators, of arriving at conclusions "borrowed from Moscow's official line"? The second question, again to paraphrase, was, "What do Russian liberals think the United States should be doing differently?" I'll answer both questions.

First, the advice to President Obama to respect "Russian tradition" and its "special path of development" (namely, autocracy) was borrowed (I hope unintentionally) from Russia's official line, amply reflected in numerous statements by its representatives. Consult the works of Foreign Minister Sergei Lavrov, for example, to see what we had in mind. There have been many other iterations of the Kremlin's official position as well, but listing them may make the reports' authors uncomfortable, so I will spare them. The esteemed senators and other authors probably did not know exactly what kind of ideas they were repeating, but at least someone among those responsible for drafting them should have known. If they didn't then that fact only highlights the need to study the Russian domestic political context more carefully in order to avoid such awkwardness in the future.

As to what advice Russian liberals at that time would give Obama: First, tell your analysts to figure out how Realpolitik toward Russia ended up producing a crisis in relations between Washington and Moscow. Only then can we talk about concrete forms of new cooperation between America and Russia.

The concept of "realism" regarding Russia and America was unlikely to have gotten a new push as a result of being defended the way it was. But at least, the one positive was that our opponents have focused attention on the problem of Russian-American relations and the need to discuss them, publicly.

In conclusion, I'd like to note an interesting fact. Soon after our debate, our opponents from the "realist" camp appeared in fact to be learning something. It would be vanity to assume that we (meaning Russian and Western critics of "realism") had influenced them. Nevertheless, some of our opponents have stopped using the arguments they had used to attack us and are instead now using ours. Consider as evidence Dimitri Simes's July 2009 article in *Foreign Affairs*: Instead of invoking the usual mantra about "common interests and challenges," he says that "U.S. and Russian interests are not identical" and "Moscow's priorities are different from Washington's."[4] On the other hand, perhaps he's fallen in with the big anti-Russian plot.

Notes

1. Anatol Lieven, *America Right or Wrong: An Anatomy of American Nationalism* (Oxford: Oxford University Press, 2004), p. 159.

2. Andrei Terechov, "Kreml' zaverboval Kissindzhera," *Nezavisimaya Gazeta*, June 16, 2009.

3. Andrei Piontkovsky and Dmitry Sidorov suggested their answers to these questions. See: Andrei Piontkovsky, "Dai Trillion" [Give Me a Trillion], http://www.grani.ru/Politics/World/US/RF/m.150448.html; Dmitry Sidorov, "Why the Rush to Engage Russia? Washington Needs a 'Timeout,' Not a 'Reset' of Relations," http://www.forbes.com/2009/ 03/31/russia-obama-iran-james-baker-opinions-contributors-kissinger.html.

4. Dimitri Simes, "An Uncertain Reset. Can the United States and Russia Find a Common Language?" *Foreign Affairs*, July 17, 2009, http://www.foreignaffairs.com/articles/65203/dimitri-k-simes/an-uncertain-reset.

53 OBAMA IN MOSCOW AND THE AFTERMATH

Considering Obama's visit to Moscow in July 2009 and the events that followed, there is little need to delve into his intentions. I'll simply focus on the impression he made on Russians. Sometimes it is important to remember how certain processes began in order to understand how they ended.

The *Economist* was on target with this simple assessment: "A meeting of pragmatism, not warmth—with potential trouble still ahead."[1] In the U.S.–Russian negotiations on hard security issues, the sides achieved as much compromise as was possible given the gulf between their views and the previous crisis in relations. By signing a conceptual framework for nuclear nonproliferation through the START follow-on treaty, as well as an agreement on transit through Russian territory for American cargo bound for Afghanistan, Moscow and Washington demonstrated a genuine interest in smoothing over their previous adversarial relations.

But perhaps much more significant was Obama's attempt to develop a new foreign policy approach. Bucking the skeptics, Obama attempted to tie engagement to addressing society while avoiding tension with the Kremlin. He was the first Western leader to speak to Russian society over the heads of the elite, meeting representatives of the younger generation, business, NGOs, and the opposition. He met with former Soviet leader Mikhail Gorbachev, who remains a symbol of change to the world but for whom there is no place on the Russian scene. Speaking to an audience numbering in the thousands in Moscow, Obama challenged the stereotypes Russian authorities sought to plant in people's minds. He disputed the contention that the United States wanted to weaken Russia: "America wants a strong, peaceful, and prosperous Russia." Regarding the Kremlin's ideas of power and politics, he said: "In 2009, a great power does not show strength by dominating or demonizing other countries." He avoided lecturing Russians about democracy. He spoke of the principles that allowed him, "a person of African ancestry," to appear before them as the president of a global superpower.[2]

Obama found the right words and the right tone. Many Russians came to see him out of curiosity, or just to see and be seen. Many in the crowd were neither romantics nor idealists, and it's not likely that most of them were free from anti-American complexes. But their expressions showed that they were impressed by Obama. Seated next to me were a Russian businessman and the director of a leading Russian theater who summed up their feelings for me: "This is a leader who thinks in new categories. Compared to him, we are people of the last generation. But our young people must understand him!" I shared their feelings. It suddenly occurred to us that Obama might become the embodiment of hope for the new in world politics.

Obama had stopped playing the traditional game. He refused to personalize U.S. relations with Russia's leaders. He was polite but aloof. He seemed to reject the policy of give and take, as in "We'll give you your 'spheres of privileged interests' if you give us help in Afghanistan." He said obliquely in an Associated Press interview that Mr. Putin "had one foot in the old ways of doing business and one foot in the new." This was a violation of the usual rules of diplomacy, but Russian observers thought it was Obama's way of showing that he had no illusions about the Russian regime. This American president was tough on the Russian national leader. He spoke with uncommon frankness, and his very style and rhetoric positioned him as a threat for leaders who still yearned for the old ways of doing things.

This, at any rate, was what the Russian liberals felt that summer in Moscow. Perhaps we were caught up in Obama mania, charmed by the stark contrast between the American president and the dreary crop of world leaders, particularly in Russia. Enchantment, like hope, is often merely delayed disappointment, but the fault is less in the object of hope as it is in those whose hopes outstrip reality. But I decided to keep a record of these feelings nonetheless in order to give you a sense of the mood among intellectuals and liberals in Moscow in July 2009.

For Obama to continue successfully in this Moscow vein required work, political will, and consistency. "Change is hard," he said, referring then to Russia's movement into a new future. The same could be said about changing the West's paradigm with regard to Russia. Both sides surely were tempted to return to the old pattern of trade-offs, anticipating tangible results (although the expected results would differ greatly). At least among the official Moscow establishment there were no illusions that "resetting" relations would work only if Washington accepted the Kremlin's terms.

It was soon apparent that the Obama administration hadn't managed to turn his welcome change of tone and attempt to appeal to ordinary Russians into a concrete new policy. Did they think about substantive changes, or only try to find what is doable? The United States reverted to the traditional formula, rejecting anything that irked the Kremlin and looking for common ground with Moscow on hard security issues. This seemed to be a version, though quite fuzzy, of tried-and-true Realpolitik, and at that time one could even maintain the impression that it worked. Washington and Moscow began clearing the "rubbish" left from the last diplomatic stage. They started post-START negotiations, with a crucial role played by former Carnegie Moscow Center director Rose Gottemoeller, the head of the American delegation. Moscow and Washington began to discuss cooperation on missile defense. There was even hope that both sides could come closer in their positions on Iran. Some American officials enthusiastically concluded that the two sides had completed the "reset" stage and had moved on to a level in which "common interests and cooperation" would prevail.

Washington, however, seemed not to want to return to pure "realism" and be accused of ignoring the value aspect. Members of the Obama administration continued to meet with Russian human rights activists and moderate opposition leaders, sending the clear message that America remains concerned by Russia's internal processes. But the meetings did little beyond encouraging Russia's beleaguered advocates for civil society. The Kremlin stopped paying attention to what it viewed as symbolic and unthreatening gestures. The two-track model the Americans were seeking—talking directly with civil society about democracy and human rights and talking with the regime about pragmatic interests—could not work. The crucial conversations about democracy needed to be held with the Russian authorities. But the Obama administration apparently felt that it could not afford to irritate the Kremlin.

Both sides found a way out of this tricky situation by including questions about values in the agenda of a Civil Society Working Group within the framework of the Obama-Medvedev Bilateral Commission. The U.S. co-chair of the working group is Michael McFaul, special assistant to President Obama and senior director of Russian and Eurasian Affairs at the

National Security Council. Before joining the administration McFaul had spent years promoting the values approach to politics. The Kremlin appointed Deputy Head of the Administration Vladislav Surkov as co-chair for the Russian side. Surkov was one of the gravediggers of political pluralism in Russia and the creator of Russia's imitation "democracy." His appointment was evidence of Russian leaders' cynical sense of humor. Who better to discuss democracy in Russia than the man who figured out how to fake it? The emergence of this new tandem demonstrates the difficulty the U.S. side experiences in pursuing an approach that attempts to be both "pragmatic" and values-based. An emphasis on the pragmatic side can easily come at the expense of values. And the Kremlin will always win playing rugby without principles.

The Russian human rights community didn't appreciate the Kremlin's sense of humor and appealed to Medvedev to reconsider his decision. Medvedev didn't deign to respond, and in December 2009, 71 American congressmen sent President Obama a letter demanding that the United States not partake of the joint working group until the Kremlin replaced Surkov. This appeal also had no effect, but we shouldn't be surprised by this. How could the White House demand Surkov's replacement after it had already agreed to deal with him?

Surkov's appointment meant that the Russian side wasn't concealing their intentions for the working group. The Kremlin wasn't about to allow any serious discussion of values or criticism of the Russian system or policy. The Russians were offering to put on a show, and they were inviting America to take part in it and legitimize it. And the United States did decide to take part, with obvious moral and political ramifications not only for the U.S.–Russian relationship, but also for the American claims of being a "normative power." No serious discussion of values would be allowed to spoil the benefits that the "reset" was meant to secure for Washington's priorities. It was an open question, however, whether the "reset" could work even in this seemingly favorable environment.

The U.S.–Russian dialogue on civil society would turn on more than just personality. The agenda was another matter. Three topics were discussed at the first meeting of the working group in Washington in January 2010. The Russian side proposed to exchange views on corruption and crimes against children, and the Americans proposed negative stereotypes and myths in bilateral relations. These are important topics, as are many others. But how could any agenda be addressed constructively when the Kremlin had erased all mechanisms ensuring the survival of civil society in Russia? Would a discussion on corruption be constructive if the working group wasn't allowed to explore the roots of corruption in Russia's system of personalized power?

Discussing their first meeting with the American side with *Izvestia*, Vladislav Surkov said, "Whenever possible, we strove to avoid questions on which it was doubtful that we will be able to agree for now." In an interview after the meeting with Radio Free Europe/Radio Liberty, Michael McFaul conceded, saying, "There was more agreement than disagreement." This was a worrisome development. How could two sides agree on any issue with respect to civil society when their countries have diametrically opposed approaches to it? What did it mean if the two sides agreed on, say, the importance of a free media or anti-corruption efforts? Did that mean that the Russian side would guarantee freedom for the media and rule of law? Given that the two sides reported coming to agreement more often than disagreement, I don't see how they could have even raised these questions, which meant that both sides were doing everything in their power to avoid irritating one another.

The next meeting of the Civil Society Working Group, held in May 2010 in Vladimir, discussed migration and prison conditions in both countries. "Now we need to work on our general approach: swapping experiences and promoting cooperation between Russian and U.S. NGOs," Surkov said, explaining the Working Group's agenda. But what experiences could representatives of such radically different systems possibly "swap"? What could Americans learn from how Russians run their prisons, or from how they deal with migration?

Russian liberals maintained a deeply skeptical view of this mechanism of interaction. As one of them wrote,

> Retaining Obama's pre-election stylistics, the meeting in Washington should have been held under the slogan, "We can not." This slogan could have become the symbol of the mythical "reset" in Russian-American relations, which exists exclusively in the imaginations of popularity-seeking politicians.[3]

The American side on the contrary, claimed to be optimistic. The representatives of the Obama administration had to say what was expected from them; they could not raise doubts about the "reset" even if they had them: "Obama believes in engagement, and he even believes in engagement with the Russian government that leads to disagreement." I agree that it's better to talk and disagree than not to talk at all. The question, however, is "What next?" What will the United States and the West more broadly do when they are forced to admit that they disagree with Russia on matters of substance?

In their talks with the Russian liberals and human rights defenders, U.S. administration officials constantly stressed that they had raised democracy issues in their conversations with the Kremlin, issuing tough statements—both private and public—when rights and freedoms in Russia were undermined. There is no doubt that the "Russia hands" in the Obama administration did their best to ride two horses, coming to agreement with Moscow on arms control, Iran, and Afghanistan while at the same time trying to find ways to demonstrate their concern on the democracy issue. There is also no doubt that Obama's adviser on Russia, Michael McFaul, a man who has devoted his life to studying and promoting democratic ideas, pushed hard to make sure values were an important component of the administration's Russia policy.

Despite all these efforts, by the beginning of 2010 U.S. administration officials themselves had to admit that their preaching (if one can call it preaching) had not changed Russian political practice (had they really hoped it would?). This failure could mean one of only two things: either nothing could change Russia's current course, or different means of persuasion were required. I've spent much of this book trying to demonstrate that the latter is true. Sure, I understand why Washington behaves as it does; how could they afford to press for Russian reforms when important strategic goals were at stake? All that awaits is for the United States to finally realize that Russia can't truly be cooperative without undergoing a genuine transformation. To be sure, Washington may be content with only limited cooperation, or even the semblance of it, from the Russian side.

Before I explain how the Russian side assessed the "reset," I should talk about how the American expert community saw it during the period from late 2009 through 2010. My impression was that, at least among security experts, there were still high hopes for the "reset" at the beginning. Many of them believed that the new START treaty would create the basis for new cooperation, even partnership. Brent Scowcroft, hardly one who could be accused of excessive idealism, said, "A new arms reduction agreement will give substance to the 'reset' in the U.S.-Russian relationship, and that, in turn, could translate into a more constructive Russian position on Iran in the United Nations Security Council and elsewhere." He even expected that "The U.S. and Russia must lead the world in reducing the risks associated with nuclear weapons."[4]

One could hear the same general thoughts being expressed at a January 25, 2010, event at the Brookings Institution in Washington, D.C., on "Resetting U.S.-Russian Leadership on Nuclear Arms Reduction and Non-Proliferation." According to the event summary, nuclear arms negotiations "create opportunities for the United States and Russia to deepen their bilateral cooperation and jointly take a global leadership role in shaping a safer and more secure world."[5] I admit these words provoked my consternation. How could two states that were built on different principles and still viewed each other through a lens of "mutually assured destruction" form "global leadership" in any area? Then again, perhaps this is mere bias or lack of imagination on my part.

Other experts outside the security community also believed that Obama's approach was working, at least in part. Anders Åslund, for example, said that "U.S.-Russia relations have improved considerably from a very deep nadir. But, it would be strange if they would flourish immediately after the war in Georgia." His criterion for claiming success for Obama's "reset" was that nothing dramatic happened in U.S.–Russian relations since it had begun. Åslund had to admit, however, that though there had been no disasters, there had been no diplomatic breakthrough, either:

> The biggest success was that we did not see any repeat of the Russian war in Georgia last summer. A follow-up agreement on START becomes the next success criterion, and that has so far not materialized. Russia's WTO accession is fundamental for any economic cooperation with the West and it seems far from materializing.

In the "plus" column, Åslund mentioned the fact that "Obama and Medvedev had a good interaction, while Putin has been left like the wolf in the forest." It remained to be seen whether the wolf would go back on the hunt.

Angela Stent's view of the "reset" was more cautious:

> When the Obama administration announced its policy of reset, there was considerable optimism in Washington that U.S.-Russian relations would improve markedly over those of the Bush administration. A year after Obama's inauguration, the results of "reset" are quite modest. There have been a total of three U.S. flights over Russia to Afghanistan; U.S. policymakers detect continuing divisions within the Russian leadership about whether it really wants to con-

clude a post-START agreement. It is not clear who within the Russian leadership has a stake in improved U.S.-Russian relations.... One senses an abiding ambivalence in Russia about whether the elite is willing to modify its view of the United States as the "Key Enemy." It takes two to push the reset button.

Watching the American scene from Moscow, I had the feeling that doubts about the success of the "reset" have been growing. One of the first to openly question the feasibility of Obama's agenda toward Russia was David Kramer. In June 2009 he wrote, "Therein lies the problem—Moscow's unwillingness or inability to reciprocate with its own reset button and its lack of introspection. Barring changes in Russia's behavior and policy, Obama's efforts to reshape relations between Washington and Moscow will face serious, perhaps insurmountable hurdles."[6] By January 2010 developments had forced Kramer to come to an even more certain conclusion: "Until there is real change in Russian behavior and policy, both internally and in its foreign policy, the Obama administration's efforts to reset relations are not likely to be reciprocated."[7]

American pundits' initial enthusiasm for the Obama administration's policy was steadily evaporating. Those who only recently had argued that the discovery of common interests would help restore trust between America and Russia were forced to admit that the road to a relationship built on trust would be a bit bumpier than they thought. Some even began to doubt that such trust was possible. Consider how the views of one expert, Andrew Kuchins, evolved over time. In a March 2009 report Kuchins co-authored with Anders Åslund, "Pressing the 'Reset Button' on U.S.–Russia Relations," he wrote that the "realistic engagement" of the United States and Russia—that is, their "productive and constructive relations"—is possible in spite of the fact that the United States and Russia "have different values." They said that

> Moscow harbors powerful motivations to improve its ties with the United States and the West to both enhance its security and facilitate its economic development. Russian leaders wish to be seen in public on an equal footing with global leaders, especially the US president.[8]

Their belief was widespread not only among the American expert community but also among some pro-Western circles in Russia. But already by the fall of 2009, Kuchins had revised his view. He admitted that

Moscow and Washington simply do not view their interests as fully aligned on the three key issues that drive the Obama administration to improve ties: Iran, Afghanistan and deep cuts in offensive nuclear arms.... Platitudes about shared interests have little relevance if you cannot agree on concrete details and action.

And one can clearly hear the frustration in his conclusion: "Despite the best intentions, Obama's 'reset button' was probably not the best chosen analogy for a policy that in all likelihood will not result in any major break-throughs."[9]

As if to confirm this skepticism, the START follow-on treaty has been delayed numerous times despite assurances from both sides that it would proceed. Achieving this cornerstone of the "reset" was proving more difficult that many had hoped. Both sides were approaching the nuclear security issue from different directions. Obama dreamed of a world without nuclear weapons; Russia's leaders viewed them as the core of their security strategy. "Russia's nuclear doctrine considers the United States its "principal adversary," reminded Ariel Cohen.[10]

Even the representatives of the Realpolitik school had to admit that the "reset" was not as smooth as it should be and did not achieve its goal. Dimitri Simes wrote,

President Obama has presented the new arms control treaty he signed in Prague on April 8 as a "historic accomplishment" in both nuclear security and U.S. relations with Russia. But there are disturbing signs that the Obama Administration is overselling progress with Russia, raising unrealistic hopes that Moscow would genuinely help in addressing the danger from Iran, the most likely nuclear threat to America and its allies.[11]

This is an admission of the fact the realist approach does not work.

Europe's view of the "reset" was even gloomier than America's, despite their still-favorable impressions of President Obama. An *Economist* editorial in January 2010 is representative: "Hitting the reset button on relations with Russia has produced nothing more than a click."[12]

Of course, how one judges the "reset" depends on one's criteria. If the Obama administration intended to limit itself to a minimalist agenda—that is, to simply stop further decline in U.S.–Russian relations—then it had succeeded for the time being. A minimalist agenda could countenance cooperation on the issue of nuclear nonproliferation, an issue on which America and the Soviet Union had worked together effectively. If, however, the architects of the "reset" policy believed that they could build a constructive, predictable, and sustainable partnership with Putin-Medvedev Russia, then they were bound to have their hopes dashed.

Analyzing the results of Obama's foreign policy in 2010, Robert Kagan concluded, "As part of its recalibration of American strategy, the Obama administration has inevitably de-emphasized the importance of democracy in the hierarchy of American interests."[13] From my vantage point in Moscow, the U.S. Russia policy proved his point. Kagan also observed that Obama's realism differed from the usual kind. The difference derived from Obama's hope that, by demonstrating America's good intentions, he could achieve diplomatic breakthroughs. By proving his moral purity and striving for the common good, Obama seemed to believe that his Russian counterparts would be encouraged to imitate him. If this was true, Obama was not a good "soul analyst" and could hardly have avoided being frustrated.

No leader in American history thus far has managed to combine realism with Wilsonianism in a way that produces good results. As I wrote this account in June 2010, developments in U.S.–Russian relations proved that, though he may be an exceptional leader in other regards, Obama had worked no miracles with America's Russia policy, even though many viewed it as a success. Yes, U.S.–Russian relations were thawing. Yet they had been even better in the fall of 2001 and spring of 2002, and that had not kept them from bottoming out.

Notes

1. "Barack, Dmitry—and (offstage) Vladimir: A Meeting of Pragmatism, Not Warmth—With Potential Trouble Still Ahead," *Economist*, July 9, 2009.

2. See "U.S.-Russia Summit Brings Series of Advances," *Washington Post*, July 7, 2009, http://www.washingtonpost.com/wp-dyn/content/article/2009/07/07/AR2009070700264 _2.html?sid=ST2009070601807.

3. Alexander Podrabinek, "Obama and Medvedev Simulate Dialogue," *Yezhenedelny Zhurnal*, January 26, 2010, http://www.ej.ru/?a=note&id=9827.

4. Brent Scowcroft, "U.S., Russia Must Lead on Arms Control," http://www.brookings.edu/opinions/2009/1013_proliferation_talbott.aspx.

5. Uncorrected event transcript: "Resetting U.S.-Russian Leadership on Nuclear Arms Reduction and Non-Proliferation," http://www.brookings.edu/~/media/Files/events/2010/0125_arms_control/20100125_arms_control.pdf.

6. David J. Kramer, "The Russia Challenge: Prospects for U.S.-Russian Relations," German Marshall Fund of the United States Policy Brief, June 9, 2009, http://www.gmfus.org/template/download.cfm?document=/doc/Kramer_Russia_Final2.pdf, p. 2.

7. David J. Kramer, "Resetting U.S.-Russian Relations: It Takes Two," *Washington Quarterly*, January 2010, p. 75.

8. Anders Åslund and Andrew Kuchins, "Pressing the 'Reset Button' on US-Russia Relations," Policy Brief, March 2009, CSIS and Peterson Institute for International Economics, Number PB09-6P.14.

9. Andrew Kuchins, "The Obama Moment," www.iss.europa.eu/nc/actualities/analysisbooks/news/back/article/the-obama-moment. Incidentally, Mikhail Margelov, the chair of the Russian Federation Council for International Relations, also admitted that "both sides have different foreign policy priorities." Mikhail Margelov, "Itogi Goda. Nie slabost' podtolknula CSHA k perezagruzkie" [The Outcomes of the Year. This is Not the Weakness That Pushed the U.S. Toward Reset], January 12, 2010, http://www.ej.ru/?a=note &id=9759.

10. Ariel Cohen, "A Nonstarter on Arms Control," *New York Times*, January 9, 2010.

11. Dimitri Simes, "Is Obama Overselling His Russia Arms Control Deal?" *Times*, April 27, 2010.

12. "Time to Get Tough," *Economist*, January 14, 2010.

13. Robert Kagan, "Obama's Year One: Contra," *World Affairs Journal*, January-February, 2010, http://www.worldaffairesjournal.org/se/util/display_mod.cfm.

54 THE RUSSIAN UNDERSTANDING OF "RESET"

How did the Russian elite understand the "reset"? You can see something of Moscow's attitude in its actions regarding the American military base in Manas, Kyrgyzstan. Even as it had begun to work with the Obama administration, the Kremlin still could not resist the petty gesture. Thus former president of Kyrgyzstan Kurmanbek Bakiev announced in Moscow the decision to close the base at Manas after Moscow promised some $150 million in aid and a $2 bilion loan. One doesn't need to be a Latin expert to know that this fits the definition of *quid pro quo*. But the Manas affair didn't end unhappily for the United States. After cashing the Kremlin's check, Bakiev turned around and convinced the Americans to agree to a higher rent. The base remained open, and Russia was left empty-handed and humiliated. Thus Russia's own satellite states can milk it for aid money with no intention of obeying its orders. The incident also reveals that Moscow isn't exactly eager to help the United States in Afghanistan. After Bakiev was ousted in April 2010, the Russian elite started again to have hopes that the new Kyrgyz authorities would "solve" the problem of Manas.

Nor did the "reset" keep anti-American rhetoric out of official Russian television broadcasts. When former U.S. senator Gary Hart arrived with a delegation from the United States in March 2009, neither he nor his traveling companions expected the on-air ambushes they received from their Russian discussion partners on Channel One. Cameras captured every angle as Hart's face turned several shades of red as he angrily tried to rebut his hosts' assertions that America's intentions were hostile. Given the overwhelming anti-American tone pervading Russian airwaves these days, he was fighting a hopeless battle. Gradually, Moscow anti-American rhetoric has been toned down. But any moment it could be raised to the familiar shrill tone.

Russia unveiled other Cold War-style tactics even as Obama and Medvedev held their early meetings in 2009. Twice in one week in March, fighter jets from Russia's Pacific fleet overflew a group of American ships. In the most serious incident, one swooped to within 500 feet (150 meters) of the aircraft carrier USS *John C. Stennis* and the command ship USS *Blue Ridge* during joint military exercises with South Korea in international waters. Soon after these incidents, Russian nuclear submarines resumed patrols along America's East Coast.

After the Obama-Medvedev summit, having decided apparently that Russia's image in the West had been repaired and the diplomatic deep-freeze sufficiently thawed, the Kremlin turned on a dime and resumed its confrontational tactics. At the July 2009 meeting of the G20 in Italy, Medvedev again threatened that Russia would deploy Iskander missiles in Kaliningrad if the United States didn't give up its plans for anti-ballistic missile defense system deployment. Medvedev then went to South Ossetia with his defense minister, apparently to show the West that Russia's position on Georgia and its "spheres of influence" was unchanged. In case the message still wasn't clear, Putin traveled to Abkhazia to reiterate it. Moscow started to build its military bases in the breakaway republics while the Western capitals pretended to look the other way.

The ruling tandem was showing the West, and America most of all, that "reset" meant accepting the Kremlin's view of order in the former Soviet regions. But the other audience for their message was the Russian public. Medvedev and Putin were reinforcing their public profile by means of militaristic symbols, almost as if they were trying to wipe out any aftertaste of Obama's visit to Moscow and the "reset" itself.

Such actions were just what Russians expected from this Kremlin. In 2009, just 28 percent of Russians surveyed felt that relations with America had improved; 57 percent thought they hadn't budged from their already strained state.[1] The cause was not inherent anti-Americanism, of course; it was the fact that official propaganda persisted in telling Russians that America remained Russia's foe.

The Kremlin wasn't planning to resurrect the Cold War landscape of 2008, however. The ruling tandem continued the "pendulum" tactics pioneered by Putin. During his visit to the United States in the fall of 2009, Medvedev maintained, "We are not separated by values barriers now.... We have practically the same view of issues of world development. We react in the same way to problems of inner life." At another venue, he felt that it was necessary to remind his audience that "NATO is a military bloc and its missiles are pointed in Russia's direction." Apparently no one had briefed Medvedev that the American missiles that could have threatened Russia were destroyed twenty-three years ago, in accordance with the Soviet-American treaty on medium- and short-range missiles.

While Russian and American negotiators continued to rejoice that they were close to reaching a compromise on a treaty on strategic offensive weapons, secretary of the Russian Security Council Nikolai Patrushev was busy announcing a shocking new Russian military doctrine. "We have limited the conditions for using nuclear weapons to fight off aggression ... not only in large-scale but regional and even local wars.... In critical situations, we do not rule out a preventive strike on the aggressor." The novelty of this announcement wasn't that Moscow was asserting the right to use nuclear weapons first in a conflict; Russian military doctrine already allowed that. The real new thing here was that Moscow was reserving a first-strike option in local wars. This was a threat heard loud and clear in the capitals of Georgia and Ukraine. Furthermore, Patrushev had promised that henceforth Russia would use nuclear weapons "depending on the probable intentions of the enemy." That meant the *siloviki* insisted on their right of making their own judgment about a foe's intentions and, therefore, the right to start a nuclear war. And counted among Russia's foes were not just the NATO countries, but certain neighboring states as well. Talk about a cold shower to douse Washington's optimistic expectations! Although it is true that the approved version of the doctrine did not contain any mention of preventive strikes, Patrushev's threat will keep leaders in other countries, especially some Russian neighbors, guessing.

All throughout these events, Russia's commentators had remained openly skeptical about the "reset." The positive diplomatic results achieved thus far had been strictly the "result of the flexibility and concessions by the Russian side," they claimed, promising that the Kremlin would make no more concessions.

Moscow returned to its favorite pastime: demanding compensation from America in exchange for being agreeable. If the Americans had hoped that the Kremlin would respond to their offers of cooperation without levying significant conditions, they were in error, to put it mildly. If two sides truly have "common interests," should one side really need to pay the other?

"Let's not kid ourselves," said Kremlin analyst Gleb Pavlovsky. "Obama is no ally of ours. Remember, Obama has no support and is on the brink of an abyss.... He needs us more than we need him."[2] That is how the Russian regime perceived the U.S. president, and, more importantly, that is how they wanted the Russian public to see him.

The same skepticism has been apparent among the Russian elite with respect to Obama's "reset" policy. "It's better not to raise expectations too high," warned Vyacheslav Nikonov. "The START follow-on treaty apparently will be signed," wrote Fyodor Lukyanov. "But the hope that this treaty will bring progress in other areas is groundless. On the contrary, the negotiations so far have only increased the level of mutual suspicion.... Russia and the U.S. continue to remain hostages of old perceptions of each other, despite the fact that they have declared dozens of times that the 'Cold War' is over."[3]

Ironically, both the liberal opposition and Russian officialdom resent Obama's "reset," although for different reasons. The former lost its hope in Obama and couldn't find in the "reset" mechanisms anything capable of constraining the authoritarian behavior of the Russian authorities. The latter, meanwhile, felt that Washington was not sufficiently forthcoming in accommodating the Kremlin's foreign policy agenda. Along the broader Russian political spectrum, skepticism with respect to the future of the "reset" has been growing. President Medvedev can be friendly when meeting with Obama, and he may even mean what he says. However, the Kremlin entourage has not concealed what it really thinks about Obama: he is the leader of a foreign state that constitutes a threat to the Russian system. In their view, Obama with his "reset" has been trying to find a new way of promoting U.S. interests and weakening Russia. That is why Russians had to be vigilant! Russians had nothing to "reset." Rather, the Russians waited for America to reciprocate for all of the compromises Russia had made in the past. And the Russians were not ready to justify Obama's Nobel Prize!

Nothing has changed in the official propaganda: Americans can't be trusted; Americans are guilty; Americans are hypocritical; and the United States is a threat! Russian TV feeds this mantra to Russian society on a daily basis. And how could it be otherwise? The Russian system continues to rest on this anti-American pillar, and the emergence of Obama changes nothing.

Putin did not miss an opportunity to demonstrate how little he cares about the success of Obama's Russia policy. In late December 2009, the Russian prime minister unexpectedly, even for his own team, made a statement designed to prove not only that he was in charge but also that

Russia was not going to make Obama's life easy. Putin chose the START negotiations that many (at least in Washington) believed were moving toward successful completion. "The problem is that our American partners are building missile defense systems, and we are not. If one is not to develop missile defense systems, then a threat appears, because having created such an umbrella, our partners may feel completely protected and will do what they want. The balance will be upset and there will be more aggressiveness in real-life politics and economics," Putin warned. He made his comments after Medvedev and Obama in Copenhagen on December 18, 2009, had announced that negotiators were close to reaching agreement on the START replacement treaty.

The Russian prime minister not only pulled the rug from under Medevedev, demonstrating not only that he had veto power, but also showing that he continued to view the relationship with the United States as a zero-sum game. His comments further demonstrated that what the observers thought to be "common interests" in reality belied the asymmetry of American and Russian security interests: Russia is replacing offensive weapons and does not want to share with the Americans information about the testing of new missiles, whereas America did not want to share information about missile defense. This asymmetry means that both sides do not trust each other. But it was Putin who did not facilitate the process of bridging the American and Russian positions. He certainly made it more difficult for Obama to demonstrate the foreign policy accomplishments that would justify his Nobel Prize. The stumbling START negotiation process reconfirmed that, for the Kremlin, the discussions are about something bigger than the formal subject of the talks. As Kremlin propagandist Sergei Markov admitted, "It's not just about an agreement on START, but about the status of the Russian Federation and whether Russia is a great power or not."[4] For the Russian political class, the confirmation of great-power status is found not in a successful agreement with the Americans, but in a nonstop process of overcoming difficulties and seeking understanding. The Kremlin was following an old axiom: the process is everything, the goal is nothing.

Discussing the obstacles for a real engagement when quite a few Western observers were praising the "reset," Paul Quinn-Judge said,

There is a semantic gulf. Words and terms mean very different things to Vladimir Putin and to his Western interlocutors. The root-cause of this semantic gap is not linguistic. It is philosophical, ideological, and sometimes even psychological. It is rooted in both suspicion of the West and, even more importantly, in the deep resentment that Putin still harbours vis-à-vis the USA as a result of Russia's perceived humiliation in the nineties. Since Munich the depth of Putin's resentment of the US in particular has become patent, open and unmistakable. He deeply resents the US, and does not try to hide this. His remarks are often infused with, to put it mildly, schadenfreude.

The constant fits and starts (no pun intended) of the START negotiations ended on April 8, 2010. Obama and Medvedev signed an arms-reduction treaty that requires them to cut their countries' nuclear arsenals by about 30 percent (the arsenal of deployed warheads, however, would be reduced by only 5 percent for the United States and 7 percent for Russia, respectively).[5] The agreement would hardly bring about the disarmament of North Korea, to be sure, but as long as the world continued to worry about such massive numbers of nuclear weapons on hair-trigger alert, even a modest treaty was a worthy goal. If anything, it proved that the two nuclear powers really do care about nonproliferation.

But with regard to the "reset," the treaty negotiations haven't been as significant. The hopes that Obama's outreach on START could lay the groundwork for forging common ground on a host of other issues, and even for a "strong partnership," have been premature. The fact that both sides restarted arms control talks is proof in itself that they don't trust each other. The negotiation process proved that the two sides were pursuing different sets of goals while merely imitating a consensus. The security problem between the United States and Russia was not as dramatic as one might have expected. Russia's strategic arsenal has been deteriorating and the number of its nuclear weapons declining even without binding treaty reductions. The American side had been prepared to replace part of its nuclear arsenal with missiles armed with conventional warheads (a plan known as Prompt Global Strike[6]). Most likely, Russia and the United States would have continued nuclear disarmament on their own, without the new treaty. Thus considerations aside from security had triggered the sudden need for negotiations, and, at the same time, they made the treaty difficult to pin down.

It's ironic that, in pursuing their separate agendas, both sides have chosen to return to the nuclear arms negotiation, a Cold War mechanism. The fact that both sides have been trying to preserve the deterrence regime proves that the substance of the relationship hasn't really changed, despite the warmer atmosphere of the meeting and the principals' bonhomie. Sore points remained. Russia viewed the relationship between offensive and defensive weapons as "legally binding" while the Obama administration vehemently denied it. Meanwhile, Moscow repeatedly warned that it could withdraw from the treaty if "quantitative or qualitative" changes in U.S. missile defense plans undermined the basis for arms control. Furthermore, there was no guarantee that the U.S. Senate would ratify the treaty, and Medvedev warned that the ratification process had to be "synchronized." A more important sticking point was the fact that Russia's insistence on "nuclear parity" trapped it back in the 1950s, meaning that the United States had to do a little time traveling in order to get Russia on board for other issues. But by doing this, Washington gave Moscow the illusion that the United States was ready to continue riding the old horses of the Cold War.

President Obama, who had announced his Global Zero disarmament strategy prior to the negotiations, needed a new treaty more than the Russian side, hence the smiling faces among the Americans and the calm and chilly reaction from the Russians. Medvedev, all smiles, was an exception to this rule. For him personally, the treaty allowed him to pretend at having the leverage and influence he lacks in reality. But even Medvedev has been looking for ways to prove that he is not charmed by Obama and trying not to arouse suspicion that he is developing pro-American feelings. During his visit to Argentina just after the nuclear summit and his very warm reception in Washington, Medvedev did not miss a chance to say, "If somebody is bothered" in America by Moscow's seeking a greater role in Latin America, "we want to spit on that." His "Spit Statement" was the most popular news on the Russian TV, being repeated over and over again—hardly without order from the Kremlin.

The feeling was that a new START treaty could hardly guarantee that the United States and Russia will dance together. We find proof of this fact in the litany of grievances Putin delivered every time he met the American officials, and in Lavrov's candid admission, "I will not say we are opponents [of the United States], but we are not friends either."[7] Regrettably, public opinion polls in Russia demonstrate that years of anti-American rhetoric have taken their toll. According to the FOM (Public Opinion Foundation), in February 2010, 14 per cent of Russians had faith in rapprochement with the United States, and 36 percent said that Russia should stay away from the United States.[8] True, Levada polls pointed to a more optimistic trend: in April 54 per cent of respondents said that they view the United States in "positive way" (in 2008 only 31 percent of respondents viewed the United States in "a positive way"). Around 31 percent defined their attitude toward the United States as "generally bad" (in 2008 55 percent said so).[9] Thus, the suspicion remained and even if the Kremlin sincerely wants to soften its line with Washington, there are serious doubts that the brainwashed population could understand that policy.

America's official optimism for the "reset" could possibly have been a forced attempt by the Obama administration to demonstrate some kind of tangible achievement in the foreign policy arena. As of this writing, the "reset" has had mixed results: on the one hand, there has been progress in controlling proliferation, reducing nuclear stockpiles, improving verification procedures, and bridging the U.S. and Russian positions on Iran; on the other hand, it has boosted the "superpower" ambitions of the Russian elite, which could annihilate any positive developments.

Some American pundits would say, "But look how our relationship has improved! We are are cutting nuclear arsenals, cooperating on stabilizing Afghanistan, trying jointly to address the Iranian nuclear program, and even created the Bilateral Presidential Commission." This only proves that Russia, like the Soviet Union before it, can cooperate on the issues that are important for the survival of its system. But let's not forget how many times seemingly constructive engagement has ended with hitting rock bottom. Moreover, the cornerstone of renewed U.S.-Russian cooperation this time around is the rejection by Washington of the value dimension. Samuel Charap counters that "... [t]he administration regularly condemns human rights abuses in Russia."[10] We in Russia would like to hear about these cases of condemnation or about how they influence the Kremlin's behavior.

Further developments in the spring and summer of 2010 might make it seem as though my skepticism is misplaced. Russia (together with China) supported U.S. sanctions against Iran, and Washington has offered Russia cooperation on missile defense. American investors have been wooed by the Russian leaders, and Russian envoys have come frequently to Washington to offer new partnership "goodies." Unexpected personal chemistry between Obama and Medvedev has created hope for new breakthroughs. Representatives of the Obama administration have praised the "concrete achievements of resetting relations with Russia." The picture seems as though it were painted by different artists, but the artists on the Russian side have not changed, and this fact is troubling.

Upon closer examination, one could find the current landscape to be controversial. True, the United States faces many challenges and has little maneuvering space with regard to Russia. Russia has not shown signs of democratic awakening, but its leadership is showing readiness for dialogue with the West. In this context, merely neutralizing Russia's assertiveness and getting some cooperation from the Kremlin on Washington's priorities could be considered success. Pretending that Moscow and Washington still play in the same league and making a few insignificant concessions are an affordable price for keeping Russia happy and relatively quiet for the time being. One could argue that a policy of tactical compromises and acquiescence could be an effective tool for managing a declining Russian superpower.

However, such tactical successes often come at the expense of strategic goals. Obama's policy toward Russia could be such a case. I would not worry, as Obama critics do, about the administration's concessions to the Kremlin or his alleged "softness." Policy is impossible without concessions, and softness can work better than machismo if it is backed up by principles. But if it isn't backed up by the normative dimension, then softness makes pursuing a strategic agenda impossible. Consider the Iranian compromise. Russia supported sanctions against Tehran only after they had been watered down. As Russian politicians admitted, these sanctions "will not hit contracts between Russia and Iran." Thus Moscow was free to continue its foreign policy duality by constraining Iran and helping it at the same time, and thus the United States took part in Russia's imitation theater, winning a symbolic victory for the "reset" policy at the expense of its concrete strategic goals.

As a price for Moscow's limited cooperation, the U.S. administration has to accept the Kremlin's terms: that is, to tacitly agree not to preach about norms and to recognize Russia's right to "spheres of privileged interests." If the Americans believe that this kind of "softness" will buy Russia's genuine cooperation, they are wrong. The Russian elites are masters of manipulation and of using every opportunity to pursue their own goals.

Russian liberals would raise another concern: Does a U.S.–Russian thaw benefit Russia's transformation? So far "the reset" creates a hospitable environment for the survival of a system of personalized power that is alien to the West. The current programs of security and economic cooperation serve that system's interests. Take, for example, the "123" civil nuclear cooperation agreement for which the Russian authorities have lobbied. Its implementation will pay significant dividends to the Russian nuclear clan, which plans to turn Russia into a giant nuclear waste dump. Optimists would say, "Well, at least Russia is pacified for the time being." But at what cost for the principles for which the United States stands?

Striking a balance between short-term tactical goals and long-term strategic ones is a really difficult task. Hopefully, the Obama administration will come to understand that if it does not feel that it has sufficient resources to sustain a transformational model for its relations with Russia, then it should at least neither pretend that pursuing a pragmatic route and a modest agenda represent a true "success" for engagement, nor sacrifice American principles along the way.

America was not the only target for the Russian elite's exercises in self-affirmation. Putin took every opportunity to hone his prized combat skills when meeting with European leaders, who make easy targets. Russian television repeatedly broadcast one meeting in particular between Putin and the leaders of the European Union. In that meeting, EU Commission Chairman José Manuel Barroso somehow managed to screw himself up and deliver what could almost be considered a rebuke to Moscow. And then Putin let him have it, delivering a tirade against the oppression of the Russian minority in the Baltic states and the "violation of rights of migrants in Europe." As Barroso and other members of the commission listened with downcast eyes, Putin took particular pleasure in reminding them, "We know of the situation of certain prison systems in individual European states." When Barroso tried to counter this attack, Putin snarled: "Are we going to continue this discussion or shall we drop it?" The team from Brussels opted for retreat. Virtually the same scene played every time the Europeans dared to mention Russia's problems. Putin assured them there were none, end of story. Naturally, the public broadcasts of these meetings were for domestic consumption. When Putin travels abroad, he usually employs a softer style, but that quick-draw machismo is always on hand if it serves the interests of the tandem.

Notes

1. See "Russians on the U.S. and the Visit of Barack Obama," http://www.levada.ru/press/2009063000.html.

2. "Pax Medvedeva: Rossiya Medvedeva vychodit iz glubokoi oborony" [Pax Medvedica: Medvedev's Russia Is Getting out of Deep Defense], http://www.kreml.org/opinions.

3. Fyodor Lukyanov, "The Trap of START," www.gazeta.ru, February 25, 2010.

4. Ellen Barry, "Putin Sounds Warning on Arms Talks," *New York Times*, December 30, 2009.

5. Michael Bohm, "The Last Tango in Prague," *Moscow Times*, April 9, 2010.

6. Craig Whitlock, "U.S. Looks to Nonnuclear Weapons to Use as Deterrent," *Washington Post*, April 8, 2010. Sergei Lavrov, reacting to prompt global strike said on April 6, 2010: "World states will hardly accept a situation in which nuclear weapons disappear, but weapons that are no less destabilizing emerge in the hands of certain members of the international community."

7. Interview with Sergei Lavrov, *Rossiyskaya Gazeta*, March 18, 2010.

8. "Dominanty, Polie mnienii," Vypusk 5 [Dominanty, The Area of Views, vol. 5], http://www.fom.ru/news?page=3.

9. "Russian Attitudes Toward the United States, the EU, Ukraine, and Georgia," http://www.levada.ru/press/2010022602.html.

10. Samuel Charap, "Assessing the 'Reset' and the Next Steps for U.S. Russia Policy," April 2010, http://www.americanprogress.org/issues/2010/04/assessing_reset.html.

55 WHY THE WEST DOESN'T WANT TO ANNOY THE KREMLIN

But the question remains why Putin's blustery attacks even work. To put the question in even broader terms, why are Western governments so intent on a policy of not annoying Moscow? I can tell you what we Russian liberals think the reason is. Now, we may be simplifying the problem. We may be far from the truth. But that should be all the more reason to discuss it.

Western politicians and commentators typically wield two arguments when they attempt to deny their ability to influence Russia's transformation. Both arguments keep true to the spirit of "realism."

Here's the first: "The West cannot transform Russia and bring it into the West. You can't expect the impossible from us." Let me quote a letter from a good Western friend who wrote to me, "Of course, you acknowledge that it is not America's role to 'promote' democracy in Russia; this is a task for Russian liberals and it will not come *deus ex machina* from above ... But it seems that Russian liberals dream that America will somehow transform Russia and integrate it into the West."

Apparently, we liberals have failed to explain ourselves clearly. Our criticism of Western policy is evidently understood as a call for the West and the United States in particular to solve Russia's problems for us. Well, allow me to clear the air.

Russian liberals believe that the 1960–1980s era of "democracy promotion" is long gone. Nor would there be any benefit in the West's repeating its 1990s-era lessons to the Russian public on the ABCs of democracy. By now Russians are capable of perceiving its advantages on their own, and they no longer need Western advisers to help them build independent institutions and a free market. If we truly needed advice on overcoming resistance to post-communist reality, we could talk to the Poles or Balts.

Every time I hear this first argument, I get the feeling that the West has an image of Russian Westernizing liberals as mendicants looking for a handout in the form of material aid and protection from the state. Indeed the same picture resides in the imaginations of the Russian authorities as well, and we liberals share some of the blame for this fact. Nevertheless, Russia has changed and the liberal agenda has changed along with it. To be sure, Russian human rights activists still cannot survive on their own, without Western help. The Russian liberal and business communities are still unable to support Russia's nongovernmental organizations in a worthy manner, despite some hopeful developments on this front. On the whole, however, Russian liberals no longer desire direct aid or advice from the West. On the contrary, liberals want to distance themselves from the political West these days, largely as a result of the Kremlin's anti-Western policy, in order to avoid accusations of being a Fifth Column. But a significant portion of liberals' desire to distance themselves is due to their disillusionment with the West's policies on Russia.

In any case, Russian liberals today (with the exception of a few radicals) do not call for the West to save Russia on behalf of the Russian people, and they don't expect the West to import values for which Russia is not ready. They do, however, believe that the West need not actively and openly support what is going on in Russia. No one is forcing Western politicians to treat the denizens of the Kremlin as bosom buddies. No one is stopping them from judging Russia's actions according to their merits, which contradict not only democratic norms but international law.

"There is no other regime in Russia, and Western governments have to deal with this one," say my Western colleagues. They must understand that dialogue with the Kremlin doesn't have to prolong the life of the traditional Russian system. The art of diplomacy and international communications in the twenty-first century have advanced to a level that permits politicians to pursue a more sophisticated course of action.

Russian liberals also reject the opposite extreme—the policy of ignoring Russia and expelling it from Western clubs as a way of forcing it to democratize. This method would only return Russia to the fortress mentality. We expect, rather, a minimalist policy from Western politicians and intellectuals—that they merely not hinder the process of Russia's renewal by actively supporting the Russian political regime and the model of cooperation it imposes on the West. I will take up this topic—what the West can refrain from doing and how it will help Russia's renewal—in the next chapter.

The second Western argument for defending a "realist" policy toward Russia is, "We have no levers of influence on Russia." This is simply not true.

Western civilization has a plethora of levers that would move Russia. The political class in particular is sensitive to pressure, because it is integrated in the Western community on a personal level. This elite lives in the West. It keeps its money there, buys equity and real estate there, takes its vacations there, bears children there, and sends them to school there. The elite makes money in Russia in order to support its lifestyle in the West. Many representatives of the Russian elite have in effect become part of the Western establishment. And they desperately want to remain a part of that establishment, hence their vulnerability to Western influence. The West can also influence the part of the Russian elite that is not directly integrated into the West by disciplining its appetite for Russian energy resources. Let me just reiterate that I am talking about influencing the Russian elite, not the broader public, which no longer needs or wants preaching from the West.

Why hasn't the West taken advantage of these levers on the Russian elite? I can name a few reasons as they appear to me from my vantage point in Russia. (But of course I'm happy to hear objections if I'm wrong.)

Some in the West fear that pushing on these levers will stoke the Kremlin's aggressive tendencies and destabilize international relations. These fears are, I admit, justified. Others fear the loss of Russia as an economic partner. Dependence on Russian energy is indeed a weighty reason to maintain pragmatic relations with Russia. Why risk the ability to fuel economic growth to utopian ideas?

There are also influential political forces in the West who believe that Russia simply can't be changed, so it would be better to deal with the elite on its own terms. This, too, is a reasonable concern.

Finally, there is the West's business community. It's probably not worth it to chastise it for wanting to maintain good relations with Russia and grease the wheels of commerce. Business has only one goal—to make money. And the regime both sets the rules of that game and is its main player.

There are other kinds of business that think about values, to be sure. The Danish pension fund PGGM withdrew $54 million in investment from state-owned Petro-China as a protest against China's behavior in the Sudan, and it was planning to break off relations with the Indian-owned Oil and Natural Gas Corporation (ONGC) for the same reason. But principled behavior like this is the exception that proves the rule in world of business.

Of course, teaching governments and societies how to behave isn't the primary role of businesses, but this doesn't absolve them of the responsibility that comes with choosing where and how to make money. When the business community agrees to obey the rules of the game proposed by the Russian elite, it has to own up to the fact that it is indirectly supporting that system.

Regrettably, there are quite a few examples when Western business, including the most powerful and influential leaders, has been actively engaged in the trade-off with the Russian authorities. German car giant Daimler had to admit to paying bribes in order to promote its production. In 2000–2005 it paid Russian officials about €5.2 million. Another example is Hewlett-Packard, which allegedly paid about $10.9 million in bribes to win a contract with the office of the Russian Prosecutor General(!).[1]

But even in Russia, Western companies could reject the informal rules of the game and follow the rule of law. This path has been demonstrated by the Swedish furniture retailer IKEA. In 2010 it fired its two top-ranking managers in Russia for turning a blind eye to a bribery case involving St. Petersburg's MEGA IKEA shopping mall. "Any tolerance of a display of corruption is completely unacceptable for IKEA. We consider the situation to be deplorable, and we'll be acting promptly and resolutely," Michael Olsson, president of IKEA, wrote in the company's statement.[2] The company prefers to freeze its investments but it never pays bribes. Not all Western companies in Russia demonstrate the same ability and decisiveness to follow a strict code of business ethics.

Far from holding their noses while conducting business with the Russian regime, certain Western firms seem to relish it, even going so far as to lobby for the regime's interests at home. These firms employ or are even led by Western politicians and public figures. Former public officials, legislators, and even prime ministers have also joined the boards of Russian state and private corporations. If they used these positions of trust to promote transparency and respect for the rule of law, they could even genuinely claim to be providing a real public good while benefiting themselves. But too often they become swept up in the profit motive and the interests of the regime, which inevitably come into alignment. Nor are private foundations immune to this process. There are quite a few Western expert and public opinion organizations that receive large amounts of financial support from Russian business interests. One doesn't have to strain one's eyes much to see the Kremlin's influence behind such generous gifts.

This gives you an idea of the forces in the West that have an interest in maintaining warm relations with the Kremlin. Many consider it impolite or politically incorrect to note this fact. Sure, people may note it, whisper to each other about it, and even condemn it, but open discussion of the topic is taboo. Nevertheless, the fact remains that in the West today there is a veritable industry—including law firms, banks, consulting firms, image makers, research centers, people in the arts, and former and acting politicians—that serves the interests of the Russian elite directly or indirectly. No other country can boast of such a formidable lobbying industry. Unable to modernize Russia, its elite has shown exceptional imagination when it comes to co-opting the West to sustain itself. Regrettably, the West itself has been all too happy to be used.

Mikhail Khodorkovsky, former head of Yukos and now an inmate in the Russian prison system, bitterly summed it up: "My country is a huge exporter of two kinds of commodities. The first export is hydrocarbons, crude oil or natural gas. The second is corruption. In years past, the victims of Russia's exported corruption became certain European and American political leaders."[3] In his May 26 *Washington Post* article, "The World's Biggest Threat Is Corruption, Not Nuclear Weapons," the most famous political prisoner in Russia makes more specific accusations: "The destruction of Yukos was driven purely by corruption.... The theft of Yukos was defended by certain German politicians, while a large Italian company played a central role as a purchaser of some stolen assets." Yes, Khodorkovsky is no neutral observer. But while he may be bitter and unfair, he now says openly what the Russian elite (not just the liberals) thinks in private.

The West's short political cycle plays a role in facilitating this state of affairs. Western political leaders have to achieve measurable results over the course of their brief terms, but a values-based approach will only yield results in the long term, long past the time any one politician could expect to reap an electoral reward. Thus it's understandable that few Western leaders want to get involved in things that will not culminate in success in the next four to eight years.

We also have to consider the historical pause that invariably follows a period of change and disruption. The world still hasn't comprehended, intellectually or politically, the geopolitical reality that arose after the fall of the bipolar world system and the collapse of communism.

Western observers admit that they do not always understand what goes on in Russia under the cover of imitation, demagoguery, and mystification. And how can you influence a society you don't really understand? As Falk Bomsdorf of the Friedrich Naumann Foundation regretfully observed:

> In the European Union, as a rule, most politicians have no idea how the Russian state functions. We don't understand how that state influences politics and the lives of people. We don't know the extent to which the state and the society in Russia are corrupt. The West does not realize that since the mid-1990s the Russian ideology is Russian nationalism and anti-Western rhetoric. Disorientation is what characterizes the perception of Russia in the West. They talk about Russia a lot there. But they have no idea what the country is and what its system is. It looks as if too many people are unwilling to make the effort to find out.

The West pays the price for this ignorance periodically, whenever the Russian regime decides to shock the international system and shake the West down for whatever it wants. Failing to understand the source of these outbursts, Western leaders prefer to make no sudden moves that might provoke this enigmatic Kremlin animal.

The truth, however, is that the Western powers are allowing the Kremlin to force Europe to return to nineteenth-century geopolitical realities. By accepting Russia, with its obsolete system, as a member of the European institutions and G8, Western states have legitimized the Kremlin's desire to reproduce the domestic rules of the game beyond its borders. The West certainly understands this trap but prefers to embrace Russia, fearing that an isolated Russia will start smashing windows, which is quite possible. But the end result is a situation in which political impotence or hypocrisy on the one side only provokes revisionism on the other side.

Such is the outcome of Brussels' approach to Russia, at any rate. Much depends on what model of relations the Obama administration will ultimately choose. But even if the U.S. president suddenly, and contrary to his advisers and past behavior, decides to start thinking about how to incentivize Russia's transformation, he won't get very far without Europe's help. But you see, I'm waxing "idealist" again. It's already become quite clear that Washington won't be experimenting with difficult policies promising uncertain results.

We find ourselves today in a situation reminiscent of the early 1990s, when the West was surprised by the collapse of the Soviet Union. The

West does not know how to deal with the country that Vladimir Putin built and whose image Dmitri Medvedev is trying to improve. Absent any real wisdom, the West contents itself with pacifying and mollifying the Kremlin. Does it absolutely need to do more?

My argument, that Western politicians and observers often misunderstand the Russian (and post-Soviet) reality and are at a loss as to how to react to it, is not the result of arrogance or any disregard for others' views, which is common among Russian intellectual circles. I see the limited intellectual ability to grasp the nature of the Russian developments on both sides. However, these limitations, it seems, are of a different nature: Russian observers (myself included) demonstrate a pathetic inability to conceive of a path from Russia's systemic uncertainty to the liberal rules of the game, whereas our Western colleagues show an inability to understand the Russian imitative paradigm and to formulate an appropriate reaction.

For all that the West doesn't know about Russia, it does claim to know that Russia is no longer a serious threat like the Soviet Union. It no longer poses an existential danger for Western civilization, which faces more troubling global challenges—from the threat of international terrorism to the rise of China. The financial, political, and intellectual resources of the West have largely been devoted to meeting these challenges, thus limiting its ability to develop a collective strategy toward Russia and the former Soviet space.

For all its provocations, the Russian elite is trying not to cross the line that would force the West to consolidate against Russia. And since there is no direct security threat from Russia, the West is willing to tolerate it—for now.

One of the most observant Russia watchers, Arnold Horelick, offered a convincing explanation for "some outrageous kowtowing going on in the West." Responding to my criticism of the West, he said:

> The most significant feature is "Russia fatigue." To most of the Western world, Russia seems uninterestingly stable and unchanging—some think Russia is "unchangeable"—stuck in a rut which most of its people find bearable though hardly inspiring, its leaders seeking to enjoy the mostly personal advantages of interacting with Western institutions, while interminably dangling the possibility of its "cooperation" on the dwindling set of issues where Russia can make a difference internationally, to the point where the possibility has lost credibility and potential partners have lost patience. The antics of the

strutting peacock Putin have become so familiar that he has become almost as boring as the soporific "modernization" lectures of his tandem placeholder Medvedev. So most of the Western political class, including its foreign policy establishments (even a goodly part of the Russia-watchers detachment), is no longer paying attention. The opposition in Russia is too ineffectual and the regime's treatment of it is not dramatically harsh enough to revive that waning attention. So there we are.

I agree: "Russia fatigue" is fast becoming the prevailing mood among the Western elite. We Russians have indeed forced the West to lose interest in us; we have provoked frustration, weariness, and the desire to forget. Does this mean that, to regain the West's attention, Russia must shock the world in its usual manner? Horelick says: "Sadly, it is probably only a bad turn of events internally in Russia or (another) ill-conceived 'foreign' adventure by Moscow that can awaken the West." Regrettably, we might be moving in this direction.

Another circumstance arose in 2009 that complicates the search for a new formula of relations—namely, the illusions arising from the "reset." Officials and analysts in Western capitals were lulled into thinking that the Russian regime had finally committed itself to a constructive course of mutual cooperation and even "partnership." They wanted to believe that Medvedev's friendly style meant that Moscow had changed course and that there had emerged inside Russia a consensus for a constructive relationship with the West. Consequently, they argued, the West should deemphasize everything that could upset or reverse this promising development.

Would that my liberal colleagues and I could have been seduced by the Kremlin's charm offensive and joined these optimists! Our lives would be so much better and pleasant. We could have finally come out of the political ghetto and participate in public life as normal citizens. Some people did join the new chorus. The stubborn minority continued to warn the world: "Don't delude yourself!" None of the "fundamentals" in Russia had changed. The system and the regime are the same. How, then, could real rapprochement between Moscow and the West be in the offing? Such litanies only annoyed the West eager to build new relations with Russia.

As critical as I am of Western policy toward Russia, I have no intention of laying all the blame at the West's feet. I've written a lot about the responsibility of the Russian elite, including the liberals, for Russia's dead end. I've written about the Russian elite's lack of a sense of duty, an understanding of national interests, and compassion for their own people. I won't repeat myself here. Today there is a need for a critical comprehension of the West's policy toward Russia from a liberal, pro-Western point of view. Many Russian liberals also need to engage in dialogue and discussion with the West. Before, we were hindered from criticizing the West not so much by political correctness as by the conviction that we could not join the chorus of criticism directed against the West by the Russian elite. But we gradually realized that we must look objectively at both ourselves and at the West's attitude toward Russia. We must make our Western colleagues aware of how we feel about the West as a political entity and what we expect from it. Mutual disaffection between the West and the pro-Western wing of Russian society is a problem for more than just Russia.

Our criticism does not mean that we think all Western politicians and experts are naïve or incompetent. Nor do we think that they understand nothing about Russia. On the contrary, often the very fact of distance and a different civilizational experience allows one to assess Russian processes in a healthier, calmer, and more objective way. I've quoted many Western authors whose opinions contribute enormously to a proper understanding of Russia. But for now, these sober voices compose an insignificant part of the expert community. Unfortunately, the Western political and expert community as a whole isn't yet ready to understand either Russia or how it may be transformed. My modest goal with this book has been to show that Russia is not alone in not finding a way out of its present historical uncertainty; the West can help it, but only if it first learns how to see the deeper Russian drama at work today.

But Western leaders who pay lip service to democracy to win points with the crowd at home only serve to confirm Russians in their cynicism, and to convince them that the West maintains a hypocritical double standard. Most unhelpful, for example, are periodic meetings between Western leaders and members of the Russian opposition and civil society such as those described by Arseny Roginsky, head of Memorial:

We've seen many Western leaders over these twenty years. More Europeans than Americans. The latter are not very eager to meet with us—representatives of civil society. Often these meetings leave a strange taste. The Western politicians ask the most basic questions, but show no particular interest in the answers.

Interestingly, Roginsky says, they always ask the same question: What can we do to change the human rights situation in Russia? "Our usual answer," he went on,

> is always this: tell your Russian partners in the Kremlin straight out that you are concerned about what is happening in Russia with the elections, with the mass media, with Chechnya.... They agree, but then nothing happens. Don't these politicians realize that their meekness (or political correctness?) is perceived as weakness by the Kremlin and discredits not so much them as the values that they claim to care so much about?

As you can see, Russian members of civil society don't think very highly of the political West.[4]

Let's ask ourselves why Western leaders, barring rare exceptions, fail to raise the question of violations of rights and freedoms when they meet with Russian leaders? They have had many opportunities to do it in an informal atmosphere—say, over dinner—that will not put the Russians on the spot publicly. Why don't they do it? Perhaps they don't consider the problem of rights and freedoms pressing. Perhaps they fear that an unpleasant topic of conversation will complicate the resolution of issues that are more important to them. Of course, if their countries depend on Gazprom, they will think twice before asking the Russian leader, "Why are journalists and human rights activists being killed all the time?" If they considered their position more closely, they would realize that Russia depends on their consumption more than Europe does on Russia's production. And that would give Europe justification to raise these questions.

One thing is clear for now: Without the support of the West, primarily the European community, Russia's transformation is unlikely. No, no, and once again, no—I am not calling for a "democratic crusade" on Russia. I know that external support of the transformation can succeed only to the extent that Russian society is ready for reform. "Russia is not ready for reform!" the Russian "protectors" and their Western allies assure us, telling us to be patient until the Russian political class matures. The point is that this class will never start liberalizing Russia of its own free will; it will do so only if external factors make it consider this course. Collective Western will could be that factor.

Formally, the Western community regards Russia as part of Western civilization, part of Europe. Russia is a member of the Council of Europe and the G8. Western politicians and experts talk about partnership with

Russia, and that is how the relations between the European Union and Russia are defined. But this "European" country retains personalized power and neo-imperial intentions, and when Europe blinds itself to that harsh fact, it in effect blesses it. By contrast, the West has ample reason not to base its China policy on the nature of the political regime there; China is not a member of the club of Western democracies. But Russia is, or claims to be. The result is a schizophrenic situation with the West in which Russia is regarded as both potential partner and potential foe. It is the ideal situation for Russia's elite to preserve its hold on power. Thus the West bears at least some responsibility for facilitating this schizophrenia.

Many in the Russian political class sincerely believe that Western talk about values is nothing more than a sop to domestic public opinion. Many in the West even share this view. "Idealists!" is the kindest insult hurled at those who keep Western and Russian "realists" from expunging values from the discussion entirely.

Yet the Russian system could become a challenge to liberal civilization. Russia has pretensions to being a civilizational alternative in its own neighborhood, and it maintains the right to dictate the rules of the game in the post-Soviet space. An incompletely reformed Russia already acts as a spoiler, demoralizing the Western political class, and it can continue to do so. The West should be interested in Russia's transformation. The question is, when will it realize that Russia's trajectory connects very concretely to the fate of Western civilization? I recognize that we need weightier arguments to convince the skeptical.

Notes

1. David Crawford, "H-P Executives Face Bribery Probes," *Wall Street Journal*, April 15, 2010.

2. Irina Titova, "IKEA Fires Two Top Managers Over Bribes," *Moscow Times*, February 16, 2010.

3. Mikhail Khodorkovsky, "A Time and Place for Russia," *New York Times*, January 29, 2010.

4. Representatives of the democratic opposition in other new independent states feel even more critically with respect to the West. Roza Otunbayeva, leader of the Kyrgyz democratic opposition, had harsh words for the American administration: "... We have been really unhappy that the US Embassy here was absolutely not interested in the democratic situation in Kyrgyzstan. It was not paying attention to our difficulties over the last two years. We were not happy that they never had the time to meet with us. We concluded that the base is the most important agenda of the US, not our political development.... They turned a blind eye...." *Washington Post*, April 16, 2010.

56 SO, WHAT SHOULD AND SHOULD NOT BE DONE?

By now I'm sure you've noticed that I like to engage in a dialogue with my readers. This is because it is very important to me to know your reaction. Have I found the right arguments? I'm taking a risk with this book by intentionally raising inconvenient arguments and casting doubt on my own position—being my own devil's advocate. I cite my opponents' arguments to demonstrate the limits of our present understanding of the problem and our need to re-examine it. I've done this because I look around today and see everywhere how the old clichés about Russia have become exhausted. We desperately need to fill these empty vessels with new content.

What, then, do Russian liberals expect from the West? We would be grateful to them if they did not behave like Italy's Silvio Berlusconi when they deal with the Kremlin, feeding the Russian authorities' sense of impunity. The West would really help us Westernizers if it could restore its image in the eyes of Russians as the standard-bearers for principles beyond that of the free flow of commerce. Russia would truly look at the West differently if Western politicians could resist the temptation to work for the Kremlin. Or if they could not resist the temptation, it would help if they paid a price for their greed in the court of Western public opinion.

It would be good if Western politicians stopped sucking up to the Kremlin, as a number of European leaders do—I don't want to name them. Television news accounts of Putin's meetings with his Western counterparts allow us to see where Russian leaders get their unbridled self-confidence. Western politicians must also stop making private agreements with representatives of the Russian ruling team, and Western experts must stop being yes-men for the Russian regime. A change in style and rhetoric, a switch to business-like cooperation without an attempt to forge personal chemistry with the Russian leaders, would constitute a real contribution to Russia's transformation.

For now, Western leaders still consider "personal chemistry" with the Russian tandem as the secret to success in Russia. It is hard to avoid the impression that they're behaving toward Russia the way the Russian regime behaves toward its people. The regime constantly talks about democracy but has shut down all political institutions; the West constantly talks about values but operates according to different principles when it comes to Russia. I don't want to appear naïve. I do understand that there is no basis (yet) for my hopes. But I can't deny myself the pleasure of dreaming a bit, and I invite you to join with me.

What else could the West do to help the new Russia?

First of all, it could restore the role it once played in the eyes of Russian society—an attractive alternative to the Russian petrostate. Democracy, freedom, and competition all working hand in hand toward sustainable economic growth—all this could give Russians an incentive to re-examine life in their society. "Practice what you preach"—that's what the West can do to support the liberal vector in Russia.

Second, a lot depends on exactly how the West engages Russia. The West still emphasizes engagement with the Russian elite, discussing security and economic issues. The Russian elite is prepared to continue this conversation infinitely, seeing it as a means of reinforcing the status quo. It's long past time to come up with a new way to organize society-to-society dialogue between Russia and the West. We need to find a form of dialogue that bolsters Russian stakeholders who have an interest in opening Russia to the West. Doing so will require creating new means of communicating with Russian society, particularly the younger generations. I can just see the shrugs: "We've heard this so many times. It's a useless idea!" If so, then that just underscores that we're still not ready to leave behind the old clichés.

Third, the West has many ways of showing the Russian elite that its prosperity and the West's good graces are intimately connected, and that the elite must observe civilizational principles at home. Of course, the West needs to be sure that its salvos fall on target. The Russian public should not suffer from the West's attempts to find a way of civilizing the Russian elite. The West must therefore learn to distinguish between the regime and the people and understand that the interests of the two do not coincide.

Fourth, the West needs to remind Russian leaders that they and their predecessors have signed international documents, including the Universal Declaration of Human Rights, that commit them to observing democratic norms.

Moreover, upon joining the Council of Europe Russia affirmed that it agrees that its domestic affairs are not solely its own private concern. Therefore Europe should pay attention to what is happening in Russian society, with an emphasis on the state of human rights and democracy. If Europe is not worried about what is going on in Russia, that in and of itself would constitute a violation of its own principles. And it could hardly be considered intolerable interference in Russia's domestic affairs if, say, Chancellor Merkel, President Sarkozy, or some other Western leader reminded the Russian leaders of their obligation to develop democracy in their country. Indeed this is the duty of every member state of the Council of Europe.

But if Western leaders fear annoying the Kremlin, they could at least resist making gestures that can be interpreted as overt support of Russian authoritarianism. I'd like to recommend that they eschew the example of French presidents, who have made cozying up to and defending the Kremlin a national pastime. Chirac's excessive courtesy toward Putin is well known in this regard. His successor, Sarkozy, has continued the treatment: He congratulated the Kremlin on victory in the last parliamentary elections, which Europeans called "not free, not honest, and not democratic."

Fifth, successful development in the newly independent states neighboring Russia might provide a good incentive for modernization. The example of a flourishing and democratic Ukraine could make a convincing argument that Russian society needs to develop a new relationship with its regime. If the Ukrainians, a people very close to Russia both geographically and culturally, could create a new system, then so could Russia. Thus the creation of a stable and democratic belt around Russia is a crucial factor in its renewal.[1] This is also something the Russian elite fears much more than the direct influence of the West on Russian society. That is why the Kremlin stubbornly persists in claiming the right to "spheres of privileged interests" in neighboring countries; the Kremlin intends them to become a *cordon sanitaire* to protect Russia from Western influences. That is why the success of the states in the Eastern Partnership program also provides a stimulus for Russian reforms.

Today the main problem for those who think about how to help Russia's transformation is how to move away from the binary "constraint or cooperation" dichotomy. That formula belongs in the past, to the Cold War. Today, even a dual-track policy, considered in the 1990s as a way of encouraging simultaneous dialogue with the Russian regime and the public, would not be enough. We need more complex multi-track mechanisms. If it has the collective will, the West is perfectly capable of stressing interests, engagement, a values-based approach, and containment of Russian traditionalists all at once. (How are they to be contained? Try the minimalist approach I mentioned earlier.)

"And that's it? Nothing more specific?" my readers may ask. I am not a spin doctor, and my work does not include being a political adviser to Western governments. I have merely tried to define an approach that could create a more beneficial external space for Russia's renewal. The specific machinery of that influence is a different problem, for different people.

Re-reading the last few lines, I thought to myself bitterly, "Well, I've just proved my own naïveté, when I'm always accusing others of it." The West is unlikely to give up a politics of situational pragmatism as long as that policy appears to be working. Why should Western leaders step out onto thin ice and start a process that could lead to a crisis in relations with Moscow? Why, indeed, especially given that the Russian elite has learned how to blackmail the West with threats of rising tensions. Any attempt by the West to change the basis of its relations with Russia's elite inevitably will give way to "the Empire strikes back!" Who needs the headache?

A Western colleague experienced in political affairs confirmed these doubts, telling me outright, "At this stage the interests of Russian liberals and of the West do not coincide. You want the West to force the Russian elite to give up the old rules of the game. But we can deal with it even with those rules." Apparently so. In that case, the West should be prepared for further "resets" to end like the previous ones. Perhaps the West can allow a "gray zone" at the eastern edge of Europe and a lone state drifting in that zone. Perhaps that's not even the worst-case scenario for the West. If so, this says a lot about Western civilization, its understanding of modern interconnectedness, and its ability to foresee the course of world events.

In the meantime, amazing developments are under way. Russian citizens—ordinary folks from Tula and Novosibirsk, Chechnya and Yakutia—have recognized the need for Western intervention in Russia's internal affairs and are forcing Europe to interfere in Russian life. How are they doing this? By appealing to the European Court to find protection from the predations of their own state. The number of suits sent to Strasbourg by Russian citizens against Russia has been growing every year. In 2000, the European Court received 1,987 appeals from Russian citizens (8 percent of the total). In 2008, there were 27,250, and they made up more than 28 percent of all the suits brought there. In 2009, the Russian appeals made up more than one out of every three suits. Russian citizens sent more appeals to the European Court than citizens of any other country, which evinces their recognition of the importance of rule of law and the fact that it does not work in Russia. They also believe, evidently, that Europe has both the right and the duty to protect them from their state.

The massive number of appeals from Russian citizens has gotten the Russian authorities thinking about how to hinder the work of the court. Frequent decisions finding Russian officials and state institutions guilty of torture, corruption, and other forms of misconduct have apparently had an effect. Until January 2010, Russia remained the only one out of 47 participating states that stubbornly and under shifting pretexts refused to ratify Protocol N14, which was supposed to speed up the work of the court. "Everyone has been very critical of Russia about it," said Thomas Hammarberg, the human rights commissioner at the Council of Europe.[2] Lo and behold, the criticism apparently paid off. On January 15, 2010, Moscow hurriedly ratified the protocol, a fact which was hailed by optimists as evidence that Russia has started to liberalize itself.

The reality was more complicated. In fact, the episode presents just another example of the Kremlin's artfulness at creating illusions and unfounded hopes. The Russian Duma reversed its long-standing opposition to reforms in the European Court only after Russia got guarantees from Europeans that Russian judges would be included in reviews of political cases against Russia, that the court would not begin investigating complaints before the cases were formally accepted, and that the court would not have any new powers to enforce its rulings. What does all this mean? It means that the Russian side gained the opportunity to influence cases at the acceptance stage, gained the possibility of affecting the judicial process, and gained the ability to block the implementation of the court's rulings. The benefits of these concessions were soon demonstrated: The court had already accepted the $100 billion case filed by the former managers of Yukos, but tricks from the Russian side constantly delayed the proceedings. By the beginning of 2010, the Yukos hearings were delayed for a third time because the official Russian representatives for the case were not available: They had grown accustomed to falling sick whenever hearings were announced.

However, nothing can stop the European Court juggernaut once it starts to move. Sooner or later, it will have to investigate the Yukos case and make a ruling, and that ruling may very well declare the seizing of

Khodorkovsky's property to be illegal. The Kremlin will then face a dilemma: Either obey the decisions of the European Court or face the threat of isolation.[3]

Thus can European institutions, against the wishes of most European capitals, force a smug Russian elite to realize that the fence it built around Russia is beginning to wobble. How quickly the Russian elite understands what many Russians already do—that their system is destroying Russia—depends on the collective efforts of the West.

Notes

1. Here I agree with Steven Pifer, who wrote, "A Ukraine that makes the political and economic transition to become a modern European democracy would provide a significant example for Russians thinking about their own future course." See Steven Pifer, "Russia and Eurasia," in *Averting Crisis in Ukraine*, Council on Foreign Relations Special Report no. 41, January 2009, p. 11.

2. Clifford J. Levy, "European Court Seems to Rankle Kremlin," *New York Times*, March 29, 2009.

3. In 2009 the Russian Supreme Court agreed with the European court's earlier judgment that the 2003 arrest of Platon Lebedev, Khodorkovsky's business partner, was illegal. Despite that, Russian authorities did not release Lebedev.

57 UNCERTAINTY AS A WAY TO SURVIVE

I t's been almost twenty years since the collapse of the Soviet Union. The new generation in Russia doesn't even remember communism. Yet Russia still has failed to acquire a new national identity that would suit the majority of its people. Nor has it found a new role on the world stage, one that would resolve the conflict between ambitions and resources. In the 1990s under Yeltsin, Russia tried to give up its grand civilizational pretensions and recognize the universality of the principles of liberal democracy. It soon became clear that the Russian elite, alas, was not ready to give up its monopoly on power and learn to function in a competitive political environment. It was still caught up in the same historical trap it had fallen into in the twentieth century. Even the liberals who ended up at the top with Yeltsin couldn't accept the fact that they couldn't cling to power forever if they wanted Russia to become a European country. (Liberals and democrats with no intention of giving up power—here was a true Russian invention.) The West, in turn, wasn't prepared to help Russia navigate out of these shoals.

Under Putin, the Russian elite began looking for a way to justify Russia's self-sufficiency and identity as a global pillar with its own set of values. The Putin era and its free-flowing petrodollars convinced the elite that they had found a way. Of course, no one had actually bothered to describe exactly what principles their alternative civilization stood for. They promised to do so, but if they ever did, then they must have kept it secretly locked away in a safe somewhere, never to see the light of day.

Some Western observers, meanwhile, were prepared to concede the Russian elite's point about proposing a distinct civilizational pillar, judging from the numerous discussions in which I took part. "Why not?" they said. "Russia has always been unique. It can't be forced into your pat frameworks. You must recognize that Russia will develop on the basis of its own values." Some Western experts and politicians believed (and some still do) that Russia could become the nucleus of a new authoritarian system opposing the West.

Admitting that Russia has a separate civilizational course means that it should also have its own principles for organizing its society and politics, as well as an independent role on the international scene. In reality the Russian political class is imitating the principles of liberal democracy in order to cover up its authoritarian and oligarchic tendencies. But no one has ever considered imitation to be a legitimate basis for an independent civilizational framework. Imitation, after all, has no substance. Nor is there any basis for considering the Russian hybrid regime something unique; there are many political hybrids throughout the world that survive by imitating liberal democracy.

Nevertheless, Russia truly is unique. There has never been a state that imitates the West even as it maintains superpower and imperialist pretensions by trying to contain the spread of Western civilization and acting as a foe of the United States. The reality is that these pretensions are just more mystification. Russia lacks both the resources and the desire by a large portion of the elite and the public to restore its empire and superpower status. But for now these phantoms, supported by official rhetoric and militaristic symbols, still haunt the nation, its people, and its foreign policy.

One can hardly consider a bluff to be a stable foundation on which to build a society. A bluff can keep a state afloat for awhile, but sooner or later, the absence of strategic orientation, values and coherent principles for organizing the society, not to mention the substitution of private interests for national ones, will lead to a state's downfall. Igor Klyamkin describes this process as it applies to Russia:

> The paradox is that modern Russia, claiming to be a civilizational alternative to the West, has no civilizational quality of its own. Unlike Western countries, it has not mastered democratic legal standards and its regime is not under the control of the law. Unlike Asian countries, Russia has lost the connection with traditional culture by destroying that culture. Russia is not a "unique civilization," but a country stuck in civilizational uncertainty. It truly is "Eurasia," but not in the sense of an organic mix of European and Asian principles but in the sense of their mechanical combination. The problem is that this combination increases the danger of Russia's collapse.

312 | LONELY POWER

During the Putin "economic miracle," Russia had at least the appearance of a good claim to possessing a special model of development. Without that miracle, however, the elite has begun to invent mythical justifications that only diminish its chances of successfully restructuring. Zbigniew Brzezinski used Arnold Toynbee's phrase "suicidal statecraft" to characterize the policies of the George W. Bush administration. I think that term is much more applicable to the activities of the Russian elite over the past twenty years.

Of course, anyone following the zigzags of Russian political thought will see that the ruling team is open to experimenting with mutually exclusive doctrines. The same people who only recently insisted that Russia wants an independent path have turned to trying to convince others that it is a part of European civilization and a liberal democracy. In 2009, Sergei Lavrov said,

> Russia was and remains an integral part of European civilization. Relations of mutual dependence and mutual influence are developing between us and other European states. We give up something, we get something in return. And now, when Europe is becoming more multinational and multiconfessional, we could help our partners in developing the skills of civilizational compatibility, which is impossible without inculcating tolerance.

I'd love to hear what Europeans think they could learn from Russia about "tolerance" and "civilizational compatibility." Civil rights? Freedom of the press? Tolerance of other religions? Or perhaps it's the Russian attitude toward "persons of Caucasian nationality." At least Lavrov's main message is clear: The Russian regime is no longer trying to present Russia as an alternative to the West—for now. This is a cardinal shift from Lavrov's previous position. In May 2010 Lavrov reconfirmed his new position, saying, "Russia is an integral part of Europe," and "Russia's foreign policy is based on [a] philosophy of cooperation."

Apparently, Lavrov was quite taken with the ideas of "mutual aid" and "mutual integration" of Russia and the West. As he informed his audience in Washington, "Socialism and liberal capitalism ... proved their insolvency. It is clear that we need something in between, something well-balanced, something not so categorical and not so uncompromising."[1] I imagine it was news to them that the era of liberal capitalism had ended. Those Western optimists who cheered the birth of the new era should have listened to the new mantra on "convergence" being chanted by the

Russian foreign minister. The Russian official establishment interprets it not as the development of European institutions in Russia but the expansion of Russian capital, interests, and rules of the game throughout the world.

Putin himself has been trying to convince the world that Russia does not differ at all from the liberal democracies. "The fundamental bases of Russia's political and economic system fully correspond to world standards," Putin insisted. He then demonstrated a rather strange understanding of world standards. Insisting that everyone, everywhere come to an agreement about who gets power, Putin explained, "When my friend Blair left, Gordon Brown became the prime minister. Did they consult the people of Great Britain? No, it was a transition of power and they were the two who made the decision."[2] It's possible he really believes this, but if so, it only goes to show the tenuousness of his grasp of the world around him. What kind of political system could form under this man's guidance?

Beginning in late 2009, the Russian regime in the person of Medvedev has started to insist that Russia is not only a liberal democracy; it is prepared to share its experiences as such with the world. In the blink of an eye, it seems, Russia has turned from an independent civilization into a missionary for Western civilization.

"The modern state is first of all a democratic state," Medvedev explained. It wasn't clear whom he was trying to convince—himself, Putin, Russia? Speaking at the United Nations in the fall of 2009, he sounded like a human rights activist, tying world politics to the protection of human rights inside individual countries. "The protection of human rights and interests, the universal application of generally accepted norms and principles must be the base for strengthening trust and stability in international relations," he said.[3] Coming from the leader of a country where gross violations of human rights are endemic, was this naïveté or hypocrisy?

The political West decided not to ponder this question, instead responding positively to the invitation to discuss democracy. The forum for this discussion, again under Medvedev's aegis, took place in Yaroslavl in the fall of 2009. Attendants included the prime ministers of France and Spain, Francois Fillon and José Luis Rodriguez Zapatero, and public opinion leaders like Alvin Toffler, Immanuel Wallerstein, and Fareed Zakaria. A-list participation like this could be interpreted as Western recognition that Russia was turning into an genuine center of intellectual debate—a democratic Mecca. Why else would such luminaries come to Russia to discuss democracy—just out of curiosity? This was a clever move on the part of the Kremlin. Who in the West could now dare criticize the Kremlin for being undemocratic? Who will pay attention to the marginalized Russians whose complaints about curtailed rights and rigged elections have become such a bore?

One sometimes gets the impression that the Western actors are proud to take part in the Kremlin's games without putting too much thought into their real roles. Let me quote Lord George Robertson, former NATO secretary-general and currently vice-chairman of the board of TNK-BP, a British-Russian joint oil venture. "The Yaroslavl Forum had great significance. This was the first forum (!) that gave the world leaders a chance to look deeply into the problems of the contemporary state," Robertson said in an interview with a pro-Kremlin media outlet. It is unclear what breakthrough ideas made this forum so "significant" and why these ideas were not presented to a broader world audience. Lord Robertson's excitement runs further. "... My old friend, vice-speaker of the Russian Duma Vladimir Zhirinovsky, participated in my panel ... He hugged me warmly and said that I was the greatest NATO Secretary-General (!)."[4] For those unfamiliar with the Russian political landscape, Zhirinovsky is the leader of the Russian ultra-nationalist party, and no one in Russia who values his reputation would admit to even knowing him. If a distinguished representative of the European political elite believes what he saying, then there is no hope that Europe will ever understand what is happening in Russia. It may happen that Lord Roberson's views are influenced by the fact that he sits on the board of a company that has ties to the Kremlin. This raises the dilemma of principles and personal interests that some distinguished representatives of the Western elite must solve. The decisions they have made so far hardly help the West to preserve its moral stance in the eyes of Russian society.

The Russian elite, which had only recently insisted on the need for a strict hierarchy of authority and rejection of the West, has changed its tune. The apologists for Putin's authoritarianism are now discussing the criteria for perfecting democracy on a world-wide scale. Medvedev himself made his job demonstrating adherence of the Russian political leadership to democratic standards. Look at his interview to George Stephanopoulos in April 12, 2010.

Stephanopoulos: I wanted to get your view on what's the single most important thing that the average American needs to know about Russia today exactly.

Medvedev: That Russia is the same normal country as America.

Stephanopoulos: What does that mean?

Medvedev: That means exactly what I said—that we have similar values. And have basically probably the same, what the regular Americans would like to have."[5]

One could wonder whether Medvedev himself believed what he said or whether he thought his audience would believe it! At his meeting in the Brookings Institution in April 2010 Medvedev again highlighted democratic principles, saying, "... We should build a long-term pragmatic relationship for the future based upon democratic values and economic freedom and common goals to counter global threats." These comments could only raise positive expectations among the American audience with respect to the Russian leader who looks so different from his older partner. Medvedev's audience should have paid more attention to how he ended his thought. "True, we have a very different history, and people see things—sometimes they see things in different ways," he said.[6] Each time the Russian leader starts to mention a "different" approach while discussing democracy, you should know: he is looking for a way to justify his country's "imitation democracy."

The ease with which the ruling tandem and its propagandists switch rhetoric and style of behavior is one more confirmation of the absence of a civilizational vector in Russia, that is, of strategy and ideological principles. Yesterday the rulers' agenda was stability. Today it is modernization. Tomorrow it could be security. None of it has anything to do with reality. Indeed, it's meant to distract people from reality.

Being everything at once and nothing in particular helps the Russian political class maintain the status quo by appealing to all public forces. But its civilizational uncertainty makes it impossible for Russia to respond to modern challenges.

How serious are the obstacles that prevent Russia from moving from the "gray zone" of uncertainty toward the liberal rules of the game? In the early twentieth century, transformation was hindered by Russia's cultural and historical baggage, its socioeconomic backwardness, and its archaic society. Today, these factors are no longer in play. Let me remind you that cultural and historical differences with the West, a lower level of economic development, and even the lack of civil society did not keep countries very different from the West like India, Japan, South Korea, South Africa, and a number of countries of Southern Europe and post-communist Europe from joining liberal civilization.

The causes for the failure of the liberal-democratic project in Russia at the present stage lie on a different plane. The first cause is the particular nature of the post-Soviet Russian elite, which for now cannot live in conditions of political competition. The second cause resides in the Soviet Union's nuclear and great-power legacies, including Russia's permanent membership in the Security Council and Russia's ambition to become one of the pillars of the world security system. This status is the main precondition for replication of a superpower identity and, consequently, for personalized power. The combination of great-power status and personalized power explains Moscow's behavior on the world stage and how that behavior reinforces Russian authoritarianism.

Russia's civilizational blurriness is manifested in the simultaneous presence of democratic slogans and authoritarian instruments, liberal, conservative, and leftist rhetoric, populism and liberal technocracy, and cooperation with Western states and hostility toward them. The Russian regime is trying to find support in the most varied strata, ranging from liberal Westernizers to extreme nationalists. The state alternately demonstrates paternalism and alienation from the public, overwhelming force and total impotence. The ruling team and the groups servicing it include *siloviki*, liberals, statists, Westernizers, proponents of dictatorship, and supporters of liberalization. The existential model for the Russian system is that of an omnivorous chameleon. It is not surprising then that the contemporary Russian project has no ideological framework; by the time you've defined it, it's mutated into something else. It is telling that the Russian political class cannot clearly articulate what it has created and what its goals are.

It is not yet clear how this civilizational uncertainty will influence the prospects of transformation in Russia. One might think that reforming an imitational system that is somewhat open to the world and allows some freedoms should be easier than transforming a strict authoritarian system. The examples of Ukraine and Serbia, where hybrid regimes eased movement toward political pluralism, are evidence of that possibility. But reforming the imitational system in Russia will likely be much harder than expected. Liberal principles and ideas were deformed here, losing their original meaning and turning into their opposites. As a result, the transformation of this system, a cocktail of mutually exclusive ingredients, is a much more daunting and uncertain task.

However, there is at least one quality of the imitational system that should give us hope. It cannot fully close itself off from the world. There will always be numerous cracks in its walls through which insiders can see the world outside and vice versa. Transparency and openness have been great engines of human progress. So, let's wait and see how Russian society handles the greatest obstacle on its path to liberal democracy: *civilizational uncertainty.*

Notes

1. Sergei Lavrov, "Russia–U.S. Relations: Perspectives and Prospects for the New Agenda," speech at the Carnegie Endowment for International Peace, May 7, 2009, http://carnegieendowment.org/events/?fa=eventDetail&id=1336.

2. Putin's speech before members of the Valdai Club, September 11, 2009, http://www.rian.ru/mm/20090911/184663534.html.

3. Dmitri Medvedev's speech at the 64th Session of the UN General Assembly, September 24, 2009, http://www.kremlin.ru/transcripts/5552.

4. Russki Institut [The Russian Institute], "Medvedev: Povorot k Progresu" [Medvedev: The Turn Toward Progress], Moscow, no. 4–6, February 24, 2010.

5. Transcript: "George Stephanoupos Interviews Russian President Dmitri Medvedev," April 9, 2010, Johnson Russia List, 2010N71, April 12, 2010, www.cdi.org/russia/johnson.

6. "Russia–U.S. Relations and Russia's Vision for International Affairs," address by Dmitry Medvedev, President of the Russian Federation, http://www.brookings.edu/events/2010/0413_medvedev.aspx.

58 THE GOAL OF POWER IS TO RETAIN POWER

As the year 2010 began, Russia continued living in the moment, afraid to peer past its imminent sensations into the far-off future. The fear, even horror, that consumed the elite and the society in early 2009, when Russia stared into the abyss of economic crisis, had abated but not disappeared fully. Society seemed impossibly weary. It continued to support the regime, but the number of Russians who had neither affection nor trust for it was growing.[1] The political class grew increasingly bewildered and annoyed by the ruling team. "I am so sick of them!" was a phrase one heard otherwise loyal insiders as they pondered the prospect of the Putin-Medvedev duo lasting beyond the elections of 2012.

Official television programming sought to amuse the people endless song, dance, and melodrama. Medvedev, Putin, and their spin doctors did their best to look confident and happy for the cameras, but Russians could see these phony smiles beginning to crack. No one knew what was coming, or what Russians would do if the government failed to address their problems. They seemed to know there was a dead end somewhere ahead, but the only thing they knew to do was move forward.

One thing was clear: The period of Putin stability based on oil prices and the memory of the chaos under Yeltsin was over. The authorities managed, albeit with difficulty, to avoid economic collapse and mass social protests during the global financial crisis. But society was gradually sobering up. There were signs that the ruling team finally realized that the Russian petrostate would pose obstacles to economic revival and even stability, something that was much more important for the regime. The raw-materials–based economy had demonstrated its limits even to incorrigible optimists. Reforms were the only way to stimulate enough economic growth to guarantee a tolerable standard of living. "Renewal or death!" became the new mantra. True, no one heard the word "change" pass Putin's lips.

For many in the political milieu, renewal meant Putin's departure. "Putin must go!" said those in the Russian establishment who blamed him for all their woes. There were more than just opposition figures voicing this demand; as a matter of reflex more than thought, many Russians view reform as a change of people rather than principles. Either way, by the first half of 2009 quite a few people in the political establishment called for the elevation of Medvedev and the concentration of political power in his hands. Even a few liberals held out hopes for Medvedev, despite the risk that his ascendance could have the effect of saving the personalized system by creating the illusion of change.

How was Medvedev responding to these developments? He tried to stay within the confines of his role as loyal Putin partner. He balanced his liberal statements with statements in the opposite direction, following his predecessor's time-tested model for ruling: one step forward, two steps back. Of modernization, Medvedev warned, "In a number of cases, the state was forced to tighten screws in order to overcome the crisis."[2] There was nothing in those words to show that the Russian president believed that getting out of the crisis required liberalization. Besides, nothing threatened the Kremlin's power. Why should Medvedev become a kamikaze reformer and risk breaking his own neck?

Medvedev did, however, make a few gestures that were taken as hopeful signs by Russian liberals and the West. In the spring of 2009, he gave an interview to the opposition newspaper *Novaya Gazeta*, met with human rights activists, and agreed with the idea of a Russian version of Hyde Park, a speaker's corner for dissidents. The president promised to initiate a review of the draconian law on nongovernmental organizations that was cutting off the oxygen to civil society. In the fall, Medvedev raised the level of his liberal rhetoric, publishing an appeal titled "Russia, forward!" on a liberal website and reiterating its theses in his annual address to the Federal Assembly on November 12, 2009. He was beginning to sound almost like an opposition figure. "Are we supposed to keep dragging into our future the primitive raw-materials economy, chronic corruption, and obsolete habit of depending on the state?" he asked. "Does a Russia overwhelmed by these burdens even have its own tomorrow? ... Democratic institutions are basically formed ... but their quality is very far from ideal." Medvedev assured the public, "In the twenty-first century our country once again needs all-around modernization. This will be the first modernization in our history based on democratic values and institutions."[3]

Attentive observers noticed something else in Medvedev's rhetoric. He wasn't basing his modernization plans on a desire to improve people's lives but on "the need for Russia to obtain the status of a world power on a fundamentally new basis." Global pretensions remained the animating factor of this "reformist" president. Having lambasted the system, he warned against rushing reforms: "We won't hurry ... The changes will be gradual ... Russian democracy will not mechanically copy foreign models." It was the old song of the Russian "protectors." The absurdity was that Medvedev was criticizing a system built by his colleague Prime Minister Putin, whom he had no intention of forcing out of power.

To make perfectly clear how the Kremlin planned to implement modernization, Vladislav Surkov, the main Kremlin political spin doctor, explained its essence: "The more money, knowledge, and technology we can receive from the leading countries, the more sovereign and strong will our democracy be."[4] Translation: Russia will take whatever Western aid it can get to maintain its system of personalized power.

Members of the Russian ruling elite made some curious proposals about how to get the West to foot the bill for Russia's technological modernization. The most original proposal belonged to Anatoly Chubais, who announced, "We are convinced that it is not realistic that we will get the most advanced technology somewhere in the world, in the West.... What should we do? We must help our business buy the high tech companies." Thus Russia doesn't need to worry about changing the rules of the game to foster innovation; all it needs to do is to buy innovation, by acquiring innovative firms from all over the world. Of course, it's not clear how these companies will maintain their innovative edge in a system that rejects innovation.

This obviously raises a host of questions. How can you hope to renew Russia while keeping personified power, a sixteenth-century governing model? How can you stimulate post-industrial development, which requires freedom and competition, by borrowing technology or buying companies in the West? Finally, how can you hope to renew Russia if the renewer (Medvedev) has no resources or support?

The backers of Russia's "reform from above" plan invariably answered, "Be patient. Medvedev will start modernization, but gradually." Apparently only the Kremlin, and not even the whole Kremlin, was prepared to believe that the cosmetic measures proposed by Medvedev would bring reform. At the start of his term in 2001–2002, Putin had also tried to implement partial reforms—fighting corruption, increasing the role of the courts, administrative reform, and diversification of the economy. The results then were as pathetic as they are now. Medvedev was re-running a failed experiment.

Nevertheless, observers, especially in the West, compared Medvedev to Gorbachev, and his reform to *perestroika*. The comparison was misleading. In his day, Gorbachev proclaimed *glasnost* and opened public discussion, thereby separating himself and the country from the old system. Medvedev, limiting himself to talk, has remained within the old system. That is the difference between him and Gorbachev. And besides, how could Medvedev begin a course of reform while he was merely the assistant to the person whose hands still remained on the real levers of power?

By early 2010, few people in Russia doubted that Medvedev's liberal rhetoric was anything more than an attempt to find a way to keep the system afloat. There was nothing new in this. Medvedev's idea of modernization was merely a reiteration of the Russian tradition of using scientific and technological innovations from the West to strengthen the state and its global role. That was exactly what Peter the Great did, for exactly the same reasons, in the eighteenth century, and exactly what Stalin did in the twentieth. Russia would borrow from the West what it needed to bridge the military and technological gap. But because it never fostered a truly innovative environment, that gap would always begin to grow anew. Medvedev was merely extending this tradition into the twenty-first century. But if they had never worked in the past, then how could they hope it would work in the high-tech present?

That reform was really about self-preservation was reinforced by the fact that the Kremlin spin doctors who had lately talked about stability were suddenly revamped as "modernizers." "The new buzzword is 'renewal,' and modernization will last for a long time," they explained. Of course, they wanted to implement modernization over such a long timeline that society simply got tired of waiting for its results.

Medvedev's address to the Federal Assembly made it clear what was really going on. "Any attempts under democratic slogans to destabilize the situation and the state, to splinter society, will be stopped," he said, chilling any hopes for a breakthrough. Medvedev let it be known that he wanted the same kind of Russian modernization that all Russian leaders had wanted before him: He wanted to perfect the system without changing its substance. Soon afterward, at the November 2009 congress of the United Russia Party, the ruling tandem made it clear that modernization would be based on "Russian conservatism." "Reform" and "conservatism" can go together just fine in the European senses of the terms. But what does "conservatism" mean in the Russian sense—a return to the traditional values of the Russian empire, or to the dogmas of the Soviet era? The Russian elite, however, understood right away that "conservatism" meant that the leaders wouldn't change a thing. Putin and Medvedev's new course was "stability and development, constant renewal without stagnation and revolution." To the Russian elite, their words signified "change that will maintain the status quo."

Medvedev's draft for a European security treaty, which he sent to European leaders in late 2009, confirmed the imitational character of his modernization scheme. In essence, his idea was an expression of Putin's 2007 demands, whose aggressiveness surprised the West. In Medvedev's version, these demands sounded more civilized, but their substance was the same. The substance of the Russian security initiative was to rebuild the European security system by removing its democratic and humanitarian dimensions. The Russian elite dreamed of a security structure that would allow Russia to maintain its great-power status through an unending process of negotiations on military and political issues. It also wanted veto power over NATO decisions, which would effectively end further expansion and protect Russia's spheres of interest. Medvedev declared that his modernization would be "the first in our history based on democratic values and institutions"; in reality it was an attempt to keep European civilization at bay. His idea of European security was a return to the geopolitics and balance-of-power arrangements of the Soviet era. This was all of a piece with "modernization from above."

James Sherr was right: The Russian proposals that Russian analysts termed "Helsinki 2" were intended to establish "Westphalia 2." I personally can't decide whether the Russian ruling duo really believed that the West and first of all Europe would agree to allow Russia to dismantle the security system that brought peace to the continent and place Russia outside the rules of the game, or whether the Kremlin as usual followed the Leninist rule: "Let's jump into the water and see what happens!"

At the beginning of 2010 the U.S. administration rejected the Kremlin proposal for the new European security architecture—not an unexpected step. Hilary Clinton in her remarks on the future of European security at L'École Militaire in Paris on January 30, 2010, said, "Indivisibility of security is a key feature of those [Medvedev's] proposals. And that is a goal we share, along with other ideas in the Russian proposals which reaffirm principles of the Helsinki Final Act and the NATO-Russia Act. We believe that these common goals are best pursued in the context of existing institutions, such as the OSCE and the NATO-Russia Council, rather than by negotiating new treaties, as Russia suggested—a very long and cumbersome process."[5] The Russian ruling team got a new pretext for hurt feelings and returned to its usual pastime of bashing Americans.

The modernization kick and new security initiatives could allow one to draw a number of conclusions about how the regime handles the economic crisis. The ruling tandem knew that it couldn't maintain control over society and find a way out of the economic crisis within the Putin paradigm of hands-on rule with a repressive bent. They needed to "humanize" the system, but only to a certain degree, so as not to undermine their monopoly on power. The twin-headed nature of the regime allowed them to follow two mutually exclusive courses simultaneously: Putin drew in the traditionalist part of the public while Medvedev worked to humanize the system in the eyes of other observers. Medvedev rebuilt the bridges to the West that Putin had burned in order to better deal with the effects of the economic crisis and new geopolitical reality. In essence, the two were reformatting the crumbling Putin consensus into a new one, which appeared to be oriented on different vectors—continuity and renewal, with the latter really being about preserving the status quo. This tactic of "playing on two pianos," even if it succeeded, could offer only a short-lived breather for the Russian personalized system.

Let me stress that this tactic didn't expand freedoms for society or for opponents of the regime; it only co-opted society and the opposition into realizing the regime's plans. In other words, they were trying to fit dissent into the framework of the system.

Even the president's defenders began grumbling early on about Medvedev's reluctance to propose any concrete steps of reform. One Moscow newspaper printed an article by an old and loyal Medvedite, Alexander Budberg, that sounded like a cry of desperation:

> We don't need to wait for the appearance of a million-strong class interested in change. It's enough to take a step down that path for the critical mass of proponents of renewal to show itself immediately....
> If the opportunities [for change] are lost, history will not forgive us.[6]

Medvedev gave no sign of heeding the call of his loyalist.

Here are just a few of the things Russian observers had to say about "modernization *à la* Medvedev":

- "Medvedev's modernization is protecting Russia from Western influence. Only Medvedev wants to defend himself from it, not like under Putin, but more gently";

- "If this modernization rhetoric is part of Medvedev's election campaign, then it's a false start. If it's serious, then it's yet another plan to replace a market economy and normal democratic institutions";

- "The president has declared, 'Russia, forward.' But which way is forward?"

Journalists asked Medvedev, "Mr. President, your words seem as if you're stepping on the brakes and telling them to go *faster, faster!*" And these were among the kinder comments.

In February 2010 Vladislav Surkov, the Kremlin's top ideologist, laid out the leadership's views on Russian modernization. Surkov's revelations were a cold shower for those idealists who had been dreaming about sweeping political changes; the leaders, it appears, had a different plan. Surkov declared the Kremlin's intention to build Russia's Silicon Valley, an "innovative city" of 30,000 to 40,000 of the brightest and most talented people from all corners of the world. The selected geniuses would live in ultramodern houses with the highest levels of comfort. Their task would be to create cutting-edge technologies to be brought to market by Russian companies. By 2015, this Miracle City, according to Surkov, would generate up to $7 billion of annual income. However, all hopes for liberalization on the path to the Miracle City had to be put aside. "There is a conception, which I endorse. Some call it 'authoritarian modernization.' I don't care what they call it ... It is crucially important to preserve political stability," explained Surkov.[7] This was a message to those who still believed that Medvedev was going to liberalize the country. His closest lieutenant wanted no doubts left: *No way! We'll follow another route, that is, innovation through political status quo.* Careful observers will have noted that Kremlin representatives have started to use the term "innovation" instead of "modernization," trying to emphasize that they had in mind only technological, not political, change.

The plan to build Russia's Silicon Valley has triggered lively competition among Russians for the best demonstration of sarcasm. Vladimir Ryzhkov, a Russian democratic politician, wrote

The real attraction of the Kremlin's Innovation City lies not in what it will accomplish for innovation but in how it will line the pockets of Russia's corrupt officials. Greedy bureaucrats are already salivating in anticipation of the hundreds of construction permits that will be required to develop a Silicon Valley from scratch. They are dreaming about the limitless bribes and kickbacks that they will be able to extort, how many registration papers and work permits for foreigners they will "sell.".... Nobody has bothered to estimate what the latest Kremlin fantasy will cost, but the price tag will clearly be in the hundreds of billions of rubles.[8]

"The principal question is whether we can do something effective and reminiscent of Silicon Valley in a country with an authoritarian regime," asked Yevgeny Yasin, a prominent liberal economist, rhetorically. Reflecting on the Kremlin's idea of involving Russian business in the construction of its Miracle City, Yasin was more than skeptical: "When a big fierce cannibal lures in little girls and offers free cooperation, it is hard to believe in the effectiveness of such a project."[9] Georgy Satarov, a former adviser to Yeltsin, had the same reaction, adding, "In recent months, the media have been overloaded with discussions of the authorities' various plans. All recent discussions of modernization have one thing in common—a complete lack of any connection to reality."[10] I would differ on one point: all of the plans for "modernization" and "innovation" are quite closely tied to a very definite "reality": the one that the Kremlin wants to maintain at any price.

If there was any ambiguity about the Kremlin's agenda, it evaporated in March 2010 at the moment Vladimir Putin appointed himself head of the government's high-tech commission charged with pushing the modernization agenda. After watching Medvedev's modernization rhetoric with an ironic gaze, the prime minister decided to take over the role of change agent in order to pursue it in his own way. Now, change would be supported by real resources. Innovative technology and political continuity had to become Putin's strategy. Putin moved onto Medvedev's turf and his message was quite clear: *Two years and billions of dollars have been spent to promote innovation and no results. It's my turn to get things done!* Medvedev has been left with his slogans but with no resources to implement them.

True, after two years in the Kremlin President Medvedev is not simply a passive decoration on the political scene. There are signs that the president has acquired a taste for politics. He definitely wants to strengthen his image as a modernizer. He continues to talk about the need to fight corruption. He pushed through a law that allowed the formation of parliamentary factions consisting of a single (!) deputy, who allegedly could represent the opposition. He even launched a shakeup of the Interior Ministry, which has been under attack for months for corruption, abuse, and human and civil rights violations. The Institute for Contemporary Development (INSOR), regarded as a presidential think tank (Medvedev heads up its board of trustees), published a report titled "Russia in the 21st Century: Visions for the Future," which stressed the need for a liberal path for Russia.[11]

However, few in Russia believe that Medvedev has the power to have an impact. According to the Levada Center, only 13 percent of respondents considered Medvedev Russia's ruler (April 2010).[12] In another survey, respondents said they did not believe that Medvedev could change things. Most doubted his intent to move beyond cosmetic change. Approximately 66 percent of respondents were convinced that Medvedev's attempts to reform the Interior Ministry would fail. Only 11 percent believed that his modernization campaign would succeed.[13]

Even Medvedev's staunch supporters from INSOR, who were calling for a liberal future for Russia, did not believe that liberal reforms were possible in the short-term perspective. "Direct and free elections ... cannot take place in their true form. We need agreements between the elite groups, but not the popular vote ... The real question could boil down to the following: Putin or Medvedev," said Igor Yurgens, president of INSOR. Yevgeni Gontmacher, another liberal from Medvedev's entourage, declared, "We believe that democratic modernization can be pursued only through authoritarian tools."[14] This conclusion hardly differs from Surkov's motto: "Consolidated power in Russia is a tool for modernization."

Asked whether the president agrees with their conclusions, Yurgens was forced to admit, "To a large extent, yes. But as a person in possession of a much larger volume of information, he is undoubtedly entitled and even obliged to disagree with many things and not to adopt an exclusively liberal standpoint. Understand this—liberal, conservative ... That is how a heart expands and contracts and it is the same with the political system. There can be no monopoly."[15] If this is how Medvedev understands the political trajectory—a step forward, a step back—there is no hope that he could become a transformational leader.

The president himself has admitted repeatedly that he and Putin have no political differences. "My union with Putin is quite effective and it brings certain benefits to our country, in my opinion.... It's good when the relations are good between the president and prime minister," Medvedev said in an interview in *Paris Match*.[16] Relations are indeed good when politicians think alike.

Medvedev, meanwhile, increasingly resembled a pathetic, second-rate actor who was merely filling air-time while the star of the show prepared to come back on stage. Indeed, more than just a star, Putin was the playwright and director, too.

At some point early on, Medvedev might have tried to break out of this pathetic role, but as time passed, his role as the Talk Man made it impossible for him to swing into action. It's pleasing to imagine that Medvedev was biding his time, husbanding his strength to make a quantum leap in reform. But there is no evidence of that. And even if he had, there is no indication that he would have replaced the system of personalized rule; all of the "system reformers" were telling him not to hurry, and in their understanding, "Let's not hurry" meant top-down governance. This would have brought nothing more than the same system with a different face.

The tandem's search for a survival strategy, meanwhile, has given rise to several paradoxes. Medvedev's appearance as a modernizer loosened Putin's hierarchy and began to delegitimize his hold on power. But keeping Putin on as national leader also kept Medvedev from becoming a serious figure, and his empty calls for modernization discredited the idea of change. These paradoxes are evidence of the dead end the regime finds itself in, largely due to its own choices. The only thing that remains unclear is whether Medvedev actually realized he was only helping to build a new Potemkin Village; I, for one, wouldn't underestimate Medvedev's intelligence in this regard. Putin of course understood Medvedev's role, and he obviously enjoyed watching him play the part.

The state of relations within the tandem has provided an inexhaustible source of speculation and jokes among Russians and Western observers. "There are more important things to study in Russia," I tried to tell the diplomats at one Western embassy. "Perhaps," they said. "But our bosses want us to give daily briefings of the relations between Putin and Medvedev." If they really were doing this, they would never understand what's happening in Russia.

To each his own, I guess. Western observers continued diligently reporting on the outcomes of the Kremlin's shadow puppet shows. Meanwhile, beyond the Kremlin stage, life went on in a massive parallel world that had less and less to do with official politics. I was worried that if people didn't look up from the puppet show, they were liable to be in for a rude shock from the real world.

As for the tandem, its time was coming to an end. After the new presidential elections, whoever is elected to the Kremlin is unlikely to share power with his prime minister, and a strong leader is unlikely to accept a secondary role. The next presidential elections were scheduled for 2012. But the Kremlin—or to be more precise, Vladimir Putin—could change that schedule at any time, if it suits his interests.

There is no need to look that far ahead, though. The Russian regime still had to get through the present election cycle, which offered little to cheer them. The exhaustion of Putin's former way of doing things was clear by now, and instability was growing throughout the entire Russian power structure, from top to bottom. This explains why the regime was trying to please the electorate, co-opt liberals and other forces, and discredit any alternatives. At the same time, the authorities were strengthening mechanisms of repression and using scare tactics against members of the opposition or local manifestations of social protest.

All of these moves served only to put off the moment of truth. Stability built on bribery and fear is never reliable. A system that has no mechanisms for preventing or resolving conflicts politicizes protest and pushes it out onto the streets.

Notes

1. In March 2010, only 22 percent of the respondents said that the Russian authorities represented "a good team of politicians that has been leading the country on a correct course." See http://www.levada.ru/press/2010032506.html.

2. "Vystuplienije Medvedeva v programie 'Vesti niedeli'" [Medvedev's remarks on "News of the Week" program], http://www.regnum.ru/news/1125119.html.

3. Dmitri Medvedev, State of the Union Message to the Federal Assembly, November 12, 2009, http://www.kremlin.ru/transcripts/5979.

4. Vladislav Surkov, "Obnovliaites', Gospoda!" [Renew Yourselves, Ladies and Gentelmen!], Itogi, October 26, 2009, http://www.itogi.ru/russia/2009/44/145418.html.

5. Hilary Clinton, Remarks on the Future of European Security, http://www.state.gov/secretary/rm/2010/01/136273.htm.

6. Alexander Budberg, "Reshajushchij moment" [The Decisive Moment], November 2, 2009, Moskovsky Komsomolets, www.mk.ru/editions/daily/article/2009/11/02/ 378750_reshayuschiy-moment.html.

7. Vladislav Surkov, "Chudo Vozmozhno" [A Miracle Is Possible], Vedomosti, February 15, 2010.

8. Vladimir Ryzhkov, "Build Innovation City and They Won't Come," Moscow Times, February 25, 2010.

9. Yevgeny Yasin, "Sviriepyi Lyudoed priglashajet k Sotrudnichestvu malen'kich devochek" [Fierce Cannibal Lures Little Girls and Offers Free Cooperation], http://www.ej.ru/?a=note&id=9889.

10. Georgy Satarov, "Chuda ne budet" [There Will Be No Miracle], http://www.ej.ru/ ?a=note&id=8990.

11. The INSOR report concluded, "Upgrading the political system has become an indispensable component of modernization.... Democracy as a system of discussion, agreement and "feedback" between the state and society reduces the risk of policy mistakes. International comparisons show that eight out of the ten best and ten worst examples of economic transformation happened under authoritarian regimes—showing that authoritarian modernization can either go extremely well or catastrophically badly. Russia simply cannot take the risk of its going badly." See http://www.insor-russia.ru/ru/news/7995.

12. About 51 percent thought that the power was shared by Putin and Medvedev, and 28 percent thought that the power was in Putin's hands. Maxim Glikin, "Putin Vernis," [Putin, Come Back], Vedomosti, April 4, 2010.

13. Vera Kholmogorova, "Nemnogie Rossianii nadeiutsia na reorganizatsiiu Ministerstva vnutrennykh del libo na natsional'nuiu modernizatsiyu" [Few Russians Are Hopeful With Regard to the Reorganization of the Interior Ministry or National Modernization], Vedomosti, March 5, 2010.

14. Yevgeni Gontmacher, "Promezhutochnye otvety" [Modernization: Interim Answers], Vedomosti, February 17, 2010.

15. Igor Yurgens, "Nie chotitie modernizirovat'sia?" [Don't Want to Modernize?] www.kp.ru/daily/24442/607772.

16. Dmitri Medvedev: "Interv'yu franstuzskomu zhurnalu Pari-Match" [Dmitri Medvedev: Interview in the French Magazine Paris Match], February 25, 2010, http://www.kremlin.ru/transcripts/6964.

59 CAN RUSSIA BE RENEWED BY LEAVING EVERYTHING AS IT IS?

The time has now come to ask the question, "What next?" What is likely to happen in Russia in the weeks, months, and years after this book goes to press? First of all, in the event that real political competition or an independent judiciary that could guarantee such competition fails to emerge, there is no reason to anticipate substantive changes in the Russian system, even if there is a change in the political regime. Thus there is no reason to hope for a reform of the raw-materials economy or for constructive changes in foreign policy.

Russia's options in general are becoming more limited every day, because the system cannot compete with Western society in innovation or ability to address global challenges. This creates a paradox of sorts. On the one hand, the Russian elite wants dialogue with West so that it can gain access to its technical and material capabilities. On the other hand, it wants to protect Russian society from the "corrupting influence" of Western values. It cannot permit real liberalization of the system because that would threaten to bring in a completely different mechanism of politics that could not guarantee the elite's monopoly on power and property in Russia. Political pluralism and competitiveness would mean the "end of history" in Russia—that is, the end of the era of personalized power and imitation democracy. The Russian elite will still be able to manage this contradictory agenda for the time being, albeit with growing difficulty.

We cannot rule out the possibility that the conservative part of the Russian ruling team will try to preserve the system and its position in it by wielding an "iron hand" and even more blatant anti-Western posturing. The "iron hand" will be more likely to come into play as the social base of the regime grows smaller, provided there is no mass demand for a liberal alternative. At discussions in Moscow in early 2010, many experts spoke of the possibility and even inevitability of this turn of events. Of course, the part of the political class oriented toward dialogue with the West, the "compradors," won't support the repressive scenario. But could it consolidate in order to prevent a stronger form of authoritarianism, or neototalitarianism? It's not clear. This isn't a potential clash of ideologies or even of political orientations, but a clash of different ways of existence for the same *rentier* class, whose individual segments structure their interests and view the West's role in securing those interests in varying ways. However, even if the *siloviki* scenario prevails, it's unlikely that the traditionalists will be able to hold on to power for long. Russia doesn't have the prerequisites for that: the willingness of the political class to isolate the country; reliable power structures; ideas to mobilize society; and the public's willingness to turn Russia into North Korea. But we can't rule out the possibility that the ruling stratum will revive a repressive regime in order to hold on to power. If it chooses that path, Russia will pay a high price.

If the preferred option of the comprador segment of the Russian *rentier* class prevailed (soft authoritarianism), their victory would change the regime and leadership but not the system-forming principles underlying the Russian state. We mustn't forget that the last time the Russian state collapsed, what seemed like an anti-system revolution brought about the revival of personalized power in a new form, under a liberal banner. A new batch of "systemic reformers" might try for a repeat of history.

Any open conflict within the Russian elite contains the seeds of hope, however weak, for the radical reform of the traditional state. Such ferment always allows for the possibility of new political forces bubbling up to the surface. In certain circumstances, the very existence of the ruling tandem could stimulate the growth of divisions within the elite, and it could even do so against the tandem's wishes. But let me reiterate: Such a conflict must meet a number of conditions before it could lead to a liberal breakthrough. First and foremost, it requires the emergence of a responsible liberal opposition that will secure society's support. Without that, a schism in the political class will lead to yet another mutation of the same old autocracy in another shape.

If they're lucky, Putin's ruling team may still retain control over the country and secure the replication of its power in 2012. As I write, it certainly has control of the situation. But even if they're not lucky—even if the Putin team loses its grip on power—the same system will probably live on if there are no deeper changes in Russian society and its moods. Such an outcome would mean that Russia would be stuck in viscous stagnation for an indeterminate length of time. If oil prices remain high, society continues to be passive, business interests willingly serve the regime, the opposition stays fragmented, and the West supports the Kremlin, then viscous stagnation is the most probable future scenario for Russia's development.

In a regime that isn't prepared to impose mass repressive measures but is also incapable of dialogue with society, it does not matter who stands as the embodiment of political power. Nor does it matter what rhetoric or governing style the regime employs. In this scenario, economic growth in certain spheres is possible, which will create the appearance of development. Grigory Yavlinksky, who described it some time ago, called this form of stagnation "growth without development." His warning came to pass: Economic growth under the previous Putin regime not only did not lead to the formation of a diversified economic model; it didn't even halt the growth of the gap between Russia and the developed world. Considering this dismal scene, Yegor Gaidar said:

> We can get out of the crisis without rethinking the political system. But creating the conditions for stable economic growth for the next twenty years without that is impossible. There is the experience of the world over the last two centuries. It shows that if you have reliably guaranteed rights to private property, free markets, and a legal system you trust—you will develop dynamically. If you don't have that, there will inevitably be problems.[1]

Not just "problems." The result of retaining civilizational uncertainty will be system rot and atrophy to the point of state implosion, putting the Russian Federation's current geographical format in serious doubt.

Unfortunately, we can't exclude the possibility of a new severe systemic collapse in Russia. With the highly centralized system re-created by Putin, dysfunction in one element can set off a chain reaction leading to a repeat of 1991. All such a chain reaction requires is an economic crisis more serious than the one that befell Russia in 2008. Even without an economic crisis, the failure of individual elements in the political system—for example, a disruption in the connection between the center and the regions—could topple the first domino. Collapse of the system can also result from a series of technological catastrophes befalling Russia's Soviet-era industrial infrastructure. The Chernobyl accident, recall, provided an important incentive for Ukraine to leave the Soviet Union, making its disintegration inevitable.

The technological catastrophes befalling Russia at the moment are less dramatic (for example, the accident at the power station serving Moscow in 2005 and a burst dam in Sayano-Shushensk in 2009). For now, these kinds of events haven't led to a public outcry against the regime. But what will happen if there are more such catastrophes? Even now, there are tragedies occurring in Russia that would have led to the collapse of the government in most normal countries: retirement homes and orphanages burn to the ground, planes crash, submarines and other ships sink, residential buildings, restaurants, and discotheques blow up, trains crash, terrorists detonate bombs in the subway—all of which exact a horrific toll in human lives. The cause for these continual tragedies is not simply obsolescent infrastructure; it's the lack of governmental mechanisms designed to protect the lives of individuals. The Russian public has borne these disasters silently, with teeth clenched, for the time being. The reason they have done so is not due to Russians' world-renowned patience, but because of a loss of faith in the government's role to save them (much less serve them). And once they've lost all faith in the government, people will start looking to save themselves.

The fact that the social protests have not yet become massive has allowed authorities to hope that they would sort it out somehow, as they had done many times before. What capacity for illusion! Several surveys have demonstrated a worrisome trend in the mood of the Russian population that could be a harbinger of more serious problems. In the spring of 2010, the Levada Center found that about 85 percent of Russians saw no opportunity to influence state decision making. Some 77 percent of the population was not prepared to participate in politics. About 62 percent stated that it relies only on itself and tries to avoid any contact with official structures. The latter figure proves that Russians have rid themselves of their traditional paternalism. The system and society are now drifting in opposite directions. The last time that happened, the Soviet Union collapsed. Keep in mind that revolutions can happen when just 1 percent of the active population takes part. In Russia, nearly 30 percent of the population is prepared to take to the streets.[2] The system is saved today by just one fact—the lack of a credible opposition. But the fact that social anger and frustration are growing faster than the political process can channel then increases the danger of degradation and demoralization daily.

At the moment, the Russian collapse scenario seems rather unlikely. But since we only understand part of what is going on, it is reasonable to keep that scenario on the table.

Using force to prolong a doomed system can only hasten its end and have devastating consequences for Russian statehood. Then again, any scenario, including a liberal one, carries the threat of breakdown, due to the fact that Russia contains civilizationally and culturally incompatible national and territorial communities. I'm referring primarily to the North Caucasus. The idea that Russia could not hold together alien elements that the present system has failed to integrate is already the subject of discussion among Russian experts.

Fear of territorial loss and statehood collapse is a substantial obstacle to reform. Even Westernizing liberals shudder to think that reforms could create a repeat of 1991. The liberal flank hasn't prepared itself for such perturbations, but I do believe that they are coming around to the conclusion that the current system is not likely to be reformed and that its transformation will lead to a new state. However, neither the Russian political class as a whole nor the public is ready for that possibility. And the public will not support reform if it believes that this will lead to territorial loss or a new state. History, it seems, continues to hold Russia in its embrace.

Let's talk about what could undermine the Russian system. The time is approaching when the Russian regime will not be able to provide the standard of living and consumer lifestyle that the most dynamic stratum of Russian society has come to expect over the past twenty years. At the same time, the regime will also have a large segment of the population still tied to the obsolete industrial structure and dependent on the shrinking budget. Thus the social base of the system, which has kept things stable throughout the Putin period, may be undermined at any moment.

There is something else that will undoubtedly keep the system fragile: the very principles on which it is presently built. The Russian system is now consuming itself. Take, for example, corruption, which until quite recently was one of the pillars of the Russian state. Today it has become a dreadful source of weakness. Corrupt police and public officials provide little support for the ruling team. The corrupt state apparatus disobeys orders from the center with impunity. The regime understands the threat posed by corruption, but taking decisive measures against it would mean rejecting the principles on which the system is built.

Or consider another factor: the elections whose management the Kremlin has now mastered. Until recently, manipulating elections and falsifying their results helped to preserve continuity of power. But falsification only works when the public agrees to play "Let's pretend!" The time may come when the public says, "Enough! We don't want to play that game anymore!" That's exactly what the people of Serbia and Ukraine did.

The rigged municipal elections in Russia in the fall of 2009, where the real turnout was no more than 20–22 percent, was a case that warrants careful examination. The authorities had to falsify ballots for the United Russia Party (in Moscow falsified ballots added 20 percent to United Russia's margin of victory). In some districts, voters intentionally spoiled 47 percent of the ballots.[3] These events tell us something new. To get support in the parliamentary and presidential elections of 2011–2012, the regime will have to falsify results on an even greater scale. At some point a regime based on such methods will lose all pretense to legitimacy. The only way it will be able to hold on to power in such a situation is repression. I've already discussed where that may lead.

No matter how hard the political class tries to keep Russia drifting through the zone of uncertainty, sooner or later it will have to acknowledge that the present pseudo-project has exhausted itself. A state that satisfies narrow vested interests while pretending that it's satisfying national ones, or that hinders societal transformation but has neither the resources for shutting out the rest of the world nor for oppressing society, is doomed, and its use of imitation to survive increases the danger of its inevitable collapse.

Notes

1. Yegor Gaidar, "Rezhim mozhet ruchnut' nieozhidanno, za dva dnia" [The Regime Can Collapse Unexpectedly, in Two Days], *Novaya Gazeta*, http://www.novayagazeta.ru/data/2009/129/09.html.

2. Levada Center, "The Relationship Between Society and Power in the Eyes of Russians," March 2010, http://www.levada.ru/press/2010031602.html.

3. "Rossijskiye vybory: vchera, siegodnia, zavtra" [The Russian Elections: Yesterday, Today, Tomorrow], December 28, 2009, http://www.liberal.ru/articles/4553; Ivan Smirov, "Marginal'naya vlast' v stranie pofigistov" [The Marginal Power in the Country of People Who Do Not Care], http://www.liberal.ru/articles/4457.

60 CAN RUSSIA GET OUT OF THE DEAD END BY ITSELF?

How will all of the above factors affect Russia's foreign policy? Keep in mind one incontrovertible fact: As the Russian authorities' adaptation is possible when it comes to domestic policy, foreign policy becomes the most conservative tool in the Kremlin's arsenal. Foreign policy also naturally attracts the most traditional, reform-resistant parts of the Russian elite. Consequently, the foreign policy community won't start thinking new thoughts until the process of the system's implosion is in a severely advanced state. During the collapse of the Soviet Union, Russian foreign policy, largely due to Mikhail Gorbachev, didn't block change or provoke an international conflict. It isn't clear how Russian traditionalists would behave in a crisis today, but the probability is high that the state would find it necessary to use foreign policy tools in a power struggle. It is hard to predict now what form that might take: conflicts with neighbors, using "hot spots" to provoke tension, new "gas wars." What is important is that a system that replicates itself by nursing its great-power ambitions will not be able to give them up easily.

"What are you talking about? Russia and the West have sorted out their problems. The 'reset' is working. Even the Russian-Polish relationship has warmed up. Russia and Ukraine are friends again," the reader would argue. This only demonstrates how appearances can be misleading. The new warmth can hardly be sustainable if the Russian elite continues to view the West as a foe that has to be deterred and the neighbors as satellites who belong to Russia's sphere of influence. The honeymoon can continue only if the Western powers accept the Russian way of dealing with the world as they do now.

As for the unexpected friendliness between Russia and the outside world, it should become a cause for concern rather than satisfaction. The new love between Moscow and Kiev is a case in point. New Ukrainian President Viktor Yanukovych has moved his country closer to Moscow, striking deals that would reassert Russia's geopolitical reach (including an extension of the lease of Russia's Black Sea Fleet in return for a sharply lower natural gas price for Ukrainians). This rapprochement, however, made in secret and haste, has demonstrated destructive impulses from both sides. It reconfirmed that energy is the only effective tool that Moscow has to build its relations with the world. In the case of Ukraine, the deal proved the failure of the elite to reform its economy and reduce its dependence on Russia. Both sides have opted to support the stagnant status quo that is so flawed that it is unlikely to endure.[1] Russia has proved once again that unless it reforms its system, its embraces will be highly dangerous for its neighbors and their leaders.

What does Russia need to do to break out of its vicious circle and take on a European identity? It must reform its state matrix. This presumes a solution to *the triad problem*: a transition to the principle of competition in economics and politics; a rejection of the principle of merging power and property; and the rule of law. In practice, these three issues mean a transition to political struggle and the inevitable end of the ruling regime and its focus on continuity and control of property. Solving *the triad problem* is impossible without a review of the Putin-Medvedev foreign policy doctrine, which justifies simultaneous cooperation and confrontation with the West in the name of realizing the interests of the Russian ruling class. Will the Russian elite, or at least part of it, be able to undergo such a radical transformation? To do so, it must first realize that the current model of Russia's development is exhausted, including the great-power ambitions, militarism, and imperial longings that are the foundation of that model.

Such epiphanies usually accompany a crisis—whether social, economic, or in the regime. There are no examples in Russian history of "preventive" reform before a crisis hits. For the time being, the current ruling team has mistaken the lack of massive social unrest and anger as a license to continue moving in the same direction indefinitely. "We'll think of something tomorrow," the denizens of the Kremlin tell themselves, but the longer they think, the greater the danger of losing control of the situation.

There is one more factor that may be just as important for Russia's transformation. I said at the beginning of this book that no liberal transformation has ever taken place without the country in question coming into the orbit of the West. In Europe, the key prerequisite for democracy has been external pressure. This was what facilitated the democratic development of postwar Germany. Accession to the European Union and NATO was the guarantee of irreversible transformation for the post-communist states in Europe. But outside influence means readiness on the part of the country being influenced to limit its own sovereignty. Russia finds itself in a situation where Europe is not prepared to expend the effort necessary to integrate Russia, and Russia is not prepared to give up even part of its sovereignty. On the contrary, retaining sovereignty has become the elite's most important tool for retaining power. Even Russian Westernizing liberals haven't dared to mention that Russia might have to give up a portion of its sovereignty to supranational European structures. For the man in the street, the very idea is blasphemous, a betrayal of the Homeland. Russian leaders see their primary mission as strengthening Russia's sovereignty and maintaining its independent path. How different they are than Konrad Adenauer, who led Germany to democracy and dared to declare in 1953, "Europe is more important than a nation!"

Another factor that simplified the formation of new rules of the game in Europe and the democratic transformation of its previously nondemocratic states was their recognition of America's global role and the need to bring it into European affairs. The Russian elite, on the contrary, continues to see the United States not only as its foe but as the main stimulus for strengthening its independent and assertive course. Yet without a new view of its sovereignty and America's role, Russia will hardly to be able to step onto the path of democratization and join the concert of liberal democracies.

Nothing to worry about, say some liberal observers in Russia, we can make Russia a modern state while taking an independent path and subordinating ourselves to no one. Alas, there is no precedent for liberal transformation without the influence of the West, and Russian development after 1991 gives no indication that that precedent is about to be broken.

Russia's authorities are desperately trying to preserve the traditionalist third of society without rousting its passive remainder out of its torpor. Money accumulated from the sale of energy and raw materials is the most effective method for keeping Russia in a state of sleepy oblivion. The government, for instance, is planning to spend an unusually large amount of money to raise pensions. Why does the government suddenly care about pensioners? Because it is entering a new election cycle and needs to bribe the most disciplined segment of society that goes to vote and usually votes for the regime. But what will the regime do when the money dries up? Of course, there is an arsenal of tried-and-true methods for manipulating public opinion—a return to a fortress mentality and containment of the West, or a search for internal enemies. This last role can be assigned to liberals, other opposition figures, oligarchs, people from the Caucasus, and so on. But while that tactic has worked for many years, where is the guarantee that it will work again?

In its day, the Soviet Union based its existence on a global project. That project was bound for nowhere, but at least it conferred an idea and passion. Today's system has only two ideas: national egotism and personal enrichment. But people are beginning to ask: Is our might a delusion? And who is going to make us rich, and how? The Russian authorities don't have the answers.

Meanwhile, the logic of history moves on. About a third of Russia could now be considered the modernist part of society—people who are psychologically prepared to live and work in a liberal system. The modernist part of Russian society and the passive strata that could join it (which, taken together, would make up about 68 percent of the population) are atomized for now and are just hoping to get by on their own. It's not clear who or what could awaken them, or what will happen when they do awaken. But I will repeat again what I have oftentimes said before: An enormous part of the Russian public is ready to accept new ways of doing things.[2] This fact may become the key to Russia's future history. A conflict of values and politics in Russia is inevitable. The question is only when it will happen and how it will be resolved.

The success of the Russian transformation will greatly depend on whether the Russian elite will be able to comprehend that continuing on the present path is suicidal. In the past, Russia has always sought its truth at the bottom of the abyss. In order to keep from falling into the abyss yet again, society must pressure the elite to take stock of its situation. For now, the public seems to be content with playing the regime's games. Those members of the elite who understand their plight remain too enmeshed in the system to speak out. For the time being, no one is taking responsibility for Russia's future.

Such people appear, however, when there is a societal demand for them. That demand will appear whenever the Russian people decide that they are tired of living a lie. The liberalization of the Gorbachev era arose spontaneously, bringing to the fore previously unknown figures who grasped the historical moment better than anyone else.

For now, the attempt to modernize Russia without changing anything may be the last Russian illusion. It is in any case an illusion that almost no one seems inclined to believe. Even those who lie for a living haven't bothered trying to make it sound convincing. The leaders are obviously confused, and we can see that they do not know where they are leading the country. The elite is trying to guess at what is ahead, while safely squirreling away their families and finances in the West—just in case. The power structure cannot halt the growing dissatisfaction in their ranks.

When dozens of policemen post their demands for reform on the Internet, and hundreds of policemen are prepared to support them—that is a rebellion, albeit a local one. When businessmen move their capital abroad because they are afraid to invest in their own country—that is an indicator of the economy's viability. When hundreds of murders, including political ones, take place and the killers are never found, when terrorist attacks occur and the authorities have no idea who is behind them—this tells us that the system is becoming powerless. When there are regions in the country that consolidate themselves on an anti-constitutional basis, like Ramzan Kadyrov's regime in Chechnya, this means that the existing state is being undermined. When people state ahead of time that election results will be falsified, this shows that no one trusts the authorities or the state. When representatives of the elite close to the authorities openly express their outrage over what is happening to the country, this tells us that the regime is losing the support of its most loyal members.

Consider the following statement:

> It's embarrassing to tell people you're from Russia. The deterioration of the nation has passed the point of no return. Normal people are fleeing the country. Over the last fifteen years we have lost 90,000 educated, qualified people a year. Multiply that by fifteen years.[3]

Who do you think said that? None other than a prominent deputy of the State Duma, former FSB colonel Gennady Gudkov. If FSB officers, the backbone of the Russian system built by Putin, allow themselves to make such public statements, then irreversible processes of decay have begun. When about 5,000 young people protesting against political murders and the spread of fascism took to the streets in January 2010, they were cruelly put down by the police. When 12,000 protesters with signs and chants saying "Putin out!" took to the streets of Kaliningrad, the Kremlin came to understand that the Russian calm could conceal bubbles that could burst any moment.

No one knows when Russian society will wake up—a year, two, five, ten years from now? But the authorities are already desperately thinking about how to defend themselves when they do. The final act in Putin's play is over, but the actors won't leave the stage.

My readers can imagine for themselves how hard it will be for the ruling team to give up power that guarantees them control over wealth that makes Warren Buffett and Bill Gates look like the proprietors of a general store. If it were only a question of the ruling team, it would be relatively easy to bid farewell to the past. Over the past decade, however, many other strata of society have formed in Russia to service the parasitic regime or offer it their support. Among the latter are pensioners, workers at Soviet-era enterprises, innumerable bureaucrats, and the technocrat liberals. (The latter, by the way, would happily offer their services to the regime in the hopes that, if they came out on top, they could make the regime more attractive.) So Russia's farewell to the past will likely be neither happy nor easy. I would love to be proven wrong in this, but I'm afraid it's just not so.

What does this mean for the West? I hope it will be able to avoid the confusion in which it found itself many times before, caught flat-footed by the rush of history. In 1991, the West didn't foresee the collapse of the USSR—a comment on the quality of its Sovietology. (To be fair, the events of that year came as a shock to Russians, too.) In 1995–1996, the West failed to appreciate the character of the system founded by Boris Yeltsin. In 1999–2008, it was mesmerized by the "Russian miracle," failing to understand the substance of the Putin regime and the kind of economic stability he created. In time, the number of inveterate optimists was reduced, but there are still quite a few who hail the idea of Kremlin modernization with their former enthusiasm and believe in the success of the U.S.–Russia "reset." These optimists are matched by others who reject the possibility of Russia's ever becoming a normal liberal country that maintains friendly relations with the West.

I hope that understanding the inevitability of the end of the present Russian system will help the West prepare for a new stage of development. "Why are you trying to scare us?" the optimists will ask. "Everything is quiet in Russia." Yes, for now things are quiet. But it's a deceptive quiet. Even if a significant part of the public and a not-so-insignificant part of the elite believe that they are living in a temporary shelter that needs to be rebuilt, that in itself is a condemnation of the system and of the Russian state. The Russian elite can keep huffing and puffing in negotiations with

Western colleagues, and society may continue to sleep (or pretend to sleep). But deep down, society is stirring.

Does this mean that the West can't count on cooperation with Russia until the country has transformed itself? Not at all: There will be cooperation on certain issues, just as there was with the Soviet Union. But don't hold out hope that this cooperation will be constructive and sustainable. It won't help Russia change; indeed at present it helps the Russian elite avoid change. The need to sustain personalized rule and its geopolitical ambitions will make all diplomatic "resets" temporary.

Does this mean that there will be no difficulties between a democratic Russia and the West? Of course not. There have been disagreements between the United States and France, for example, or between the United States and various coalitions of European states, or between states within Europe. But despite such disagreements, a democratic Russia and the West would be able to entirely abandon the regime of *mutually assured destruction*, a development for which the entire world could breathe an extended sigh of relief.

***

I've come to the end of my conversation with you, my readers, but I would like to leave you with one thought.

Russia must do its own work to reform itself, but this hard work will only pay off if the West gives Russia a helping hand. If it isn't prepared—and at the moment, it is not—then Western Civilization will have proven, first, that it has lost the sense of mission it once had and, second, that it is no longer equal to challenges on a global scale. Russia—adrift, isolated, *interrupted*—is an opportunity for the West to prove that its global destiny is far from over.

Notes

1. Edward Chow predicted that "the new agreement ... could again threaten the supply of gas to Europe." See Philip P. Pan, "Ukraine's Extension of Russian Base's Lease May Challenge U.S. Goals in Region," *Washington Post*, April 28, 2010.

2. In the early 2010, 49 percent of Russians believed that "the people have the right to fight for their rights even if it goes against the interests of the state." Only 23 percent of Russians believed that Russia does not need a democracy and 31 percent said that the power structure has to guarantee the well-being of Russian society, whereas 48 percent emphasized the need to strengthen civil society and human rights. See http://www.lev-ada.ru/press/2010012601.html; http://www.levada.ru/press/2010012105.html.

3. Quoted in *New Times*, November 30, 2009.

INDEX

ABOUT THE AUTHOR

Lilia Shevtsova is a senior associate at the Carnegie Moscow Center, where she chairs the Russian Domestic Politics and Political Institutions Program. She is also an associate fellow at the Royal Institute of International Affairs (Chatham House). Shevtsova is the author of *Yeltsin's Russia: Myths and Reality*, *Putin's Russia*, and *Russia: Lost in Transition*.

CARNEGIE ENDOWMENT FOR INTERNATIONAL PEACE

THE CARNEGIE ENDOWMENT FOR INTERNATIONAL PEACE is a private, non-profit organization dedicated to advancing cooperation between nations and promoting active international engagement by the United States. Founded in 1910, its work is non partisan and dedicated to achieving practical results.

Following its century-long practice of changing as global circumstances change, the Carnegie Endowment is undertaking a fundamental redefinition of its role and mission. Carnegie aims to transform itself from a think tank on international issues to the first truly multinational—ultimately global—think tank. The Endowment has added operations in Beijing, Beirut, and Brussels to its existing centers in Washington and Moscow. These five locations include the two centers of world governance and the three places whose political evolution and international policies will most determine the near-term possibilities for international peace and economic advance.